Economics and Business environment

W. Hulleman

A.J. Marijs

Noordhoff Uitgevers Groningen/Utrecht

Fifth edition

Cover design: G2K Groningen - Amsterdam
Cover illustration: G2K, met dank aan TheNounProject

If you have any comments or queries about this or any other publication, please contact:
Noordhoff Uitgevers bv, Afdeling Hoger Onderwijs, Antwoordnummer 13, 9700 VB Groningen, e-mail: info@noordhoff.nl

The greatest care has been taken in the realization of this publication. Author(s), editors nor publisher can be held liable in case any information has been published incompletely or incorrectly. They shall be pleased to receive any adjustments to the contents.

0 / 18

ISBN 978-1-032-04877-2 (hbk)
ISBN 978-90-01-88943-2 (pbk)
ISBN 978-1-003-19498-9 (ebk)
NUR 781

Preface

The economic business environment has a considerable influence on company turnover and returns. An increase in the degree of competition, a period of economic decline or a strong increase in the exchange rate of the euro involve risks for European companies. These risks are discussed and analysed at length in the annual reports of many European companies.

What should students who will be taking up future managerial positions within European companies know about the business environment of these companies?

This book offers a twofold answer to this question.

In the first place, in their future careers, students will need to be able to independently follow and analyse economic developments. They will need to be able to do such things as interpret the economic and financial pages of newspapers, as well as relevant economic publications by banks, national governments, the European Union and global international organisations. To do this requires a basic knowledge of the terminology generally employed in these publications. For this reason, this book avoids complicated economic jargon and mathematical analyses as much as possible. The theoretical perspectives contained in this book are concerned with the analysis of industries as well as macroeconomic and international economic developments. The theory is well illustrated by means of tables, figures and case studies that give an impression of recent developments within the European economy.

In the second place, students will need to have an insight into the way in which the business environment influences the company returns. Companies run risks that may be associated with developments within the industry (industry risks), or be the result of developments within the national or the global economy (such as business cycle risks, interest rate and exchange rate risks and country risk). In order to analyse these risks, the managers of companies will firstly need to determine the extent to which companies' results are exposed to economic developments and, secondly, they will need to be able to make a prognosis of future developments in the industry and in the national and global economy. The material in this book will provide the student with both these skills.

Educational material for a tertiary institution has to conform to a number of criteria. Firstly, it must allow independent processing of the subject matter. Secondly, the material must be practical and directly applicable to professional practice. Tertiary institutions often take thematic approaches to education, where the emphasis is not on the individual disciplines but on themes or practical problems. This book fits in with that approach, because it takes the business environment as its basis and only to a lesser degree economic theories. Nevertheless, the emphasis is still on the economic elements of the business environment. This is in keeping with the philosophy of Adam Smith, the founder of economics, who saw a certain amount of specialisation increases productivity within society (which includes the field of education).

In the fifth edition, text, tables and figures have been updated.

We thank all those colleagues and students that have given their opinions on the study material, whether invited or not. Their remarks have been an incentive to improve on the educational material.

Zwolle, Hattem, Autumn 2017

A.J. Marijs

W. Hulleman

Table of contents

Study guide

Central to this book is the issue of what influence the business environment
has on company results. Chapter 1 discusses the concept of the business
environment and the role that economics as a science can play in analysing
the business environment.

The rest of the book is made up of four parts. Each of these deals with a
particular aspect of the business environment (see figure).

Companies and their enivronment

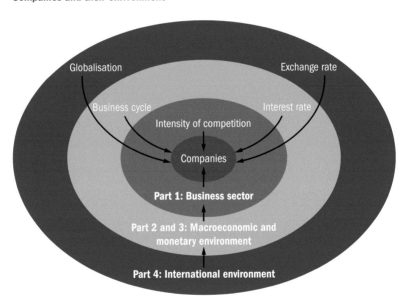

Part 1:   The company in the business sector

Part 1 deals with the immediate environment within which companies
operate; that is, the particular industry. Chapter 2 deals with price
formation within markets. Market price is a function of supply and demand.
The factors that determine supply and demand will also be treated.
Any change in supply or demand will have an effect on the degree of
competition between businesses. However, even in industries with a high
intensity of competition, there will always be businesses which will succeed
in making good profits. They will have succeeded in doing so because of
their competitiveness. Those factors which determine the competitiveness
of companies within an industry will also be treated in Chapter 3.

Part 2:   The macroenvironment of companies
Central to Part 2 is the macroenvironment. Chapter 4 deals with the supply side of the European economy. Some of the issues that will be dealt with include how production within the economy is organised, how production is gauged and over what sectors of the economy production is carried out.

Chapter 5 discusses the demand side of the economy. To what destinations do the products of an economy go? What relative amounts are purchased by private consumers, businesses, government authorities and foreign consumers? Developments within macroeconomic demand have a repercussion on the business cycle. Those factors that affect the business cycle are dealt with in Chapter 6. The business cycle has a considerable effect on the both government income and expenditure and on business results. As such, Chapter 6 also deals with the government and business policies in relation to business cycles.

Part 3:   The monetary environment of companies
Part 3 deals with the monetary environment of companies. Chapter 7 deals with money supply and demand. Too rapid monetary growth can have the effect that private consumers and companies start spending too much, with inflation as the result. The monetary policy of the European Central Bank is directed towards preventing inflation. The means at its disposal are also dealt with in Chapter 7.

Interest is the price one has to pay in order to borrow money. Chapter 8 deals with the factors that determine the money market and long-term interest rate within the Euro zone. Interest rate fluctuations can have a considerable effect on company profits. As such, Chapter 8 also deals with interest rate risk.

Part 4:   The international environment of companies
Liberalisation of international trade and capital flows and improvements in transportation and telecommunication technology are meaning that the distances and borders between countries are increasing less important than they used to be. Chapter 9 deals with the main trends in global economy as well as the background against which international trade has arisen and what effects it is having. This chapter also deals with how trade and capital flows are reflected within the balance of payments.
International trade and investment involve currency market transactions. The exchange rate is set by the currency market. Chapter 10 deals with the factors that determine the exchange rate. Exchange rate fluctuations have a considerable effect on business profits and turnover. As such Chapter 10 also deals with exchange rate risk. Companies that intend to internationalise their operations face the problem of finding a suitable sales market. Central to Chapter 11 are country selection procedures according to the so-called filter method. These procedures allow a suitable target market to be selected from a large number of potential sales markets. Chapter 11 also deals with one of the main risks of doing business outside Europe, namely, country risk. This is the risk that business partners of European companies will not be able to fulfil their international obligations in hard currency as a consequence of government measures.

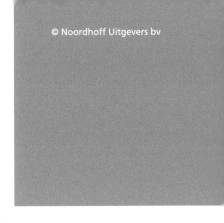

1

Economics and the business environment

What is economic activity and what academic discipline studies it? What is the relationship between the business environment and economics? Economic phenomena are regarded as belonging to the so-called business environment.
This chapter will address the following key question: what role does economics play in the business environment?
On the next page, a situational sketch is used by way of an introduction to these issues.

People always have needs of one form or another, and they fulfil these needs with available resources. This is termed economic activity. Economic activity is the subject of many branches of economic research, and is dealt with in Section 1.1.

Section 1.2 deals with the objectives of economics within the framework of the business environment. It delineates that business environment with these objectives in mind. The main issue is what external factors determine business results. Political developments in market areas, technical innovations, major shifts in customer demand and changes in work ethics all have a major effect on companies. The contribution that economics could make to analysing these aspects is illustrated in a diagram.
Section 1.3 treats the relationship between absolute and relative changes in variables. The importance of the absolute change in economic variables will always be manifestly evident (for example, the employment figures over a number of years). However, the relative changes to these variables are often just as significant (for instance, the percentage of employment growth during a specific year).

1

CASE

The economic conditions under which the management of an airline have to operate are crucially important. Knowing these conditions can be the key to success. The top management level may have to find answers to the following questions: if there is an economic slump, what is the effect on tourist spending likely to be? What will happen to the oil prices? Will the prices of American competitors' tickets drop dramatically if the exchange rate of the dollar drops? Can we still afford our pilots' wages, or will we have to buy bigger planes instead? Should we invest in new machines if the interest rate rises and lending becomes more expensive? The top management needs to make sure there is sufficient expertise in these fields to understand those symptoms and developments that have a direct bearing on the company's achievements. They will need to ask themselves whether there are ways and means of avoiding negative effects.

1.1 Economic activity and economics

Human beings need things like food, warmth, shelter, safety and self-development. These needs can be partly fulfilled by the supply of goods and services. The ready availability of goods and services to fulfil needs is termed prosperity. Human needs are virtually unlimited, while production is limited by the availability of resources like land labour, and capital. The excess of human needs over what can be produced is termed scarcity. Resources such as raw materials, machines and labour, which are used in the production of goods and services can be used for a variety of purposes. Labour can, for example, be used for the production of food, consumer electronics, education or safety (the judiciary and police). Raw materials and machines can also be put to a variety of uses. Since they can be put to a variety of purposes, they can be described as scarce or in short supply.

Prosperity
Resources
Scarcity

Economic activity

Economic activity occurs when people (consumers, managers) make choices to maximise their prosperity using scarce resources. Economic activity occurs everywhere in society: consumers obtain an income by going out to work; a company buys products, uses them to make other products and sells them; a bank employee buys shares on behalf of a customer; a town planner makes plans for a new city suburb for the city council; a sales employee of a company obtains a big international order.

Economic activity takes place within and between various organisations. In the examples mentioned, there is an interaction between consumers and companies, government institutions and companies and companies interacting with companies in other countries.

Science of economics

The science of economics is concerned with the study of economic activity. The field is so complex that it has had to be divided up into several subdisciplines. These can be roughly divided into two groups: those that study the internal process within companies (such as financial accounting, management accounting) and those that study the relationship with the environment or the environment itself (such as marketing and macroeconomics).

Company employees are rarely able to resolve the problems they encounter merely by having a knowledge of one of these fields alone. A problem often has both internal and external causes. This is illustrated in Example 1.1.

EXAMPLE 1.1

A sales employee has noticed that the sales of a product are increasing at a lesser rate than was anticipated. There may be a number of reasons for this. Perhaps competitors have brought a similar product but with a better price-quality ratio onto the market. Maybe the costs have become too high because of inefficient production methods (which may then constitute an economic, a business management or even a technical problem). Perhaps competitors have increased their advertising or improved their distributing organisation (aspects that are investigated in marketing). Perhaps the product is sensitive to cyclical trends and the economic growth in the sales area is suffering a setback. Sometimes customers abruptly change their spending pattern, which will affect sales. A product may have suddenly become too expensive for buyers in certain countries because of changes in the exchange rate. These are all aspects of the problems that fall under economics.

All these factors could play a role and may even exert a simultaneous influence on sales.
The sales employee would like to take measures to turn the tide.
To do that he will first have to find out what the causes of declining sales are.

TEST 1.1

What measures could the company in Example 1.1 take to reduce costs that are the result of a wage rise?

Economic activity in a country can be studied on various levels. One way of doing it is to study the options open to all the companies and households within a country. Another is to analyse the economic activities of a group of companies or households who make or buy a similar type of product. The relationship with other countries is also important for the economic processes within a country.
All these topics belong to the field of economics. A distinction needs to be made between the following:

- Industry analysis
- Macroeconomics
- Monetary economics
- International economic relations.

Industry analysis is the study of the characteristics of markets and business sectors that companies come into contact with, the supply and demand of goods and the changes that occur in supply and demand when prices change. These subjects are dealt with in chapters 2 and 3.

Macroeconomics deals with economic activities at a national level, such as the total consumption, all company investments, company imports and exports and the government of that country. These subjects are dealt with in chapters 4, 5 and 6.

Monetary economics is concerned with the phenomenon of money and the role that banks play in the economy. The extent of lending and the interest rate are variables that monetary economics tries to explain. The tasks of monetary authorities are also part of the field. These subjects are dealt with in chapters 7 and 8.

Economics

Industry analysis

Macroeconomics

Monetary economics

International
economics

International economics is the study of the international trade between countries, international capital flows and monetary relations between countries. These subjects are dealt with in chapters 9, 10 and 11.

European Union

Much of the data in this book is concerned with the 28 countries that make up European Union (EU), and with the 19 countries that use the Euro as their common currency.

In 1957, six countries came together to form the predecessor to the EU, the European Economic Community (EEC). These countries were Belgium, France, Luxemburg, Italy, the Netherlands, and West Germany. They were joined in 1973 by Denmark, Ireland, and Great Britain, at which point the collaboration became known as the EU. Subsequent additions to the EU were Greece in 1981, Portugal and Spain in 1986, Sweden, Austria, and Finland in 1995, many countries from the east and south of Europa (being Cyprus, Estonia, Hungary, Latvia, Lithuania, Malta, Poland, Slovenia, and the Czech Republic) in 2004, Romania and Bulgaria in 2007, and Croatia in 2013. There exists a lot of tension within the EU. In June of 2016, the population of the United Kingdom, by a small majority of the votes, elected to withdraw from the European Union. The government accepted and assumed this standpoint, thus requiring it to trigger a process of withdrawal. Since there are many uncertainties surrounding this process, the hows and ifs concerning the way in which the withdrawal is to be enacted are still highly uncertain.

Figure 1.1 shows the EU member countries by their share in the EU's total production in 2015. Total production in the EU in 2015 comes to approximately 15,000 billion Euros against approximately 10,500 billion in

FIGURE 1.1 Gross domestic product in the EU, 2015

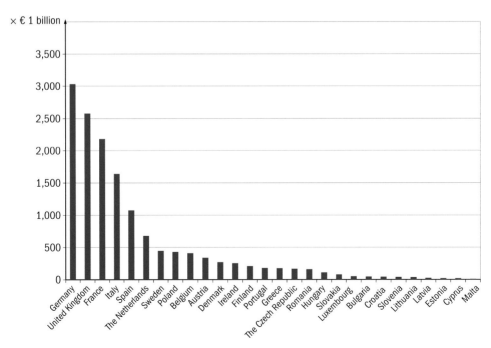

Source: Eurostat, consulted December 5, 2016

© Noordhoff Uitgevers bv   ECONOMICS AND THE BUSINESS ENVIRONMENT   **15**

Euroland. In comparison, production in the US is close to €16,200 billion; production in Japan is €3,700 billion. The four largest countries in the EU are responsible for approximately 65% of the total EU production (see Figure 1.1).

1.2 Business environment

Having a general overview of the business environment is essential to understanding how economic variables affect companies. Section 1.2.1 deals with this issue. Section 1.2.2 gives an overall view of the connections between the economic environment and the business economic variables.

1.2.1 The business environment

The term 'business environment' covers all the changes in the environment of a business that can have an effect on the company results. These effects can relate to buying, selling, market developments, competition, staff management and the like.

The factors relating to the business environment that can have an effect on the results of a company are usually presented in a standard way, based on the extent to which the company can influence the environment. A distinction can be made between factors relating to the direct environment, indirect factors and macroenvironmental factors (*see* Figure 1.2).

TEST 1.2
List the factors that are likely to affect a large company in the food retail sector under direct, indirect and macroenvironmental factors.

The direct environment is made up of the buying or selling markets on which the company operates. Entrepreneurs are in ongoing contact with market players (suppliers, distributors and final customers), collecting information to effect as advantageous a quality-price ratio for their raw materials and products as they can. They continually collect information to improve the reliability of their delivery of the products. One of the ongoing tasks of the sales department is to try to obtain as much information about the sales market as it can in order to improve on the effectiveness of advertising campaigns. A lot of different departments are involved, all of which have to put a lot of energy into detecting any tendencies within the direct environment. It is the only way a company can exert a favourable influence on it.

Direct environment

Ongoing contact

Market players

Every company has an incoming flow of goods and services: raw materials, labour and capital, each with their own buying market. Every company also has an outgoing flow: the products or services that are supplied to the various sales markets. Depending on the company, these markets will have different characteristics in terms of the nature of the competitors and the type of clients. This also means that the company itself has to constantly adapt its approach. If there are many companies operating within the same business sector and competition is stiff, there will be less margin for stipulating the price than in a situation where there is little competition. If the clients are consumers, a different promotional approach is required than if the clients are other companies. The indirect environment consists of employer and employee organisations, the government and cultural elements such as public opinion and the media. There is usually no need for company departments to keep a daily check on its indirect business environment. The company will be represented by one or more of the employer organisations, who in turn lobby

The nature of competition

Indirect environment

FIGURE 1.2 The business environment

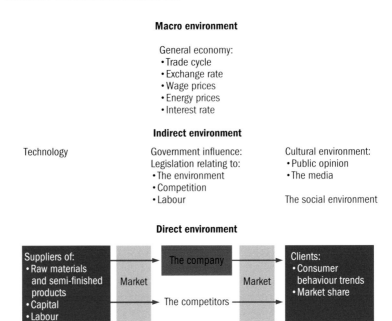

Macro environment

General economy:
• Trade cycle
• Exchange rate
• Wage prices
• Energy prices
• Interest rate

Indirect environment

Technology

Government influence:
Legislation relating to:
• The environment
• Competition
• Labour

Cultural environment:
• Public opinion
• The media

The social environment

Direct environment

Suppliers of:
• Raw materials
  and semi-finished
  products
• Capital
• Labour

Market

The company

The competitors

Market

Clients:
• Consumer
  behaviour trends
• Market share

Little influence

with the government on behalf of the employer organisations. The company can exert little influence on the indirect environment, but the influence of the indirect environment on the company can be very great indeed.

Public opinion

Companies are increasingly having to take public opinion into account. This is a task for the public relations department or the public relations manager. The media can easily sway public opinion one way or another and as such, the task should be approached warily. Many companies have issued directions on how to handle situations where public opinion might play a role, such as environmental calamities or product safety. Public opinion may have an immense influence on a company, whereas the effect that a company can have on public opinion is usually very small.

Social environment

As one would expect, the social environment exerts a considerable influence on a company, as the following illustrates.

Many companies have difficulty finding staff. For a long time a poor coordination between supply and demand on the labour market was held responsible for this. It was thought that the education and mentality of the working population was insufficiently geared to the requirements of employers. It has now been shown that the company's working conditions can play an important role in how successful a company is on the labour market. Improvement of working conditions and the company's image can help to improve the situation.

TEST 1.3
When applying for a job, would you take note of the working conditions in a company? Would you also want to find out about the rate of turnover of the company's products?

Technology exerts a powerful influence on competition. Products are replaced at a rapid rate. A product lifecycle of a few months is no longer unusual in industrial markets. Technological advancement is accelerating, as are the associated risks.

For those companies that provide their own technological advancements through research and development, this factor is one that belong to the direct business environment. For those companies that rely on other firms for new technological developments, technological advancement is an indirect business environment factor.

The macroenvironment belongs to the wider company environment. This environment takes in economic trends, variations in exchange rates and the price of raw materials and demographic developments. While these factors can have a major bearing on a company, individual companies cannot exert any influence on them: they are virtually uncontrollable. Because of the disastrous effects they can have on company results, an economic slump or lowering of the exchange rate of an important export country are the entrepreneur's nightmare. There is however no way in which an entrepreneur can influence these variables.

Consequently, it is important that managers have an idea of the influence macroeconomic variables can exert on returns, costs and profits. They can then more easily assess the competitive position of their own company.

1.2.2 The influence of economic variables on a company's results

Those aspects of the business environment that fall within the field of economics exercise a considerable influence on the results of companies. This is shown in Figure 1.3.

Many of the variables that are shown in Figure 1.3 are dealt with at length in this book. The illustration aims to show how varied the influence of economic variables is on businesses.

In Figure 1.3 the different parts of a profit and loss account have been related to economic variables. Some of these variables, such as the national and international economic situation, the wage and salary bill, government influence, the amount of capital investment and labour productivity are dealt with in the section dealing with the macroeconomy.

Exchange rates, exchange rate systems, interest theory, capital market, central bank monetary policy and the like usually fall under monetary economics or international economics. Managers operating in an increasingly internationally focussed environment should possess some knowledge of these matters.

Apart from macroeconomic, monetary and international variables there are variables in Figure 1.3 that belong to the fields of business economics or industry analysis. Amongst these are various market structures and circumstances, the competitive position of companies and technical developments. The relationship between suppliers and customers and especially the question of whether these relationships can be described as networks or clusters is a business economics issue. The competitive strength and the profitability of companies depend on this kind of variable.

Managers should not try to solve business economic problems in isolation from other changes in the business environment. However, if environmental variables are seen as unchangeable, this sometimes happens. Costs, sales

Margin notes: Technology · Macro-environment · Profit and loss account · Changes in the business environment

and interest are sometimes viewed as being constant for long periods (for instance, when an internal returns account is drawn up). Such an approach obviously simplifies the reality far too much. In reality, there may be major fluctuations in these variables. Managers would be far better off working with **predictions relating to environment variables** and taking their risk to the company seriously. A **policy** of reducing the effects of changes in economic trends, currency, prices of raw materials, wages and interest is essential for many companies. Companies are often able to determine their relationship to their suppliers and clients, the currency in which they lend their capital, where they are based, how they can make their range of products less susceptible to trade cycles, and so on.

FIGURE 1.3 The influence of general economic variables on business results

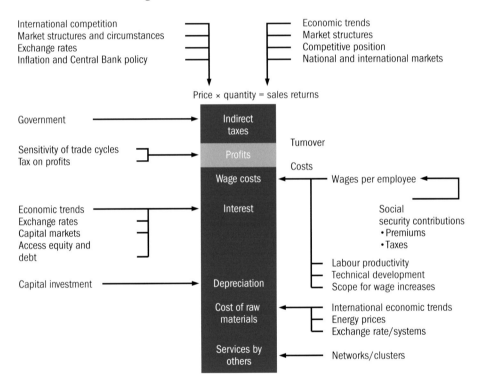

1.3 Absolute and relative data

The concepts of volume, price and value are interrelated. The turnover of a company over a certain period consists of the sales multiplied by the price. Turnover is a variable that denotes a value and sales is a variable that denotes either volume or quantity.

It is not only the absolute amounts of quantity (volume), price and value that are interrelated, the changes within each of the variables are also related in a certain way. This can be illustrated as follows.

We will assume that the data in Table 1.1 applies to a certain company.

TABLE 1.1 Quantity, price and value

	Quantity (in tons)	Price (in euros per ton)	Value (in euros)
Period 0	1,000	20	20,000
Period 1	1,050	22	23,100
Changes in % compared to period 0	5	10	15.5

Both the quantity and the price have increased in period 1 as compared with period 0. Multiplying price and quantity gives the value per period. The percentage change to each variable is calculated by dividing the increase by the amount in period 0 and multiplying that by 100. This produces a percentage of change between period 0 and period 1 of 15.5%. There is also another (but less accurate) way of determining the value increase, namely by adding the percentage change in quantity and price together.

It is a rule of thumb that the relative change in a variable that is a product of two other variables is approximately the same as the sum of the changes to the component variables. If a variable is the quotient of two other variables, the relative change is the difference between the relative change to the component variables. The reader can check this in Table 1.1, where price can, for example, be expressed as a quotient of value and quantity.

The change in value obtained in Table 1.1 by adding the percentages of the changes in quantity and price together is 15%, a discrepancy of 0.5% compared to the calculated change in value of 15.5%. The smaller the percentages of change in quantity and price, the smaller the degree of inaccuracy, also known as the discount factor. If the degree of inaccuracy is very small, it can be disregarded.

The increase in value of a variable is known as a nominal increase. The nominal increase in the example is 15%. The change in quantity is known as the real increase and is 5% in the example. The nominal increase is therefore equal to the real increase plus the price increase.

Nominal increase

Real increase

With economic variables, it is equally important to make a distinction between nominal and real changes. The total wages can be defined as the number of employees multiplied by the wages per employee. A change in the total wages can be broken up into a change in the number of employees and in the wages per employee. If an increase in the total wages is the result of a rise in wages, a quite different economic picture emerges than if the increase is due to an increase in employment.

We will assume that Table 1.2 gives an estimate of the total wages for a certain year.

TABLE 1.2 Volume and price changes to the total wages (example)

	2017 in 2017 prices	Volume increase	2018 in 2017 prices	Price increase	2018 in 2018 prices
	(1)	(2)	(3)	(4)	(5)
Total wages	200	2%	204	5%	214.5

The first column gives the value of the total wages in 2017. From column 2 it can be deduced that there is an increase in employment of 2%. The total wages would have been 204 if the wages per employee had remained constant. In that case the price increase would have been zero: the total wages in 2018 would have been the same as in 2017. This is why column 3 is headed '2018 in 2017 prices'. If the volume increase is added to the price increase (column 4) the result is the value of the total wages in 2018 (column 5). The wage per employee has risen by 5%.

In this case the rise in the total wages is approximately the same as the volume increase plus the price increase: 2% + 5% = 7%; 7% of 200 = 14. If the percentage increases in volume and prices are small they may be added up to determine the increase in value. Here, the discrepancy is 0.2, which is 0.1% of 200, a negligible difference.

The relationship between total wages, wages per employee and number of employees

The relationship between total wages, wages per employee and number of employees can be expressed in an equation:

$$W = W_{emp} \times N$$

in which:

W = the total wages
W_{emp} = the wage per employee
N = the number of employees

The relationship between the changes can be expressed as follows:

$$g_W = g_{Wemp} + g_N$$

in which:

g_W = the relative increase in the total wages
g_{Wemp} = the relative increase in the wage per employee
g_N = the relative increase in number of employees

Glossary

1

Business environment	The company environment that exerts an influence on the results of a company. Three types of environment can be identified: 1 Direct environment 2 Indirect environment 3 Macroenvironment.
Economic activity	The quest for maximum prosperity using limited resources.
EMU	The Economic and Monetary Union, consisting of those countries that have the euro as their currency.
Macroeconomics	Sub-discipline of economics, mainly concerned with the study of the connection between economic factors such as national income, employment, consumption, investments, inflation and the like.
Scarcity	The excess of human needs over what can be produced given the limited availability of resources.

PART 1
The company in the business sector

2
Markets

What are markets and how can they be demarcated?
What is consumer behaviour like within particular markets?
What connection is there between demand and the prices of goods? Why do
entrepreneurs go for certain products?
How are prices determined?
On the next page, a situational sketch is used by way of an introduction to
these issues.

Section 2.1 contains a description of markets and products. While
companies are in competition for customers, not all companies are in
competition with each other.
Companies that provide similar products to the same market are
particularly in competition with each other for a share of the market. This
is why it is so important to look at businesses per sector, as this section
does. Markets are not independent units: they are part of a conglomerate
governed by rules and regulations – the economic order.
Section 2.2 deals with the demand for goods and services. Consumer demand
is dictated by consumer needs, consumer income and the price. The main
issue is to what extent demand is affected by changes in price or income.
Section 2.3 deals with the supply of products. Supply is dependent upon
the cost and the price of products. Costs are an important aspect of
competition. Companies with high fixed costs are much less flexible than
companies with high variable costs.
The interaction between demand and supply within the market place
results in prices. This is the subject of Section 2.4. How stable prices are is
dependent on certain market conditions. Government influences on prices
are also dealt with.

CASE

Accell Group profile

Accell Group operates in an international market of bicycles, characterised by a fixed seasonal pattern that can vary by country. The bicycle season in our primary markets, Europe and North America, runs from September to August. At the start of each new season, Accell Group releases its annual collections of new bicycles. These are introduced at, among other things, major international bicycle conventions.

In the area of bicycle, the assortment covers all of the important bicycle categories using high-quality products within the middle and upper segments.
The most important bicycle categories for Accell Group are urban bicycles, recreational bicycles, sport bicycles, and e-bikes. The assortment by make and by collection year consists of an average of 80 different models and 500 to 700 products (men's and women's models, different frame heights, colour schemes, etcetera).

Other aspects that differ by country are popularity, preference, tastes regarding types of bicycles, and look & feel, or design. In order to be and remain successful on the various bicycle markets, it is essential for Accell Group to operate close to each market. To that end, in each country we combine nationally strong brands with international (sport)s brands. The international brands focus on specific sectors and niches, with preferences and tastes of end-users the world over being more homogenous.

Market data is gathered and analysed at the group level. Important changes in consumer behaviours, preferences, and trends are shared with country organisations. This helps us to achieve 'efficiency in inspiration'. It prevents research from needlessly overlapping, and ensures an optimised exchange of additional market information and ideas generally unavailable to small-time players.

Source: Accell Group N.V., Annual Report 2015, p. 8,9

2.1 Market, product and the business sector

Products find their way from suppliers to those parties that demand them (Section 2.1.1). Producers can be divided into business sector according to the similarity of products and production processes (Section 2.1.2). Since markets are an integral part of society, producers and consumers have to conform to all kinds of regulations, in order to ensure safety and public health as much as possible (Section 2.1.3).

2.1.1   Markets and products

Producers offer goods and services on the market to parties that have a demand for them. Demanders and suppliers negotiate with each other

Negotiation   to establish the required quantity, quality, terms of delivery and price of a certain product. This negotiation can be relatively direct, as is the case on daily markets and in retail situations, but it can also be indirect, as is the case on currency and share markets, where buyers and sellers negotiate with each other via telephone lines and computer screens. The area encompassed by the relationships between the buyers and sellers of a product can be described as that product's market: the market for television sets, the oil market, the grain market, and so on. The main function of markets is to set prices. Prices are an important indicator of supply and demand. Consumers compare prices in order to be able to satisfy their needs within their budgets. Entrepreneurs decide on the basis of market prices what products they will produce. Markets come in many shapes and forms and the prices of countless numbers of different products are in a process of negotiation. A market can be defined in countless different ways. Demarcating a market in geographical terms and defining the product itself are two ways of approaching the problem of describing a market.

Prices

Geographic dimension

For some products there is a world market where prices are established that apply to all buyers and sellers. Prices of raw materials such as ores, metals, coffee and grain are determined on a world-wide basis. Producers, traders and large-scale buyers take daily note of the prices and negotiate with each other via exchanges, forward markets and the like. A world market has its counterpart in the local market. Local markets can be very small indeed. Many retail trade firms and the hotel and catering sector (to take two examples) compete on the local market only since they are dependent on the customers coming to them. Other products have a national market or markets that are restricted to a few countries. Health insurance firms, for example, are affected by national legislation that limits the market to national borders.

World market

Local markets

National market

The notion of the relevant market is a very important one for companies. A relevant market is that part of the market that they service. Many producers of furniture sell their products in the country they are situated in and almost never further abroad. Although there are furniture markets all over the world, the competition of the furniture manufacturer is likely to be restricted to competitors within his own country. In this case the relevant market is the national market.

Relevant market

The product

Suppliers and buyers trade in products on markets. Products come in all shapes and forms, however. The beverage market illustrates this diversity. Consumers quench their thirst by drinking and there are many drinks on the market that can fulfil that need. These can be divided up into various categories: soft drinks, dairy products, alcoholic beverages and hot drinks. Those products that fall under the category of soft drinks can be termed a product group. Soft drinks can be divided up further into colas, fruit-based drinks and mineral water. The other product groups (milk drinks, alcoholic drinks and hot drinks) can likewise be divided up further. Is it the beverage market we want to refer to, or is it the soft drinks market, the cola market or even the Coca-Cola market? Are we referring to the dairy product market, or the milk market, the pasteurised milk market or even the full-cream or reduced fat milk market? In theory, a market consists of products or product variations that cater to the same need. In practice, the notion of market is not a uniform one, and may refer to any or all of these products and product groups, depending on the reason for analysing a certain market.

Product group

2

TEST 2.1
The term 'clothing market' is sometimes used. Do you think this is accurate enough? Clothing is a textile product, and the term 'world textile market' is often used. In what context would this be an accurate term?

2.1.2   Industry and the production chain

Business sector

Companies that make the same sorts of products using similar production methods are called a business sector. Companies that belong to the same business sector are in competition with each other to satisfy the same client needs.

Companies that belong to the same business sector usually produce a group of products, for whose manufacture the same raw products or the same production processes are used. They sell these products on various markets. Dairy companies, for instance, produce fresh milk, powdered milk for industrial use, milk products such as ice-cream and milk-based desserts, butter and cheese. For the manufacture of all of these products the same raw material, made into various different end products sold on various markets, is used. The company nevertheless still belongs to the business sector of dairy products. A base metal industry makes use of a number of raw materials such as iron ore or aluminium ore to produce a variety of products that are sold on various different markets. Nevertheless, steel producer Corus still belongs to the sector of base metal industries. The conclusion can therefore be drawn that a business sector is usually more than the suppliers of one particular market. Rather, a business sector usually supplies a group of markets.

Group of markets

Individual companies may belong to a number of different business sectors. If dairy factories also own a soft drink factory (they do, after all, understand beverages) they are part of not only in the dairy product business sector, but also the soft drink sector. Very large companies such as Shell, Bayer and Nestlé are part of a number of different business sectors.

NACE

The statistical institutes in EU countries have the task of classifying businesses according to their economic activity. Companies which manufacture the same type of product and apply the same production processes, are grouped. These institutes use the Nomenclature Statistique des Activités économiques dans la Communauté Européenne (NACE). In the NACE, all production activities of companies and governments in Europe are classified into twenty sections, each identified by a letter (see table 2.1). For civil and hydraulic engineering, and road building, a further division is presented. Each independent company division is assigned a four-digit code, which indicates the main activity performed by this division. The institutes determine the main activity based on the relative added value.

Sections
Groups
Classes

The CBS does not attribute these figures arbitrarily: it classifies the businesses according to a set system. The letter of the code indicates the sector the business belongs to. Each sector consists of sections (the first figures of the code) which in turn are subdivided into groups (the second figures of the code). The groups are in turn subdivided into classes (the third figure of the code).

Department stores, for example, are indicated by code G.47.19.1. Department stores are stores that sell a general range of non-food items (the Hema and Bijenkorf stores, for instance).

TABLE 2.1 Classification of industries

Primary sector	
A	*Agriculture, forestry and fishing*

Secondary sector		
B	Mining and quarrying	
C	Manufacturing	
D	Electricity, gas, steam and air-conditioning supply	
E	Water supply; sewerage, waste management and remediation activities	
F	Construction	
	42	Civil and hydraulic engineering, road construction (no earth moving)
	42.1	Construction of roads, railways and works of art
	42.11	Construction of roads and motorways
	42.11.1	Construction of roads and motorways
	42.11.2	Paving works
	42.12	Construction of railways and underground railways
	42.13	Construction of works of art

Tertiary sector	
G	Wholesale and retail trade; repairing of motor vehicles and motorcycles
H	Transportation and storage
I	Accommodation and food service activities
J	Information and communication
K	Financial and insurance activities
L	Real estate activities
M	Professional, scientific and technical activities
N	Administrative and support service activities

Quartairy sector	
O	Public administration and defence; compulsory social security
P	Education
Q	Human health and social work activities
R	Arts, entertainment and recreation
S	Other service activities
T	Activities of households as employers; undifferentiated goods – and services – producing activities of households for own use
U	Activities of extraterritorial organisations and bodies

Source: CBS

CBS-code

The sector: wholesale and retail trade; repair of motor vehicles and motorcycles
The section: retail trade
The group: general range of non-food items
The company class: department stores

G.47.19.1

Table 2.1 shows the sectors with a subdivision according to the first two figures of the Classification of Industries.

From raw material to final product, each product passes through a number of business sectors. Each subsequent stage is part of what is referred to as the production chain. Every business sector within the production chain adds some value to the product.

Production chain

Value adding

Value adding is subject to change. One important trend in value adding is a shift in power to those sectors that are closest to the consumer. The ongoing segmentation of markets has meant that power within the food, tobacco and beverage industry production chain is shifting from the producers to the retailers. Big retail chains possess more finances to collect or buy the necessary information than small ones, which means that the trend has, in turn, a bearing on competitive position within the retail trade.

2.1.3   The economic order

The economic conduct of companies and consumers is governed by a variety of rules. Companies attempting to make a profit are restrained in many ways, ranging from habits, customs and the prevailing morality to legislation, trade regulations and the like. Regardless of his spending pattern, a large part of the consumer's spending is governed by rules. Collectively, these rules regulate economic practice, and are consequently referred to as the economic order.

The economic order is the sum of the collective values, norms and institutions that determine economic activities.

Values, norms and institutions

Values

Worth striving for

Values are intangible things that are regarded as worth striving for. They have a bearing on what we want to achieve. If large parts of a community hold certain values we call them collective values. In economic behaviour, both economic and moral values play a role. Economic values include profitability and employment. Moral values have to do with how we view our human existence. Every society has collective opinions that have to do with basic ideas about what people are. The prevailing values in Europe include those of equality, liberty and solidarity.

Moral values

Norms

Norms are rules that are derived from values. They are a guide for human behaviour in concrete situations. Norms are all-pervasive. They govern such things as table manners, how one generation treats another, dress, traffic behaviour, and behaviour in recreational and working situations. Deviation from the collective norm usually lead to sanctions, since values and norms are embodied in laws and regulations. A great number of bodies have been created to transform laws into concrete regulations and to supervise them. They are responsible for professional and product codes, building regulations, environmental regulations, safety norms for people and materials, and so on. The judicial entities, the regulations and the bodies that formulate and enforce them are called institutions.

Institutions

TEST 2.2
In the United States, there has been a campaign by consumer organisations to boycott products from the Third World produced by means of child labour.
Which values and norms lie at the basis of this? What institutions are required to realise the objectives?

Table 2.2 shows the connection between values, norms and institutions.

TABLE 2.2 Values, norms and institutions

	Function/ description	Type	Examples
Values	Intangible things worth striving for	Economic Moral	Employment, productivity Equality, liberty, solidarity
Norm	Behavioural rules		Etiquette, behaviour toward staff
Institutions	Motivation and sanction	Prescriptions	Laws and regulations
		Institutions	Employer and employee organisations, government, police, judiciary

Government interference in the economy is aimed at maintaining the prevailing economic and moral values. If the behaviour of individuals is not supportive of the prevailing collective values or even rejects them, the government will intervene in the economic process. The extent to which the economic order is affected by market mechanisms and regulations will differ from one order to another.

Markets differ according to the extent that they are affected by price mechanisms or regulations. Some markets are largely unaffected by regulations. The companies that operate on these markets consequently have a great freedom of action. The furniture industry, for instance, is largely free to choose its own designs and materials. Other markets, such as health care, are much more highly regulated. Figure 2.1 shows the importance of the market mechanism and regulation for a number of product groups.

Markets
Regulations

FIGURE 2.1 The relative importance of the market mechanism and regulation on a number of markets

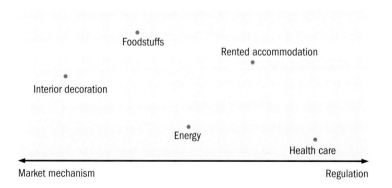

The market for interior decoration is relatively unregulated, although the producers usually lay down quality regulations and guarantee provisions via employer organisations. Since foodstuffs could be detrimental to public health, production is governed by product regulations and safety

prescriptions. Energy is a very important aspect of the economic process. Without electricity, oil or gas, economic activity would be unthinkable. As such, governments do not leave the production of energy entirely to the market process. In some markets, such as the market for rented accommodation and that for health care, the consideration that housing and medical care also have to be accessible for the financially weak plays a role. This consideration is based on a value: that of equality of people. Lack of accommodation and medical care contravenes human dignity.

TEST 2.3
The government interferes heavily with those industries that bring out products that are detrimental to public health, such as the tobacco industry. Another way of combating the detrimental effects of smoking would be to leave the tobacco industry free and to recover any damage via the courts. Could the latter be regarded as being a free market? What norms and institutions are involved?

2.2 Demand

Companies make products to cater to the needs of their target groups. They do this to make a profit. The profit is partly dependent on consumer demand, and a strong drop in demand can be disastrous for the results. Consequently, companies need to have an insight into the purchasing behaviour of their customers. They will at least want to know the following: do consumers spend a large or a small part of their budget on our products? Do they consciously decide to buy our products or instinctively? Are our products easily replaced by other products? Can big changes in sales be expected if the prices of products or the incomes of consumers change? Are our products susceptible to changes in fashion or a change in consumer lifestyle? The answers they get will give an insight into consumer behaviour. When they analyse consumer behaviour, producers are looking for the underlying causes for the demand for their products. These causes are also known as demand determining factors. They can be listed as follows:

Insight into purchasing behaviour

Demand determining factors

- Consumer needs (Section 2.2.1)
- The price of the product (Section 2.2.2)
- The price of other goods (Section 2.2.3)
- The income of consumers and the size of the population (Section 2.2.4).

2.2.1 Consumer needs

Satisfaction of needs

Customers usually buy goods and services for the satisfaction of needs. The individual has all kinds of needs. They can be divided into basic needs or needs of a less crucial nature. The satisfaction of basic needs is a necessity for physical survival. Food, clothing, accommodation and medical care are products that fulfil basic needs. The less crucial needs are the need for safety, social relationships, the desire to be appreciated and self-fulfilment. Goods and services in the fields of transport and communication, education, self-development and recreation fill such needs. The consumer's pattern of consumption is what he or she purchases to satisfy all these needs. Consumers satisfy their basic needs first and subsequently their other needs. This is why consumers with a low income spend proportionately more on their basic needs than consumers with a higher income. With

Pattern of consumption

growing prosperity, consumers are better able to satisfy their non-basic needs.

Almost all consumers in the industrialised countries are able to satisfy both types of need to a greater or lesser extent and with a great variety of products.

Their individual patterns of consumption can consequently vary greatly. Some consumers satisfy their need for self-development in participation in art activities, others look for personal development in sporting activities. Many goods that are intended to satisfy the basic needs have as a side effect that they satisfy other needs as well. Clothes are usually more than merely protective garments: they also indicate the group that the wearer would like to be associated with or the position that the wearer holds at that moment. In many professions clothing is used to differentiate between people's roles. Food and home decoration may also be used in that way. Companies often highlight the social and cultural aspects of the satisfaction of needs in their advertising campaigns.

Individual patterns of consumption

TEST 2.4
What influence is segmentation of markets likely to have on competition?

The decisive factor in patterns of consumption is the consumer's preferences. These preferences determine consumer spending priorities, and are influenced by a number of social and psychological variables. These include such things as the age category the consumers belong to, their upbringing and their education. The age category determines such things as preferences for certain types of music, reading, clothing, furniture and entertainment outside the home. Fashion (and clothing in particular) is an area that demonstrates the effect of consumer patterns particularly well. If the current fashion prescribes a certain colour and shape, this will affect demand. Consumers follow the fashion out of a need to satisfy their social needs. Adherence to fashion is often a prerequisite for belonging to a certain group. Clothing norms are particularly strict amongst young people.

Preferences

Fashion

Changes in consumer preference may have a decisive effect on company sales. A sudden switch to wooden floorboards and parquetry can turn out to be disastrous for the carpet industry. Changes in consumer preference are very often the result of psycho-social phenomena that cannot be explained by the science of economics. Other trends are less erratic because they are associated with changes that take place within society slowly, demographic and lifestyle trends being the main ones.

Changes in consumer preference

Demographic trends

The consumption of many products is age-related. One age group distinguishes itself from another via clothing, drinking habits, sports and entertainment. The population of the industrialised countries is ageing: there are relatively many people in the older age groups and relatively few in the lower age groups compared with the population in the non-industrialised countries. This has consequences for the demand for many products. The consumption of beer, for instance, declines when people become older. A beer manufacturer knows that the average consumption of beer will drop when the average age of the population rises. Breweries can only increase their sales if they export to countries with a strongly growing population and consequently beer manufacturers invest heavily in those countries. Older people do, however, have needs of their own: health care, for instance.

Age-related

Growth of expenditure in this area is typical of countries with an ageing population.

Education

The incomes of highly educated people are often higher than those of people with a lower level of education. Consumers with a high education are more self-confident and less inclined to follow mass fashion trends than consumers with a lower education. They want meaningful experiences. They find these in travelling, education, health and relationships. The need to accumulate possessions becomes less pronounced, and the more highly educated consumer is less prepared to pay for them. This partly explains the falling share of durable consumer goods in total consumption as incomes rise. Companies have to take increasingly notice of cultural trends. Consumers are becoming increasingly conscious of the circumstances under which products are being made. They may have an aversion to production processes that have a highly negative effect on the environment and products that have been produced by, say, child labour.

Lifestyle trends

Lifestyle trends arise when more or less coherent patterns of norms and values exert an influence on the behaviour (including the purchasing behaviour) of individuals. A lifestyle involves more than purchasing behaviour alone. It also includes ideas about society derived from the values that one holds. The main lifestyle trend is increasing individualisation.

Individualisation

A lot of products used to be geared towards the needs of the family. Nowadays, the emphasis is more on individual needs. This is increasingly the case with food, which is increasingly tailored to suit the individual. This explains why food retailers are increasingly selling food in smaller quantities which require less preparation. Ready to serve meals and even hot meals are increasingly the order of the day. Many consumers spend their free time as individuals, with the family playing only a minor role. There are many products on the market that enable consumers to select their own entertainment program. An increase in the living area per person, individual rooms for family members and personal audio-visual equipment is enabling consumer markets to become more segmented.

TEST 2.5
Supermarkets and department stores are increasingly offering catering services. How does this reflect the change in consumer patterns? How is this likely to effect competitive relationships?

This is frequently referred to by companies as 'custom made products through mass individualisation.' Customers are increasingly able to tailor the products to their own needs. They can choose their own mortgages, have their paints mixed exactly to their own specifications and choose their coffee to their own taste by selecting the blends and having them mixed in the shop. Value addition has shifted to the link in the production chain that is closest to the consumer. The role that service plays is also becoming more important. Companies that make the most advantage of these trends have a competitive advantage.

Companies market their products to enhance the chance of these products being successful. They not only react to changing consumer preferences, they also create demand and manipulate it. Product range improvement and innovation is high on the company agenda, and largely explains the ongoing change within consumer preferences. Consumers are increasingly counting on product improvement, meaning a shortened product life cycle: the period during which a product is sold. The risk of unsaleable stocks due to a change in taste by the public is quite real. Companies need therefore to be constantly aware of trends in consumer behaviour and new products in their field because the effects of these on their own sales could be very great indeed.

Marketing and consumer preferences

Product improvement

The demand for many products and services is seasonal. The demand for soft drinks, ice-cream, tourist services and the like peaks in summer, while other products, such as skates, heating oil and gas, umbrellas and rubber boots usually peak in autumn and winter. A consequence of this is that the companies concerned will either have large stocks in the off season, or suffer from overcapacity. This usually has a negative effect on prices. Conversely, a peak in demand will mean that the production capacity is likely not to be adequate.
Fluctuations in sales as a result of climatic circumstances are virtually unpredictable. They belong to those coincidental factors that have an influence on the financial results of enterprises. Erratic sales patterns are accompanied by planning problems and stock risks.

Seasons and climate

Government measures can have an effect on buying patterns. The government makes the consumption of certain items (such as a third-party insurance for car owners and health insurance for most of the population) compulsory.
Other types of consumer behaviour, such as the consumption of alcohol and smoking, is discouraged by means of publicity. In the same way, some other types of consumer behaviour (such as healthy food and hygienic behaviour) are encouraged. Industries try to keep track of government policy via employer organisations. Industries whose interests are opposed to those of the government are usually well organised. They will negotiate environmental measures and regulations relating to packaging, health and safety. The reports of these trade organisations often devote a lot of space to describing the effects of government on their sector.

Government measures

2.2.2   The price
Price is an important factor in determining demand. Consumers usually compare the price of goods when they are surveying what is available. With most products, the price has a negative effect on the quantity demanded. When the price drops the quantity demanded becomes larger and vice versa. The relationship between price and the quantity demanded can be expressed as an equation [1]:

$$q = -2p + 600 \qquad\qquad [1]$$

in which:
q = the quantity demanded
p = the price

2

The relationship between the price and the quantity demanded is termed the demand function. The demand function can be shown in a graph in which the quantity is plotted along the horizontal axis and the price along the vertical axis. The resultant curve is termed the demand curve (see Figure 2.2).

Demand curve

FIGURE 2.2 The demand curve

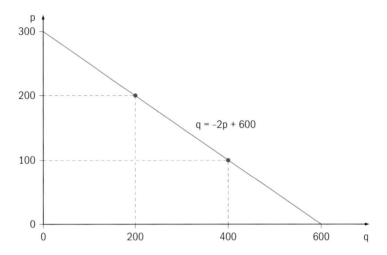

TEST 2.6
The demand for some goods rises when the price rises. Explain why these goods are termed 'snob' goods.

There are two causes for the inverse relationship between price and quantity demanded: the substitution and the income effects.
A price change for one product will have an effect on the demand for other products. If a product is lowered in price the consumers will be tempted to use more of it, to the detriment of those products that have not had their price lowered. This is called the substitution effect. Consumers will, for example, make use of a drop in the price of soft drinks to buy more of those instead of tea or light alcoholic beverages, for example.
Lowering the price of a product means that the consumer can buy more of these products, assuming his or her income remains constant. The purchasing power of that person's income will have increased by the price drop. This is termed the income effect of a price change.

Substitution effect

Substitution and income effects together explain why a fall in prices results in an increase in quantity demanded.

Price elasticity of demand

Whether and to what extent the quantity demanded is sensitive to a price change depends on the type of product. It is important for companies to know to what extent the quantity demanded will react to price changes. A variable that provides information about this is the price elasticity of demand. Price elasticity of demand is the relative change in the quantity demanded as a result of and divided by the relative change in price. Relative changes can be expressed as a percentage change. The price elasticity of demand can be expressed in the following way:

$$E_{pq} = \% \, \Delta q \, / \, \% \, \Delta p \qquad\qquad [2]$$

in which:
E_{pq} = price elasticity of demand
$\% \, \Delta q$ = the percentage of change in quantity demanded
$\% \, \Delta p$ = the percentage of change in price.

If the price changes from 100 to 101 (+1%), the quantity will drop from 400 to 398 (–½ %) according to equation [1]. This results in:

$$E_{pq} = -0.5\% \, / \, 1\% = -0.5 \qquad\qquad [3]$$

The price elasticity of demand is – 0.5. This means that a rise in prices by 1% will result in a drop in demand of 0.5%. The price elasticity of demand can also be described as the extent to which demand changes when there is a price change of 1%.

TEST 2.7
Under what circumstances could the price elasticity of demand be a positive figure? Can you name products for which this would hold?

Price elasticity is not constant along the whole curve: it constantly changes value. Along the first part of the curve – at high prices and low demand – the price elasticity is high. A small relative price change will result in a large relative change in demand. A drop in price at p = 250 of 1% to p = 247.5 will result in a quantity change of 5%, namely from 100 to 105. The price elasticity of demand is therefore –5. This is called the elastic part of the demand curve, or the elastic demand.

Elastic demand

When we go down the curve the price elasticity decreases in absolute terms. At a price of 150 and a quantity of 300 the price elasticity is exactly –1. Below this point is the inelastic part of the curve, with an elasticity of between –1 and 0. In this part of the curve the relative change in quantity is smaller than the relative change in price. This is termed inelastic demand.

Inelastic demand

The prices of most consumer goods are relatively constant. Prices usually only rise by a few percent each year. That part of the curve where prices and quantities originate is known as the relevant part of the curve. The relevant part of the curve usually only shows whether demand is elastic or inelastic. The elasticity is not only dependent on the position on the curve, but also on the slope of the demand curve. This is shown clearly in Figure 2.3.

Relevant part of the curve

Slope of the demand curve

FIGURE 2.3 Demand curves with different slopes

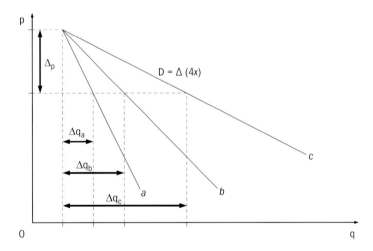

Curve *a* in Figure 2.3 is a steep curve. If the price is changed by p the change in quantity is small. The curve is inelastic in the relevant part of the curve.

Curve *b* has a greater elasticity than curve *a*. A change in price by p causes a greater change in quantity than in curve *a*.

Curve *c* is very flat. A price change of p results in a very great change in quantity. Curve *c* is very elastic in the relevant part of the curve.

Basic goods

Luxury goods

The price elasticity of the demand for basic goods is much smaller than that for luxury goods. When they are satisfying basic needs, consumers cannot react to price rises by stopping demand. Foodstuffs such as potatoes can show a very big fluctuation in price without any real change in demand. On the other hand, the sale of luxury goods such as cars is much more sensitive to price changes. It is easy for consumers to adjust their pattern of consumption when luxury items go up in price.

Elastic and inelastic demand may very well occur on the one market. Industries very often consist of a few very large enterprises and many small ones. If small companies raise their prices the customers will look for other suppliers and they will lose their market. Their demand curve is elastic. Large companies can sometimes raise prices without their customers looking for other suppliers. They control such a large part of the market that customers do not have an alternative. If they were to move to a competitor then that competitor would in turn see fit to raise prices. This is one of the reasons why companies try to increase their share of the market.

Price elasticity of demand is important for turnover. Entrepreneurs can use price elasticity to determine the effects of a price change on turnover (the product of price and quantity). Entrepreneurs dealing with an inelastic demand will see their turnover increase with a price rise. A price rise of 1% that is accompanied by a drop in sales of less than 1% will result in a rise in turnover. The increase in turnover is roughly equivalent to the sum of the changes in price and quantity.

EXAMPLE 2.1
At a price of 100, the quantity (according to equation [1]) is 400. The turnover is therefore 40 000. A price rise of 1% results in a drop in sales of 0.5%. The turnover increases from 40 000 to 40 198 (101 x 398). The turnover has risen by about 0.5% by a price rise of 1% and a sales drop of 0.5%.

In the elastic part of the curve, entrepreneurs can generate greater turnover by lowering the price.

TEST 2.8
What will the change in turnover be if a price of 250 drops by 1%? Use equation [1].

Table 2.3 describes the relationship between the price elasticity of demand and turnover.

TABLE 2.3 The relationship between price elasticity of demand and turnover

Demand elasticity	Price	Turnover
$-1 < E_{pq} < 0$ (inelastic demand)	increase	increase
$E_{pq} < -1$ (elastic demand)	increase	decrease

2 Position

A shift along and a shift of the demand curve

Changes in the quantity demanded that are the result of a change in prices can be read from the demand curve. This is referred to as a shift along the curve. From equation [1], it is easily deduced that a price rise from 100 to 101 will result in a quantity change from 400 to 398. However, the demand curve can change position as well: for example, because the needs have changed. If the need for a product increases, customers are prepared to buy a larger quantity at the same price. During a heatwave, the demand for soft drinks will increase, even though the price remains the same. In the graph, this is indicated by a shift to the right of the curve. The demand function also changes. Because of the increasing need for a product the demand will increase at every price level. If at every price the demand increases by 50, equation [1] becomes:

$$q = -2p + 650 \tag{4}$$

Figure 2.4 illustrates the shift in the demand curve.

FIGURE 2.4 A shift in the demand curve

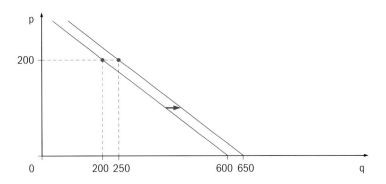

As we have seen, a shift in the demand curve is often caused by trends in consumer preferences. The influence companies can exert on these trends is usually relatively small.

2.2.3 The influence of substitute products

The demand for a certain product can change because of a price change in other goods. We have already encountered the term 'substitution effect' in this connection. The relationship between the sales of one product and the price of another product can be shown by cross-price elasticity.

$$E_{pq} = \%\Delta\, q_y\, /\, \%\, \Delta p_x \tag{5}$$

where:
E_{pq} = the cross-price elasticity
$\%\, \Delta q_y$ = the demand for goods y
$\%\, \Delta p_x$ = the price of goods x

There are several ways in which the prices of other goods can affect the demand for a product. The cross-price elasticity can be positive, negative or zero.

A positive cross-price elasticity will cause the demand for goods to increase if the price of other goods – termed substitute goods – rises. A rise in the price of cars will result in a decline in car use and an increase in the use of public transport. Car transport and public transport are substitute goods. Synthetics, wood, metal and glass in the building trade are another example of substitute goods. In a sense, they are in competition with each other. The use of one material will be to the detriment of the others. The height of the cross-price elasticity is an important indication of competition within a market: the higher the cross elasticity, the greater the competition.

Positive cross-price elasticity

A negative cross-price elasticity will cause the demand for certain goods to decrease when the price of other goods rises. A raise in the price of petrol will have a negative effect on the sale of cars. There is a negative cross-price elasticity between the price of petrol and the demand for cars. Goods with a negative cross-price elasticity are referred to as complementary goods.

Negative cross-price elasticity

At a cross-price elasticity of 0 both goods are mutually completely independent.

Cross-price elasticity of 0

Income and size of population

Changes in income have an effect on the demand for goods or services. This is illustrated by the income elasticity of demand. The income elasticity measures the percentage of change in the quantity demanded as a result of a percentage change in income:

Changes in income

Income elasticity

$$E_{qY} = \% \, \Delta q \, / \, \% \, \Delta Y \qquad\qquad [6]$$

where:
E_{qY} = the income elasticity of the quantity demanded
$\% \, \Delta Y$ = the change of income as a percentage.

At an income elasticity smaller than 1, the change in demand is smaller than the change in income. This is the case with basic goods. The demand for food increases somewhat with an increase in income, but not as much as the increase in the income itself. When the income elasticity is greater than 1 the change in demand is greater than the change in income. This is the case with luxury goods. The demand for things like tourist trips increases greatly with increasing incomes. Finally, there are goods that have a negative income elasticity. When incomes rise the demand for these goods – termed inferior goods – will decrease.

TEST 2.9
Many articles for body care have a low-income elasticity of demand in Europe, whereas in Asia they have a high-income elasticity. Can you use this fact to explain why Unilever (foodstuffs, toiletries, soap) is seeking to expand its markets mainly in Asia?

The income elasticity of many goods and services will decrease with increasing prosperity. Goods change from being luxury goods to being basic goods. A lot of products that are basic goods in a prosperous society are luxury products in developing countries. Business sectors that produce products with a low-income elasticity in rich countries can profit from attractive growing markets by exporting to developing countries with a high percentage of growth.

2.3 Supply

Modern society produces thousands of different types of product. The production processes for these goods and services are very varied. Some products – such as motorcars – are produced by extremely large companies; other products – such as agricultural products – by small enterprises. Some products – paper, for example – require a large quantity of raw materials while others – such as software – almost none. Some products call for very large capital installations – chemical products, for instance – while other products – among which retail trade services – require a large amount of manpower. Some products – such as medical operations – can only be produced by highly trained people, whereas other products – cleaning work, for instance – can be produced by unskilled labour.

The thing all goods and services have in common is that they are produced with the aid of the production factors of labour, nature and capital. Production processes differ to the extent that they make use of each of these factors.

Producers purchase the production factors in certain proportions on the relevant markets. Purchasing production factors involves costs to the producer. The various types of cost are discussed in Section 2.3.1. The differences in production methods lead to differences in the cost structure. Some business sectors have a relatively high variable cost, others have a high fixed cost. Competition within a business sector is closely related to the cost structure. Section 2.3.2 explains this.

2.3.1   Cost categories

Capital goods

Not dependent

Production volume

Companies engage certain production factors such as capital goods and part of the labour for a long period. Costs that are not dependent on the production volume are termed constant or fixed costs. Fixed capital goods such as machines or buildings usually remain in the possession of the same company during their whole life span. Many companies also engage part of the production factor of labour for an extensive period. Almost every company has its core workers that have accumulated a lot of know-how and experience over the years and which represents a considerable value for the company. Experts that bring in specific knowledge and experience are especially indispensable for a company. They distinguish themselves from their colleagues by adding their own distinct value to the enterprise. They are referred to as specialised or heterogeneous labour. A company cannot manage without such employees. In many production processes (particularly in the service field) knowledge is the only important production factor. Developing computer programmes, doing technical research and trading on international financial markets are some examples of such processes. The dismissal of staff members that carry out these activities could endanger the continuity of the company or even make production impossible.

The costs associated with the deployment of fixed capital goods and heterogeneous labour are termed constant or fixed costs. These costs are not related to the volume of production.

Variable costs are dependent on the production volume. The number of employees varies within many industries. For example, in the building trade, workers are often employed for a specific project only. The costs associated with the use of raw materials and semi-manufactured goods are usually variable costs. Companies order these materials when they

Core workers

Specialised or heterogeneous labour

Knowledge

need them for the production process. The costs will vary according to the volume of production.

In the short term, some production factors (such as land and capital) are fixed. Other factors of production (such as labour) are variable. The law of increasing and diminishing returns states that if more of the variable production factor is added to the fixed production factor, the extra production will at first increase and after a certain period it will decrease. The law of increasing and diminishing returns to scale applies to most companies if viewed in the short term. Any company will have a number of fixed costs that are directly related to the machines and buildings that the company is utilising at that particular point. A company cannot expand the supply of capital goods in the short term, so the fixed costs will remain constant.

Law of increasing and diminishing returns

If the company is producing a small quantity of goods, only a small quantity of variable production factors such as labour and raw materials are required. The variable production factors cannot be deployed optimally with a small production quantity; work productivity will be low, causing the variable costs per unit to be high.

When production increases, labour can be used more efficiently, causing the cost per unit product to decrease.

Finally, when all production capacity is fully put to use, the additional labour will be less productive, causing the variable costs to rise again.

Example 2.2 illustrates the reasons for the decreasing and increasing changes in the average variable costs.

- -

EXAMPLE 2.2

A department store sells various types of products in a number of departments. Every department has a cash register. Customers select their purchases from the racks and take them to the nearest cash register to pay for them. Sometimes they ask for information about products.

It is very quiet in the store during the morning. Few cashiers are needed, fewer even than the number of cash registers. The cashiers tend to use the nearest cash register, depending on the needs of the customers. The number of sales per employee is small, and the labour cost per item sold is consequently high.

As the number of customers gradually increases, sales also increase, meaning a need for extra staff. The manager satisfies this need for extra staff by employing people from a pool of temporary staff during certain parts of the day. The manpower can now be employed more efficiently because all cash registers are manned. Sales will now increase proportionally more than the labour costs. The variable costs will increase more slowly than the sales. The quotient of the variable products and the production – the AVC (average variable costs) – is lowered by the deployment of extra staff. There will be a decline in the average variable costs.

During the course of the afternoon, sales rise even more. All cash registers are constantly in use. There are rows of waiting customers at every cash register. It is, of course, not possible to increase the number of cash registers at such short notice. The manager can speed up the flow through at the registers by putting on even more staff. An extra employee is placed at every cash register to remove the security tag from the articles and to help by packing and so on. The extra staff means that each cash register is doubly manned. The sales do not double, however.

Labour productivity drops. Although the total number of sales (the production) increases, the labour costs increase even more. The labour costs per unit rises again, causing the average variable costs to also increase again.

From example 2.2 it can be shown that labour as a variable production factor is used inefficiently at low sales. When there is an increase in customers more people have to be deployed to increase the production per staff member. When there are very many customers the company has to put on more staff in a less efficient way, causing the sales per staff member to decrease again. The graph of the average variable cost will show a u-shape. Table 2.4 shows the fixed and the variable costs of a company at various production levels. The law of increasing and diminishing returns to scale is applicable to Table 2.4.

TABLE 2.4 Production and costs

Q (1)	FC (2)	VC (3)	TC (4)	AC (5)	AFC (6)	AVC (7)	MC (8)
1	600	200	800	800	600	200	200
2	600	360	960	480	300	180	160
3	600	450	1,050	350	200	150	90
4	600	570	1,170	293	150	142.5	120
5	600	710	1,310	262	120	142	140
6	600	966	1,566	261	100	161	256
7	600	1,260	1,860	266	86	180	294
8	600	1,600	2,200	275	75	200	340
9	600	2,160	2,760	307	67	240	560
10	600	2,800	3,400	340	60	280	640

Q = product quantity
FC = fixed cost
VC = variable cost
TC = total cost

AC = average (total) cost
AFC = average fixed cost
AVC = average variable cost
MC = marginal costs

Table 2.4 shows the fixed (FC) and the variable costs (VC) at a certain volume of production. The sum of FC and VC is the total cost (TC). Since the variable costs will increase as production increases, so too will the total costs rise.
The average total cost is the quotient of the total cost and the production quantity. It decreases until a production quantity of 6 is reached and then increases.
The average fixed cost and the average variable cost can be calculated by taking the quotient of the fixed and variable costs and the production quantity. The marginal costs are the extra costs per product unit. The extra cost of producing the first product is 200, the second product costs an extra 160, the third costs 90 extra, and so on.
Figure 2.5 shows the average and marginal cost curves. The AFC curve drops steadily because the fixed costs have to be divided by an increasing production quantity. The average variable costs drop initially to a minimum and then rise again. The marginal cost curve drops more steeply than the

AVC and also rises more steeply after the minimum. An extra product that costs less than the average will lower the average; an extra product that costs more than the average will raise the average. The MC curve crosses the AVC curve at the lowest point.

FIGURE 2.5 Average and marginal costs

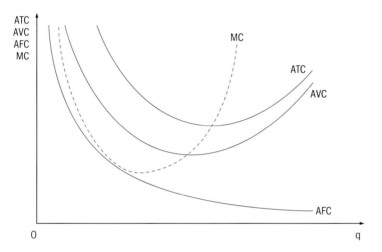

The firm has a production capacity of 10 units. Nevertheless, the average cost isn't at its minimum at this production rate. The lowest point of the AC is reached at a level of production of 6. This point is called the business optimum.

Business optimum

The supply curve

As Figure 2.6 shows, the marginal cost curve is of great importance for determining the quantity supplied. It shows the average and the marginal cost curves of a certain product, with some prices indicated on the vertical axis. In Figure 2.6 the prices are a factor that the enterprise itself cannot exert any influence over. Prices are determined by the market. In this case, the individual firm cannot influence prices by altering the production level. Consequently, the price curve is horizontal. The company's extra revenue marginal revenue is thus also constant and the same as the price on the market.

Marginal cost curve

Using Figure 2.6 we will try to find out what the output of the company will be when there is a market price of p_3. We will assume that the company is aiming for maximum profit. If the price is p_3 profits will be at their maximum when the company produces quantity q3. As the figure clearly demonstrates, putting more products on the market or taking some off will have an adverse effect on profits.

Maximum profit

If the company's output is less than q_3, profits will decrease. Since the products that are taken off the market will nevertheless have provided a profit, the marginal costs are less than the marginal revenue. If the company has an output of one unit more than q_3, this extra unit will cause a loss because its marginal costs are greater than its marginal revenue. An output

FIGURE 2.6 Marginal costs and the output quantity

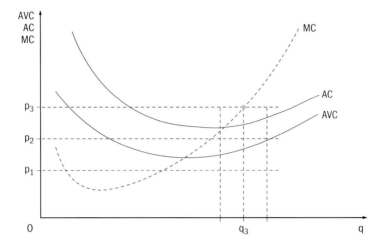

of a quantity q_3 at a price of p_3 is therefore advisable. The company will then have an output for which the marginal revenue and the marginal return is the same ($MR = MC$).

MR = MC

In this example, the total revenue is $p_3 \times q_3$. The total cost is a product of the average cost and the quantity ($AC_3 \times q_3$). The difference between total revenue and total cost is the profit. A company can only make a profit if the price lies above the AC curve. If there is a price of p_2 in between the AC curve and the AVC curve, the price will be insufficient to cover the average total cost and the company will operate at a loss. The company might

Loss

decide to accept the loss for the time being and continue production, because the variable costs and a part of the fixed costs can be retrieved. If the company ceased production the loss would be even greater, because then the loss would be the same as the fixed costs.

At the price of p_1 the company will cease production, since in that situation the variable costs are no longer covered. By ceasing production, the company will incur less loss than by continuing production.

Supply curve

The relationship between output and price is referred to as the supply curve. The marginal cost curve above the AVC curve is the short-run supply curve and the marginal cost curve above the AC curve is the long-run supply curve.

TEST 2.10
A road construction firm has low orders at a certain point in time and decides to tender for a certain project. According to the financial department the company will make a loss on that project of approximately €100,000. Under what circumstances is this tender a rational choice?

In the above analysis of the supply curve we have assumed that the price is a fixed factor and that the company can sell the whole of its production on the market at that price. This is only the case if the market is extremely large compared to the company's output. This is usually not the case: the company is usually so big that it covers a sizeable part of the market.

Sales can only be creased by lowering the price. The relationship between price and quantity demanded is the firm's demand curve. If the firm has a monopoly, the firm's individual demand curve will coincide with the market demand curve. Table 2.5 gives an example of an inverse relationship between price and quantity demanded.

Firm's demand

TABLE 2.5 Average and marginal revenue for a company able to influence the price

Quantity sold	Price = AR	Total revenue	MR((revenue/)sales)
0	100	–	–
10	90	900	90
20	80	1,600	70
30	70	2,100	60
40	60	2,400	30
50	50	2,500	10
60	40	2,400	–10
70	30	2,100	–30

The price is the same as the average revenue because the price represents the revenue per product unit. The marginal revenue is the revenue per extra unit sold. The marginal revenue will be lower than the average revenue if the average revenue is decreasing. The low return on the extra product will lower the average revenue. In other words, the MR curve declines more rapidly than the AR curve, as Figure 2.7 demonstrates.

Average revenue
Marginal revenue

The profit maximising output is also the output at which MR equals MC. As long as the marginal revenue of a unit produced and sold exceeds its marginal costs, profits will rise with increased production.
If MC exceeds MR, profits will fall and production will have to be reduced.

FIGURE 2.7 Sales at a decreasing firm's demand curve

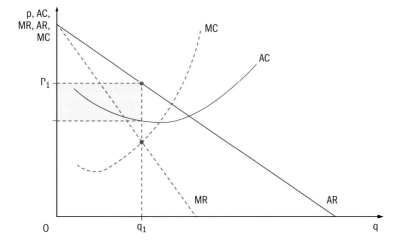

2.3.2   Cost and competition

Having dealt with average costs, important conclusions can now be drawn in relation to the difference in competitive conditions in the various business sectors. The following will now be looked at:
- Differences in cost structure;
- Differences in company size.

Differences in cost structure

The cost structure can vary considerably from one industry to another. A cost structure is the relationship between the various types of costs, especially the average fixed costs and the average variable costs. Some companies have a small proportion of fixed costs compared to the variable costs - software and consultancy firms, for example – whereas other businesses - such as chemical and steel producers – have a high proportion of fixed costs. Figure 2.8 illustrates a business with high fixed costs.

FIGURE 2.8 AVC and AC with high fixed costs

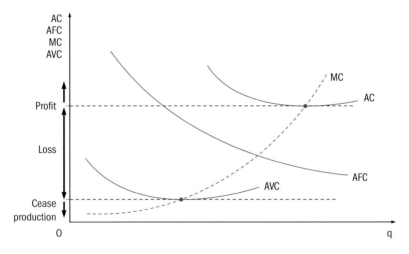

Figure 2.8 demonstrates that when demand and production decrease, the price can drop considerably before the company needs to cease production. If the price drops to below the level of the average total cost, losses will increase sharply.

If demand recovers, production levels can be increased and utilisation of capacity improved. Profits will only be made at a high production output. The flat slope of the AC does, however, mean that profits will increase rapidly with increased sales. The profits of businesses with high fixed costs usually show great fluctuations.

Capacity utilisation Figure 2.8 illustrates why capacity utilisation is so important for the results of businesses with a high proportion of fixed costs. A decrease in demand leads to a decrease in output. The AFC will therefore increase. The prices of products on markets that are served by industries with a high proportion of fixed costs can show great fluctuations. Price changes of 50% to 100% are no exception on industrial markets such as those for chemicals, metals and paper.

Industries with a high proportion of variable costs are much better able to adjust their costs downwards in the event of price drops. This type of business is prevalent in the services sector.

Difference in business size

The size of companies belonging to the same industry can vary greatly. Differences in business size will lead to differences in the cost structure. This factor is crucial to the intensity of competition within an industry. The following situations are typical.

Firstly, in some business sectors, both small and large businesses have higher costs than medium-sized businesses. In the car industry, small companies can make considerable savings in the purchasing, marketing and machinery areas if they grow in size. Very large businesses often have immense organisational problems that make their costs higher than those of medium-sized car manufacturers.

Figure 2.9 shows seven businesses (K1 to K7), each with a different production output and average total cost curve. These businesses make the same product and are therefore part of the same business sector. In this business sector, the average cost decreases when the stock of capital goods and the production output increase. These are advantages of scale. The advantages of scale increase up to business K4, after which disadvantages of scale come into force.

The disadvantages of larger businesses could be caused by organisational problems in the planning of production processes threatening the profitability. If prices are the same for every business, K4 has the largest profit per product unit. The other businesses produce with a higher average cost and have a lower profit margin.

If small businesses survive in a business sector like this it is usually because they serve a section of the market. On that section of the market they can often command a higher price for a qualitatively better product. Apart from big producers of audio-visual products that serve the mass market, there are many that serve not only the smaller consumer markets, but also the producer markets.

Intensity of competition

Advantages of scale

FIGURE 2.9 Economics of scale and diseconomies of scale in an industry

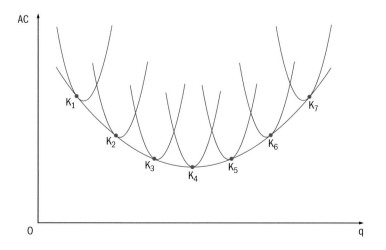

Secondly, there may be only small differences in average cost between large and small businesses. In such a case, the minimum value of the average cost curves is at roughly the same level. This makes it difficult for businesses to gain a competitive advantage from the average cost, which creates a greater degree of competition between large and small businesses. Entry into a business sector becomes very easy because entrepreneurs can start with only a small output. The retail trade, professional services and the building trade are some examples of such sectors.

Figure 2.10 shows a business sector where the minimum cost is not dependent on the size of the business. Expanding output will not bring any economies of scale.

FIGURE 2.10 Output without economies of scale

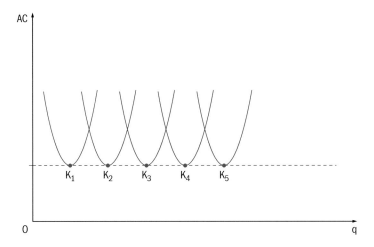

Thirdly, in some business sectors the average cost initially increases with higher capital goods stock, after which it becomes fairly level, as is illustrated in figure 2.11.

FIGURE 2.11 Minimum efficiency scale

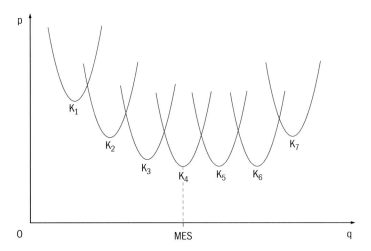

In Figure 2.11, business K4 has achieved the lowest possible average cost. Businesses K5 and K6 are much bigger, but they cannot produce at a lower average cost. Their capital goods stock does not enable higher productivity. This capital goods stock might consist of the same types of machinery that K4 has, only they have more of them. K4 has reached the minimum efficiency scale (MES): the smallest production output with the minimum level of cost. The height of the MES determines how easily businesses can enter the business sector. If the MES is low, the business sector can be entered at a low cost. When the MES is high the threshold for entering is also higher. Industries in business sectors with a low MES include assembly industries such as the metal products industry and the newspaper industry. Economies of scale mean that companies can reach such a size that the business sector only has room for a few businesses. This occurs when the entire market is only a few times the size of the MES. This is an important barrier to entry to that particular business sector. They know beforehand that it will result in overproduction and that prices will constantly be under pressure.

Economies of scale

Few businesses

2.4 Market price

Demand and supply meet at the marketplace. We will illustrate this by drawing the collective demand and supply curve in the one graph, giving the equilibrium price and equilibrium quantity (*see* Section 2.4.1). If we include the factor time, it will be seen that while some markets reach equilibrium at a certain point, others never reach it. The government exerts an influence on some products by prescribing a minimum or a maximum price. This is the subject of Section 2.4.2.

Collective demand and supply curve

2.4.1   Demand and supply

The suppliers of every industry offer their products on the market. Every supplier has his own supply curve. In Section 2.3 we determined the individual supply curve. That is the relation between price and output for an individual company. If we add all the individual output at a certain price by all the suppliers we obtain the collective supply curve. In a similar way we can obtain a collective demand curve from all the individual demand curves. If we assume the collective demand function to be

$$q_d = -300p + 6000 \qquad\qquad [7]$$

the collective supply function is:

$$q_s = 150p + 1500 \qquad\qquad [8]$$

in which:
q_d = the quantity demanded
q_s = the supplied quantity
p = the price

The market is in equilibrium if demand and supply are equal. If we equate demand and supply we will find that the equilibrium price is $p = 10$ at an equilibrium quantity of $q = 3000$. Figure 2.12 shows demand and supply.

Equilibrium

What happens if there is a change such as an increase in demand because of a change in income or preferences? The answer is that the demand curve will shift to the right, as is illustrated in Figure 2.12. An increase in demand causes an increase in price. The suppliers will react by increasing their supply. The supply changes along the supply curve.

FIGURE 2.12 The collective demand and supply curve

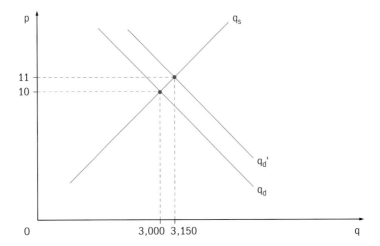

After the shifting of the demand curve from q_d to $q_{d'}$, a new equilibrium price of p = 11 comes into being with an equilibrium quantity of 3150. The market is in equilibrium again.

TEST 2.11
What factors would lead to a shift in the supply curve? What are the effects on equilibrium?

Instability
In our description of the processes that lead to a new market equilibrium we have made the assumption that supply can immediately adjust to a change in price, which is by no means always the case. It usually takes some time before businesses have adjusted their production processes to cope with the increase in demand. There is usually a time gap between the increase in demand and the increase in supply. Figure 2.13 shows how the adaptation process takes place.

In Figure 2.13 there is a position of market equilibrium at point 1. Subsequently the demand curve shifts from q_d to $q_{d'}$. If the supply does not increase in the short run, the supply curve will rise vertically through point 1 and the price will rise to p_2. The suppliers take that price as the basis for their production planning for the next period. They will want to bring quantity q_3 onto the market (see point 3). The consumers, however, are only prepared to pay a price of p_3 for a supply of that magnitude. Since the suppliers cannot change their production at such short notice, they will have to sell the supply q_3 for the price of p_3. For the next period, they take the price p_3 as the basis

Time gap

FIGURE 2.13 Delayed adjustment of supply to price changes

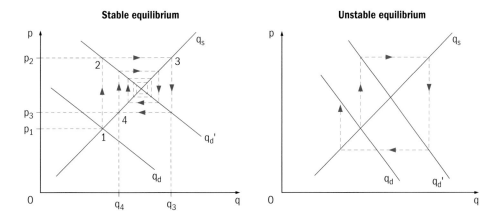

for the production planning whereby quantity q_4 is brought onto the market (see point 4). This process will continue until equilibrium is reached at the intersection of the new demand curve $q_{d'}$ and the supply curve q_s. A new equilibrium, termed a stable balance, is reached in this situation.

Stable balance

Figure 2.13 shows an unstable balance on the right. Such a situation can arise with a highly inelastic demand in combination with a supply that needs a period of time to adapt. After a sudden rise in demand customers are prepared to pay a high price for the available supply. During the following period, supply adjusts to the increase in price, after which prices drop steeply. The prices will still be higher than before the last rise in demand and the fluctuations will accelerate. Both prices and quantities will move increasingly away from market equilibrium.

Unstable balance

This type of development can be seen on agrarian markets. Producers of agrarian products cannot adapt their production in the short term, but have to wait a number of months (meat) or a whole year (potatoes) for the next harvest. The demand for agrarian products is usually very inelastic. The demand for potatoes, for instance, changes very little when the price changes. In those business sectors where market imbalance is accompanied by high fixed costs, losses may be experienced for very long periods of time.

2.4.2 Government influence on prices: maximum and minimum prices

The government exerts an influence on the price of a number of products by fixing a minimum or a maximum price for them. As well as this value added tax (VAT) and excise duties have an influence on prices.

Maximum and minimum price

The government regulates a number of markets in order to protect consumers and producers. It does so by fixing maximum prices (to protect consumers) or by fixing minimum prices (to protect producers). Government influence can be readily detected in demand and supply curves. Figure 2.14 shows a maximum price that is situated below the market equilibrium. Only in such a situation will a maximum price affect the market process. If the equilibrium price is lower than the maximum price it will be the equilibrium price that determines demand and supply.

Maximum price

FIGURE 2.14 Maximum price

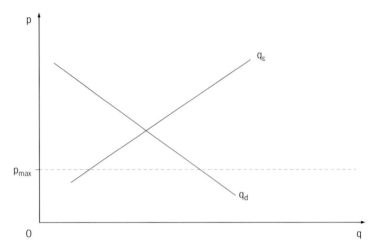

If a maximum price is below the level of the equilibrium price consumers
pay less than in a free market situation. The demand is therefore also
greater than at market equilibrium. The supply is less than it would be at
market equilibrium (*see* figure 2.14). There is a demand surplus. In this

Demand surplus

situation, the market would not be able to supply an equilibrium quantity.
There would be consumers prepared to pay more for a product than the
maximum price and there would be suppliers prepared to supply them.
The government would have to ration the demand by a system of permits.

**System of
permits**

A possible effect of maximum prices is the development of a black market.
Buyers can resell products at a higher price. A rationing system and market
supervision involve extra costs for the government. A government will
need good arguments to interfere in markets in this way. There are good
arguments to be found, for instance, for government regulations on the
rental housing market.

FIGURE 2.15 Minimum price

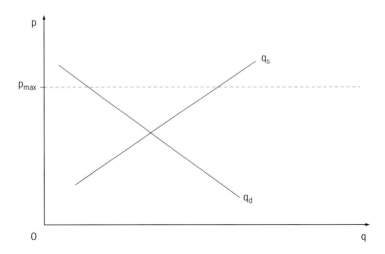

Minimum prices that are higher than the equilibrium price protect the producer from low prices. One example is the EU agricultural policy. Minimum prices have been set for a variety of products. Governments that set minimum prices for certain products do so in order to keep the production of those products in their own country. Consumers are the victim of minimum prices because they pay a higher price and consume less than on a free market. Figure 2.15 shows that minimum prices are associated with a supply surplus. This surplus has to be taken off the market in one way or another. This can be done by destroying the products, by storing them or by subsidised export. All these measures involve high costs that have to be met from general funds. To keep these costs down the government could issue production quotas to a limited number of producers. These quotas form an entry restriction.

Excise and value added tax

The government imposes a tax (VAT) on most goods and on top of that excise duties on some products. Producers regard the taxes that they have to pay an effect on the position of the supply curve. If the tax is a certain percentage it has an effect on the slope of the curve, as is illustrated in Figure 2.16.

FIGURE 2.16 The effect of VAT on the supply curve

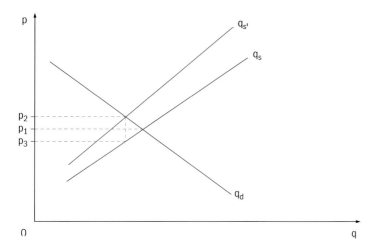

Figure 2.16 shows that taxes cause the equilibrium price to increase and the supply quantity to decrease. Producers try to shift the tax burden onto the customers by raising prices. The consumers then pay price p_2 whereas they were paying price p1 before the introduction of the tax. The tax is equal to the difference between p_2 and p_3. After paying the tax, the producers are left with price p_3. They will therefore not have succeeded in transferring all of the tax to the consumers. The extent to which producers are able to transfer taxes to the consumers is dependent on the price elasticity of demand and supply in the market equilibrium. If consumers can easily change to another product (in other words, if the demand curve has a flat slope) producers are likely to end up with a greater share of the tax. If the supply curve has a flat

2

slope, taxes are more easily transferred to consumers, meaning that they are likely to end up with a greater share of tax money.

Different rates

Products are taxed at different rates. The government imposes a lesser amount of VAT tax on basic goods than luxury goods. Excise duties can also vary greatly: there is a high excise on tobacco and alcohol, for example.

Substitution effect

These indirect taxes can cause a strong substitution effect because they affect products that satisfy the same needs to a different extent. Alcoholic beverages with a high excise can be replaced by beverages with a low excise. Entrepreneurs need to be very aware of the effects of indirect taxation on their products and substitute products.

Subsidies

Subsidies for goods and services form another impediment to the market mechanism. The housing market is a good example of a market where an enormous distortion of prices takes place because of subsidies. The subsidised rental costs of people with a low income make the benefits high for this group and corresponding low for the owners. Tax deductions for mortgage interest payments have the effect that the prices of houses are higher than they would otherwise be. This is favourable for the financial position of higher income groups.

Glossary

Average cost	Total cost divided by production output.
Basic needs	Needs that must be satisfied for physical survival.
Business optimum	The production quantity at the lowest average total cost.
Business sector	A group of businesses that make the same type of product using the same type of production methods.
Consumer preferences	Consumer buying behaviour priorities.
Consumption pattern	How the consumer usually goes about satisfying his / her consumption needs.
Cost function	The relationship between cost and production output.
Cross-price elasticity	The relationship between sales or output of a product and the price of another product.
Demand curve	The relationship between price and quantity demanded.
Demand function	The relationship between price and the quantity demanded of a product.
Economic order	All the norms, values and institutions that determine economic activity.
Economies of scale	The cost advantage gained by increasing production capacity.
Elastic demand	A price elasticity of demand less than −1.
Fixed cost	Costs that are not dependent on the size of production in the short term.
Homogenous labour	Labour for routine jobs that usually only require a low level of education. This type of labour is regarded as a variable cost.
Income effect	The increase in the purchasing power of income that comes about as a result of a decrease in the price of products.
Income elasticity of demand	The change in demand for a product divided by the change in income.

Inelastic demand	A price elasticity of demand between 0 and –1.
Inferior goods	Goods with a negative income elasticity.
Law of increasing and diminishing returns	Average variable costs initially decrease and subsequently increase as the production output increases.
Lifestyle	The more or less coherent patterns of norms and values that influence the behaviour of individuals (including their purchasing behaviour).
Marginal costs	Costs associated with the increase of production by one unit.
Market	The sum of the relationships between the demanders and the suppliers of finite goods.
Minimum efficiency scale	The minimum capacity at the lowest average total cost.
Norm	A guideline for human behaviour in concrete situations.
Other needs	Those needs that are related to matters of security, social relationships, the desire to be appreciated and self-development.
Overutilisation	Production greater than normal utilisation of the production capacity allows.
Planning curve	The curve that connects the minimum values of the long-run average cost curves.
Price elasticity of demand	The relative change in demand for a product divided by and the result of a relative change in price.
Production chain	The series of business sectors a product passes through from initial producer to consumer.
Seasonal pattern	The change in demand as a result of climatic factors.
Specialised labour	Labour usually characterised by a high level of education and which is regarded as a fixed cost.
Substitution effect	The choice of a certain product as a result of a decrease in the price of another product.
Supply curve	The relationship between the price and the quantity supplied
Underutilisation	The state of the production capacity not being fully utilised.
Value	Those intangible things that we regard as worth striving for.
Variable costs	Costs that vary according to production volume.

3

Competition

What parties within the environment does the firm have to compete against?
What factors determine intensity of competition and the competitive
position of a business?
What policies can a business adopt to strengthen its competitive position?
Why do industries change so much during the course of time?
On the next page, a situational sketch is used by way of an introduction to
these issues.

Section 3.1 discusses the competition for market share that takes place
between businesses in the same industry. They not only have to compete
with suppliers and customers for the added value in the production chain
but they also have to compete with businesses wanting to enter the industry.
Section 3.2 deals with those industry aspects that determine the intensity of
competition and the structure of the market. The number of companies within an
industry and the degree of product differentiation determine the market structure.
The market structure gives rise to particular types of business 'conduct', which
in turn exert an influence on the business results (performance) in particular
industries. Business conduct and performance are treated in Section 3.3.
Section 3.4 deals with changes in the structure of an industry that are
caused by products and industries having their own product life cycle. The
competitive process will be different for each phase of the product life cycle.
Section 3.5 deals with a method of analysing industries that mainly looks at
the environmental factors that affect industries. These include the role that
government and the economic order plays, and the influence exerted by
customers and the mutual relationships between businesses. Such factors
give an impression of the way the particular circumstances within a certain
country influence the competitive position of businesses. One could even
describe it as competition between countries.

3

CASE
A certain business makes all kinds of synthetics and possesses a number of injection moulding machines. The business is not very big, but it does have a few researchers on its staff who have close connections with the local technical university. This enables the firm to make highly innovative products. It has good contacts with customers who make office machines and copying machines and also supplies the car industry. Competition is relatively fierce because the large synthetic industries are envious of the good competitive position of the firm and regularly bring similar products onto the market. The customers are also constantly negotiating prices because they are experiencing high price pressure on their own markets. This forces the firm to ensure that its production process stay efficient. What it should in fact be doing is expanding to ensure future economies of scale, but there are few candidates for a takeover and the ones there are, are expensive. However, its current competitive position is quite good, because the researchers have enabled the firm to enter the market for metal parts. The director and owner of the firm is nearing sixty and is thinking about selling the firm to a large competitor. There are good reasons for this: while he has a business that is running well now, there is no guarantee that this will be the case five or ten years from now. Right now, the firm is probably worth as much as it ever will be.

3.1 Intensity of competition and competitiveness

The intensity of competition, the battle for the favour of consumers and the added value in the production chain are a source of ongoing concern among businesses. Companies have to constantly assess where they stand in relation to suppliers and consumers. Section 3.1.1 deals with the various types of competition, and competitive position is treated in Section 3.1.2.

3.1.1   Intensity of competition
Businesses produce products, and products are traded on markets (Figure 3.1).
Businesses that belong to the same industry are in competition with each other to satisfy the same customer needs. They all vie for a share in the market: a share of the sales made by all the players in a particular industry. Since they have to service as many customers as possible, this is likely to be to the detriment of other industry members. This is termed internal competition.
Businesses are also in competition with customers and suppliers: external competition. This type of competition is aimed primarily at obtaining as large a share possible of the added value and the profit margin within the production chain.
A further influence on competition in an industry is the threat of other businesses that want to enter the industry or businesses bringing products onto the market that are capable of replacing existing products. This type of competition is called potential competition: it is a future possibility.

Internal competition

External competition

Potential competition

FIGURE 3.1 Types of competition and main determining factors

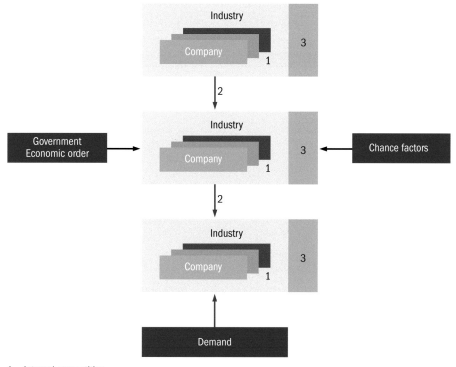

1 = Internal competition
2 = External competition
3 = Potential competition

3.1.2 Competitive position

Competition is one way that companies try to get some return on their invested capital. The amount of the return will depend on the company. An important factor is the difference in intensity of competition in those industries the companies belong to. The higher the competition within an industry, the lower the average profitability within that industry.
The return can also vary within an industry. Factors such as how effective management is, the quality of the machinery, staff expertise, the size of the market share, the size of the company, the geographical location of the company and the location of its markets, technical ability and other related factors will all play a role. Figure 3.2 shows the relationship between intensity of competition and the competitive position of the individual business.

In Figure 3.2 the degree of competition is plotted along the horizontal axis and the profitability along the vertical axis. In industry X, the average return at competitive degree x is amount R. Individual businesses could obtain higher returns (company X_1) or lower returns (company X_2). Company X_1 has a better and company X_2 a worse competitive position than the average company in this industry.

Return

FIGURE 3.2 Intensity of competition and competitive position[1]

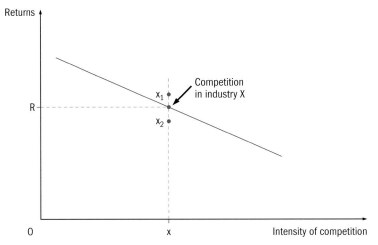

1   See also: H. Daems & S. Douma, *Concurrentieanalyse en concernstrategie*, Kluwer, 1989

The competitive strength of a business is frequently measured on the basis of its profitability in comparison to other industry members. A good indicator is the return before taxes as a percentage of output. Competitive strength should not only be gauged on the basis of profitability. The competitive position is the extent to which the company is able in the long run to satisfy all stakeholders. These include not only owners and employees but also customers, suppliers and the government.

All stakeholders

Not only businesses but also industries are in competition with each other.

Competitive position of an industry

The competitive position of an industry is frequently gauged by means of a number of variables, including average profits, its contribution to export, how many people it offers employment to and its contribution to the domestic product. Strong industries are better able to perform than weak ones.

TEST 3.1
A bank receives two loan applications. One is by a firm with a return of 5%, while the industry average is 7%. The other application is from a firm with a return of 4%, while the industry average is 2%. Which application represents the better proposition for the bank's credit department?

3.2 The structure of the market

The circumstances under which businesses operate vary considerably. Some produce for saturated markets, others for growing markets. Some have high variable costs and others have high fixed costs. Differences in circumstances cause considerable differences in intensity of competition. In this section, the factors that determine competition are delineated with a view to analysing their influence on intensity of competition. Section 3.2.1 describes a model – the SCP model – that can be used to analyse industries. Section 3.2.2 deals extensively with structural aspects. They are crucial to determining intensity of competition and are known as competition determining variables. Section 3.2.3 deals with market structures based on the number of businesses that operate on the market and with product differentiation.

3.2.1 Structure, conduct, performance

There are two sides to any market: the supply side and the demand side. The demand side consists of consumers or one or more purchasing industries or both. The supply side is an industry with certain characteristics. The market structure is dependent as it were on the circumstances that determine the conduct – the modus operandi – of the company. If the industry is made up of a large number of companies, these companies will not be able to exert an influence on the prices but will have to accept the price that originates on the market itself through the interaction between supply and demand. The number of companies is a structural feature that has an influence on the entrepreneur's conduct. Structural features are preconditions for any business conduct. Companies develop their goal-directed activities (the results) within the limits imposed by these preconditions. This section will deal with the structural features of a market.

Circumstances

Entrepreneur's conduct

Market structures are constantly changing and consequently the industry is too. The SCP method (structure, conduct, performance) aims to define the mutual influences exerted on the structure of the industry and a company's business conduct. According to this method, the particular business conduct of entrepreneurs and companies is not only determined by the structure of the industry, but in turn it also exerts an influence on that structure. The company's conduct not only brings about a certain performance or result, but the result will in turn determine the approach. Companies could, for instance, use high profits for takeovers, with the ensuing possibility of a concentration within that industry.

SCP

Figure 3.3 shows the relationship between structure, conduct and performance, often called SCP.

FIGURE 3.3 Structure, conduct, performance

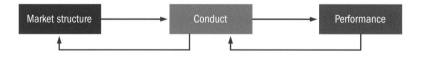

Table 3.1 lists the variables that determine the structure, conduct and performance according to the SCP method.

3

TABLE 3.1 The market situation: structure, conduct, performance

Structural features

Supply features

Number of suppliers:
- Supplier concentration
- Scale of the suppliers

Type of product:
- Homogenous or heterogenous

Cost structure of production:
- Capital intensity
- Nature of economies of scale

Entry barriers:
- High fixed costs
- Product heterogeneity
- Limit pricing
- Patents
- Forward and backward integration
- Strategic overcapacity

Demand features
- Increase in demand
- Concentration of customers
- Proportion of consumption goods in output
- Foreign demand: export share

Conduct
- Profit maximisation
- Innovative conduct
- Entry and exit

Performance
- Profitability
- Increase in added value
- Increase in domestic sales
- Increase in foreign sales
- Innovative performance
- Employment
- Productivity

Source: largely derived from: G.B. Dijksterhuis, H.J. Heeres and A. Kleijweg, *Indicatoren voor dynamiek*, ESB, 19 July 1995

TEST 3.2

In some countries, the food retail industry consists of only a few large firms.
Nevertheless, price wars with low returns as a result are very frequent. Explain why this might be so.

3.2.2 Competition-determining variables

The structural features that are summed up in Table 3.1 are competition determining variables. We will look at them one by one.

The number of suppliers

The intensity of competition is dependent on the number of suppliers on a market.

When there are many suppliers operating on a certain market, each company has only a small share of the market and therefore little influence on the price that is reached on the market. The suppliers have little market strength. They have to accept the market price and adjust their output in such a way as to obtain the maximum profit. They could be described as price takers and quantity adapters.

Market strength

If there are only a few companies on the market, the suppliers can exert a much greater influence on prices and quantities. As price and quantity makers they have much more market strength.

One criterion for measuring the market strength of the biggest companies in an industry is the concentration ratio. The market concentration CN indicates the market share of the biggest N suppliers. A C_4 of 60% means that the four largest suppliers have a combined share of the market of 60%. C_3, C_5, etc. can be explained in the same way. The concentration ratio says something about the largest companies, but does not give any information about the other suppliers. They could be a few large ones, but they could also be a large number of small ones.

Concentration ratio

Many markets have a few big suppliers and a large number of small suppliers. The big companies service the major part of the market with a standard product for which they themselves fix the price. Big companies are often the price leaders. Small companies try to find customers who are interested in a divergence from the standard product, such as a particular technological innovation. They make use of market niches.

Market niches

The nature of products

In some markets, the products that are traded are the same. These are termed homogenous products. Homogenous products are products that from the consumer's point of view are no different to each other. Heterogeneous or differentiated products are products that are sold on the same market, but are different in the eyes of the consumer. Where this applies it is called product differentiation. Product differentiation could involve changes to the technical features of an existing product. In particular, the construction of industrial goods is frequently changed to comply with the specific wishes of certain customer groups. Doing this could enable a supplier to corner a segment of the market.

Product differentiation

Technical features

Companies could also develop a completely new product, a process termed product innovation. The new product will supersede the existing products. This could give rise to a completely new industry that will initially have a monopolistic character.

Product innovation

Product differentiation can also involve differences between products that are not so much concerned with the technical aspects of the product, but with other aspects such as packaging, advertising, and acceptance by consumers. In the eyes of the consumer, different packaging or advertising may make the product itself different. Many goods and services can be sold on specialised markets simply by adapting the packaging or advertising to various customer personality types. Design, packaging and advertising can be designed to appeal to consumer preferences for the sporty, youthful, fresh, erotic or some other fashionable trend.

Other aspects

How heterogenous products are, is dependent on a variety of product features and production processes. Table 3.2 lists the main ones.

TABLE 3.2 Industry features and product differentiation

Homogenous	Differentiated
Products features and production processes:	
Mass production	Tailor made assembly
Intensive use of raw materials	Intensive use of know-how and R&D
(low-tech)	(high-tech)
Process innovation	Product innovation
Start of production chain	End of production chain
(basic goods)	(end products)
Features of the competitive process:	
Price competition	Quality competition
Little advertising	A lot of advertising

Large plants

Some companies install large plants to make products by means of mass production techniques. Some examples of this are the petroleum and chemical industries (petrol, fertilisers and raw materials for chemical processes). There is also some large-scale production in the services sector: in the communications sector, for example, the service provided by telecommunication companies, which consists for the main part of providing the required telephone connections as well as the energy to make them operational. The distribution of gas, water and electricity is also an example of large-scale servicing. The banking industry also provides products that have a mass and homogenous character. These services are **Commodity** usually called commodity services because the production has many of the **services** hallmarks of the mass production of homogenous goods. The production **Mass production** process is highly computerised, the technical innovations are aimed at a **Product** reduction in costs, the products are almost completely standardised and **differentiation** almost no product differentiation is possible.

The products that are made by intensive use of raw materials are usually at the beginning of the production chain and they are usually more homogenous than end products. Companies that make these products usually use a lot of raw materials and add little value to them themselves. This is why they are referred to as low-tech products. Homogenous basic goods are used to make differentiated end products. Grain and milk are relatively homogenous products that are used to make various products. Grain is made into pasta, all kinds of bread and cakes. Milk is the basis for a variety of cheeses, drinks and desserts. End products frequently consist of a combination of a large number of basic products. Car parts, for instance, contain all kinds of metals and synthetics. The closer the production is to the consumer, the greater the possibility of differentiation.

Process innovation is aimed at making the competitive position stronger by reducing costs. Not only producers of goods, but also producers of services can reduce costs by improving their production processes. The retail trade, for example, can reduce its stock on hand by improving the logistical process, thus lowering costs. Improving the logistical process brings with it economies of scale and consequently there is a tendency to concentration in many sectors of the retail trade. Product innovation requires a great deal of R&D, marketing efforts and the like. This means that companies add a lot of value to products. This is why they are referred to as high-grade products.

TEST 3.3
Why would labour costs and profits form a relatively high part of the price of high-tech products?

Differentiated products can compete on the basis of quality. Customers are prepared to pay a higher price for products of a higher quality.
Price competition is often keen when it is almost impossible to add exclusive features to products. Sometimes it is possible to differentiate between homogenous products by advertising. For products such as washing powders, soft drinks (cola) or petrol, which have a high degree of similarity as far as their technical aspects are concerned, the differentiation lies mainly in the brand name of the producer. In prosperous countries, these brand names are heavily promoted in advertising campaigns, whereby they take on an enhanced importance in the awareness of consumers. This is why brand names often represent greater value than the other assets of a company.

Cost structure of production
The company cost structure has been treated in Chapter 2. For an analysis of competition, the main elements are as follows:
- The relationship between fixed and variable costs. Companies with high fixed costs are very sensitive to underutilisation of production capacity. This usually leads to heavily reduced selling prices.
- Differences in cost patterns between large and small companies within the industry. When there is no economy of scale, competition is particularly fierce.

Entry barriers
Entry barriers may prevent companies from developing activities in an existing industry. These impediments will affect potential competition.

Beginning of the production chain

3

3

In industries where entry impediments are great there will be little threat to profits from newcomers on the market.

High fixed costs

High fixed costs are an important entry barrier since the entrants will have to invest heavily. They know beforehand that any additional supply could cause pressure on prices. Their entry could mean that all suppliers will suffer losses. This situation could last for a long time because it will be difficult to edge competitors out of the market. Exiting the market involves high costs as well. Dismantling and selling factories will involve enormous losses. The exit barriers are also considerable in capital-intensive industries.

Production heterogeneity

Production heterogeneity is also an important entry impediment. Companies that service a segment of the market tend to create customer loyalty. Newcomers find it difficult to build up the same loyalty. Customer loyalty

Brand awareness

is often attained by means of brand awareness. Existing companies make use of sales-creating measures that have been used in the past and they therefore have more economies of scale than newcomers. Entrants will be faced with large initial losses.

Share of the market

Sometimes a cost leader active within a market deliberately keeps the price below that of his competitors in order to safeguard his share of the market. This strategy has an impact on the market structure because it tends to lead to market concentration. Competitors who suffer losses will be forced to leave the market and potential entrants will be frightened off. A lowest cost strategy combined with lowering prices is an effective entry deterrent. Existing patents can also constitute a barrier to entering an industry. Companies can use patents to obtain a monopoly on production for a long period. Patent availability is for many companies a precondition for their

R&D

R&D. Companies naturally want their R&D expenditure to bear results. If the results of their research could be applied immediately by other producers, R&D would be a costly joke. This issue is very important in the pharmacy market. It is difficult to enter a market where the big companies protect their production by means of patents.

Forward and backward integration

In some markets, forward and backward integration is used by companies to increase their market position in relation to their own customers and suppliers, but also to threaten off prospective entrants to the market. The newcomers have to reckon with the fact that they have a horizontal

Strategic overcapacity

competitor on their supplier and customer markets. Finally, strategic overcapacity in an industry is a way of creating barriers. Existing companies will only make use of this capacity when other companies try to enter the market. Entrants will have to consider that over and above the extra supply that they themselves bring onto the market they will be faced with an extra output by the existing companies, and this will exert a lot of pressure on prices. Because of their high initial expenditure, the entrants will face considerable losses, and this will make survival unlikely. In industries that require high investments, the costs involved in leaving the industry are especially great, which makes entry to the industry particularly risky.

Demand features

Demand factors are a crucially important aspect of competition within any industry. These factors include increase in demand, customer concentrations, the proportion of consumer goods in the total output and export share.

TEST 3.4

If you were to start a business, would you rather be active in a saturated market or in a growing market?

Increase in demand is a crucial aspect of competition analysis. Growing markets are very attractive for companies, since even though the share of the market will remain the same, sales can increase. No price concessions have to be made to increase output. This is why the internal competition is less than within markets with little growth. Customers in strongly growing markets cannot exert much pressure on prices either. Any increase in supply is often not or not entirely sufficient to cope with the increase in demand: there is a degree of scarcity, therefore. Suppliers have greater market strength than demanders. Where this occurs, it is termed a seller's market. Competition is relatively small on markets with a high growth rate. Growth can be the result of a trend or of the business cycle. High growth rates resulting from a certain trend are characteristic of industries that apply new communication technology. The high growth rate will not be permanent, however. After some time, sales will decrease because of saturation of the market (as has notably happened with the mobile telephone market). Companies that have invested heavily during the growth period might then encounter cost problems that could bring them in serious trouble. There will be underutilisation of production capacity due to a drop in sales. Cyclical trends occur in the chips industry, to take one example. A utilisation rate of less than 50% is not uncommon during a decline. Influences on the performance of businesses exerted by the business cycle that currently prevails in a country is dealt with extensively in Chapter 6.

Companies may also supply to other industries. Their business customers will form a more or less consolidated group. A concentration on the demand side is an important cause of fierce external competition. The market strength of customers is proportional to the degree of concentration. When concentration is high they can more easily pass on any decrease in sales price onto their suppliers. Customers with a large amount of market strength can also impose conditions such as product quality standards on their suppliers. They can even prevent an increase in concentration on the supply side. Big customers will, for instance, prevent their suppliers forming cartels or collaborating in other ways in respect of prices and quantities supplied. The same principle holds for input markets: the more consolidated they are, the more market strength the suppliers will have.

The proportion of consumer goods in the output will provide an indication of how consolidated the customers are. Concentration will be very low on consumer markets because the numbers of consumers that purchase goods and services are large. The public utility firms (water, gas, electricity), banks, insurance companies and newspapers are all big companies that supply consumers directly. However, many companies that make consumer products supply the wholesale or retail trade directly rather than the consumer. In the retail trade in particular, industries can be highly amalgamated. They can also increase their market strength by forming purchasing combines. In their advertising, many producers of consumer goods approach the consumer directly, thus reducing the disadvantages of a concentration of the intermediate layers. It looks increasingly as though only those producers with strong brands will survive such fierce competition.

Chapter 6 will describe production as it takes place in the open and in the protected sector. The open sector consists of companies that sell many of their products on international markets and the protected sector consists of

Margin notes:

Increase in demand

Growing markets

No price concessions

Seller's market

3

Concentration of customers and suppliers

Market strength

Consumer products

Foreign export

companies that are almost exclusively active on the domestic market. The first group includes industrial and transport companies. They frequently have to deal with very large foreign competitors that can profit from cost advantages within their home markets. There is likely to be constant price pressure, especially when production takes place in low-wage countries. On the domestic market, they also often have to deal with international companies, which means that they often face stiffer competition than companies in the protected sector.

3.2.3   Market structures

Companies that supply products to the same market are in competition with each other for a share of that market. Some markets are characterised by a lot of businesses players; on other markets, there may be only a few or even a single player. Some markets tend to sell homogeneous products; others are characterised by greater variety.

Number of suppliers

Product differentiation

In the microeconomic literature, markets are usually classified according to the number of suppliers and the extent of product differentiation. These criteria are used to classify the markets in Table 3.3. All other factors that determine competition have been disregarded here.

TABLE 3.3 Market structures

Nature of products		
Number of suppliers	Homogenous (Undifferentiated)	Differentiated
Many	Perfect competition	Monopolistic competition
Few	Undifferentiated oligopoly	Differentiated oligopoly
One	Monopoly	–

Perfect competition

A market with perfect competition has many suppliers. They produce homogeneous products. Typical markets are sugar beet, milk, grain and the market for dollars. These markets are very large, compared to the sales of each individual supplier. The price is established by supply and demand.

Price is a given

The price is a given for individual suppliers, a fact on which they cannot exercise any influence. Individual suppliers of dollar assets cannot increase prices by withholding their dollars from the market. The price will not change, due to such a small change in quantity. However, they can decide to withhold their dollars if the market price is too low, and offer them at a later time when prices are higher. Suppliers in markets with perfect competition are price takers and quantity adapters. In Figure 3.4, a situation of perfect competition is shown.

In the left-hand section of Figure 3.4, the collective supply and demand curves are shown. An equilibrium quantity of 3,000 and an equilibrium price of 10, are achieved. In the right-hand section of Figure 3.4, the equilibrium price is shown as a horizontal line. The market prices are shown for every supplier. It is irrelevant how much an individual supplier offers. The price will remain constant. The price is equal to the sales per unit product, or the average revenue. As the price is constant, the average revenue is equal to the

FIGURE 3.4 Market balance and individual balance

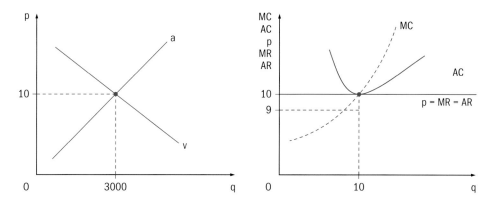

marginal revenue (see also chapter 4). The company will receive the same price for every product.

Based on the market price, the entrepreneur determines the quantity he will offer to maximise his profit (see right-hand of Figure 3.4). The company that strives to maximise its profit, will offer a quantity for which the marginal costs are exactly equal to the price of 10. At a price of 10, the manufacturer will therefore offer 10 units on the market. This is a very small quantity compared to the size of the market (3,000), and proves again that the individual supplier has little influence on the price.

In Figure 3.4, the average total costs (AC) curve is also drawn. The total cost (100) can simply be calculated with the aid of Figure 3.4 by multiplying the costs per unit (10) by the number of units (10). The company therefore has neither profit nor loss for a revenue of 100.

In markets with perfect competition, there is most of the time, much information with regard to prices and products. Prices are set at auctions or public markets (stock-exchange, money markets) and are often published in trade journals. By definition, there are hardly any entrance barriers. This is only possible if the fixed costs are low. Usually, there are many small companies that are active in markets with perfect competition.

In Table 3.4, structure, behaviour and result are schematically presented for the market of perfect competition.

TABLE 3.4 Perfect competition: structure, behaviour and result

Structure	Behaviour	Result
Many suppliers	Adapt quantity	Price equal to minimal costs
Homogeneous product		
Full information		
No entry barriers	No price, product or advertising competition	No profit in the long-term
Low fixed costs	No individual innovation	

In practice, companies do not all have the same cost curves. There are many differences between companies, and this will lead to cost differences, due to dissimilarities in management and geographical location. Hence, some companies can be more profitable than others. These are the so-called

**Entrepreneurs'
premiums**

entrepreneurs' premiums: profit opportunities which derive from individual differences between companies.

Monopolistic competition
In the market of monopolistic competition, there are many suppliers who offer slightly different products. The market is monopolistic because each producer is the only provider of his own specific market. He therefore

**Control over the
price**

has a certain control over the price. The market is characterised by the competition, as the product varieties compete with the varieties of other suppliers. Hence the term 'monopolistic competition'. The control over price is fairly limited. A good example of monopolistic competition is the

Clothing market

clothing market in a particular city. Usually there are many suppliers, who in addition are also located in a shopping centre.
There are dissimilarities in clothing, reflecting an obvious taste difference. Nevertheless, consumers make their eventual choice based on the price. If a clothes shop sets its prices too high, sales will decrease. On the other hand, sales can increase due to a price reduction.

**Furniture retail
trade**

Another good example of an industry with a monopolistic competition market is the furniture retail trade. There are a very large number of suppliers. They each attempt to exploit their different product characteristics. In Figure 3.5, a situation of monopolistic competition is shown.

FIGURE 3.5 Monopolistic competition

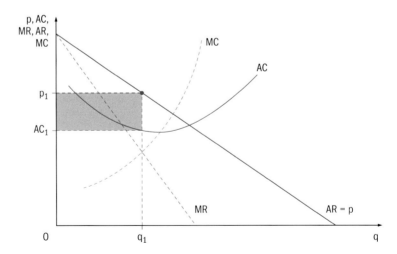

Demand curve

The demand curve shows the relationship between price and quantity demanded. The demand curve applies for this market form however, to a company, and therefore shows the relationship between the price and sales

Price sales curve

of this one particular company. It is therefore called the price sales curve or the average revenue curve.

In the market of monopolistic competition, there is a demand curve for every product. These individual demand curves have a declining development: buyers wish to buy more at a lower price. The differences between the products are so small, that they are easily substitutable. The demand curve is therefore relatively flat. A price increase will lead to a steep drop in demand, as consumers can easily switch to an alternative.

Easily
substitutable

In Figure 3.5, the marginal revenue curve is also shown. In markets without perfect competition, these do not coincide with the average revenue curves as they do in a market with perfect competition. In decreasing average sales, the revenue of an additional unit is lower than the average revenue. The lower revenue of the additional product, will lower the average. The MR curve will therefore decrease faster than the AR curve (see also chapter 4).

In Figure 3.5, besides the revenue curves, the average and marginal cost curves of the company are also presented. The profit is at maximum if the marginal revenue is equal to the marginal costs. At the point where MR = MC, the company will offer q1. Quantity q1 corresponds with price p1. The total revenue is p1 × q1. The total costs are the product of q1 and the related average total costs, AC1. The variance between both is the profit, the brown area in figure 6.3. The company therefore generates profit. Owing to the small scale of the individual suppliers, there are few entry barriers. Potential entrants see their opportunities and also enter the market. Due to this, the profit will reduce.

Most markets of monopolistic competition are fairly easily accessible. This market form occurs also in the retail trade and the service industry, such as hospitality and advertising agencies. Starters require very little capital to set up a business. It is usually fairly easy to obtain the required knowledge.

Entrepreneurs operating in this type of market, have more options to compete than entrepreneurs in markets with perfect competition. As mentioned already, they can reduce their prices to influence their sales. It is also possible to attract customers by advertising and further product differentiation. Individual advertising campaigns and technical development therefore, play a much larger role in this type of market than in a market with perfect competition. There are many options to achieve entrepreneurs' premiums.

In conclusion, in Table 3.5, the structure, behaviour and result of entrepreneurs operating in a monopolistic competition market are shown.

TABLE 3.5 Monopolistic competition: structure, behaviour and result

Structure	Behaviour	Result
Many suppliers	Price-setter	Many options for entrepreneurs' premium
Heterogeneous product	Concentration	
Incomplete information		
Minor entry barriers	Competition through price,	No industry profit in the long-term
Many customers	product, advertising	

Oligopoly

In the oligopolistic market, there are only a small number of suppliers. They can take each other's activities into consideration. This concerns for example, manufacturers of large product markets supplying for example, cars and consumer electronics. Most industrial markets are oligopolistic by nature. There can be two suppliers, but also twenty. If there are few suppliers, this is known as a *narrow oligopoly* and if there are more suppliers, it is a *wide oligopoly*. The suppliers attempt to keep as much as possible all knowledge on their products and production processes a secret to their competitors, then they can use their competition advantage. This market form is characterised by incomplete information. Manufacturers are continuously busy renovating their products and production processes. Technical development plays an important role in this.

Economy of scale

High entry barriers

Economy of scale and a high minimum efficiency scale assure high entry barriers. The number of suppliers is always limited and constant. The number of customers in oligopolistic markets however, can vary strongly. Some producers only have a customer for certain products, such as in railway construction, where a few suppliers only have the rail company as a buyer. Other producers have many customers, such as car manufacturers. As mentioned, oligopolistic suppliers take each other's activities into consideration. In Table 3.3, a distinction was made between a homogeneous and heterogeneous oligopoly. As the latter type is dominant, and producers of homogeneous products will do their utmost to distinguish themselves

Heterogeneous oligopoly

from one another, only the heterogeneous oligopoly will be further discussed.

Assume that there are two companies offering a particular product at a certain price. Let us further assume that one of the two changes the price. This will not only have sales consequences for that company but also for the other company. If for example, company A decreases its price, its sales will increase and the sales of company B will decrease. Company B will take immediate action by also lowering its price. If company B further sets a price lower than that of company A, the sales of A will decrease rather than

Price war

Action and reaction

increase. Company A will also have to further decrease its price. This will result in a price war, which sometimes occurs in this type of market. The pattern of action and reaction is typical for the oligopolistic market.

As price wars are negative for both companies (A and B), they will usually avoid using their price-setting as a competing instrument. Businesses often only compete by introducing new product characteristics and advertising campaigns. There is no price rigidity. In Figure 3.6, the price sales or demand curve of company A is shown.

Assume that company A offers quantity q1 on the market at price p1. A price increase would result in a severe decrease in demand. The customers would go to company B. If company B does not change its price, it will be able to take over a large amount of the demand. If company A lowers its price, the sales will increase, but less than expected, because company B also reduces

Kinked demand curve

its price. There is actually a inked price sales curve or kinked demand curve. Left of point (q1, p1), the curve is much more elastic than at the right-hand of the point (q1,p1). Company B also has a kinked demand curve. Both companies will maintain their prices, also if they do not generate maximum profit.

FIGURE 3.6 Price sales curve in an oligopolistic market

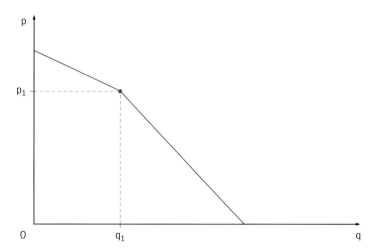

This situation can be clarified with the aid of game theory. Total sales will reduce.   Game theory

In Table 3.6, an example based on game theory is provided, showing the various behavioural options of two businesses A and B, operating in an oligopoly. In the matrix, the profit of company A is shown left, before the profit of company B.

TABLE 3.6 Behavioural problems of oligopolists

Company B	Company A		
	Same price		Price increase
Same price	(8,8)		(4,12)
		Profit (A,B)	
Price increase	(12,4)		(10,10)

The situation at which both companies end up has the following options:
a   Both companies can achieve more profit by selling less. The price will increase and so will the profit (area 4).
b   One of the two companies, for example A, increases its price, while B maintains the same price. The sales of A will decrease and B will take over part of the market of A. The profit of A will decrease and that of B will increase (area 2).
c   Both companies do nothing and the profit will remain constant (area 1).

Both companies will benefit if they both increase their prices and reduce their sales (option a). For the companies this is beneficial, but not for society as a whole. The sales, and therefore the consumption, will decrease if prices increase.

For each individual company however, it is best to do nothing while the other increases his price (option b). As they are suspicious of each other, they will both wait and do nothing (option c).
Both companies are trapped in the suspicion they have towards one another. This theory was first applied to the behaviour of prisoners, and is therefore called the prisoners' dilemma

Prisoners' dilemma

Option *a* will lead to an optimum situation for both companies, however they will have to make a mutual agreement on their behaviour. They will adjust their behaviour or even enter into a cartel agreement. A cartel agreement is a cooperation between companies with regard to price-setting, market-sharing, etc. Such agreements are prohibited in most countries. Nevertheless, as cartel agreements in oligopolistic markets are very profitable for the companies involved, there will be many such agreements in this type of market.

Cartel agreement

The European Commission tracks down cartel agreements. Companies which enter into a cartel agreement can turn themselves in and the European Commission reduces their fine. This makes it attractive to become a whistle blower on cartel agreements, and due to this, companies have become even more suspicious of one another.

Markets of monopolistic competition often become oligopolistic markets. Due to concentration in the industry, such as the retail trade, large business chains emerge, benefiting from economies of scale.
In Table 3.7 the characteristics of an oligopoly are summarized.

TABLE 3.7 Oligopoly: structure, behaviour and result

Structure	Behaviour	Result
Few suppliers	Reaction to competitors	Price rigidity
Heterogeneous/homogeneous product		
Incomplete information	Competition through product,	Profit, but not maximized
Entry barriers	advertising	
Few/many customers	Cartel agreements	

Monopoly

In a monopoly market, one supplier offers a particular product. There are three types of monopoly: the legal monopoly, technical monopoly and natural monopoly. In the legal monopoly, the government has left the production of certain types of goods and services to a company. This is, or was until recently, the case for public utilities, gas extraction, exploitation of the natural gas network, the Dutch Railways and exploitation of the cable and telephone networks. The government sets guidelines and directions with regard to the obligation to supply, price-setting, etc. Legal monopolies can also occur by patenting of certain products. Over a certain period of time, the government can grant the production rights to companies which have performed the technical development. In an economical, or technical monopoly, the company concerned has the availability of production factors which no other company has. In a natural monopoly, there is an 'endless' economy of scale. It is nearly impossible for other companies to enter the market, because one large company supplies the entire market and has an endless economy of scale during production. Even if there would

Legal monopoly

Technical monopoly

Natural monopoly

be a few suppliers, the smallest would be pushed out of the market very quickly. The market maintains the monopoly in a 'natural' manner. This monopoly may occur in mining and quarrying.

A monopolist is the sole supplier of a market. He influences price. This can be noticed in the decreasing development of the price sales function. A monopolist can set combinations of prices and quantities on the demand curve. In the event of a decreasing price, demand will increase. The price sales curve shows for every quantity, the average sales revenue of the company. In Figure 3.7, the average and marginal revenue and costs are presented.

FIGURE 3.7 The average and marginal revenue and costs of a monopolist are presented

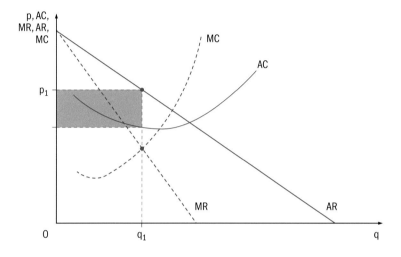

A monopolist that strives to maximise his profit, will offer a quantity for which the marginal costs are equal to the marginal revenue. This corresponds to price p1, which is on the AR curve.
The profit of each product, is the difference between the price and the average costs. The total profit is the profit of each product, multiplied by the number of products (the brown area in Figure 3.7).

In concluding this paragraph, the structure, behaviour and result of the monopolistic market are summarised in Table 3.8.

TABLE 3.8 Monopoly: structure, behaviour and result

Structure	Behaviour	Result
One supplier	Profit maximisation	Short and long-term profits
Homogeneous product	Price limits	
Complete information		
No entry barriers		
Few/many customers		

3.3 Business conduct and business results (performance)

Businesses engage in a wide variety of activities in order to achieve their objectives. Short-run profit maximisation (Section 3.3.1) is one of these. Companies can do this by obtaining the highest price possible or by reducing their costs to the lowest level possible. The continuity of the company is another important objective. Companies need to safeguard their long-run profitability. Being innovative (Section 3.3.2) or consciously making adjustments to the structure of the industry (Section 3.3.3) are two possibilities to consider.

3.3.1   Profit maximisation

Profitability requirements

Companies aim for maximum profit. This aim is usually formulated in certain profitability requirements. These requirements are based on premises such as average industry profit margin and past profitability. In order to improve on or maintain profitability, companies may take short-term measures such as raising prices or lowering costs.

Pricing

An increase in costs is the main reason for a decrease in profits. Companies will try to recover their costs by raising prices. Not all businesses can do this, however. It can only be done if specific requirements are met. Table 3.9 sums these up.

TABLE 3.9 Passing on increased costs in the selling price

Industry features	Possibilities for passing costs on	
	Easy	Difficult
Market structure	Monopoly	Perfect competition
Degree of internationalisation	low	high
Average capacity utilisation	high	low
Price elasticity of demand	low	high

Market structure

The market structure a company is working in is significant. A monopolist (the electricity company in a certain region, for example) can pass on the raised energy costs in its prices without too much difficulty. Only companies with sufficient market strength can use price as a weapon in the battle for maximum profits. In particular, such price-setting behaviour is possible in markets with a high level of concentration. Companies with relatively little market strength have their hands tied as far as their prices are concerned. Their prices are at the mercy of the market and are determined by supply and demand. A company such as a small transport firm, whose market is highly competitive, will have to be much more reticent to pass on increased oil costs in its prices.

Price-setting behaviour

Degree of inter-nationalisation

The degree of internationalisation also plays a role. Companies with high import and export ratios are limited in their ability to pass costs on.

Overcapacity

A third factor of importance is overcapacity. Overcapacity also limits the possibility of passing costs on. The companies concerned would be more inclined to lower prices in order to increase capacity usage. Finally, the price elasticity of demand plays an important role. Petrol for private use has proven to be a relatively inelastic product. This is a favourable condition for oil companies to pass on the raised cost of energy in the price of petrol.

Price elasticity of demand

Cost strategies

Companies that aim for maximum profit would be better off trying to keep their cost levels below those of their competitors. Such a strategy is termed a lowest cost or cost leadership strategy. It is a particularly suitable strategy for large companies within an industry that can profit from economies of scale. There are two ways open to them to make use of such an advantageous situation.

Cost levels

Economies of scale

In the first place, they can fix their prices at the level of their competitors. This means that they can create a higher profit margin than their competitors. However, this creates the threat of new entrants. Potential entrants will be attracted by the high profit margins and will try to corner a piece of the market for themselves. The business conduct of these entrepreneurs will cause the market structure to become less tightly amalgamated. Loss of market share and the decrease in market prices will force the producer concerned to keep on lowering his costs. In order to increase their share of the market, companies that have adopted a cost leadership strategy could also lower their price to below that of their competitors. This type of price setting is termed limit pricing. A company with a market share of between 40% and 100% can attain a price leadership position comfortably. The other companies in the industry will adjust their prices to those of such a company. If a lowest cost strategy with on-going price decreases to below the level of the competitors is successful, the competitors will in the end be forced to leave the industry and the industry will become a monopoly. Despite the advantages of limit pricing it is not always a good thing. With an inelastic demand, decreases in price will lead to decreased returns despite increased sales. This could affect profits in the entire industry. Such a situation is described as profit erosion by price cutting. Such a business practice is obviously not suitable for every market. Companies on oligopolistic markets will often elect to adopt a certain price rigidity which gives the industry some degree of stability. This is all the more important if entrepreneurs are not certain about the cost levels of their competitors. Table 3.5 summarises the lowest cost strategy.

Higher profit margin

New entrants

Share of the market

Limit pricing

Profit erosion

Price rigidity

TEST 3.5
A manufacturer of metal products is experiencing a lot of competition from the eastern European countries. The company is considering a cost leadership strategy. How wise is this in your opinion?

In general, companies that follow a cost strategy correspond to the identifying features in the left-hand column of Table 3.10.

TABLE 3.10 The lowest cost strategy

Costs leadership in combination with	Consequences
Prices at or above the level of competitors	High profit margin for the cost leader
	Possibly more competitors (deconcentration)
Prices below the level of competitors	Large share of the market and high profits for the cost leader
	Competitors leave the market (concentration)
	Profit erosion in the industry through price cutting

Investments

Investing is one way that companies can lower their costs. Companies that invest a lot are able to keep on increasing their productivity since they are able to introduce the newest techniques that supplying firms have developed.

Innovation

Companies that want their profits to continue will put more emphasis on product differentiation than on cost control. Costs associated with the development of new products, markets and distribution channels will be unavoidable. Being innovative is at the expense of short-run profitability. Chapter 4 treats innovative company conduct in more detail.

Being innovative

In general terms, companies that follow a product differentiation strategy correspond to the characteristics set out in the right-hand column of Table 3.2.

3.3.2   Entry and exit

Companies can strengthen their competitive position by taking over other companies and disposing of some of their divisions. Industries and production chains where this happens frequently are relatively dynamic. This section deals with these dynamics.

When companies within an industry expand at the expense of other companies or acquire an interest in other companies, this is termed a horizontal concentration. When a decreasing number of suppliers obtain an increasing share of the market the market will be more consolidated. One effect of concentration is that decisions about production are made in increasingly fewer places. The main reasons for wanting to consolidate are outlined below.

Increasing market share

Increasing market share is one important reason for concentration. Companies can strengthen their position considerably if they are the market leader and thus occupy a strong position in relation to their customers. Customers are less able to force market leaders to make price concessions than companies with a small share of the market.

Training economies of scale

As machines make large-scale production possible, companies can reduce the price of their products correspondingly. As transport improves, goods can be transported over greater distances at lower costs. The result is that companies can service a greater geographic area, and eventually a particular market will be serviced by fewer companies. Companies that become too small to produce for the lowest cost are forced to collaborate with others.

Getting rid of overcapacity

Industries whose markets are shrinking are usually eventually faced with overcapacity. The constant pressure on prices that this exerts causes the whole of the industry to suffer losses. With concentrations, the weakest companies are removed from the market, thus reducing any overcapacity.

Purchasing technology

Merging of businesses results in one firm's inventions becoming available to other firms as well. Some big multinationals have made it a policy to take over businesses that in the recent past have made inventions.

Until now we have been dealing with concentration within an industry. Companies can also be active in other industries. Such concentrations can be described in the following terms:
- Forward and backward integration
- Diversification
- Conglomeration.

For the sake of completeness, it should be mentioned that the corresponding trend away from concentration is termed specialisation.

These will be explained in the following sections and the trends that give rise to them will be discussed.

Many individual companies do not restrict their activities to one industry but are active in several links of the production chain. Manufacturers may, for instance, take over the wholesaler of their products (forward integration) or they can take over their own suppliers (backward integration). Integrated companies control their suppliers or their customer markets either partly or wholly. Oil companies like Shell control the whole value chain from initial producer to consumer.

Integration

The main reason for integration is to eliminate the market strength of the opponent. If a company has to cope with customers with strong bargaining positions on its selling markets it could try to take over one of them. Companies that want to know more about their end markets frequently also resort to forward integration. The closer they are to their final customers the faster they can react to changing needs, thereby reducing uncertainty about demand trends.

Supplier markets can also be highly uncertain, especially in relation to price levels. For example, prices of raw materials can vary strongly as a result of changes in demand, which are frequently cyclical. Price rises of more than 50% are not uncommon in the raw materials market. Companies that produce their own raw materials will not be affected by these price increases. On the other hand, they will not profit from a decrease in prices either. Consequently, some companies try to be independent of the market for half of their raw materials, thereby reducing the risk of price fluctuations as much as possible.

Improving the quality of the end product is another reason for integration. There is an increasing trend for companies to tighten their grip on their suppliers. If companies regard the quality of their supplies as inadequate they may start their own supply companies or take over supply companies. Such activities are potentially able to invigorate the entire production chain.

Diversification is the process whereby companies introduce goods and services from another production chain into their package of products. When this involves goods and services in the same link of the production chain, this is termed parallelisation. To take an example: a wholesale meat company considers the markets that are available insufficient and so it expands its range of products to include dairy products. Companies frequently resort to diversification to increase their efficiency. Conglomerates of companies may be active in diverse and completely unconnected industries and links of production chains. Conglomeration was a trend in the 1970s, when it was thought that there were immense economies of scale to be had through computerisation, which at that time could only be afforded by large companies. Since computerisation is no longer restricted to business of a certain size, most conglomerates have now been disbanded.

Diversification

Conglomeration

Specialised companies are active in one or more industries. Companies that specialise usually start off by determining the fields in which they have unique expertise. They formulate a number of core activities and divest themselves of other activities. Increasing pressure of competition often forces companies to specialise. Competition may cause activities that are not part of the core activities to incur losses. In particular, companies that operate on the world market encounter a lot of competition. They usually

Specialisation

3

have to produce on a very large scale in order to keep their costs low. They also have to put immense effort into research and development in order to keep on bringing new products onto the market. If the companies can focus strongly on their core activities they can meet both of these requirements.

Table 3.11 gives an overview of industry activities and their main causes.

TABLE 3.11 Activities in various industries

Activities	Aim	Background causes
Integration	Improving market knowledge and market strength	Segmented end markets
	Improving the value chain	Fluctuating prices of raw materials
		Increasing importance of product quality
Diversification	Improving efficiency	Company too big for markets
	Spreading of risks	Increasing product differentiation
	Complete range of products	
Conglomeration	Economies of scale	Not a current trend
Specialisation	Profitable core activities only	Increasing competition through internationalisation

Horizontal and vertical concentration is often brought about by various legal means. The following options are available:
- A takeover or merger;
- A consortium or cooperation arrangement;
- A voluntary chain, purchasing combine or franchise organisation;
- A joint venture;
- A cartel.

A takeover of companies by other companies has already been mentioned. This is what happens when a big company buys up a much smaller company and absorbs it into the larger one. Equal partners combining **Merger** their activities into one company is termed a merger. In both cases, the companies lose their independence.

In some forms of cooperation, however, the companies involved do retain their independence.

Consortium A consortium is a type of partnership between companies that is of a temporary nature. It is usually aimed at carrying out a specific project, such as a large infrastructure construction (a bridge or a tunnel, for example). Financial companies sometimes form a consortium to issue a large loan. **Cooperative** A cooperative is a collaborative arrangement between companies (usually in different parts of the production chain) to work together with the aim of controlling supply or customer markets. The agrarian sector has a great number of purchasing, sales and production companies that collaborate with each other. They come into being to improve the market strength of independent but very small agrarian firms. Purchasing combines are **Purchasing combines** largely confined to the retail trade industry. They primarily strengthen the competitive position of small businesses threatened by the big supermarket chains. These chains can price sharply because they can force their suppliers to reduce their prices.

A voluntary chain is an association retailers can join that originates from a wholesaler. The association does communal purchases and part of the sales promotion. Voluntary chains only occur in the retail grocery industry.

Voluntary chain

A franchise is a contract between a franchisor and franchisee in which it is stipulated that the franchisee may exercise some of the rights of the franchisor, such as using a brand name, using a certain method of production or producing and selling a certain product. Franchise contracts are often made between manufacturers and importers or retailers. Some examples are to be found in the petrol and car industries.

Franchise

A joint venture is a joint subsidiary of a number of companies. Joint ventures are usually started if a certain activity is particularly risky. They enable the risk to be spread over a number of companies. Joint ventures are often started to profit from the specific know-how that various companies have. European companies that want to enter the Asian market can do so by starting a joint venture with an Asian company. The European company can provide the technical expertise while the Asian company can provide knowledge of the market and distribution channels.

Joint venture

Cartel agreements can be made between various companies in order to limit competition. Cartelisation is common, but it is illegal unless the consumer profits from it. Any exceptions to the ban have to have been clearly laid down by law.

Cartel

Table 3.12 gives an overview of the options available for concentration.

TABLE 3.12 Concentration: the legal options

Types	Most common sector	Reasons
Merger/takeover	Almost all sectors	Economies of scale
Consortium	Industry, building trade, banks	Spreading the risks of large projects
Cooperative	Agrarian sector	Obtaining market strength in relation to customers and suppliers
Voluntary chain/franchise	Retail trade	Economies of scale in purchasing and sales promotion
Joint venture	Industry	Bringing in various types of skills and know-how
		Spreading risks
Cartels (no legal option)	All sectors	Obtaining market strength

3.3.3 Performance

Performance variables are variables used to measure business and industry performance.

As Figure 3.3 shows, company performance is both determined by and is the reason for a particular business conduct. If market conditions are such that companies are able to make large profits, they will take the opportunity to take over some of their competitors and to enter other sectors or take similar courses of action, thereby changing the market structure.

Performance variables can be classified as micro or macroeconomic variables.
Microeconomic variables include profitability, sales opportunities and innovative performance. Macroeconomic variables include the contribution of the industry to the added value of a country and to employment.

TEST 3.6
In the second part of the 2010's, many companies used high profits to buy out competitors against very high prices. Suggest why and outline the risks they ran.

Profitability
Earning capacity

Profitability is the main variable for measuring the performance of companies and industries. Earning capacity can be estimated using all kinds of variables. For most business economic purposes, the most important factors are the rate of return a company can generate on shareholder equity as well as the total assets. The profit margin is also an often-used criterion. The average profitability of companies can differ from one industry to another, depending on the competition determining factors. The profitability of companies within the same industry can also show some variation. These differences can be analysed by comparing a particular company against the industry standard. The competitive position of individual companies can thereby be ascertained.

Sales
opportunities

The extent of demand is not only a structural variable. Industries can exert a major influence on demand by exporting, advertising and product innovation.
These means are effective in warding off other products. Demand is therefore also a performance variable. Increases in demand within the industry as a whole and sales increases by a particular company can vary. Suppliers who have developed a large amount of competitive strength and whose business conduct is successful will be rewarded by an increase in sales that will be higher than the increase in demand on the market. This may result in an increase in

Market profits

the share of the domestic market or in market profits on foreign markets.

Successful product development

The rewards gained by product development is also an important tool for gauging the extent to which suppliers can be innovative in their product development. One way of measuring that success is by looking at the number of patents and comparing this number to other industries.

Added value

Added value indicates the contribution an industry makes to the national income. An increase in added value that exceeds the growth of the national income indicates that the industry is performing strongly. The added value of an industry can also be compared to that of industries in other countries to determine a country's competitive position.

Employment

The employment growth in an industry can be compared to that in other countries. If an industry in a given country is very competitive, the employment rate will rise faster than in other countries. This is a positive indicator for overall employment in a country.

Labour productivity

Labour productivity is the basis for the prosperity of a country. In those industries where labour productivity is high, wages will also be high. The opposite is also true: if wages in a country or in an industry are high in comparison with other countries, they will have to be compensated for by high labour productivity. If this is not the case, the companies' costs will be too high to compete with companies in other countries. These industries will then gradually disappear.

3.4 The product's life cycle and industry structure

The structure, business conduct and performance of an industry will alter during the various phases of a product's life cycle. A life cycle is based on the assumption that the sale of products follows a standard pattern throughout the course of time. After a slow introductory phase start, there will be a period of rapid growth, after which sales growth stabilises (the maturity phase). This is followed by a decline phase in which sales decrease. The life cycles of products are subject to considerable variation. Some products last a few months before being superseded by new inventions; others last for centuries. Some products disappear from the market altogether, while others remain and their sales are about equal to the replacement demand.

The consecutive phases of a product's life cycle are accompanied by standard patterns of development within the industry.

Standard pattern

3

Introductory phase
Sales of a product that has just been put on the market are usually low. The fact that it is unknown to the customers means that demand will be low. The marketing expenses per product unit will have to be high to make the product a success. The other costs will also be high. The R&D expenses of the development stage will still exert a strong influence on the cost price, but production itself will also initially be small-scale and knowledge-intensive. The introduction phase is usually characterised by start-up losses. For the entrepreneur, this is a tense period during which it must become clear whether the product will catch on and whether the investments will eventually be recovered. The number of product suppliers will be small, with one particular supplier likely to have a monopoly on the new product. During the introductory phase, entrepreneurs will be highly innovative in their business conduct. If there are other suppliers doing research into the same product they will frequently seek cooperation in joint ventures in order to share the risks. Vertical integration is another way of safeguarding supply and output channels and of absorbing them into the innovative process.

Marketing expenses

R&D expenses

Start-up losses

Monopoly

TEST 3.7
Philips very rarely brings completely new consumer products on the market by itself. Instead, it tends to develop them jointly with Asian competitors. Suggest why it does this.

Growth phase
The growth phase is characterised by a rapid increase in sales since the product has become better known. Because of its exclusivity the product has a high elasticity of demand. Growing markets are very attractive for new entrants. The share of the market that the various suppliers have may fluctuate strongly because customers have not yet become attached to a particular brand or producer. Demand is frequently greater than supply, causing delivery problems. Companies move from a loss to a profit situation and profits rise rapidly. The market structure changes to a oligopoly with relatively many suppliers, a so-called wide oligopoly. All these suppliers

Exclusivity

New entrants

Profit situation

Oligopoly

Improving products and processes

Decrease in costs

work on improving products and processes with two aims in mind: firstly, to create their own segment of the market through product differentiation, and secondly, to make large-scale production possible by standardising the product and by improving the production processes. Production consequently becomes increasingly capital intensive. Because of the enormous decrease in costs, price competition, an important feature of the next phase, also starts to play a role.

Maturity phase

Everyday article

Replacement demand

Overcapacity

Forward and backward integration

During the maturity phase, there is a decline in growth: the market has started to become saturated. Income elasticity drops sharply because the product has become an everyday article. There are some new buyers, but the major part of the demand consists of replacement demand. The decline in growth frequently comes as a surprise to suppliers. During the period of intensive growth, the companies will have made large investments on the basis of the expected sales and the future market share. There is a very real chance of overcapacity, and especially in industries with a high capital intensity, high pressure on prices will result. Profits will no longer increase: at best, they will stabilise. Companies will be forced to carry efficiency to the extreme and cost cutting and redundancies will be common occurrences. Through amalgamations, mergers and takeovers the number of suppliers will be reduced to a reasonably constant level. The shares will stabilise. The market structure will become a narrow oligopoly with only a few suppliers. As well as horizontal concentration, companies will try to improve their competitive position by controlling the supply and sales markets. Forward and backward integration will occur. During this phase, a company may start to transfer production to low wage countries. This holds especially for products that can be sold on the international markets.

Decline phase

New products of the same type

Little R&D

Structural overcapacity

Stagnation monopoly

Depending on the emergence of new products of the same type, during the decline phase, sales will be reduced to the level of replacement demand. Some industries will disappear completely after a while; others will remain. Only a few suppliers will be left, and they will have transferred their production to low-wage countries as much as possible. The companies that are left will have to survive as best as they can. During the decline phase, companies pay little attention to R&D. Profits are usually low because of a structural overcapacity. During the decline phase, many companies call on the government to help them downsize. The market structure during this phase is known as a stagnation monopoly.
Table 3.8 shows the processes of concentration and deconcentration within industries during the various phases of the product's life cycle.

Although the product's life cycle can be used to analyse the dynamics of an industry, there are important objections to doing so.
Firstly, as we have already noted, many products stay in the maturity phase for a very long time, during which demand stabilises at the level of replacement demand. Developments that take place in such an industry are thus difficult to explain from the point of view of the product's life cycle because the level of sales does not alter.
Secondly, market analysis on the basis of the product's life cycle is mainly done in respect of industrial markets, which explains why the market structures *monopolistic competition* and *perfect competition* are missing

in Table 3.13. In the service sectors, the monopolistic competition market structure is common and in the agrarian sectors, perfect competition often occurs. These markets usually are governed by completely different dynamics.

TABLE 3.13 Industry changes and the product's life cycle

Phases in the product's life cycle	Market structure	Rivalry/cooperation
Introductory phase	Innovation monopoly	Joint ventures
		Vertical integration
Growth phase	Wide oligopoly	Competition based on quality
		Price competition
Maturity phase	Narrow oligopoly	Horizontal and vertical concentration
Decline phase	Stagnation monopoly	Cartelisation
		Government influence

TEST 3.8
What phase is the retail clothing industry going through at the present time?

There is a third reason as well: the product's life cycle is about products rather than industries. Industries usually produce more than one product, and when these products are superseded, companies always try to replace them by new ones. Manufacturers of black and white television sets do not go out of business when their product disappears: they simply produce one that will be more successful. The industry also remains, therefore. Notwithstanding this, a major part of the changes in competitive relationships can be explained from the product's life cycle. The transference of the production of low-grade products on saturated markets to low-wage countries is one such change (see Chapter 9).

3.5 Porter's diamond

The American economist M.E. Porter has developed a method of comparing the competitive strength of industries in different countries. Porter is of the opinion that the competitive strength of industries is mainly determined by environmental factors. These factors can be classified according to the strength of the production factors, the influence of government, the economic order and the degree to which industries reinforce each other by means of networks. Those environmental factors that are largely regionally determined cause some industries to have considerable competitive strength on international markets, while other industries are barely able to resist international competition. Porter therefore highlights the importance of regional differences in the analysis of competitive relationships. This is why he refers to the competitiveness of countries. His method is often used to compare industries in different countries. Porter's method is illustrated in Figure 3.8.

Environmental factors

Regionally determined

In Porter's diamond, the mutual influences on each of the elements is important. The government can, for instance, exert an important influence on the quality of production factors, thus stimulating high-tech production.

Mutual influences

FIGURE 3.8 Porter's diamond

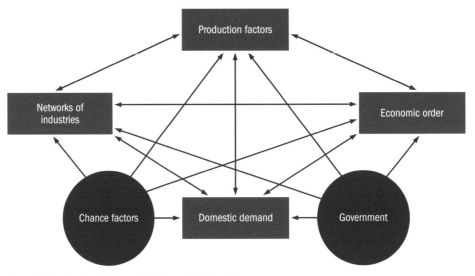

Source: M.E. Porter, *The Competitive Advantage of Nations*, London 1990, p. 127

A similar interaction holds for all elements in the diamond. This is why the model is a useful tool for studying the dynamic aspects of industries. The various elements of Figure 3.8 will be explained below.

Basic production factors

Production factors can be classified as basic production factors and advanced production factors. See also table 3.9. The basic production factors include the climate and the geographical position of the country, the presence of raw materials, capital and unskilled labour. Each country has these to a greater or lesser extent. They are, as it were, the inheritance of each generation and are enduring. In the Netherlands, production factors include position on the shore of a busy sea, the presence of rivers, a mild climate and a relatively large population.

Advanced production factors

Competitive strength depends largely on advanced production factors. These include skilled labour, education and research, physical infrastructure and telecommunications. These production factors come into being via ongoing investments made by the whole of the population. These are partly dependent on the political climate in a country and the amount of government interference. Countries use these advanced production factors to distinguish themselves from other countries.

A country's competitive strength can be boosted by human endeavour.

This can lead to areas of expertise that would at first glance seem unlikely to be developed. Incentives are often provided to encourage basic production factors to be combined with advanced production factors in order to obtain a relative advantage. Porter uses the Dutch cut-flower industry as an example of this: adverse climatic conditions were overcome by advanced hothouse technology and an advanced trading system (the Dutch auction system). In combination with the natural gas basic production factor, these high-tech production factors have led to a leading position on the world market.

We have already seen that companies can compete not only by reducing their costs, but also by increasing the quality of their products. Porter points out that for countries as a whole, the second way is much preferable to the first. Continual wage restraints are likely to have the effect of countries competing with products that are largely the result of basic production factors. There will be too few incentives to invest in advanced production factors. The added value of production will be low, therefore. Such a country will eventually lag behind in the international competitive race. Countries with a high wages level are forced to maintain their competitive advantage by keeping the level of expertise, R&D and the infrastructure high.

Quality of products

Wage restraints

TABLE 3.14 Production factors

Nature of the production factor	Consequences for competitive strength
Basic production factors (climate, population size, geographical position, natural resources)	Low-tech production Competition based on costs
Advanced production factors (education, knowledge, R&D, infrastructure)	High-tech production Competition based on quality

Domestic demand
The competitive strength of industries is influenced quite strongly by demand on the domestic market. Demanding and discerning customers force producers to provide high quality products and to regularly bring new products onto the market. Entrepreneurs must be constantly alert to new developments and be at the forefront of innovation. This is especially valid for those companies that serve the producer markets. Their customers are sometimes market leaders on the domestic as well as on the international market, which also offers the supplier a chance to create an internationally important position for himself. This situation also occurs on some consumer markets. Many American and Japanese producers have obtained

Discerning customers

a competitive advantage because their customers set international trends and thus have had an effect on other countries. American consumers are trendsetters in a great many fields, including audio-visual software (films, music) and cosmetics. Japanese products are often extremely compact because Japanese houses are very small. Japanese companies have therefore been able to make a name for themselves as producers of compact products. A single European market as a necessary condition for European companies to build up sufficient competitive strength is often used as an argument for the unification of Europe.

Discerning consumers who are willing to try new products are favourable for the competitive strength of companies. They make it possible for companies to quickly bring differentiated products onto a growing market, thereby building up an entry barrier against foreign producers and at the same time obtaining a favourable position in relation to international markets.

Large domestic market

Economies of scale

A large domestic market is important for the competitive strength of companies since it enables them to profit quickly from economies of scale. Economies of scale are only profitable for companies that can make use of them first. Companies that know their markets well have an advantage in this respect. As soon as other companies expand the size of their production the advantages will be eroded by the price concessions that will be necessary because of the increase in output.

Table 3.15 summarises domestic demand.

TABLE 3.15 The domestic demand

Aspects of demand	Consequences for competitive strength
Critical demand	Stimulates product innovation
Demand quantity	Economies of scale

Networks of industries

Products are never only produced by a single industry. As we have seen in Chapter 1, several industries in a production chain are always involved. A particular industry can only be competitive if the previous and the next links are strong and produce high quality goods. The value addition must be optimal within every link of the production process. Only when there is a strong relationship between suppliers and contractors in networks can high competitive strength be achieved. Networks can be described as non-market-based cooperations between individual companies in which an exchange of nonmarket-based expertise takes place. Parties along the production chain can thereby connect information about customers and potential new producers further along the production chain, making reactions to market changes potentially more effective and more direct. The competition between companies in the industry and in the production chain will thereby change into competition between different production chains. This tendency is especially obvious in the car industry. Production chains of contractors and suppliers of Asian, European and American car producers are in competition with each other.

Value addition optimal

In a vertical network of companies (in other words, with mutual relationships within the production chain), there is a final producer who supplies products to the final customers. They can be consumers or producers of capital goods. The final producer is a producer in his own right: he produces new products independently and uses independent R&D to do so. Final producers usually design and manufacture only the strategic parts of their products. Such a final producer is also known as an *Original Equipment Manufacturer* (OEM). An OEM may be a car manufacturer, a manufacturer of railway carriages or a company that markets photocopying machines.

OEM

An OEM obtains his non-strategic products from a main supplier. The main supplier is expected to be able to develop products in conjunction with the contractor. This is termed co-design. The main supplier has to be able to supply complete modules rather than individual components. For example, a main supplier has to be able to supply complete undercarriages for trains or a complete door system for cars. To do this he needs to be able to solve problems and individually implement technical improvements in those fields that the OEM does not regard as belonging to his core tasks. Selecting his own suppliers is an important aspect of the main supplier's task. He and the final producer will have to determine which of the potential suppliers has the quality and capacity to satisfy the demand.

Main supplier

Co-design

Main suppliers obtain many of their products from specialised suppliers. These are companies that can supply high quality products with a high degree of delivery reliability. They must be able to monitor the quality themselves and ensure that the main supplier receives a quality product. Cooperation in product production is called co-makership.

Specialised suppliers

Co-makership

In turn, specialised suppliers farm out their production to jobbers. These are companies that only produce on the basis of detailed job descriptions provided by the specialised supplier or by the main supplier. This type of company is often called a screwdriver factory to indicate the low-tech nature of the production activities. The further back along the production chain the less important the role of knowledge in the production process.

Jobbers

Networks of companies have leaders and followers. A leader initiates developments within the network. This does not necessarily have to be the final producer: the task can just as readily be taken over by a wholesale or retail company close to the customers. Such things as the specifics of what the customer wants can thus be passed on to the final producer. The initiating function can also be taken over by companies at the start of the production chain, where material technology often leads to completely new products.

Leaders, followers

Networks play an especially important role in producing innovative or improved products. The regional aspect of networks is of prime importance. Research and development are often regionally determined. When new products are being produced, contact is often required between the research departments of companies that make final products, machine industries and producers of raw materials. There must be contact between the financial department, banks and accountants. These contacts often function better at a regional than an international level. If all these relationships are effective, it is to the advantage of business as a whole.

Regional aspect

Main suppliers in particular tend to look for their suppliers in the direct vicinity, because frequent personal contact between parties is very important.

Table 3.16 shows the features of the various companies within a network.

TABLE 3.16 Features of companies in a network

Companies	Features
Jobbers	Production to specifications
	Low-tech
	Low added value
Specialised suppliers	Subcontracting capacity
	Quality control
	Reliability of delivery
Main supplier	R&D activities
	Supplying modules
	Selection of materials
	Organising suppliers
Final producer	Technology and product development
	Manufacture and assembly of strategic components
	Marketing activities toward the consumer

Source: partly based on D. Jacobs and A.P. de Man, *Clusters en concurrentiekracht*, Alphen aan den Rijn 1995, p. 118

Business cluster

Networks of companies do not stand alone: they are supported by service institutions such as banks, accountancy firms, advisors, research institutes and government institutions. Together, they are referred to as a business cluster. A business cluster is a definable group of companies and supporting institutions within an industry or a group of connected industries. It is characterised by both cooperation and competition (D. Jacobs & A.P. de Man, *Clusters en concurrentiekracht*, Alphen aan den Rijn 1995, p. 20). In clusters product innovation is of greater importance for competitive strength than the lowering of production costs. Business clusters are effective if they succeed in taking leading technological positions. The dissemination of knowledge is quicker within a particular regional area than outside of it. Business clusters consequently possess a strongly regional character.

Product innovation

Economic order

USA

The economic orders of the United States, Europe and Japan differ in certain aspects. Employees in the USA are highly individualistic. There is a culture of individual capitalism with a strong emphasis on personal freedom. Employees are prepared to accept considerable personal risk and change their employers frequently. Europe puts much more emphasis on institutionalised solidarity. Equality as well as freedom is valued by the average worker. These values are reflected in the social market economy. In Japan, group cooperation is regarded particularly highly by employees. This has led to a type of group capitalism: a desire to harmonise the interests of all non-market-related groups. In Europe and Japan employees stay much longer with one employer and the right of dismissal is less flexible than in the USA. According to Porter, no one system is superior to the others. Each economic order promotes in its own way the competitive strength of the various industries. It could even be risky to transfer an element of one economic order to another in order to increase competitive strength. The Japanese system of motivation in which individual values are made completely subordinate to the company is only possible within the Japanese religious context. If American companies were to try to make their employees' personal philosophy subordinate to a system of motivation it would be doomed from the start. The individualistic tradition is far too deeply rooted in American society.

System of motivation

TEST 3.9
How do you view the effect of education on an individual's preparedness
to take risks? How is your point of view likely to affect the competitive
strength of industry?

Company objectives and strategies to achieve them vary from country to
country. In the United States, maximum profit is an important objective for
many companies since shareholders judge the managing board on their
quarterly results. Consequently, nearly all industries in the USA comply
with the demand for high profitability. In Japan, the growth of the company
is the main objective and profitability is merely a precondition for growth.
Shareholders invest their money in the company for a long period so it can
achieve a considerable amount of internal growth even with low profits.

Company objectives

The economic order also governs competitive relationships on the domestic
market. A lot of rivalry on the domestic market is a prerequisite for strong
positions on international markets. Companies put pressure on suppliers
and on their marketing and R&D networks to perform as well as they can.
Porter is of the opinion that a group of innovative companies can create a
fertile environment for lasting and strong competitive advantage. Intense
competition can have an invigorating effect on the entire value chain.
The other elements of the diamond are also affected by this. Networks of
companies are enlarged, production factors improve, and customers can be
discerning because they have greater choice. Vigorous competition on the
domestic market is therefore a much more favourable condition for entering
foreign markets than one big company that dominates the domestic market.

Domestic market

Chance factors
Random events can cause a shift in the interplay between the elements of
the diamond.
Major technological breakthroughs can change economic relationships
dramatically. The rise of chip technology made it possible for all kinds of
small companies to compete with big companies. In some business sectors
(such as the administration and advisory sectors), the major part of the capital
goods consists of computers with accompanying software. In the field of
electronic data processing there are almost no economies of scale to be had.

Technological breakthroughs

Changes in the exchange rate and sudden price changes affect international
competitive relationships, and they may force industries to make massive
changes. The instability of the world's exchange rates has forced companies
to build production plants in all of their major market areas in order to have
their costs and their revenue in the same currency.

Changes in the exchange rate

The last chance factor is the weather. The production and sale of many
goods are sensitive to weather influences.

Weather

Government
The last of the elements in the diamond is the government. All government
measures, including product regulations, taxes and subsidies, can enhance
or diminish the competitive strength of the economy. Government also
affects production through its education policies, technology policies,
capital market policies, environment laws and the like.

Government can exert an influence on networks by establishing expertise
centres that pass on technical knowledge from company to company. It
can also encourage clustering of companies via its research institutes and
universities.

Glossary

Advanced production factors	Production factors that have to be developed, such as expertise and training.
Basic production factors	Production factors that a country has by nature, such as geographical position, climate and size of population.
Business rivalry	Competitive behaviour.
Industry	Companies that produce similar products using similar production methods.
Cartel	A collusive agreement between independent companies to curtail competition.
Cluster	A definable agglomerate of companies and service institutions within an industry or an agglomerate of connected industries, characterised by both cooperation and competition.
Co-design	Product development by the supplier in conjunction with the contractor.
Co-makership	Cooperation in product production.
Concentration	Merging of companies leading to a situation in which production decisions are made in fewer decision centres.
Cooperative	An association that carries out a business on behalf of its members.
Commodity services	Mass-produced services that usually have a homogenous character.
Competition	Vying to win customers' favour.
Competition-determining factors	Those factors that have an influence on intensity of competition.
Competitive behaviour	Business conduct by means of which companies vie for as large a share of the market as possible.
Competitive strength	The long-term extent to which a company is able to satisfy all stakeholders, including not only proprietors and employees, but also customers, suppliers and the government.

Conglomeration	Development of activities in various industries and in various stages of the production chain.
Consortium	Cooperation by several companies on a specific project.
Cost leadership	A strategy in which companies strive to keep their cost levels below that of their competitors.
Decline phase	The phase of the product's life cycle during which sales decrease.
Differentiated market/ product	Similar products that are different in the eyes of the customers.
Diversification	The development of activities in a different production chain.
Dynamics (of an industry)	Changes within an industry. Also the ability to obtain or retain sufficient competitive strength in the long term.
External competition	Competition between industries within a production chain.
Franchising	Cooperation between companies whereby one company offers other independent companies the right to sales promotion, products and services at a charge.
Growth phase	The phase in a product's life cycle in which the sales of a product increase rapidly.
Heterogeneous product	A differentiated product.
Homogenous products	Similar products that are not different in the eyes of the customers.
Innovation monopolist	A company that is the first to bring a product onto the market, thereby creating a monopolistic position for itself.
Innovative competition	Developing a completely new product, thus creating a new market.
Integration	Expansion of activities into other stages of the production chain.
Internal competition	Competition between firms that belong to the same industry.
Introductory phase	The first phase in a product's life cycle during which the product is introduced onto the market.
Joint venture	A joint subsidiary of a number of companies.
Lasting competitive advantage	Advantage by which a company can distinguish itself from its competitors for a certain period.

3

Limit pricing	A strategy in which a company keeps its prices below the cost level of its competitors in order to ward off new entrants to the market.
Market structure	The aspects of the market that determine the business conduct of a company.
Market structure	Classification of markets according to number of companies and product diversity.
Market	The collective relationships between suppliers and demanders of a particular product.
Maturity phase	The phase in a product's life cycle in which the growth of the sales stagnates and declines.
Merger	The joining up of two similar companies to form one new company.
Monopolistic competition	Market structure with many suppliers and differentiated products.
Monopoly	Market structure with only one supplier.
Networks	Systems of mutual relationships between suppliers and contractors independent of the market process.
Oligopoly	Market structure characterised by few suppliers and a homogenous product (undifferentiated oligopoly) or a differentiated product (differentiated oligopoly).
Parallelisation	Developing activities at the same stage of another production chain.
Patent	A monopoly on production for a set period.
Perfect competition	Market structure characterised by many suppliers and a homogenous product.
Potential competition	Competition that may arise from the entry of new companies into the industry or by products that are capable of replacing existing products.
Price leader	The company that sets the price that other companies in the industry conform to.
Production chain	The industries that a product passes through from primary producer to final consumer.
Product's life cycle	A description of the sales of a product according to a natural growth pattern.

Profit erosion	Decrease in profits cause by price cuts.
Stagnation monopoly	Monopolistic market structure during the decline phase of a product's life cycle.
Value system	The added value of the production chain as a whole.
Voluntary chain	An association which individual retailers can join that originates from a wholesaler.

3

PART 2
The macroeconomic environment of companies

4

Producing

How can we measure and compare prosperity?
What does producing have to do with the satisfying of needs and prosperity?
How do producing and procuring an income relate to each other? What
role do capital, labour and natural resources play in producing goods and
services?
How should the supply side of an economy be structured?
What economic factors determine capacity for growth and long-term
competitive power?
On the next page, a situational sketch is used by way of an introduction to
these issues.

Section 4.1 shows how national prosperity can be compared by means of
the Gross Domestic Product per head of population. Prosperity can be
viewed as consumers all over the world having access to products such as
those produced by Unilever.
Section 4.2 deals with added value and stakeholder compensation. Unilever
adds value to products and sells them on markets. From the returns on
the sales it pays the company's stakeholders. These stakeholders are the
suppliers of raw materials and intermediate products, employees, owners of
the capital and the government.
Production factors are the subject of Section 4.3. In order to produce goods
and services, companies need production factors and the purchasing of
these production factors leads to costs. The main cost item for companies is
labour costs.
Capital, labour and natural resources are not always available in sufficient
quantity. They have to be constantly renewed. Long-term economic growth
is limited by the production factors of labour and natural resources.

In Section 4.4, production is classified into six sectors: agriculture, manufacturing, construction, trade, financial services and public services. The competitive power of the economy is also treated. Strong competitive power within the economy depends on adding a lot of knowledge to products, and we will see which products satisfy this prerequisite.

CASE

Unilever produces all kinds of toiletries for hair, mouth and skincare, including soap, toothpaste and cosmetics. The company is also active in the food and beverage area. It makes ice-cream, drinks, margarines and bakery products. The company also plays an important role in the international market for cleaning products. The company sells all of these articles to wholesalers and retailers around the world. Regardless of their wealth, people in every country appear to need the products and are prepared to pay for them. The returns are consequently more than sufficient to cover costs. The company buys in raw materials such as vegetable oils, sugar, water, fine chemicals and all the other ingredients that the company does not produce itself. The difference between sales and purchases – the added value – is sufficient to provide the employees' wages and interest and profits to the financiers. There is also enough money left to replace worn out machines and buildings.

4.1 Prosperity

People who have a lot of goods and services at their disposal to satisfy their needs are prosperous. Companies and the government make these goods and services: they are producers. There are big differences between the prosperity of one nation and that of another. However, not everybody even within the same country can afford to be a consumer of the same number of products. There are big differences in prosperity in most countries and also between countries.

Gross Domestic Product

The capacity to satisfy needs by means of goods and services is termed prosperity. Goods and services from natural resources cannot satisfy needs without first being processed. Value has to be added to them. That process we term production. The total production of a country is termed the Gross Domestic Product (GDP) The GDP is the main criterion for comparing the prosperity of countries. In order to add value to products, labour, machinery, buildings, and raw materials from natural resources are needed. These are the production factors of labour, capital and natural resources. Companies use these production factors to make products they can sell. The returns on these products can be used to remunerate the owners of the production factors: the employees, self-employed people with a firm of their own and the financiers. The income that results from the use of production factors is always the same amount as the value that is added to the goods and services.

Sections 4.1.2 and 4.1.3 will explain why this is so, but we can summarise it by saying that the total production in an economy is equal to the total income earned. This is why the terms *production, added value* and *income* may be used interchangeably.

Firstly, though, the difference in prosperity between countries will be discussed.

4.1.1 Differences in prosperity

This section deals with the prosperity differences between countries and with the growth of prosperity.

The GDP per head of population is often used to determine how prosperous a country is. It can be calculated by comparing the GDP of a country with the size of its population. Table 4.1 represents the size of the world's population and the absolute and relative GDP for selected regions and countries.

Table 4.1 also shows the GDP at purchasing power parity (PPP) per capita of selected countries, expressed in US dollars.

TABLE 4.1 GDP per capita in different regions (2014)

	Population x 1 million	%	GDP billion $ PPP	%	GDP/capita PPP x 1$	GDP/capita kkp World = 100
World	7259.7	100	108477	100	14,942	100
UK	64.6	0.9	2550	2.4	39,500	264
Denmark	5.6	0.1	264	0.2	46,850	314
Sweden	9.7	0.1	454	0.4	46,870	314
US	318.9	4.4	17823	16.4	55,900	374
Japan	127.1	1.8	4847	4.5	38,120	255
South Asia	1721	23.7	9119	8.4	5,298	35
East Asia	2264.1	31.2	33742	31.1	14,963	100
Latin America	626.3	8.6	9534	8.8	15,226	102
Africa (sub-Sahara)	974.3	13.4	3309	3.1	3,396	23
China	1364	18.8	17967	16.6	13,170	88
India	1295	17.8	7293	6.7	5,630	38
Russian Federation	143.8	2.0	3237	3.0	22,160	148
The Netherlands	16.9	0.2	824	0.8	48,860	327

Source: World Bank, *World Development Indicators*, 2016

The dollar cost of purchasing an item varies from country to country. Holidaymakers can buy more for their money in the Czech Republic or Indonesia than in Switzerland or Japan. The purchasing power of the dollar varies from country to country. We must therefore adjust the incomes for these differences in purchasing power. This adjustment produces the purchasing power parity.

To compare the GDP of different countries, we must therefore:
- determine the GDP per capita;
- convert the GDP in a common currency, for example US dollar;
- adjust for differences in the purchasing power of the currency per country.

Distribution of wealth

The statistics in table 4.1 also give the distribution of income in the world. The figures in table 4.1 give us some idea as to the world's distribution of wealth. Above-average wealth is found in the countries at the top. There, the income per capita is above global average. The richer regions hold approximately 45% of global wealth, with less than 15% of the world's population actually living there. China and India are home to approximately 37% of the world's population, and 23% of the world's GDP. In the United States, GDP per capita is around 10 times that in India. Compared to the US, the GDP per capita in Europe and Japan is around 33% lower. The purchasing power of many African countries is only a fraction of the average income in the US. The personal income in poor countries is often less than the pocket money of children in rich countries.

Table 4.2 includes data relating to EU countries.

TABLE 4.2 GDP and growth in the EU, 2012, pps

	GDP/capita €	EU=100	Average real growth per capita (%), 2011-2015
EU	28800	100	0.94
Luxembourg	78048	271	0.56
Ireland	41760	145	6.54
The Netherlands	37152	129	0.36
Austria	36576	127	0.44
Germany	36000	125	1.24
Denmark	35712	124	0.66
Sweden	35424	123	1.38
Belgium	33696	117	0.4
United Kingdom	31680	110	1.26
Finland	31104	108	-0.42
France	30528	106	0.5
Italy	27360	95	-0.92
Spain	26496	92	-0.14
Malta	25632	89	2.9
Czech Republic	24480	85	1.56
Slovenia	23904	83	0.32
Cyprus	23328	81	-2.12
Portugal	22176	77	-0.5
Slovakia	22176	77	2.52
Estonia	21312	74	3.84
Lithuania	21312	74	5.6
Greece	20448	71	-3.44
Poland	19872	69	3.8
Hungary	19584	68	2.2
Latvia	18432	64	4.8
Croatia	16704	58	-0.12
Romania	16416	57	2.86
Bulgaria	13248	46	2.1
United States	42624	148	1.6*
Japan	28512	99	0.7*

* growth of GDP, 2000-2014, source: WDI, 2016
PPS = purchasing power standards

Source: Eurostat

The wealth in the European Union (EU) is approximately equal to that of Japan. Rich EU countries, have approximately 15% less wealth than the US. Luxemburg has a much higher wealth per capita but Luxemburg is a very small country with a large bank sector, which traditionally has high added value. The Netherlands is high in the ranking, and retains a strong position.

Wealth in the EU is more evenly distributed than wealth in the world as a whole. The difference between the country with the highest (Luxembourg) and the lowest (Bulgaria) is admittedly a factor of 6 but Luxembourg is only a very small EU country. The poorest countries have an income level of about half the average GDP in the EU. Prosperity in Southern Europe is about 60% of that of the richest countries in the EU.

Prosperity growth

Needs

Infinite

Most countries aim for a growth in production, also known as economic growth. It enables them to meet the increasing needs that are a result of population growth. But it is not only the newly born that need more products. Many economists believe that the needs of the individual are infinite, or in any case, much larger than can be met by the resources available. This is even more relevant for people in poor countries. In the light of the wealth in the richer countries, the unsatisfied needs of people in countries with a low level of prosperity are very great indeed. Countries with a low level of prosperity can make up their disadvantage by means of a high growth rate, which will make the population better able to satisfy their needs in the future.

Prosperity differences within a country

Not only are there great differences in prosperity between countries, but also within countries. In many rich countries, some groups of people can barely satisfy their basic needs. The US has extremely impoverished suburbs where people have great difficulty in obtaining even such basic commodities as food and medicines. While the degree of acceptance of large differences in income depends on local norms and values, the international community has, however, laid down the minimum requirements that the individual needs to be able to satisfy before his or her existence can be regarded as a dignified one. These norms are set out in the Declaration of Human Rights. These rights include the right to food, clothing, shelter, education and medical care.

Table 4.3 shows the division of income in a number of countries.

TABLE 4.3 Share of income or consumption in selected countries

	Year	Poorest 10%	Poorest 20%	Richest 20%	Richest 10%
Netherlands	2012	3,4	8,9	37,1	22,6
United States	2013	1,7	5,1	46,4	30,2
Sweden	2012	3,2	8,7	36,2	21,5
Chili	2013	1,7	4,6	56,7	41,5

Source: http://worldbank.org/table/2.9, consulted 4 January 2016

A completely even distribution of income would mean that every 20% of the population would also earn 20% of the income. One of the most uneven income distributions of the world is in Chile, where 56.7% of the income goes to the 20% of the population with the highest income and only 4.6% to the poorest 20%. Sweden and the Netherlands have the most even distribution of income. The other countries are somewhere in between. The distribution of income has an effect on the level of income in a country. An important reason for the difference in income is the difference in labour

Labour productivity

productivity. People who make a high contribution to productivity want to receive a high amount as well. Otherwise they would not be prepared to produce as highly. A very even distribution of income would not be representative of the differences in labour productivity and would be detrimental to prosperity. If income is not in proportion to the labour productivity supplied, much productive capacity will be lost. A very uneven distribution of income results in the poorest groups of the population having insufficient opportunities to have access to such elementary facilities as healthy food, *education* and medical services. Their well-being is not sufficient to enable them to function in an economy, even at the most minimal level. Large differences in income are frequently accompanied by illiteracy in the lower income groups. Illiterates will remain in the underprivileged group and there is a great chance that their children will too. This prevents the production factor of labour from being used in an optimal way. *Power* is another important factor in the division of income. Groups of people with high incomes have at the same time considerable power, which they then use to perpetrate the existing division of income. It can be concluded that both a highly uneven distribution of income and a too even distribution of income have a negative effect on the level of prosperity.

TEST 4.1
Discuss the desirability of a society with a comparatively uneven division of income.

4.1.2   Welfare

Prosperity and welfare are closely related. Prosperity has been defined as the availability of goods and services. Well-being is more an indication of the sense of contentment and satisfaction that people in a given society have. While a certain amount of material satisfaction of needs is required for a happy life, this is not enough. Human happiness is also dependent on the satisfying of immaterial needs such as access to education and a healthy life.

The United Nations has developed an instrument to measure the welfare of a population. It is called the Human Development Index (HDI). The HDI goes from 0 (minimum welfare) to 1 (maximum welfare). The HDI includes the following elements:

Human Development Index (HDI)

- A long and healthy life: life expectancy at birth;
- Education, measured in terms of access to primary, secondary and tertiary education;
- A reasonable living standard: per capita income.

An individual's sense of well-being has a lot to do with the expectation of a long and healthy life. Life expectancy is a reflection of the medical facilities in a country: the better the medical facilities the higher the quality of life. Access to education allows people the opportunity for self-development and gives them a chance to provide an active contribution to the culture and economy of a country.
Table 4.4 shows the HDI scores of a number of countries in various continents.

TABLE 4.4 HDI scores of various countries (2012)

Ranking	Country	HDI
1	Norway	0.944
5	The Netherlands	0.922
6	Germany	0.916
8	United States	0.915
17	Korea	0.898
20	Japan	0.891
22	France	0.888
44	Hungary	0.828
60	Panama	0.789
72	Turkey	0.761

TABLE 4.4 HDI scores of various countries (2012) (continued)

Ranking	Country	HDI
74	Mexico	0.756
75	Brazil	0.755
90	China	0.727
145	Kenia	0.584
188	Niger	0.348

Source: UNDP, *Human Development Report 2015*, p. 208

Norway has the highest score, Niger the lowest. Countries that have a high position on the GDP list also score highly on the HDI list. Placement within each list is, however, not identical. The United States and Luxemburg, both of whom are among the countries with the highest per capita GDP, score lower on the HDI list.

TEST 4.2
Is the pursuit of prosperity or the pursuit of happiness the main human endeavour?

4.2 Added value

GDP

The GDP is the sum of all the productive activities that take place within the borders of a country. Production can be measured in a variety of ways. We can determine the GDP of the EU by adding the added value of businesses and governments within the borders of all the combined countries. This is the production approach to determining production.

Remuneration

Labour, capital and natural resources are needed to produce. The owners of these factors will have to be paid for them. It is therefore also possible to measure production by adding together all the remuneration that the production factors receive. Measuring production in this manner is called the income approach.

Expenditure

People spend the income they receive on goods and services. Total expenditure is therefore the same as production. Adding together all the expenditure to determine production is called the expenditure approach (Figure 4.1).

The first two approaches will be dealt with in this section, the last one in Chapter 5.

FIGURE 4.1 Measuring production

Businesses produce, and in doing so, they add value to products (1). Households put their production factors at the disposal of businesses and receive an income in return (2). In turn, these households spend their income on businesses (3).

Production and income approaches

Businesses make products. To be able to do this they buy raw materials, hire labour and buy capital goods. These they put into making products saleable. The returns on the sales will have to be divided among the various stakeholders in the production process (see Table 4.5).

TABLE 4.5 Production in the EU and in the Netherlands (2015)

	EU (x € 1 billion)		The Netherlands (x € 1 billion)	
Revenue from sales (production value)		27680		1347
Purchases		12972		670
GDP$_{mp}$		14708		677
Cost price increasing taxes -/- subsidies		1756		70
GDP$_{bp}$		12952		607
Depreciations		2560		112
NDP$_{bp}$		10392		495
Wages	6967		332	
Profit, interest	3425		163	

Source: Eurostat and CBS

The return on sales by a business is not the same as the production or the value added. To start with, the company has to pay for its purchases. The value of raw materials and semi-manufactured goods has been added by other companies. What remains is the gross domestic product at market prices (GDP$_{mp}$). The government imposes a tax on the added value (VAT). This tax causes the cost of products to rise. Businesses pass on these costs in their selling prices (GDP$_{mp}$). This is what the term 'at market price' refers to. The businesses pay the price-raising taxes to the government. On the other hand, the government provides subsidies that lower the costs of, for instance, the railways, swimming pools and public libraries. If we deduct these amounts from the GDP$_{mp}$ we get the gross domestic product at basic prices (GDP$_{bp}$). The term 'basic prices' refers to this figure reflecting the costs of the production factors. Depreciation is one of the major ones. This is the reserves set aside to deal with wear and tear on machines and buildings. Companies can use depreciation to replace worn out machines and buildings. If we deduct depreciation from the GDP$_{bp}$, the amount left is the net domestic product at basic prices (NDP$_{bp}$), and this is what is used to pay for wages, interest and profits.

Return on sales

VAT

Market price

GDP$_{mp}$
GDP$_{bp}$

NDP$_{bp}$

The wage costs consist of the wages and salaries as well as the social security contributions that employers and employees pay in regard to them. Companies pay interest over the capital they borrowed to the lenders of that capital and profits to the providers of risk-bearing capital.

Wage costs

Profits are the difference between the returns from sales and the costs of the production process. Seen from the company's point of view, there is a

Profits

world of difference between wages and interest on the one hand and profits on the other. The first two are usually contractually laid down expenses. When a firm has contracted a certain amount of labour and has borrowed an amount of money from the bank or rented premises, it has an obligation to pay the sum agreed on. Profit distribution is a different matter. Providers of risk-bearing capital will have to wait and see whether there is actually any profit being made. Profits can change as a result of fluctuations in returns and costs. If for some reason or other the returns of a company decrease, the profits will also decrease if the costs remain the same. Profits, therefore, are a balancing item, used to balance out returns and costs. Profits are consequently sometimes regarded as a remuneration for the production factor of entrepreneurship. The more a company is able to combine production factors, the higher the reward for the entrepreneur's risk.

Entrepreneurship

If Table 4.5 is read from the top down, this is the production approach to the GDP. If it is read from the bottom up, this is the income approach.

Profits, balancing item

Because profits are a balancing item, the sum of all the remunerations of the production factors is equal to production. GDP measured according to the production approach will always be the same as GDP measured according to the income approach.

'Gross National Income' (GNI)

The term 'Gross National Income' (GNI) is used to refer to total production and total income. There is a difference between the two terms. The domestic product derives from production factors that apply within the borders of a country. The national income is that income that is derived from the production factors that are owned by the population. An investor who has made all of his investments in other countries and who gets all of his income from abroad is not contributing to the GDP but is contributing to the national income.

Government Production

The government is actively involved in the production of all kinds of goods and services, including the construction of roads, dikes and pipelines, designing urban development plans, government buildings and education, part of the medical care, judiciary and law and order. All of these are valuable services: society cannot function without them.
It is a fact, therefore, that not only do companies produce, but also that the government adds value to products. To this end the government buys goods and services from firms and takes on employees to add value to them. The government plays an important role in public safety and in safeguarding the legal system. Preventing crime and trying the accused are part of this. Resources and manpower have to be put into action: safety is also a matter of production. It involves buying such things as uniforms, police cars, buildings, computers and paper. As well as this the government employs people with a specific education and training to carry out certain tasks: police tasks, for example. A public service is a combination of all of these elements: policemen doing their beat in a police car, for example. The effect of this is preventative: society is safer because potential criminals are deterred.

Government adds value

Added value

The added value of government production cannot be measured in the same way as for businesses because the government does not sell its products on markets. International agreements deem the added value of the government to be the same as the sum of the wages and salaries paid to government employees.

Sum of the wages

4.3 Production factors

For the production of goods and services by businesses and the government, the production factors of capital, labour and natural resources are needed.
Before natural materials are suitable for human consumption they have to be transformed by means of labour, machines and buildings. Each of these production factors will be dealt with in turn.

4.3.1   Capital goods

The production factor of capital – stock of capital goods – consists of all the goods that are used or used up in the production process. This is illustrated in Example 4.1

Stock of capital goods

EXAMPLE 4.1

In a certain economy, a number of firms each have a share in the production of pinewood furniture: a forestry business, a sawmill, a furniture factory and a furniture retailer. The production of furniture involves foresters, furniture makers, salesmen and a variety of other related occupations. They all play a part in transforming trees into usable products. For this purpose they use machines such as saws, transport, lathes, templates, computers and various types of building. In short, they make use of capital goods. They add value to products by combining production factors, ultimately creating furniture that can be delivered to customers.

Durable capital goods are long-lasting goods. There are various types of capital goods. The production process needs industrial buildings such as factories, offices and shops. Houses are also regarded by Eurostat as belonging to the category of capital goods because they satisfy the need for acceptable living conditions. Other durable goods are machines, tools and means of transport. An extensive infrastructure of land, roads and waterways is also needed. Roads waterways and pipelines are indispensable for the transport of goods. Dikes are necessary to protect the country against flooding. All of these capital goods are used in the production process and are therefore subject to wear and tear. They have to be replaced regularly. In order to do this, replacement investments are needed.

Durable capital goods

Floating capital goods are incorporated into the final product. In Example 2.1 the saw mill has an amount of raw material in the form of trees to be made into planks and beams. These are termed semi-finished products.
They have been processed, but are as yet not suitable for consumer use. They need further processing into furniture via a production process in the furniture factory. The raw materials and the semi-finished products are part of the stock of capital goods that are processed into the end product. They are transformed into products with a higher added value.

Floating capital goods

Raw material

Consumables

During the course of the production process, companies also make use of consumables such as energy. What these have in common is that they are used up during the production process. If the furniture factory were, for instance, to purchase and use natural gas, this would not be visible in the end product.

Apart from stocks of raw materials, consumables and semi-finished products, companies might also have stocks of finished products. While it is in the company's interests to spread production evenly over the whole year, a seasonal pattern in sales could be one reason for having stock. Furniture sales, for example, peak in spring. The furniture manufacturer would be best off spreading production evenly over the whole year because otherwise there would be a much greater production capacity needed in spring than in the rest of the year. This would involve extra costs in machinery and buildings that would be superfluous for the rest of the year.

Capital coefficient

Companies can make use of capital goods to make products. The capital coefficient indicates the amount of capital goods needed to produce one unit of the product. A capital coefficient of 3 indicates that three billion euros in capital are needed to produce 1 billion's worth of the final product.

As one would expect, the service sectors have a low capital coefficient. Consultants can earn a lot with a low-tech computer. The same is true for construction and trade, catering industries and repairs. Those sectors that depend on physical networks or buildings that have a long lifespan have a high capital coefficient. Other sectors such as industry occupy an intermediate position.

For long-term economic growth, stocks of capital goods have to increase. Investment is dealt with in greater detail in Chapter 5; here we will briefly comment that businesses in sectors with a low capital coefficient can increase production without large investments being required and that sectors with a high capital coefficient will have to invest heavily before production can be increased.

Table 4.6 shows that a sector with a low capital coefficient with the same output and investment rates grows faster than an industry sector with a high capital coefficient.

TABLE 4.6 Growth with different capital coefficient

Sector	Output	Capital coefficient	Capital goods	Investment	Output growth	
					Absolute	%
1	1,000	2	2,000	100	50	5
2	1,000	5	5,000	100	20	2

4.3.2   Labour

The availability of the production factor of labour is dependent upon the size of the population and the participation rate.

The EU has about 508 million inhabitants (1 January 2015). Not all of a country's inhabitants are, of course, candidates for the labour market. The labour market draws primarily upon people between the ages of 15 and 65. The people in this age bracket are referred to as the working-age population. Of the working-age population, not everyone is a candidate for the labour market either. Those people in the age of 15 to 65 who *are* candidates for the labour market (both the employed and the unemployed) are the work force. The work force as a percentage of the working age population is the participation rate. The participation rate in the EU was about 70% in 2015. The participation rate is an important indicator of what part of the working age population can be deployed in the labour process. Since the population growth in the EU is stagnating, raising the participation rate is an important method of involving a sufficient number of people in the labour process in time to come.

Working-age population

Work force

Participation rate

There is another important variable for analysing the labour market, namely the employment rate. The employment rate is the ratio of employed to working-age people. (See Table 4.7.)

Employment rate

TABLE 4.7 Employment rates in the EU (2012)

	Total	Part-time
Total	70	19
Male	76	8
Female	64	32

Source: Eurostat

The employment rate in the EU is approximately 70%. More men than women take part in the labour process and a much higher percentage of men have a full-time job than is the case with women. The employment rate indicates which part of the population contributes actively to the production process. Countries with a low employment rate are less efficient in the use of their population than countries with a high employment rate.

The GDP, labour demand (the number of employed) and labour productivity are closely related. Labour productivity is production per worker. The amount of production is employment multiplied by labour productivity (See Formula 1).

The relationship between the three variables can be represented as follows:

Labour demand and GDP

$$GDP = Lp \times Ld \qquad [1]$$

In which:
GDP = Gross domestic product
Lp = Labour productivity
Ld = Labour demand or employment

In the EU, the GDP is about €13,000 bn (2012) and there are about 217 m people employed. Labour productivity therefore is about €60,000.

If we apply the rule that a change in a variable that is the product of two other variables is approximately the same as the sum of the change in the component variables, we can also write the equation thus:

$$g_{GDP} = g_{Lp} + g_{Ld} \qquad [2]$$

In which:
g_{GDP} = the percentage of increase in production
g_{Lp} = the percentage of increase in labour productivity
g_{Ld} = the percentage of increase in employment

In order to obtain growth in production, an increase in the number of employees or an increase in labour productivity is therefore necessary. The European work force is hardly increasing. Growth is therefore hampered by the availability of people on the labour market. From what has been said before, it follows that for a long-term increase, an increase in the degree of participation is needed or an increase in labour productivity.

Unemployment

Someone is regarded as being unemployed if he or she is 15 or older, is looking for work and does not have a job. The percentage of unemployed – the proportion of unemployed compared to the numbers of employed and unemployed added together – was 9.4% in the EU in 2015 (see Table 4.8).

TABLE 4.8 Unemployment in the Netherlands and in the EU (2015)

	The Netherlands	EU
Total	6.9	9.4
Women	7.0	9.1
Men	6.2	10.3
Long-term unemployment (share of unemployment percentage)	3.0	4.5
Unemployment 15-24 year olds	11.2	21.9
Unemployment among low-skilled workers	9.3	16.3
Unemployment among high-skilled workers	3.7	5.2

Source: Eurostat

Long-term and short-term unemployment

The difference between long-term and short-term unemployment is important. It is normal for the number of jobs to decrease and unemployment to increase in periods of slow-growing expenditure and production. Temporary unemployment as a result of low expenditure is far less harmful than long-term unemployment. When the economy picks up, the temporarily unemployed usually get back to work relatively quickly. People who are unemployed for a long time run the risk of never returning to the labour process because knowledge and skills date quickly. This is damaging to the long-term growth potential of the economy. The same applies to youth unemployment and unemployment of those with a low level of education. The longer those in these categories stay outside the work process, the greater the chance that they will remain outside for a very long time. The figures in Table 4.8 show that there is above-average unemployment among younger people and those with a low education level.

Figure 4.2 illustrates demand and supply on the labour market.

FIGURE 4.2 Demand and supply on the labour market

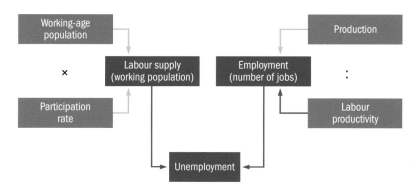

The price of labour is the wage per employee. Wages are an important cost item for companies. About 80% of added value consists of labour costs. Entrepreneurs keep a very close check on labour costs for that reason. For companies, the remuneration per employee is the best labour cost criterion. The wage cost per employee includes the gross wage of the employee as well as the social security charges that employers have to pay on top of that. Wage determination is for a large part dependent on supply and demand on the labour market (see Figure 4.3). If there is high unemployment in the business sector, the employees will have little market power and wage increases will be minimal. When there is a limited labour market, however, the employee organisations will be able to force sizeable wage increases. Employers and employees usually negotiate to compensate for the rise in the prices of consumer goods. Adjusting the wages to the raised prices prevents a decrease in the purchasing power of the wages. The parties usually also negotiate any extra production that requires their labour. Price compensation and increased labour productivity are together termed the wage scope. A number of factors relating to the structure of the working population tend to raise the gross wage. These include an increase in the average level of education or age of the working population. The wage level is often related to the education level or the age of the employee. If both the average education level and the average age of the working population increase, the effect will be an increase in the average wage cost per employee.

Labour costs and competitive position

Changes in wage cost per employee

Raised prices

Labour productivity

Wage scope

Level of education or age

TEST 4.3
In the light of demographic developments, how are wages in the EU likely to develop?

Government taxes and social security charges have an effect on wages. Government policies in relation to social security benefits and pensions can affect wages.
Figure 4.3 shows those factors that have an influence on the wage cost per employee. The words in brackets indicate the direction in which that variable could develop. The arrows indicate a positive effect on the wage cost per employee. For example, a tightening of the labour market creates a tendency for wages to rise.

FIGURE 4.3 Causes of changes in wage cost per employee

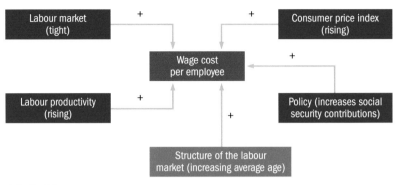

+ Positive influence

Labour cost per unit

Competitive
position

Cost per unit

For the competitive position of a firm, it is not the wage cost per employee, but the wage cost per unit of production that is important. The wage cost per unit is equal to the wage cost per employee divided by the labour productivity. If a worker were to cost €70,000 per year and produce 3,500 units, then their costs per unit would be €20.

At the macroeconomic level, the development of the wage cost per unit is also dependent on the wage cost per employee and the labour productivity, but taken for the economy as a whole. Changes in either of these variables will result in a change in the wage cost per unit. In the following equation, this change is represented as a function of the wage cost per employee and the labour productivity.

$$g_{Lu} = g_{We} - g_{Lp} \qquad\qquad [3]$$

In which
g_{Lu} = The percentage of change in the wage cost per unit
g_{We} = The percentage of change in the wage cost per employee
g_{Lp} = The percentage of change in labour productivity

The wage cost per unit increases as a result of an increase in wage per employee and drops as a result of an increase in labour productivity.

- -

EXAMPLE 4.2

This can be made clear by using some figures. Let us assume the following figures:
- Total wage bill = €350 billion
- Labour productivity = 10,000 units per employee per period
- Labour demand = 5 million

The average wage cost per employee is €70,000 (€350 billion: 5 million)
The wage cost per unit can be calculated by dividing the average cost per employee by the production per employee.
The wage cost per unit is therefore €70,000: 10,000 = €7. The equation shows that an increase in the wages bill by 10% and an increase in the

labour productivity by 5% will result in an increase in the labour cost per unit of about 5%. (In our example, the wage cost per employee will then be €77,000 and the labour productivity 10,500).

In the economy, wages not only have an effect on costs but also an effect on spending. If all the wages in a country increase, businesses will find that their sales will increase. This is, of course, particularly the case for businesses that produce products with a high elasticity of demand. This is the case with luxury goods. Companies that are largely oriented toward export or concerned with the production of primary goods and services will experience the increased wages mainly as a cost item. Figure 4.4 summarises the influence of wages on company profits.

Effect on costs

Effect on spending

FIGURE 4.4 Wages bill and company profits

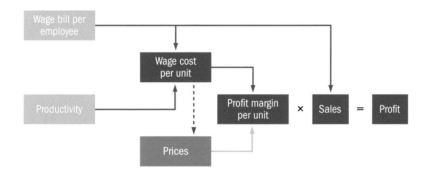

The wage bill per employee and the labour productivity together determine the wage cost per unit. Companies that have sufficient market power can pass a rise in wage cost per unit on in their prices. The profit margin per unit is dependent on this. Sales are affected by the possible effect on sales of the wage rise. The profit margin and the sales together determine the profitability of a company.

4.3.3 Natural resources

For various reasons, the production factor of natural resources is important for the satisfaction of needs and for production.

Natural resources provide raw materials. Metal ores such as iron, aluminium, copper and precious metals are important raw materials. Energy generating primaries such as coal, oil and gas play an important role in production. Europe is largely dependent on imports for these products.

The price of raw materials has a major effect on the returns of companies. This is particularly true for fluctuating oil prices. Figure 4.5 shows the effect of oil prices on company profits.

Raw materials

FIGURE 4.5 Oil prices and company profits

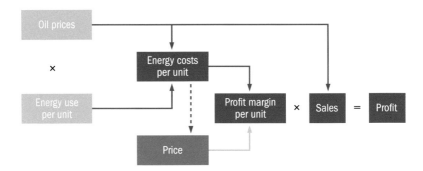

The oil price multiplied by the energy consumption per unit gives the energy costs per unit. Companies can react to rising energy prices by reducing their energy consumption. This is, however, usually not a viable short-term alternative and it makes companies relatively powerless in relation to price increases. The next step in counteracting a rise in costs is to pass on the rise in cost in prices. This can only be done when there is sufficient market power: in other words, if the companies have a large market share, if there is no overcapacity, if the demand is inelastic, and so on. The difference between price and costs per unit is the profit margin per unit. Sales can be affected by increases in the oil price: the spending effect of the price rise. Consumers will tend to replace energy-high products by other products if they are available. A rise in oil prices also has the effect that consumers have less money left over for other products. Products that do not need much energy to produce could even suffer a loss in sales as a result. The result of the profit margin per unit multiplied by the sales is the total profit. The geographical position of a country in relation to other countries determines the transport opportunities for a large part. The main areas of industrial activity are centred around the seaports and along big rivers. However, big changes in the location of companies are occurring. Modern industrial products and services are less dependent on transport than on telecommunications. These companies prefer to be located in areas that the production factor of labour regards as pleasant. The old centres of industry are in areas of housing shortages, traffic congestion and environmental problems. The new centres are in places in the vicinity of recreational facilities and attractive nature areas.

Geographical position

Climate
Agriculture is reliant on climate and soil conditions. The agricultural sector in each of the EU countries is adapted to that country's natural conditions.

Recreation
Nature provides possibilities for recreation. Recreation requires a suitable climate and sufficient space for each individual. These spaces can be found away from the urban conglomerates in forested areas, near beaches, in hills and mountains.

Water and air
Nature is also important for satisfaction of the need for water and air. In this respect, nature is one of the basic necessities of life, since life is impossible without water and sufficient clean air. Large investments in the purification of air and water and for the processing of waste materials are necessary. Another role that nature plays is in the taking up and breaking down of waste materials that are released during the production process.

Long-term growth possibilities

Economic growth throughout the world (and the EU is no exception) is limited by the effect it has on the environment. The alarming condition the environment is in has brought about fundamental changes in the way people think about the environment.

In the past, the main issue was how to use the possibilities offered by nature as effectively as possible. The long-term effects on the environment were of lesser concern. Nature was viewed as a commodity to be used freely as long as other possibilities for its use were not destroyed. We are becoming increasingly aware of the fact that the environment is a scarce commodity. The human activities of production and consumption have had such a damaging effect that despite the crucial importance of the environment for not only future production but also for the quality of life, long-term provision of goods and services and a guaranteed quality of existence is under threat. Long-term economic development that maintains the quality of the environment is called sustainable development. It requires a sustainable GDP. A sustainable GDP may, however, involve negative economic growth with a reduced demand for raw materials, energy and space.

Environment is a scarce commodity

Sustainable development

TEST 4.4
What are the options for sustainable environmental growth?

Sustainable development is part of company policy in an increasing number of companies. It is being applied not only to the production factor of natural resources but also to the factors of capital and labour. Dealing responsibly with production factors has become increasingly important for companies. Sustainable entrepreneurship – people, planet and profit forming the guidelines for company policy – aims at making a profit without damaging society (people) or the environment (planet) now or in the future. It is profit that is the determining factor, since it rewards the production factor of capital and ensures continuity of the company. The planet aspect refers to protection of the environment against direct damage by the production process and to ensuring future resources. The people aspect refers to dealing with employees and the relationship between the company and society. Table 4.9 illustrates the interpretation Shell has given to sustainable entrepreneurship.

TABLE 4.9 Shell and sustainable entrepreneurship

Sustainability principle	Explanation
Generating robust profitability (profits)	Good financial results are important for the continuity of Shell and contribute to the community's prosperity
Providing value to the client (profits)	A good relationship with the client is a necessary condition for the sustained future of Shell
Protecting the environment (planet)	The sustainability of human existence is dependent upon the quality of the environment
Management of resources (planet)	Sustainable management of resources is necessary for satisfying the needs of future generations.
Respecting and protecting people (people)	Respect for personal and cultural differences and protection of people against injury and damage caused by the Shell's products and activities

TABLE 4.9 Shell and sustainable entrepreneurship (continued)

Sustainability principle	Explanation
Working for the benefit of local communities (people)	Shell's 'social residency permit' depends on the contribution Shell makes to the wellbeing of the local community
Cooperation with stakeholders (people)	Taking account of, listening to and reacting to those who have an interest in Shell

Source: based on *The Shell Report*, 2001

4.4 **The structure of the European economy**

Businesses and the government produce in order to satisfy needs such as those for food, clothing, housing, transport, recreation, education and safety.

4.4.1 **The ten sectors of the European economy**

Eurostat classifies production under ten sectors. Figure 4.6 shows the structure of production in the EU in 2015.

FIGURE 4.6 Structure of Gross Value Added in the EU, 2015

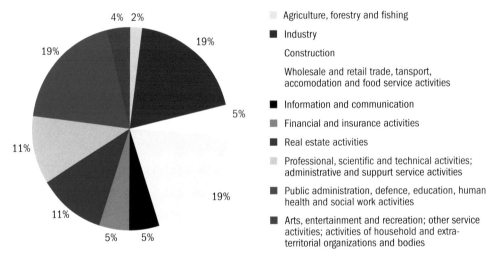

Source: Eurostat

Advanced economies

Agrarian sector

Industrial sector

The relationships between the various sectors in Figure 4.6 are typical of advanced economies. The production of the agrarian sector is a small part of the total production. The same holds for the industrial sector. The share of both these sectors has decreased dramatically during the course of the twentieth century, while the services sector has increased proportionally. Our society is often called a post-industrial society with a large service component of more than 70% of the GDP. All these activities consist of the whole economy except agriculture, industry and construction.

There are a number of reasons for the growth of the services component. **Services**
Firstly, there are physical limits to the need for goods. Prosperity is at such a
level that consumers have enough goods and demand is only replacement
demand. The goods markets are therefore often saturated markets with a
low-income elasticity. After basic needs (food, clothing, housing) have been
met, consumers increasingly tend to want to satisfy those needs that are met
by the service sectors (travel, sport, education, entertainment).
Secondly, because of the increasing free trade and high wages compared
to the low-wage countries, there has been a production shift to other
countries within the sectors that are price-sensitive. This development has
been stimulated by the sharp drop in the cost of transport. Many industrial
companies have disposed of their production department or have relocated
it and have become head-and-tail companies that develop products and
market them, but farm out production or relocate it to areas with lower
costs. The competitive advantage of advanced economies is no longer the
availability of physical production factors such as raw materials, capital
goods and unskilled labour, but specialised elements of production such as
an efficient organisation, advanced technical know-how, innovation, brand
name development and customer-directed service (see also Section 4.4.2).

There is a relationship between the sectional division of production and
that of labour. Figure 4.7 shows the sectional division of employment in the
EU.

FIGURE 4.7 Structure of employment in the EU, 2014

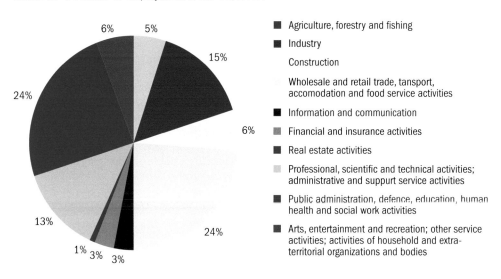

Source: Eurostat

The biggest sectors also provide the greatest employment. Public services
and trade, transport and communication together account for 48% of the
total employment.
It is interesting to compare the contribution to employment against
the contribution to the GDP. The agriculture sector provides 5.0% of
employment, against 1.8% of the GDP. Employees in the agriculture sector

produce less than the average, therefore. Financial services and insurance activities contribute 2,6 to employment and 5,1% to production. The added value per employee in this sector is therefore higher than the average, and consequently five times greater than that of the agriculture sector.

4.4.2   Knowledge and innovative activities

Specialise

Increased international competition has forced economies to specialise in areas where the competitive power of their businesses is the greatest. What these businesses are depends not only on the features of these businesses, but also on the macroeconomic environment variables, of which knowledge and innovation are the main ones for large parts of the European economy.

This section will examine some macroeconomic features of the competitive power of an economy.

Not every sector has been affected to the same extent by the internationalisation of the economy. The construction sector, large sections of financial services, business activities and public services have little to fear from increasing internationalisation. These are called protected sectors.

Protected sectors

The sectors that are particularly subject to international petition are manufacture, wholesale trade, transport and some financial services. This is the open sector. Agriculture is still protected by the European agriculture policy, but after this policy has been revised it will be part of the open sector. Companies that are part of the open sector are at the mercy of daily international competition and under increasing pressure to raise their labour productivity and to be innovative with their products.

Open sector

The macroeconomic key factors to company success are dependent on the development level of the economy. For convenience's sake we will refer to three development levels, each related to the GDP per person. Countries with low incomes usually have factor-based growth. Their economic development is based on a larger deployment of the basic factors of land, raw materials and unskilled labour. At this stage, their competitive power is largely dependent on the availability of these factors and their price. The technology employed is simple and is completely based on an imitation of technologies that have been developed in other countries. The contribution of the government to their competitive power is in this early stage of economic development mainly to provide a stable political and economic climate and a good working market for production factors and goods. For the latter, a reliable judicial system is very important. Countries with factor-based growth are often dependent on the export of raw materials and labour-intensive products. Practice shows that the export output of these countries is very sensitive to fluctuations in economic conditions, prices of raw materials and exchange rates.

Development level

Factor-based growth

As the economy develops, the driving force behind economic growth is taken over by the increasing influx of foreign direct investments (investment-based growth). These foreign investments mean that the countries become more integrated into the world economy and they are able to import technology from abroad. The combination of relatively low cost of production factors and imported technology enables these countries to produce standard goods and services efficiently. The priority of the government lies at this stage in trying to attract foreign investments. Apart from a stable political and economic climate, investments in the

Direct investments

physical infrastructure and effective laws and regulations are required. Although at this stage technology still comes from abroad, these countries are increasingly able to improve on existing technologies. Some Asian countries are wizards in imitating and improving imported technology. In countries with investment-based growth, the most successful sectors are industry and services that have been farmed out (by high-wage countries). Countries with investment-based growth are very dependent on the influx of capital from abroad. For this reason, they are very sensitive to financial crises in the world economy. They are also susceptible to sector-specific shocks because they often specialise in a limited number of industrial sectors. Taiwan, for example, is one of the world's greatest producers of semiconductors for the computer industry. If world-wide sales of computers decrease for some reason or other, the Taiwanese economy will be badly affected.

The changeover to the last stage of economic development is the most difficult one. During this stage, self-developed technologies are the motor behind economic growth. Any country that wants to permanently grow in an innovation-based manner will have to excel in technology in a number of sectors. The government can create the preconditions by providing good education, stimulating research and development and taking away financial and legal restrictions for techno-starters. Innovation-based growers obtain their competitive power from high productivity growth. During this stage, companies have to invest continually in research and development and in the training of their staff ('life-long learning'). Experience tells us that in the technology field, innovation prospers best in a climate in which suppliers, contractors, service companies and universities work together in so-called clusters. Innovative clusters are as strong as their weakest link. If one of the participants in a cluster is no longer able to function at the limit of his technical abilities or is relocated abroad, the competitive power of the whole of the cluster is jeopardised. A shortage of highly educated personnel can become an impediment for innovation-based growth.

Innovation-based

Table 4.10 summarises the features of the various stages of economic development.

TABLE 4.10 Various stages in economic development

	Low income	Middle income	High income
Nature of the growth	Factor-based	Investment-based	Innovation-based
Motor behind the growth	Mobilisation of basic production factors (land, raw materials, unskilled labour)	Influx of direct foreign investments, including modern technology	Self-developed new technologies (product and process innovations)
Basis for competitive power	Low costs of basic production factors	Efficient production of standard products	Productivity
Government priorities	• Political and economic stability • Efficient markets for production factors	• Physical infrastructure (ports, roads and telecommunication) • Legislation (customs, taxes, company law)	• Stimulation of research, development and higher education • As few restrictions on techno-starters as possible

TABLE 4.10 Various stages in economic development (continued)

	Low income	Middle income	High income
Technology	Standardised, obtained by importing, imitation and direct foreign investment	Imported and improved where necessary	Own development in at least a number of sectors
The main sectors for growth	Agriculture, fisheries, mining, labour-intensive industrial production	Industry and the export of outsourced services	Innovative clusters of business sectors in cooperation with universities
Sensitive to	Fluctuations in the economy, prices of raw materials and the exchange rates	Financial crises and sector specific shocks	Disintegration of innovative clusters
Examples	Ghana, Bangladesh	South Korea, Poland	United States, Finland

Renewal of products and production processes

The countries of the EU can be classified as falling within the second and third stages of economic development. For companies and business sectors to be competitive, regular renewal of products and production processes is required. This enables them to enter into new markets and to keep their costs under control.

The easiest way in which companies can innovate is by investing. By buying new machines, companies buy, as it were, the technologies developed by other companies. New inventions are thus disseminated throughout production sectors.

Immaterial investments

Alongside material investments, immaterial investments in new products and for the renewal of production processes are also needed. Immaterial investments are expenses that contribute to a company's ability to produce goods and services now or in the future. These investments include the following:

- R&D;
- Exploitation of titles to ownership;
- Brand names;
- Schooling, know-how;
- Participation in networks and clusters.

Where innovation is concerned, there are two main schools of thought: that of technology push and that of demand pull.

Technology push

The technology push view assumes technology to be a more or less autonomous process. The technology departments of companies and government institutions invent new products that are made by the production department. The marketing and sales departments then introduce the product to the customers and sell them. The product is pushed, as it were, from its first development through the whole production process and all the way to the customers. The physical invention and production are the key elements. R&D plays a crucial part in this view. The company might even patent the invention and exploit its right to ownership by making use of the monopoly position: asking high prices or allowing other companies to do part of the production, but at a price.

In the demand pull view, the demands and needs of the customer are crucial.

Demand pull

In this view, innovation by companies and the government is not a more or less autonomous process, but one that is directed by demand. Demand pulls the innovative activities along, as it were. Innovation not only involves the technical development of new products, but also the development of communication with the market, new distribution channels and training of staff. Not only the product and the price, but also the other P's of the marketing mix – promotion and place (distribution) – are included in the innovative process. It would be more accurate to talk about innovative activities than technical development.

Company R&D can be carried out by employing researchers and building or hiring laboratories in which to do the research.

As a rule, expenditure on R&D by companies increases when the national income of the country increases. If national prosperity increases, consumers will demand ongoing improvement in the quality of the products they buy. They will be more discerning in their spending, forcing companies to vary the production package they offer. This makes innovation essential for maintaining the competitive position of companies. The development of new products gives companies an opportunity to open up new markets that are less sensitive to general fluctuations in the economy and to competition from other companies. This means that companies that invest the most in R&D also have the strongest competitive advantage. R&D expenditure in a country thus gives an indication of the competitive position of its industries and consequently its long-term growth potential.

R&D and GDP

Figure 4.8 represents the total R&D. The figure clearly reveals, in percentage terms, that the US and Japan spend approximately one third more of their GDP than the EU. Their R&D expenditure per unit output is approximately 50% higher.

Differences in knowledge intensity give rise to a division into high-tech, medium-tech and low-tech products. The R&D expenditure per unit or the R&D expenditure as a percentage of output is usually taken as a criterion.

High-tech products are products that are continually being improved. Companies that make these products often have a research budget that is higher than 7% of their output. The development of their products takes place in countries with a high human capital and requires relatively few raw materials. Companies also vie for development of efficient production processes for these products. Traditional products are low-tech. They require a lot of raw material and low-trained labour and usually require little marketing. Many of these products are subject to intensive price competition from imports from low-wage countries. Medium-tech products occupy an intermediate position. They include high-quality consumer goods and intermediate products for the high-tech sectors.

High-tech products

Low-tech

Medium-tech

FIGURE 4.8 Total R&D expenditure as a % of GDP, 1981-2015

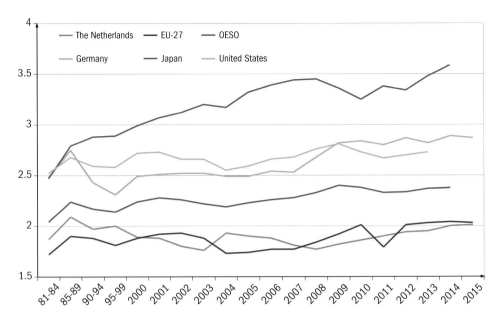

Source: Eurostat and OECD

On the basis of these considerations, we can classify the industrial sectors as in Table 4.11.

TABLE 4.11 Classification of industry into high-tech, medium-tech and low-tech sectors

High tech	Medium tech	Low tech
Microelectronics	Electrical machinery	Oil
Electronics	Chemicals	Basic metals
Pharmacy	Car manufacture	Foodstuffs
Aircraft manufacture	Non-electrical machinery	Metal products
Instrument making	Rubber and plastics	Textiles etc.
New materials	Glass, stone, clay	Transport
Biotechnology		Paper and printing
Robot technology		Wood and furniture
		Other industries

Source: Slabbers and Verspagen, *Een beoordeling van de Nederlandse technologische positie op basis van kwantitatieve factoren*, Maastricht 1994, p. 29

The fastest growing sectors of the economy of the EU indicate the importance to the economy of long-term technological development:
- Office machinery and computers;
- Aeronautics and astronautics;
- Motor vehicles and motor vehicle parts;
- Pharmaceutical products.

All of these are business sectors in which growth is mainly stimulated by research or marketing.

The demand-pull view of technical development involves more than inventing new products and implementing production processes alone. This view is also concerned with developing and applying new raw materials, sales outlets, markets and sales methods.

An information process is required to trace the needs of clients (both businesses and consumers) and to find out whether the company possesses the necessary potential for meeting these needs or can develop it. Such an approach calls for a smooth exchange of information between company and client: an information diffusion process. To achieve reasonable quality in this information diffusion process, planned organisation of the stream of information is necessary. Companies are increasingly obliged to organise this aspect of their external environment. This is evident in long-term supplier customer relationships in which products are made in communal projects (co-design, co-makership, *see* Chapter 3).
A large proportion of the European industry is concentrated along a belt that runs across the south of the Netherlands, Belgium, the south of Germany, the north of France and the north of Italy. Many industrial businesses are organised in international networks.

Information diffusion process

TEST 4.5
Airbus has meant that Europe has a self-generating aircraft industry. What are the consequences of this for information within the Airbus network and within the industry as a whole?

4.4.3   Long-term growth potential
The EU is striving to achieve a minimum annual long-term growth rate of 3%. We have already referred a few times to the long-term growth potential of the economy, though in terms of the various production factors. In this section, these will be looked at jointly, and it will become clear that the conditions for long-term economic growth are mainly aimed at raising labour productivity. Labour productivity is the source of prosperity. Differences in labour productivity are largely responsible for the difference in prosperity per capita between countries and in remuneration for the production factor of labour. Improvements in the production factors of capital and natural resources are therefore also aimed at raising labour productivity.
In the long run, the growth potential of a country is determined by two factors: growth of the working population and growth of labour productivity. Economic growth that is the result of employing more labour is called factor-based growth. Imagine that at a certain point in time the entire working population of Europe is able to be involved in the production process. From that moment on, Europe will be dependent on the second determining factor behind growth potential: an increase in labour productivity.
The economic growth will then have to become innovation-based instead of factor-based.

Labour productivity

Six elements are important for the growth potential of a country: human capital, entrepreneurship, market structure, innovation, environmental planning and sustainability. The policies of the government and industry should be aimed at reinforcing these elements. This would enable optimal use of the labour potential to be made and a basis created for sustainable growth sustainable productivity growth (*see* Figure 4.9).

Figure 4.9 shows that the growth potential can improve by better use of the labour potential or by raising labour productivity. The EU is striving to achieve a participation rate of 70%. Ultimately – after all available labour has been put into action – productivity growth is the only factor determining economic growth. The question is how the other elements mentioned in Figure 4.9 could contribute to productivity growth.

FIGURE 4.9 Long-term growth potential

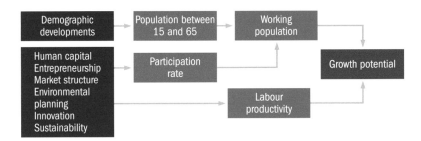

Human capital
In the field of human capital, it is important to avoid a situation in which shortage of well-educated staff inhibits economic growth. There is a quantitative and a qualitative aspect to human capital. In order to achieve higher growth potential, the labour potential must be deployed better and trained better.

Entrepreneurs
It is important for the growth potential of the economy that entrepreneurs starting on new activities be given room to manoeuvre, both literally and figuratively. They should have actual access to sufficient industrial space and space on motorways, railways and waterways. In the densely populated areas of Europe, opportunities for habitation, employment and recreation are limited. Good environmental planning is consequently an essential aspect of the growth potential. In a figurative sense, it is important that entrepreneurs not be hampered unnecessarily in their movements by rules and regulations. Entrepreneurship may also be hampered by too little availability of venture capital or excessive taxation pressure on profits.

Competition
Competition on well-structured markets forces entrepreneurs to make tight pricing policies and to be innovative. If the government improves market structures by, for instance, abolishing entrance barriers to markets or by better control of restrictive trade agreements between entrepreneurs, they can increase the competitive pressure on markets. This gives entrepreneurs

Sustainability
a greater incentive to increase their productivity. The growth of the European economy will have to be less factor-based and more innovation-based in the future. Innovation is therefore perhaps the main determining factor for European growth potential. The EU is striving to achieve a minimum R&D expenditure of 3% of GDP. Product and process innovations demand a high application of ICT and knowledge. Both the government – via a good public education infrastructure – and industry – through

investment in human capital and in research and development – will have to contribute to this.

Finally, it is important for the sustainability of economic growth that the growth be accompanied by as little social and ecological damage as possible. Economic growth is not sustainable if it leads to great social contrasts or interferes with the growth potential of future generations.

For high and sustainable growth potential, a good balance between social, ecological and economic interests is therefore essential.

TEST 4.6
Give a concrete example of an economic development that has caused social damage.

Glossary

4

Added value	Adding to the commercial value of a product by the use of production factors.
Capital coefficient	The stock of capital goods needed for 1 euro's worth of production.
Capital goods	Goods that are used or consumed during the production process: • *Durable capital goods* have a life span of more than one period • *Floating capital goods* are used up in one period.
Cluster	A cooperative partnership between businesses, the government, research organisations and commercial service institutions for the purposes of innovation.
Competitive position	(Of Europe) All those factors that determine the chances of European products on foreign markets.
Depreciation	The costs associated with the use of durable capital goods during a certain period.
Diffusion of knowledge	Spreading of knowledge and information.
Export-oriented business sectors	Business sectors that export a relatively large amount of their produce.
Factor advantage	A production factor of such a quantity or quality that a lower cost level or a higher quality of production is possible.
Gross Domestic	The production of goods and services within a country's borders.
Product	A distinction should be made between GDP at basic prices and GDP at market prices. See the entry *National income* for the difference between the two.
Intermediary deliveries	Mutual deliveries between businesses of products that need to be processed further.
Labour productivity	The production per employee per period.

National income	The sum of the remuneration of the European production factors. A distinction needs to be made between: • *Gross national income at market prices*: Gross national income at basic prices including the difference between indirect taxation and cost-price-decreasing subsidies • *Gross national income at basic prices*: the sum of the remuneration of employees, gross operating surplus, mixed income and depreciation.
Networks	A far-reaching collaborative agreement between supplying and contracting businesses.
Participation rate	The working population (both the employed and unemployed) expressed as a percentage of the population between the ages of 15 and 65.
Production	Adding value to products by the use of labour, natural resources and capital.
Production capacity	Maximum production taking into consideration the quantity and quality of production factors.
Production factors	Resources used for production: labour, natural resources and capital.
Prosperity	The satisfaction of needs by means of scarce goods and services.
R&D	Research and development for the purpose of creating new products and production processes.
Sector	A part of industry arranged according to the nature of the activities: • *Market sector*: businesses that sell their products on markets where there is price formation, at least to some extent • *Primary sector*: agriculture, forestry and fishing • *Secondary sector*: industry and mining • *Services sector*: commercial services • *Government sector*: non-commercial services • *Open sector*: firms that export the major part of their production • *Protected sector*: businesses that do not export any of their production or only a minimal amount.
Sustainable entrepreneurship	Conducting a business in such a way that no damage is done to the present and future production factors.
Sustainable growth	Growth of the GDP on the condition that the environmental factors are not damaged.
Taxes on production and exports	Indirect taxation, especially value-added tax, import and excise duties.

4

Technology push	The philosophy that technical development is a prerequisite for production and marketing.
Unemployment	The difference between the supply of and the demand for labour.
Well-being	The extent of experiencing happiness.

5

Expenditure

5.1   **Consumption**
5.2   **Investments**
5.3   **Government expenditure**
5.4   **Foreign expenditure**
5.5   **The circular flow of income**

The main issues that will be addressed in this chapter are as follows:
- On what do the various sectors expend their money?
- Why do they need to expend this money?
- What causes an increase in expenditure?
- How do production, income and expenditure relate to each other?

Production was the main subject of Chapter 4. It dealt with the supply of goods and services.
Chapter 5 is all about expenditure. We will deal with the following four sectors: consumers (Section 5.1), businesses (Section 5.2), the government (Section 5.3) and foreign countries (Section 5.4). Expenditure is also referred to as the demand side of the economy.

Figure 5.1 shows the distribution of expenditure over the sectors.

In Section 5.5, the production and expenditure of the four sectors will be looked at within the framework of the circular flow of income. Production and expenditure are interrelated. Entrepreneurs and the government tailor production to customer demand. Participants in the production process derive an income from production, which they in turn can spend.

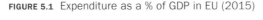

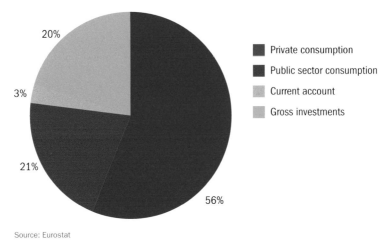

FIGURE 5.1 Expenditure as a % of GDP in EU (2015)

Legend:
- Private consumption
- Public sector consumption
- Current account
- Gross investments

Source: Eurostat

CASE

Philips makes products for consumers, the government and companies. What follows is a random selection from Philips' product package.

For the consumer market, it makes the following: light bulbs, batteries, televisions, radios, videos, vacuum cleaners, irons and all kinds of other domestic appliances.

For the business market Philips makes light fittings, automobile headlights, automobile radio systems, automobile electronics, chips, x-ray machines, professional TV systems, business communication systems, software on CD and so on.

The government purchases systems for communication, security and medical applications.

It is not only European parties but also consumers, businesses and governments outside the EU that buy Philips products.

5.1 Consumption

This section focuses on consumption. It will deal particularly with the macroeconomic consumption pattern and the factors that determine the growth of consumption.

Household expenditure is called consumption. We only call goods consumer goods after they have been bought by consumers. A piece of furniture that is still in the shop awaiting purchase belongs to floating capital (stock). Only after it has been bought do we speak of consumption. Consumers purchase a set number of goods and services to satisfy their needs. This is termed a consumption pattern. Consumption patterns vary considerably. Consumers use a variety of different products to satisfy their needs. Consumer preferences differ. One consumer might have eating habits that cause him to consume a lot of fruit and vegetables, another consumer to frequent snack bars and a third consumer to dine in

Consumption pattern

Consumer preferences

restaurants. Some consumers spend a lot of money on durable consumer goods while others have a preference for travel.

Adding up all of the various items of expenditure of individual consumers gives us a macroeconomic consumer pattern. Figure 5.2 shows the macroeconomic consumer pattern for the EU.

FIGURE 5.2 Consumption pattern EU, 2015

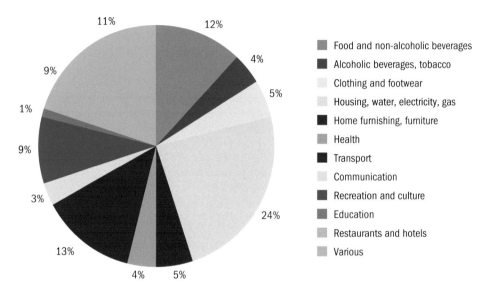

Source: Eurostat

Changes in consumer patterns
Chapter 2 has already dealt at length with consumer patterns, so a short commentary on Figure 5.2 will therefore do for our purposes.
It is important for companies and industries to know what changes are occurring in their expenditure, because these changes will affect their own sales. Companies that were producing for growing markets in the past will find that their markets are becoming saturated, which will have consequences for competition.
In Chapter 2 we have seen that the income elasticity of expenditure can differ   *Income elasticity*
greatly. Foodstuffs have a lower income elasticity than services. At a constant increase in income, the ratio between expenditure on foodstuffs and services will change in favour of the latter. In 1994, consumers spent 16.1% of the total consumer expenditure on food; by 2012 this had fallen to only 12%. This drop is related to the low-income elasticity of foodstuffs. In the same period, expenditure on hotels and restaurants rose by a quarter. This reflects the high-income elasticity of this expenditure, in which the service component is much larger than it is for the sale of foodstuffs by retailers.
Economic agencies often predict both long-term and short-term changes in consumption on the basis of income developments. These are the main influences. In the short term, a few others – distribution of income, capital development, consumer confidence and the interest rate – also play a role (see Figure 5.3).

FIGURE 5.3 Determining factors of changes in consumption (in the short term)

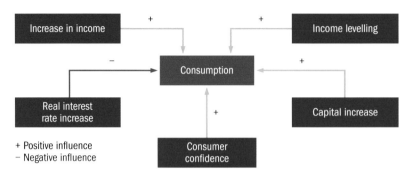

Consumer confidence Consumers receive an income. The height of that income together with prices determine how many products they can buy. The price of consumer goods may rise year by year. This is termed inflation (see Chapter 6). An increase in income during a particular year says little about the quantity of products that people can buy in that year. This brings us to the concept of purchasing power. Purchasing power can be defined as available income corrected for inflation (see Formula 1).

$$\% \ \Delta\text{purchasing power} = \% \ \Delta\text{income} - \% \ \Delta\text{prices} \qquad [1]$$

Real

Nominal

Income bracket

Marginal consumption ratio

With a 4% rise in income and an inflation of 3%, purchasing power will therefore increase by 1%. Increase in purchasing power is also known as real increase in income: in other words, an increase in the quantity of products consumers can buy. Income that is not corrected for price increases is called nominal income. As a general rule, a real rise in income equals the nominal income increase minus price rises.

The extent to which the sales of a product profit from an increase in income is in the short term also dependent upon the income bracket in which the increase took place. In order to understand how this works, we need some insight into the concept of the marginal consumption ratio.

The marginal consumption ratio gives an indication of how much of every extra euro earned is consumed. If consumers spend 75 cents of an extra euro earned, the marginal consumption ratio is 0.75. The marginal consumption ratio is significantly lower for high incomes than for low incomes. As such, the distinction between wage income, social security income and other income is a significant one.

EXAMPLE 5.1

Marginal consumption in the Netherlands

If wage income increases by €1, consumption will increase by 72 cents. The marginal consumption ratio will therefore be 72% or 0.72. An increase in social security income by €1 will result in a rise in consumption of 95 cents. A rise in capital income of €1 will only cause a 40-cent increase in consumption. For companies with income-sensitive sales it is therefore very important to know what income bracket their products are intended for.

People with a low income consume a large part of their increase in income. Companies that market bulk goods for the low and middle segments can profit considerably from an increase in income within the low income brackets.

TEST 5.1

In a certain year, the United States government tried to stimulate the economy by lowering dividend taxes. How effective a measure is this in your opinion?

While a rise in income or purchasing power is a necessary prerequisite for an increase in consumption, on its own it is not enough. If consumers have little confidence in the general economic future or their own economic future, their willingness to buy will be low. Consequently, they will not spend the increase in their income, but save it. Situations like this often occur during stock exchange crises or threats of war. Only when confidence returns will consumers spend their savings. Consumer confidence is therefore also an important factor affecting consumption. Consumer confidence measures the consumer's own feelings about his financial situation and his economic environment, and can be gauged on the basis of a number of questions put to a group of consumers. Figure 5.4 represents the index for the EU between 1985 and 2013.

Consumer confidence

The answers to each question are expressed as a percentage of the total number of answers. The consumer confidence index is the average of these outcomes. The minimum value is −100, the maximum +100. Figure 5.4 shows that periods of low consumer confidence (1993, 2003, 2009 and 2013) coincide with periods of economic depression.

Consumption growth is also dependent on two other factors, both of which have a small effect on consumption: real interest and capital increase. Real interest is the difference between nominal interest and inflation. If the real interest increases, consumption will decrease. The reason for this is that loans become more expensive. Consumer credit will decrease and so consumer expenditure will also decrease. This affects travel, tourism and durable consumer goods in particular.

Real interest and capital increase

Real interest

Loans

Consumers possess capital that they invest in savings accounts, shares, houses and the like. A rise in capital value (as, for instance, the result of an increase in share prices) will lead to an increase in consumption. Households can utilise any increase in the value of their homes by raising the mortgage and using the funds obtained in this way for consumption purposes.

Capital

FIGURE 5.4 Consumer Confidence Index, EU (1985-2016)

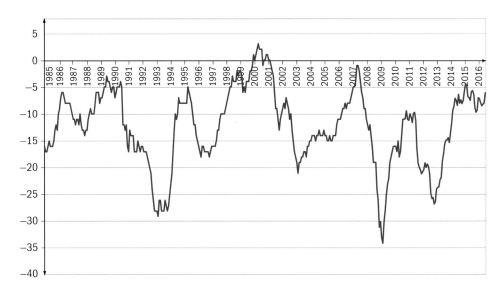

Source: ECB, Eurostat

5.2 Investments

Investing is buying capital goods for the benefit of production. Companies buy various types of goods for their production, including raw materials and semi-finished products that are only used once during the production process. An increase in capital associated with these things is termed investment in floating capital goods or stock investments.

Planned stock investments

These investments can be planned or forced stock investments. Firms often buy in extra supplies of raw materials or allow their stock of finished products to mount up when they expect sales to increase, thus causing the quantity of floating capital goods to increase.

Forced stock investments

Forced stock investments also occur. Normally, production is equal to demand. However, a situation will sometimes occur in which companies overestimate their sales, and the expectations that they had initially prove to have been too rosy. They will have produced more than the demand and will not be able to sell part of their production. The effect will be that production within that particular economy looks higher than expenditure, but this is deceptive. These companies will now have to make expenditure of a type that business sectors are not willing to make. They will be forced to invest in stock they are not able to sell. These stock investments mean that in retrospect (that is, after the economic process has been completed), expenditure will always be exactly the same as production and income. This is also the reason why establishing the GDP via the production and income approach is the same as via the expenditure approach.

TEST 5.2
What will happen during the period to come if companies have to make forced stock investments during a certain period?

Companies also buy goods that can be used for long-term production: buildings and machinery that are used for the production process and consequently gradually diminish in value through wear and tear and becoming outdated. The purchase of these products is termed investment in fixed capital goods. Investments in fixed assets can be divided into replacement investments and expansion investments. Replacement investments are those investments that companies need to make to replace their old machinery after it has been in use for a number of years: purchasing capital goods because of wear and tear. The fact that machines wear out during the production process means incurring costs, and these costs companies pass on in their sales prices. The proceeds of their sales enable companies to buy new machinery. If they fail to do this, they will have to cease production when the machines wear out. Replacement investments are therefore necessary in order to keep production going. They are financed from depreciation. Expansion of capital goods stock is a second reason for investment. Unlike replacement investments, expansion investments are aimed at increasing the production capacity. Companies that make expansion investments during a certain period thereby increase the capital goods stock that was present at the beginning of the period. Companies can finance expansion investments through loans (borrowed capital) or retained profit (equity capital).

Replacement investments

Expansion investments

The various types of investment, the reasons for them and the financial sources are shown in Table 5.1.

TABLE 5.1 Investments

Type	Reason	Financing
Replacement investments	Wear and tear of capital goods	Depreciation
Expansion investments (fixed assets)	Expansion of capital goods stock	Reserves or loans
Stock investments		
• Planned	Expected increase in sales	Reserves or loans
• Forced	Unexpected decrease in sales	Reserves or loans

We can now differentiate between gross and net investments. Gross investments are net investments plus replacement investments. Net investments consist of expansion investments in fixed assets and stock changes. When companies buy new machinery, adjustments are usually made to the existing stock of capital goods. These adjustments often have the effect that there is less labour required per machine, which will result in an increase in labour productivity. This can be described as a laboursaving technical development. The purchase of such machinery is termed investments in depth. If no labour-saving technical developments take place and the new machines produce the same quantity of products per employee per period as the old machines, this is described as investments in width.

Gross and net investments

Investments in depth

Investments in width

Economic research institutes often explain the development of investments using the following variables:
• Sales expectations;
• Degree of capacity utilisation;
• Profits;
• Interest rate.

Companies make investments with a view to future expansion of production (see Figure 5.5). The future production will depend on the future sales. Companies have sales expectations about the quantity of products they could sell in a certain period. These expectations are often based on the estimated growth of the GDP at home and abroad. The higher the expectations, the more a company will be prepared to invest.

Sales expectations

FIGURE 5.5 Investment growth

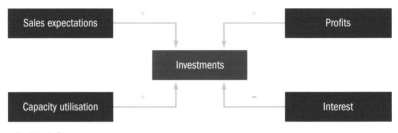

+ Positive influence
− Negative influence

Degree of capital utilisation

The degree of capital utilisation indicates the percentage of time that machines and other capital goods are actually being used. If the degree of utilisation is high, companies can only increase production by expansion of the stock of capital goods.

Interest

Investments and interest affect each other negatively. If the interest rate rises, investments will decrease. Companies invest in order to produce. The sale of products provides profits which companies regard as the return on investment: the internal rate of return.

A company could also invest the available amount at a lower risk on the capital market in order to obtain interest income. Investing on the capital market is an alternative for investment. If the interest on the capital market rises, companies will postpone many investment projects with a low internal rate of return.

Profits

The higher the profits, the easier it is for companies to finance investments from their own resources. As well as this, companies with high profits have easier access to loan capital markets, which makes it easy for them to borrow capital.

TEST 5.3
Why would investments during an economic boom period be less dependent on interest rates than during an economic recession?

Labour income ratio
We have seen that the proportion of profits to the added value of a country is important for the level of investment. The labour income ratio (LIR) and the capital income ratio give an indication of the proportion of labour and capital in the added value. The LIR indicates the share of the gross added value that is apportioned to the remuneration for the production factor of labour. The remaining share of the added value is for depreciation, interest and profits. The closer the LIR approaches 100%, the less is left for the

owners of the capital. As a rule, a LIR percentage of 80% is regarded as sufficient to allow entrepreneurs to finance investments using the remaining profits. The level of investments is sufficient under these circumstances to safeguard the growth potential of the economy.

The formula for LIR is:

$$LIR = \frac{W}{GDP} \qquad [2]$$

in which:
W = Wages
GDP = Gross domestic product

The quotient of the real production and the labour demand (the number of employees) is equal to labour productivity.

The change in LIR as a percentage can be expressed as follows:

$$g_{LIR} = g_{Wemp} - g_p - g_{lp} \qquad [3]$$

Change in LIR as a percentage

in which:
g_{LIR} = The change in LIR as a percentage
g_{Wemp} = The change in wages per employee as a percentage
g_p = The change in the cost of the added value as a percentage
g_{lp} = The change in labour productivity as a percentage

If we assume that in a certain year the wages rise by an average of 6%, inflation is 3% and labour productivity increases by 2%, then the LIR will increase by approximately 1%.

It follows from formula [3] that entrepreneurs will have to pay a larger part of the added value in wages if the wages per employee increase. If, however, they are able to raise the price of their products, returns will increase. If the costs remain the same, the added value will increase and the proportion of wages to the added value (LIR) will decrease. A rise in labour productivity will also result in a lower LIR. If the employees make more products the added value will rise. At equal remuneration, the percentage of wages to the added value will decrease and the proportion of profits will increase.

The relationship between investments and LIR
Investments and LIR have an effect on each other. Profitability is roughly inversely proportional to the labour income ratio. That part of the added value that is not paid out in wages is, after all, the remaining income: profits and interest. Since investments are dependent on profitability, it is logical to assume that changes to the LIR have an influence on investment behaviour. This relationship can be expressed as follows:

$$LIR \uparrow \rightarrow I \downarrow \rightarrow Lp \downarrow \qquad [4]$$

Conversely, investments also have an influence on the LIR. Companies can improve on their labour productivity by investing in new capital goods.

This will cause the LIR to decrease. The relationship between investments and the LIR can be expressed as follows:

$$I \uparrow \rightarrow Lp \uparrow \rightarrow LIR \downarrow \qquad\qquad [5]$$

5.3 Government expenditure

The EU governments spent 50% of the GDP in 2012. The government's 'products' include public administration, security, education, infrastructure, medical services and the like. Approximately 25% of the GDP is earmarked for social security expenditure. This consists primarily of a transferral from households whose income is derived from wages, profits and interest (primary income) to households that do not have a primary income. These households are dependent on the social security system.

Countries have governments to do particularly necessary tasks which cannot be left to individual citizens or businesses. Government expenditure is related to the following duties of government:
- Allocative duties
- Redistributing duties
- Regulatory duties.

In this section, we will mainly deal with the government's allocative duties. Section 6.3 will deal with the other duties.

Allocative duties

Allocative duty

We have already seen in Chapter 2 that the government produces: it adds value to products. To do this it buys goods and services from businesses and takes on employees to add value to them. This could be described as the government taking possession of the means of production in order to produce certain goods and services with them. This is the government's allocative duty. It is how the government can provide services to its population. The government itself therefore pays for the government services it provides free or at less than the cost price to its population.
The government buys such things as uniforms, arms and police cars. Those goods that last less than a year are material government consumption (Cgov). Those goods that last longer than a year are termed government investments (Igov). As well as this the government hires labour: policemen, for instance.
For them the government pays salaries, termed the government's labour consumption. (NDPgov). Total government expenditure can be expressed in the following formula:

$$G = NDPgov + Cgov + Igov \qquad\qquad [6]$$

in which:
G = Government expenditure
Cgov = Material government consumption
Igov = Net government investments
NDPgov = Salaries of government personnel

The combination of uniforms, weapons, cars and personnel in, for instance, the form of patrols or the arrest of lawbreakers provides security. Security is a public good; nobody can be excluded from the security that the government provides thereby. The same holds for the protection that dykes provide against floods. Once the dyke is there it is impossible to exclude people who are not willing to pay for them from the protection they provide. As well as these public goods there are also so-called quasi-public goods. These could also be provided by businesses, since those that do not want to pay for them can be excluded from them. These include museums, swimming pools, public transport and theatres. The government regards these provisions as being so important that it is prepared provide them to the population below cost price. These businesses receive their income partly from government subsidies and partly from payment by the public.

Public good

Quasi-public goods

5.4 Foreign expenditure

The countries of the EU trade with each other. This is termed intra-EU trade. The countries of the EU as a whole also trade with countries outside the EU. This is termed extra-EU trade. The present section only deals with trade by the EU with other areas. Figure 5.6 shows export and import per area.

Noticeably, a large share of export and import is aimed at other highly industrialised regions the world over, the US and Japan or countries near Russia. The figure also demonstrates clearly that China has become the EU's production workshop. The European Union had a major surplus on the trade balance compared to the US, and a major deficit compared to China. The deficit in Russia has to do with importing energy.

FIGURE 5.6 Extra-EU trade, by region, as a percentage of the total trade in goods, 2015

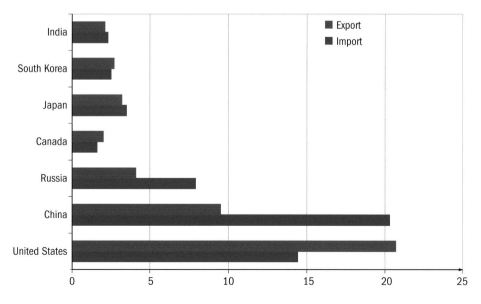

Source: Eurostat

Figure 5.7 shows the distribution of extra-EU trade according to product.

Figure 5.7 shows that the EU has an import surplus of raw materials, especially energy. This is set off by an export surplus in chemical products, machines and means of transport. In these products, therefore, companies within the EU have a competitive advantage.

The visible trade balance deficit in 2015 was 140 billion euros, approximately 1% of the GDP. The deficits and surpluses within the trade balance are caused to a large extent by oil prices. The energy supply of the EU depends partly on oil imports. The consumption of oil is very inelastic in the short term. Price rises have little impact on the quantities imported. A doubling or tripling of the oil prices has an immediate and negative effect on the export balance.
In addition to the trade in goods, there is also an international trade in services. In 2015 this amounted to approximately €830 billion. Services mainly involve such things as travel, transport and business services (such as market research and advertising). The EU has a slight services surplus of approximately €145 billion in 2015.
The export of goods and services together amounted to around 2,600 billion euros in the year 2015, approximately 18% of the GDP. For the US this was 15% and Japan 17%. The degree of openness of the major economic regions in the world is therefore comparable. Individual countries in the EU (and especially the smaller members) can be much more open, with export ratios up to 60%.

FIGURE 5.7 Extra-EU trade, by product, 2015 (% of total)

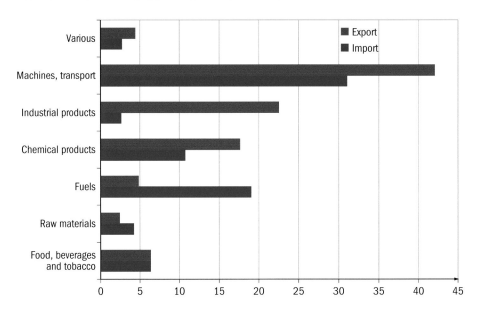

Source: Eurostat

Export changes

Export developments are influenced by two types of factors: the state of the global economy and the competitive position of industry. The main export areas of the European Union are the other industrialised countries, especially the United States. Much attention is therefore paid to the economic situation in these regions, as well as to the exchange rate of the dollar and the Japanese yen. An improvement in economic activity in the US together with a high dollar exchange rate could stimulate the EU's exports greatly, causing production, employment and expenditure to increase. During the initial stages of an economic revival, the economy of the US frequently acts as a booster for the European economy.

Economic
situation /
exchange rate

In the long term, the competitive position of the European companies on the export market is dependent upon the factors that have been dealt with in the previous chapters. Figure 5.8 gives a summary of the factors that affect export.

Innovative activities lead to a higher labour productivity. Wage developments and the development of labour productivity together determine the wage costs per unit (see Section 4.2.2). This last variable determines the pricing of export products. The wage costs per unit and pricing of competitors in other regions will vary. Ultimately, customers will make a choice after comparing the various products and prices. This is what determines the competitive position of European entrepreneurs on export markets.

FIGURE 5.8 Factors that affect export

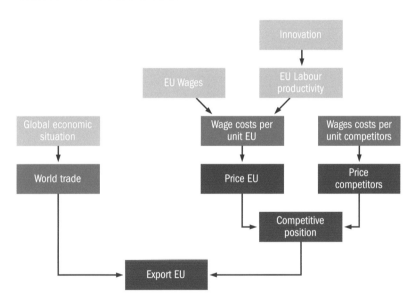

5.5 The circular flow of income

In the previous sections we have treated the expenditure of consumers, industry, the government and foreign countries. Figure 5.9 shows the transactions between the various sectors in the form of a circular flow of income. A circular flow of income represents the cash flows between the various sectors during a certain period of time.
The cycle shows that the outgoing flow of cash of one sector is the incoming flow of cash of another sector. For example, consumptive expenditure by households creates income for the sector companies. In the circular flow of

Inflow and
outflow of cash

income, the sum of the outgoing cash flows of the sectors is equal to the total of the incoming cash flows.

Figure 5.9 shows the main variables that affect production and expenditure. The left-hand side relates to supply in the economy, the domestic product and imports. The right-hand side relates to the expenditure. There are four sectors: consumers, the government, industry and other countries. Each sector has its own tasks in the production or the expenditure of income. These tasks can be easily deduced from the circular flow of income.

Left-hand side = production

Right-hand side = expenditure

The consumers provide the government and industry with a means of production for which they receive an income. From that income, they pay taxes to the government. The remaining part – the disposable income – they spend for the major part on consumer goods. What remains they save. The government and industry produce goods and services. The income flow to the consumers, who receive that income because of the productive activities they engage in, is indicative of this fact.

Disposable income

FIGURE 5.9 Circular flow of EU income, × € 1 mld

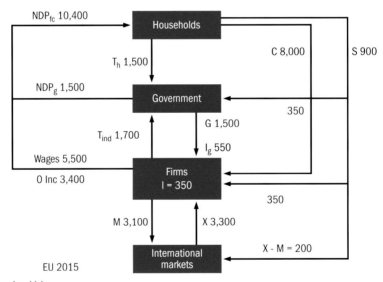

In which:
NDP$_{fc}$ = net domestic product at factor costs
T$_h$ = taxes households
c   = household consumption
S   = savings
NDP$_g$ = net domestic product government
NDP$_f$ = net domestic product firms
T$_{ind}$ = indirect taxes –/– cost price reducing subsidies
G   = government consumption
I$_g$ = net government investments
I   = net investments of companies
O Inc   = other income: profit and interest
M   = import
X   = export

Source: Eurostat

Production is augmented by import goods and services from other countries to meet the overall demand. The other countries buy export goods and services from the European industries.

The figures that are shown in Figure 5.9 are roughly those of the economy of the EU in the year 2015. The amounts are in billions of euros.

The circular flow of income is in a state of balance. In Chapter 4 we have seen that production and income are equal to each other because the level of profit adjusts itself automatically. If companies sell less than expected, they receive less profit than expected. This causes income to decrease at the same rate as production. If companies sell less than they produce, they have to make the expenditure themselves in the form of stock investments. This also means that production and expenditure are equal to each other. If companies regard their profits as being too low or if they have to make forced stock investments they will adjust the production process.

Balance

TEST 5.4
What would happen to the market if entrepreneurs underestimated demand?

We will now deal with the flow of cash within the cycle in more specific terms.

Consumers receive a remuneration from industry and government for making the means of production available (NDP_{bc} =10,400). They spend this income partly on consumer goods (C = 8,000) and pay taxes to the government (T_c = 1,500). The rest they save (S = 900).

Consumers

The government receives direct taxes from the consumers (T_c = 1,500) and indirect taxes minus cost-price decreasing subsidies from industry (1,700). The government expends its money on material government consumption and government investments in industry ($C_{gov} + I_{gov}$ = 2,050). As well as this, the government pays out salaries to the households of government employees (NDP_{gov} = 1,500). The government budget shows a deficit of 350.

Government

Industry receives money from sales to consumers (C), the government ($C_{gov} + I_{gov}$) and other countries (X). It pays income to consumers (NBP_{ind}), indirect taxes to the government and money to other countries to pay for imports (M = 3,100). Foreign countries lend 200 from the EU.

Industry

The other countries receive an amount for the imports (M) and pay out an amount for exports. The other countries will borrow to cover any deficit or invest any surplus on the EU's capital markets. When there is a deficit on the current account, as is the case in Figure 5.9, there will be a capital flow from the other countries to the EU and when there is a surplus on the current account there will be a capital flow in the other direction. In Figure 5.9 the EU has lend 200 to other countries. A number of equations can be derived from Figure 5.9. Consumers spend their income on consumptive expenditure, savings and taxes:

$$NDP_{bp} = C + S + T_c$$
$$10,400 = 8,000 + 900 + 1,500 \qquad [7]$$

If we add the indirect taxes minus the cost-price reducing subsidies to both sides of equation [7], we get equation [8]:

$$NDP_{mp} = C + S + T$$
$$12,100 = 8,000 + 900 + 3,200 \qquad [8]$$

The cycle is in a state of balance, because the incoming and the outgoing cash flows of each sector are equal to each other. It also follows that production or income is equal to expenditure. This is shown in equation [9]:

$$NDP_{mp} = C + I + G + X - M$$
$$12,100 = 8,000 + 350 + 3,550 + 2,300 - 3,100 \qquad [9]$$

If we add depreciation to NBP_{mp}, the amount obtained is GDPmp. We then have to add the depreciation to the net investments on the right-hand side of equation [9]. This will give us the gross investments and equation [9] becomes equation [10]:

$$GDP_{mp} = C + I_{gr} + G + X - M$$
$$14,600 = 8,000 + 2,850 + 3,550 + 3,300 - 3,100 \qquad [10]$$

We can also write equation [10] another way. This gives us equation [11]:

$$GDP_{mp} - (C + I_{gr} + G) = X - M$$
$$14,600 - (8,000 + 2,850 + 3,550) = 200 \qquad [11]$$

The left-hand side of equation [10] represents production minus domestic expenditure. The right-hand side shows the net exports. If the domestic expenditure is greater than production, the deficit will have to be imported from abroad. In other words, if a country has a deficit in its balance of payments, its domestic expenditure is greater than its production and the country is living beyond its means. It has to borrow from abroad in order to import. An expenditure cut will create a decrease in imports and as a result exports and imports will be equal again.
Equation [11] elucidates another important aspect of the cycle: the relationship between government spending and the balance of payments. If the government increases its spending, domestic expenditure will increase.
If production remains the same, imports will also have to increase. Stimulating expenditure by the government will therefore result in a deterioration of the balance of payments. If the government alleviates the taxation pressure, the disposable income of households will increase, resulting in a rise in consumption. In that case too, if production remains the same, imports will have to increase in order to satisfy all expenditure requirements.

The following equation [12] can be deduced from equations [8] and [9]:

$(S - I)$	+	$(T - G)$	=	$(X - M)$
Savings balance of the private sector		Government savings balans		Export balance

National savings balance [12]

Equation [12] shows the main elements of the macroeconomic situation of an economy. The words in Equation [12] indicate that the sum of the savings balance of the private sector (industry and households) and that of the government (together the national savings balance) is equal to the export balance.

Macroeconomic situation

TEST 5.5

What can be expected to happen in a country where savings are insufficient to finance investment?

5

The balance of private savings (S) and private investments (I) is known as the savings balance of the private sector (S – I). Earlier we stressed the importance of savings for the financing of investments. If there is a positive savings balance, there will be no impediments to future investment. Investment is important for the growth of the capital goods stock, which in turn is a prerequisite for the growth of production.

Savings balance of the private sector

Government income (T) reduced by the government expenditure (G) gives us the balance of the government's budget. An assessment of this budget is relevant for macroeconomic policies. Governments of countries with large deficits will sooner or later have to carry out expenditure cuts, which will be to the detriment of government services. Government demand for all kinds of goods and services as well as the demand for labour will diminish as a result of government cuts.

Balance of the government's budget

Export (X) minus import (M) is the export balance (X – M). Deficits or surpluses on the balance of payments are dependent on (among other things) the competitive power of industry on foreign markets.

Export balance

The multiplier

We can analyse the consequences of an increase in expenditure using the circular flow of income. Let us assume that at a particular moment a certain company makes a new investment and for that purpose places orders with machinery factories and building contractors. The machinery factories and building contractors subsequently start producing. They attract the means of production to do so (labourers, machines, buildings) and they remunerate them. The domestic product and income increase.

The households that receive the remuneration will spend in such areas as the foodstuffs retail trade. This branch will in turn remunerate employees, who in turn will spend money. This elicits more production and income. The original extra investments will therefore have set in motion a whole chain of income building and expenditure. The result will be a greater increase in production, income and expenditure than was the case with the original investment. This is referred to as the multiplier effect of expenditure. A multiplier is an increase in production and income as a result of a stimulus to spending.

Multiplier

For governments, high multiplier situations have a very attractive side. Such a situation offers an opportunity for governments to encourage vigorous economic growth and need only a small increase in government spending. The expenditure by the government must, of course, be balanced by income in order to avoid the government deficit becoming too great. A high multiplier situation causes income to rise rapidly as a result of government expenditure. Taxes will also rise, since they are dependent on income.

The rise in tax receipts that is associated with an increase in G is called the beneficial budgetary effect of government expenditure.

Beneficial budgetary effect

Extent of the multiplier

The extent of the multiplier is dependent upon imports, taxes and savings. A country will have a high multiplier when citizens save and import relatively little and also pay relatively little tax.
If the company places the orders that are related to the extra investment entirely outside the EU (by, for instance, buying the machinery in Japan) it will stimulate production in Japan. The investment stimulus will not be noticeable in Europe. The higher the imports are, the more the investment stimulus will be diverted to other countries. It is also true that the higher taxes and savings are, the less spending is done.

The multiplier is therefore smaller when the proportion of imports, taxes and savings expressed as a percentage of the GDP is greater.

Glossary

Budgetary deficit	The negative difference between government expenditure and income.
Consumption	Expenditure by households on goods and services.
Expenditure	Expenses associated with goods and services. They can be divided into consumption, investment, Government spending, import and export expenditure.
Government expenditure	The spending of a government on salaries and materials, both on materials that last more than one year (government investments) and materials that do not last longer than one year (government consumption).
Investments	Purchase of fixed and floating capital goods, including stock building. The following terminology is used: • *investments in width*: investments that do not involve a rise in labour productivity • *gross investments*: all the investment goods bought in a certain period • *net investments*: gross investments minus depreciation • *investments in depth*: investments that involve a rise in labour productivity • *replacement investments*: the purchase of capital goods to replace worn out capital goods • *stock investments*: that part of the net investments that consists of floating capital goods.
Nominal	The value of a particular variable in a particular period, usually compared to an earlier period.
Real	The volume of a particular variable during a particular period, usually compared to the previous period.
Savings balance	The difference between savings and net investments • *National savings balance*: The sum of the personal and the government savings balances which is equal to the balance of the current account of the balance of payments • *Government savings balance*: The difference between savings and net investments by the government • *Savings balance of the private sector*: The difference between savings of industry and private households and investments by industry.

Savings	The difference between income (excluding taxes) and consumptive expenditure.
Subsidies	Unrequited transfers by the government to other sectors.

6

The business cycle and policy

The following issues will be addressed in this chapter:
What is the relationship between company sales and the business cycle?
What are the causes and effects of inflation?
What policies does the government pursue in order to cope with business cycles?
What are the main features of an economy?
What opportunities do companies have to react to economic trends?

Chapters 4 and 5 have dealt with the reasons behind changes to macroeconomic variables.
These developments result in alternating periods of higher and lower economic growth.
This is known as the business cycle and is the subject of Section 6.1. The causes and the various types of cyclical waves are dealt with, and the section concludes with an analysis of business cycles within the EU. One of the main problems of cyclic economic situations is inflation. Governments implement inflation-restricting policies because a wide-spread general rise in prices has some negative effects on the economic process. Section 6.2 treats the causes and effects of inflation. Government income and expenditure have an important effect on business cycles and vice versa. Section 6.3 explores the theme of the interconnections between government and business cycles. Research institutes use certain models to predict developments in macroeconomic variables. Section 6.4 treats one of the prediction tables widely used by governments and industry to base their policies on. Section 6.5 deals with those parts of industry that are liable to suffer from a cyclical downturn and the policies they could implement to prevent negative effects.

CASE

A building firm carries out various activities within a variety of markets. The firm has a house construction unit which includes a large department concerned with the construction of new dwellings and a relatively small department dealing with maintenance work on homes and business buildings. The firm also builds offices and factory buildings. The customers for the latter are mainly big companies such as investment institutions, pension funds and industrial enterprises. The firm also competes regularly for government tenders. These may be buildings or civil engineering works. The firm's long-term strategy is such that it needs to keep track of developments within the various markets. There could be considerable variation in the growth of demand within these markets over the course of time. The market for new housing is likely to boom on some occasions, while at other times the market for office buildings will flourish. The firm might sometimes find that a large part of its profit is obtained from large infrastructural projects. The latter market is not a fast grower, but is profitable in times of economic depression. In order to be able to switch to the most promising market in time, some insight into the various markets is necessary. The firm needs to know the reasons for the fluctuation in demand on the various markets. The demand for houses appears to be mainly associated with changes to the nominally available household income and the interest rate. The fluctuations in the demand for office and factory buildings are associated with the growth of the GDP. Companies invest in new buildings when they are optimistic about their own sales. Government expenditure is dependent on the financial position of the government.

The financial department of the firm keeps a close track on sales developments as described in the daily press and trade association publications. This gives management a general view of the economic developments that apply to the sales markets.

6.1 The business cycle

The phase of the business cycle in which a country finds itself can be determined from an analysis of the growth of the GDP. The business cycle is the more or less regular fluctuation of expenditure and production in relation to production capacity. If expenditure and production exceed the production capacity there will be a positive output gap or overexpenditure. This situation is accompanied by a high GDP growth rate. If the reverse situation applies, there will be a negative output gap or underexpenditure. The GDP will grow very slowly, or perhaps not at all.

Output gap

Business cycles have an important effect on government finance, on the business results of many companies, on employment and consequently also on the income of many households.

Section 6.1.1 looks in detail at the types of business cycles, Section 6.1.2 looks at the various phases of business cycles and Section 6.1.3 deals with business cycles in Europe.

6.1.1 Kondratieff, Juglar and Kitchin

Economic theory has identified three different types of business cycles, each with its own cause and length. They are called after the people who identified them: Kondratieff, Juglar and Kitchin (see Table 6.1).

TABLE 6.1 Business cycles: causes and duration

Name of the cycle	Main cause	Duration
Kondratieff (long wave)	Major product and process innovation	47-57 years
Juglar	Investments in fixed assets	7-11 years
Kitchin	Investments in stocks	3-5 years

Kondratieff

The Kondratieff cycle is the cycle with the longest duration. This so-called long wave is caused by major breakthroughs in technology, such as the Industrial Revolution, the building of railway lines or the invention of electricity (see Table 6.2). The application of such new technology stimulates investments, productivity and economic growth to such an extent that an upward movement in the cycle is initiated. When the main possibilities of the break-through technology have been exploited, economic growth drops back to a lower level. We then have to wait for a new technological breakthrough to initiate a new 'long wave'.

Break-through technology

TABLE 6.2 Economic 'long waves'

Period	Main breakthrough	Evolving country/region
1782-1845	Industrial Revolution	England
1845-1892	Building of railways	Mainland Europe
1892-1948	Electricity	United States
1948-1992	Petrochemicals	Japan
from 1992	IT/Telecommunications	China

Source: prof. J.J. van Duijn in *Safe*, July 2000

Since the 1990s, the driving force behind the upsurge in the economic wave has been the revolution in information and telecommunication technology (ICT). ICT has brought all kinds of new growth markets into being, including the mobile telephone industry and the Internet. ICT has also led to wide-spread increases in infrastructural services. To create a world-wide communication network requires considerable investment in hardware and software. These investments have not only contributed to higher economic growth, but also to an increase in labour productivity. This has allowed the inflation in the rising phase of a long wave to stay low. The expectation of many economists – that the application of ICT would lead not only temporarily but permanently to a combination of a high growth rate and low inflation – has not come true. The 'New Economy' has had to relinquish its claim to lasting validity. Those economic laws that are based on cyclic economic movements are still valid.

Because of its long duration, the Kondratieff cycle is of minor importance for daily business in industry. When mention is made of a business cycle in company annual reports or in the media, it is usually the Kitchin cycle or the Juglar cycle that is referred to. The main cause of both these cycles lies in the investment behaviour of entrepreneurs.

Kitchin
The Kitchin cycle is the shortest one and is caused by stock investments. These investments can be adjusted quickly to sales expectations. If sales expectations are unfavourable in the short term, companies will diminish their stocks. If sales are low, a company can manage with a smaller stock of products in storage to meet demand. The company can also use the capital that is freed by lowering the stock pile for other purposes. The stock investments of companies will decrease, with a lower level of expenditure and production as a result. If, however, companies expect an increase in sales, they will anticipate by increasing stock, which will stimulate a higher level of economic activity.

Juglar
There is a similar logic behind the investments in fixed assets (machinery and industrial buildings) that are important for the Juglar cycle.

TEST 6.1
ICT enables more efficient management of stock (for instance, just-in-time delivery). What effect is this liable to have on the development of future business cycles?

6.1.2   The phases of a business cycle

Progress of a
business cycle

Figure 6.1 illustrates the progress of a business cycle. The trend line shows the rise in production capacity in time. The actual level of expenditure and production fluctuates around it. If the actual production is greater than the production capacity overexpenditure will result, and if vice-versa, under expenditure.

Four business cycle phases have been identified:
- The upturn phase
- Economic boom
- The downturn phase
- Economic recession (depression).

Upturn phase

The upturn phase of a business cycle is characterised by increasing growth in expenditure. This also causes production to increase. In the beginning companies are able to take care of the increase in production with their current staff, which is very much to their advantage. This causes a considerable initial rise in labour productivity. Any shortage in staff will be taken care of by overtime or hiring temporary staff. Only when the sales growth has been going on for some time will companies put on more permanent staff.

FIGURE 6.1 The business cycle

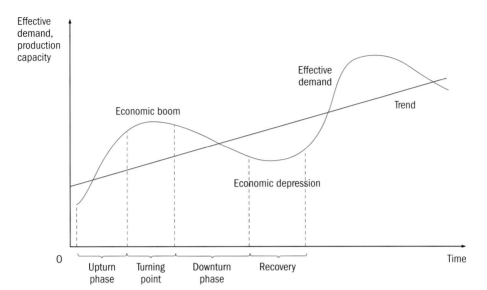

The increase in demand in the upturn phase can initially be easily dealt with by increasing production. During the phase of a negative output gap, production is less than the production capacity. An increase in production is possible within the means available. The average fixed costs will decrease and the profit margins will increase, even if prices remain the same. This is why this phase is called the quantity cycle: the quantity changes but the prices do not change yet.   **Quantity cycle**

The upturn phase ultimately results in a period of economic boom.   **Economic boom**
Capacity usage will have increased to such an intensity that the production processes cannot keep up. The demand for goods and services exceeds the production capacity, which enables companies to raise their prices. The quantity cycle will have turned into a price cycle. It is not only the prices of   **Price cycle**
end products that are raised. Because of the great demand for raw materials and labour during an economic boom, the prices of raw materials and wages also rise.

An economic boom is characterised by an atmosphere of optimism: both entrepreneurs and consumers look to the future with confidence. This contributes to the high level of consumption and investments. The demand for credit is also high and the interest rate rises.

During an economic boom, the turnabout is already looming.   **Turnabout**
Overconfidence in the future means overestimation of the market. The supply of goods and services on the market rises fast, causing prices to increase more slowly or even decrease. Furthermore, wage costs rise quickly when the labour market becomes stretched. Returns on the expenditure made will be disappointing.
Companies will not be tempted to invest as quickly in new machinery and buildings. The diminishing desire to invest is reinforced by the rise of interest rates during an economic boom.

Companies with marginal returns are the first to feel the effects of the turnabout. These could be companies with a high break-even point, which means companies that need to have large sales to make a profit. A small drop in sales or sales growth brings these companies into the red. During the initial stages of an economic recession some of these companies will go bankrupt. The optimistic view of the future gradually makes way for prudence and pessimism during this stage.

Downturn phase

The downturn phase is characterised by exactly the opposite symptoms to those during the upturn phase. Expenditure decreases, causing the inflation rate, production, employment rate and profitability to drop. Lack of confidence in the future by entrepreneurs leads to a low level of investment. The downturn phase of the business cycle ushers in decreased and possibly even negative economic growth. In the press and in business, this stage is often termed a recession.

Recession

A common definition in economics is that an economy is in a recession when the gross domestic product decreases two quarters in a row. In this book, we will apply a less strict definition, and use the terms cyclical downturn and recession as synonyms.

During a recession, the conditions for recovery of the economy evolve almost automatically. While investments may have dropped to a very low level, companies will have to replace their worn-out and outdated machinery and buildings sooner or later. The capital goods industry and to a lesser extent the building industry will be stimulated to a modest extent by this. A cyclical downturn also causes the interest rate to drop, because inflation has decreased and the demand for credit has diminished. The competitive position of exporters will also improve, as wages, prices and interest rates decrease during a cyclical downturn.

TEST 6.2
During the 1990s, many entrepreneurs thought that a period of uninterrupted economic growth had started. What influence would that have had on investments and on the downturn that nevertheless did come?

6.1.3   The business cycle in the EU
The business cycle can be measured in terms of volume changes in the GDP. These are shown in Figure 6.2.

From figure 6.2, it can be derived that there were peaks in 1994, 2000, 2006 and 2010. Downturns occurred in 1993, 1996, 2003, 2009 and 2013. The downturns in an economic cycle show alternating deep and less deep declines. In practice, the economic cycle appears to have an M-shape development. This can be seen clearly in the period between 1993 and 2003. The economic cycle describes an entire M, from one steep decline to another steep decline over approximately ten years. In this ten-year period, the Juglar cycle can be identified. The Kitchin cycle is the less deep decline in between (1996). When an economy starts to recover businesses will wish to build-up their inventories again. This is an incentive for production. After a certain period of time, the inventories are at a sufficient level again and the inventory investments will decrease. This is the cause of the temporary dip in growth.

FIGURE 6.2 The economic cycle in the EU, 1992–2018

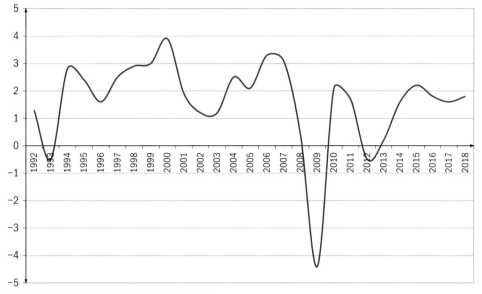

1 2016, 2017 and 2018 are predictions by the European Commission.

Source: European Commission

The recession of 2009 is an incident in the economic cycle, due to the credit crunch. After this incident, the ten-year economic cycle picks up again. This is the reason why 2012/13 shows another low. The economic cycle will revive again until 2020 and in 2023 another low will occur. This is the normal development of an economic cycle. In between, other incidents can occur, due to political or economic tensions.

For governments and companies, the predictions of the economic cycle are very important. Predictions can be made with the aid of indicators. Indicators show in advance how certain variables, in this case the GDP, will develop in the near future. The European Commission sets out surveys to producers and consumers on a monthly basis to assess the economic cycle, as shown in figure 6.3 for the euro zone. In these surveys, questions are posed with regard to the variables on production and consumption in the near future. In figure 6.3a, the indicators for the building and manufacturing industries for the euro zone are shown. The industrial sector exhibits the largest fluctuations in production during an economic cycle. The growth of industrial production can therefore also be considered as an indicator for the entire economic cycle. The producers' confidence is an indicator for the production during the following months.

Significantly, the indicator for the building industry is severely lagging after 2009, in comparison with that of the manufacturing industry. The manufacturing industry exports a major share of its products outside the euro zone, whereas the building industry mainly depends on customers in Europe. This difference reflects the difference in growth in the world. Growth outside the euro zone is higher than within the euro zone.

Indicators

Furthermore, figure 6.3b provides information on consumer spending. For this purpose, the confidence in the retail trade and consumers' confidence was measured. The confidence indicators are important for future sales.

FIGURE 6.3a Confidence indicator for the building and manufacturing industries (euro area)

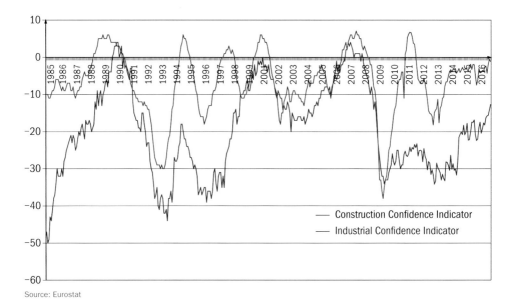

Source: Eurostat

FIGURE 6.3b Confidence in the retail trade and consumers' confidence in the euro area

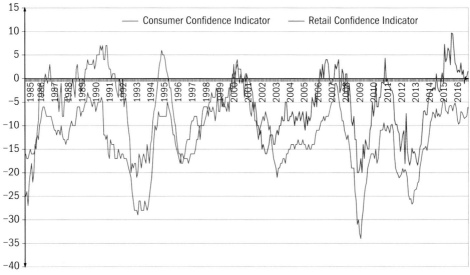

Source: Eurostat

CASE 6.1

The business cycle and the stock exchange

The business cycle exerts a major influence on the stock exchange. In the first place, the state of the economy is vital for the overall stock exchange sentiment. A phase of economic boom is generally speaking favourable for the exchange because of increasing industry profits. On the other hand, investors have to be aware of the danger of an increase in inflation. When inflation increases, the interest rate will rise too. A high interest rate is unfavourable for stock exchange rates, because it means that interest-bearing alternatives to investment in stocks and bonds are becoming more attractive.

The business cycle not only affects the general stock exchange sentiment, but also the attractiveness of some sectors to investors. In stock exchange terms, this is known as the problem of sector allocation: at what moment in the cycle should the stake of certain sectors in the investment portfolio be increased or decreased? The figure below provides the answer to that question. It has to be kept in mind, however, that the stock exchange always anticipates actual economic developments. In other words, the price of shares in a particular listed company increases before sales, production and profits increase.

Business cycle and investment in sectors

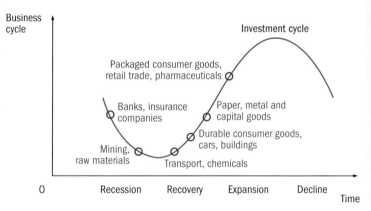

Source: Rabobank, *Ups and Downs*, August 1997

During a cyclical decline, defensive stocks such as banks, insurance companies and publishing houses are attractive. The profitability of these companies is relatively insensitive to business cycles. For banks and insurance companies there is the added advantage that decreasing interest rates are favourable for lending operations such as mortgages. The turnaround period of the cycle is a good time to buy shares in mining and materials such as steel. After all, before they expand their production, companies have to buy their basic materials first. A phase of economic recovery is usually heralded by growth in exports. Sectors that export a large part of their production (such as the chemical industry and transport) profit from the early stages of an economic recovery. The revival of exports is followed by an increase in investments and consumption. Those sectors that target these expenditure categories will only profit from the economic recovery at a later stage of the cycle.

The credit crisis of 2008/2009

Fig. 6.2 shows the low points of the economy in 1993 and 2003. If low points occur every ten years, the next one can be expected in 2013. The world was, however, taken by surprise by the severe slump in production in 2008 and 2009. This slump has been labelled the Global Financial Crisis. The crisis can be described on the basis of the causes, the effects and the policies that governments adopted to overcome the crisis.

Causes

Low interest rate

An important cause of the financial crisis was the low interest rate and the strong economic growth in the world in the last decade of the 20th and the first years of the 21st century. In 2001, terrorists destroyed the Twin Towers in New York, in which the cream of the United States' businesses were housed, with the purpose of striking the North American economy in the heart. In answer to the threat to the economy the Central Bank of the US lowered the interest rate to a historically low level. Banks were able to lend money cheaply from the Central Bank and put it out against a low interest. In this way businesses and private individuals were able to invest and buy houses against a low interest rate. The economy flourished, consumption and production were stimulated and the growth figures of the GDP were high. By abolishing a lot of regulations that limited the granting of loans, many people were able to profit from the economic upturn by being able to start a business or buy a house.

Large savings

A second cause of the financial crisis was the large savings in several parts of the world. In particular, consumers and businesses in China, Germany and the Netherlands had saved so much that there were insufficient possibilities in these countries themselves to invest these savings. The liquid assets found a way abroad and especially to the United States, where there were sufficient opportunities to invest in real estate and shares. With the incoming money, the US was able to buy products in other countries, enabling those countries to have access to their money, which they could invest again in the US in shares and real estate, the price of which kept on rising. China, Germany and the Netherlands are countries with large surpluses in the balance of payments that are accompanied by large excess liquidity; the US is a country with large deficits on the balance of payments and a large liquidity shortfall. Added to this were the liquid assets that the oil-producing countries received and that also found their way to where the profits to be expected were high.

Globalization of banking

The third cause was the globalization of banking and the remuneration system of banks. The large banks of the world have subsidiaries on almost every continent. This facilitates the flow of capital in the direction where expected profits are the highest. Banks made use of the possibility to bundle loans to people who financed their house by means of a mortgage into larger amounts and to sell these on to other banks all over the world. This provided the banks with more money they could spend on the housing market. Banks were able to insure the bundled mortgages with other parties and these insurances were also separately negotiable in the international finance markets. In this way, large streams of capital easily found their way onto the American housing market. Repackaging, insuring and trading mortgages became a goldmine for bank employees. They were able to convince their managers, the bank directors, the government and the public at large that in this way they were adding value to their products. One of their arguments was that because of their activities the world's capital could be used more productively and through their bonuses they pocketed part of the profits. What they forgot was that the profits had not yet been realized, but would have to be produced by the countless house owners who would have to pay the interest and repayments on their mortgages over the next thirty years. Should the house owners no longer be able to do that, the banks would be confronted with the losses, while the bankers had already received their bonuses.

Bonuses

Consequences

And exactly that happened in the course of 2007. An increase in inflation as a result of an increased demand for commodities in the world forced the Central Bank of the US to increase the interest rate. Because of the increase in interest, house prices stopped rising and instead declined slowly. House owners who had trouble paying their interest and paying off their debts had to leave their houses. The banks were saddled with large residual debts, exacerbated by the fact that in many states in the US, house owners who leave their house are no longer obliged to pay off their mortgage. That led to a general crisis of confidence in the banking sector.

Inflation

The banks no longer received their interest and repayments because of the ever-increasing number of bad debts. They covered the bad debts with their own capital, which shrank before their eyes. The owners of the banks' own capital, the shareholders, lost confidence in the banks and banking shares dropped rapidly, making it impossible for the banks to attract own capital on the capital markets. Banks finance their mortgages by attracting savings from the public. The public lost confidence in several big banks and withdrew their savings. Banks that lend out money on the long term must be able to attract savings on a regular basis. This requires the confidence that the bank can pay back the savings at any time. If there is a crisis of confidence and savers withdraw their money, a bank can go bankrupt within a matter of days. This is called a run on the bank. To make matters worse, the banks also lost confidence in each other and were not prepared to lend money to each other any more: the interbank market collapsed.

Crisis of confidence

Run on the bank

The globalization of banking led to waves of distrust in the banking sector the world over. Economies where there was no sign of decreasing house prices or reduced economic activity noticed that even their banks were being hit hard because of the collapse of the housing market in the US. Banks became more cautious with giving credit, causing economic growth everywhere to decrease. The terrorists who attacked the economy of the US in 2001 achieved great success: not only the economy of the US but also that of Europe and many other countries were hit badly, not so much by the action of the terrorists but because of the failing policies of governments afterwards.

During the course of 2008, this led to the global conviction that international banking would not be able to survive without outside help. But banks are indispensable in modern economies: without them, people and businesses cannot draw or transfer money. There would be no possibility of granting credit or withdrawing savings. Other financial institutions too, including insurance companies and pension funds, could easily be swept along in the downfall. The economic process would come to a standstill with severe consequences for food supply, energy production, the transport of goods and so on. Many of the big financial institutions in the world are just 'too big to fail': they cannot be allowed to go bankrupt.

'Too big to fail'

Policy
Governments have taken a number of measures to save the banks and to avoid the crisis getting out of hand.
In the United States and in Europe, governments have taken over banks, provided capital support or founded banks to take over bad debts. The Dutch government has become the owner of the Dutch part of the ABN Amro bank and of Fortis by buying shares from unsuccessful takeover bids by some foreign banks. The ING bank and some other banks have had to accept financial support in order not to become insolvent.
The central banks in Europe and the US have taken over the interbank money market. The interbank money market is essential for alleviating liquidity shortages at very short notice. The fluid assets that banks were no longer prepared to lend to each other because of the high risk could now be obtained from the central bank. One of the tasks of central banks is to ensure that the economy is not faced with liquidity shortages. They have brought back the interest rate to a very low level and consequently the costs of the loans that the banks obtain from the central bank are very low. The central bank also buys government bonds from investors such as banks and pension funds. In turn, they receive liquid assets that they can use to issue more loans. In this way, the amount of money can be increased. This is also known as printing money.

Printing money

Throughout the world, governments have allowed their deficits to increase in order to stimulate their economy. Initially they have deliberately not reduced spending or even increased it, even though tax receipts have decreased because of the crisis. This has in fact stimulated economies, but has also led to debts that were overall twice the size of the deficits before the crisis. This has caused the national debt to increase considerably and at some time in the future governments will have to reduce the deficits and debts.

National debt

The financial crisis has consequently posed significant risks to present and future economic growth. In the first place, banks now have a weak balance, causing them to have a high risk perception in relation to loans. They will not easily put out loans with a high risk factor. This reduced credit facility limits economic growth and increases the chance that businesses and home owners will not be able to pay back their loans.

Weak balance

Secondly, governments now have to cut expenditure in order to prevent deficits and debts from mounting up too high. Apart from actual debts, many governments have given guarantees not only to banks but also to citizens. The Dutch government, for example, has a risk of more than €100 billion because of home mortgages. The government gives guarantees to mortgage providers should the mortgagees not be able to meet their obligations. Government debts and the risks governments run because of debts by others are impeding economic recovery.

Cut expenditure

An added problem is that the risks associated with interest payments and the repayment of debts are mounting in many European countries. Some

countries have such high deficits and debts that the international financial
world has insufficient confidence in the creditworthiness of these countries.   **Creditworthiness**
The interest rates in these countries have therefore risen sharply. At the
same time, these countries have a deficit on the balance of payments
current account, which increases doubts about their creditworthiness.
Countries with deficits are having to borrow to pay for their imports, and
as a consequence they are earning too little currency to pay back their
government's debt. This is causing severe tension in the Euro zone and
some fear that the union will disintegrate, increasing the risk for businesses
who want to do business in the Euro zone. This uncertainty is also having a
dampening effect on economic growth.

Thirdly, governments all over the world are being pressured to support
domestic industry. Politically, stimulating the economy is highly risky if a   **Domestic**
part of the extra spending disappears to other countries via imports.   **industry**
Citizens find it hard to understand why they should pay taxes for
employment abroad. Governments therefore tend to support their own
industry and to erect trade barriers. This is detrimental to world trade and
damages economic growth.

Furthermore, there is a 'double-dip recession'. Economic growth occurs in cycles   **'Double-dip**
of about ten years. The last normal economic low was in 2003. It is in the line of   **recession'**
expectations that there will be an economic low in 2012/13. This economic low
actually did occur. This recession is extra-large because the balances of banks
and other businesses were still weak after the recession of 2009.

Governments have got so deeply into debt that they are unable to save the
banks again, and they cannot stimulate the economy artificially once again.

6.2 Inflation

Inflation is an increase in the average consumer prices, or in other words,
an increase in the general price level. This is the other side of monetary
depreciation. When the price of goods and services rises the consumer
receives increasingly less for a unit of currency. The currency loses its value.

Statistics bureaus measure the level of inflation on the basis of an increase
in the price of consumer goods. Since 1995, Eurostat has used the
'Harmonised Indices of Consumer Prices' (HICP). The HICP publishes
details of the previous month every month, thus making it possible to
monitor the development of inflation very closely.

Figure 6.4 shows inflation in the US, the Euro zone and Japan.

The inflation figures of the EU and the US have not varied very much from
1993 onward. Sometimes inflation is a little higher in one region, at other
times in another. Inflation in Japan was on the whole lower than in the US or
the Euro zone during the period under review.

We shall now look at the causes for inflation.   **Causes for**
inflation

A rise in consumer prices in an economy can be caused by one of the
following:
- An increase in expenditure that exceeds production capacity
- An increase in wage costs
- An increase in the price of raw materials and semi-finished products

- Government measures relating to value added tax, excise and prices of government services
- An increase in profit and capital costs (interest and depreciation).

FIGURE 6.4 Consumer price index, Japan, US and euro area (1993–2018)

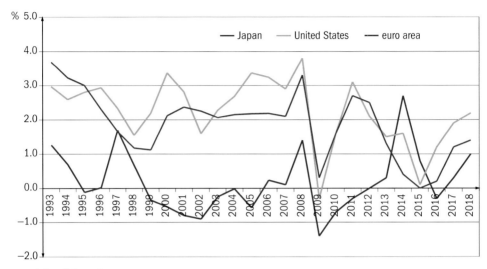

2016, 2017 and 2018 are estimates.

Source: OECD, *Economic Outlook*

These causes we will now look at in detail.

Demand-pull inflation

Demand-pull inflation is the result of overexpenditure and occurs during periods of economic boom. In this phase of the business cycle the production capacity is completely utilised and there is a positive output gap. Companies have an opportunity to raise their prices because demand exceeds supply.

Positive output gap

Companies will try to pass on the rise in costs in their prices to avoid a decrease in the profit margin. This can be described as cost-push inflation. A rise in costs could have various causes.

Cost-push inflation

If wages increase faster than labour productivity, this will cause the labour costs per unit to rise. Entrepreneurs pass these costs on in their prices. Employees will thereupon demand compensation in their wages for the price rises, because otherwise the purchasing power of their wages would decrease. With constant nominal wages they would buy fewer products if the prices of products increased. Price compensation in wages leads to a constant escalation of prices and wages: a wage/price spiral. Wage increases usually occur in situations of low unemployment. At the international level, it is assumed that wages are put under upward pressure when unemployment is less than 5%.

Labour costs per unit

Wage/price spiral

TEST 6.3

How will the profits of companies that have to give compensation for price rises in the wages they pay be affected if they cannot raise their own prices?

The effect of fluctuations in the price of raw materials such as oil and mineral ores on the costs of companies can be considerable. Most of the raw material markets quote their prices in dollars. As well as uncertainty about the price of the raw material itself, European companies also have to deal with the uncertainty of the dollar exchange rate. A decrease in supply on the raw materials market combined with a rising dollar exchange rate is very disadvantageous to companies that import a lot of raw materials. High raw material prices result in price increases for semi-finished products and eventually for end products.

High raw material prices

Government measures

The government has an influence on various types of prices. In many countries, it determines the rental prices for houses and the prices of medicines. It also determines the height of social security benefits and the security contributions associated with the benefits. These contributions are imposed on wages and therefore have an influence on the wage costs that entrepreneurs have to pay for attracting labour. The government also determines the tariffs for indirect taxes such as excise and VAT. These cost-price-raising taxes have an effect on prices. A rise of 1% in VAT will cause an almost overall increase in inflation of approximately 1%.

Government measures/ prices

Tariffs

Because of the negative effects of inflation, some central banks – in the Euro zone, the European Central Bank (ECB) – will aim at keeping inflation down to a maximum of two percent (see Chapter 7). The ECB makes use of inflation indicators to predict the development of inflation in the near future (see Table 6.3).

TABLE 6.3 Inflation indicators

Inflation indicator	Manifests itself after a while as
Output gap	Demand-pull inflation
Low unemployment (< 5%)	Rising wages (cost-push inflation)
Wages and labour productivity	Labour costs per unit
Prices of raw materials/Producer prices	Prices of finished products (cost-push inflation)
Decrease in the exchange rate	Rising import prices (cost-push inflation)
Actual inflation	Expected inflation

The public becomes accustomed to inflation. The current rate of inflation gives rise to expectations about the future level of inflation. If there has been a low level of inflation in the past, large increases in prices are less likely to be accepted. For companies, this constitutes an important barrier to implementing price increases. This is why the current rate of inflation acts as an indicator for future inflation.

6.2.1   Inflation and its effects

Inflation is closely intertwined with the degree of power exercised by market players. Scarcity on the goods market will allow entrepreneurs to raise their prices; scarcity on the labour market will encourage trade unions to demand higher wages.

Certain groups within the economy could profit at certain moments from inflation. Employers are generally served by price increases, whereas

Profit from inflation

employees are interested in wage increases. As a rule, the strongest group will get the best results, whether this be the employers or the employees.
Inflation intensifies the emphasis that groups lay on their own interests to the detriment of the public interest.
A dangerous situation will arise if the behaviour of various groups is governed by the effects of inflation. Wage demands will in turn be

Hyperinflation
counteracted by increases and a situation of hyperinflation will develop. While wage and price developments may keep an even pace, some income groups will still suffer from the effects of inflation.

Inflation and income distribution
Inflation has an effect on income distribution. Some groups with a fixed income will see their purchasing power diminished by inflation. Investors in bonds and people on pensions that are not corrected for inflation are especially vulnerable to the effects of inflation.

The government's vested interest in inflation
An additional problem is that the government has to a certain extent a vested interest in inflation. Governments are usually the largest debtors in the economy. They have to make ongoing repayments of fixed amounts of these debts. These amounts have to be financed by income from taxation. When prices and wages increase, taxes do too, because they are linked to the level of income. It is therefore easier for the government to meet their payments, as these do remain constant. Monetary depreciation makes repayments cheaper all the time. The government repays its debts with euros that are worth less than the euros it borrowed in the first place.

TEST 6.4
Could the government stimulate inflation? If so, how would it do this?

Companies and monetary depreciation
The fact that repayments have a lesser value than the amount that was borrowed applies, of course, to all debtors to a greater or lesser extent. It is not only the government but also businesses that profit from depreciation of their debts. This has an effect on production. If companies see their wage bill increasing while the value of repayments on borrowed money

Replace labour by capital
decreases, they will be encouraged to replace labour by capital. Companies will be more inclined to invest in machinery than to take on extra staff.

Real and nominal interest
Inflation favours debtors in another way. In times of inflation, the real interest is lower than the nominal interest. Real interest is defined as the nominal interest less the inflation rate. The lender will, of course, demand a higher interest rate to compensate for the disadvantage of monetary depreciation. This does not alter the fact that in times of high and variable inflation rates, the real interest might be very low at times, or even negative.

Risk effect of investments
Inflation also increases the uncertainty within the economy. This is especially relevant for investments. Rising wages and prices affect both costs and returns, and there is no certainty as to which factor will have the upper hand. The higher the rate of inflation, the more difficult it is to determine the expected internal rate of return on an investment. Because of this uncertainty, there is a good chance that investment projects will not be carried out. This will result in lower profit margins on exports or a loss of a share of the market. In both cases the profits of the European exporters will drop.

6.3 The government

In the EU, 'the government' comprises the supranational, national and local authorities as well as the social security administration agencies.

Because of its income and expenditure of around 50% of the GDP, the government exerts a great influence on expenditure, production and income distribution.

We will deal further with the duties of government and expenditure in Section 6.3.1. Section 6.3.2 will deal with government income. The influence government income, its duties and expenditure have on the business cycle is the subject of Section 6.3.3.

6.3.1   The duties of government and government expenditure

In Chapter 5 we saw that the government has various duties to perform. These can be categorised as follows:
- An allocative duty
- A redistributing duty
- A regulatory duty.

Its allocative duty consists of providing collective and quasi-collective goods and services and has been dealt with in Chapter 5. We shall only treat the redistributing and regulatory duties here.

The government has a redistributing duty to pass income on. The government levies taxes and requires contributions from households that receive an income from the means of production, and passes the money on to households that cannot contribute any labour, capital or natural resources. A large part of government expenditure is aimed at more even distribution of income. Social expenditure in 2014 amounted to 28% of the GDP (more than €4,000 bn). The social involvement of the government can be delineated as shown in Figure 6.5.

Redistributing duty

FIGURE 6.5 Categories of social security benefits, EU, 2014

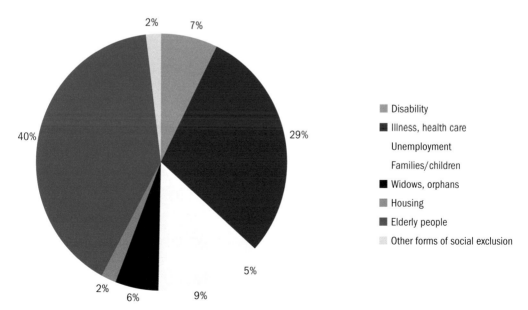

Source: Eurostat

Only the two largest items will be treated here. The largest item in Figure 6.5 is pension benefits. The affordability of pensions is being threatened by the strong increase in the ageing population. Those countries whose pensions are for the largest part being paid for by the current working population will be faced with an ever-increasing pension burden when the proportion of the employable population compared with the total population decreases. Two solutions to this problem are lowering pensions or increasing the pensionable age. These measures are meeting strong resistance from pensioners, who constitute a growing part of the electorate. Another option is letting the active population themselves save for their pension during their working life. This means that for a large number of years they will have to cope with an additional financial burden.

The next biggest benefit item is the cost of health care. Health care is regarded as a part of social security benefits, but it is, in fact, an aspect of government production. After all, it is the government that provides health care to its population. Health care and pensions face very much the same problems. An ageing population and increased medical options means that the demand for health care is increasing. The governments of the EU are trying to limit these costs by imposing maximum prices on medicines, by increasing competition in the health care sector, by imposing contributions on the client him or herself, and other similar measures.

The government's regulatory duties have to do with the economic order. The economic order lays down the principles that the government has to pursue in its policies. These policies are of two kinds: macroeconomic policies and microeconomic policies.

The government interferes in the economic process with the following macroeconomic aims in mind:

- Adequate economic growth (Chapter 4)
- Adequate distribution of income (Chapter 4)
- Full employment (Chapter 4)
- Stable price level (Chapter 7)
- Balance of payments equilibrium (Chapters 9 and 10)
- Care for the environment (Chapter 4)

These topics are dealt with in the chapters listed.

As well as this, the government has a duty to regulate the markets in the broadest sense of the word. Its policies are aimed at obtaining markets that function well. For instance, the government makes sure that there is sufficient competition by preventing cartelisation and monopolies. The government also issues separate regulations for those markets that are particularly important: the labour market, markets for agricultural products, financial markets, the rental housing market, the pharmaceutical market and the like. This particular government duty – to determine what markets are to be regulated and the way in which this is done – characterises the economic order of a country (see also Chapter 2).

In previous chapters, several aspects of government expenditure were dealt with in detail. In addition to government spending, the government also makes transfer payments. These are payments for social security. The division of government expenses is shown in Figure 6.6.

Margin notes:

Pension benefits

Health care

Regulatory duties

Macroeconomic aims

Microeconomic policies

Social security

FIGURE 6.6 Government expenses in 2012 in percentages of GDP, EU

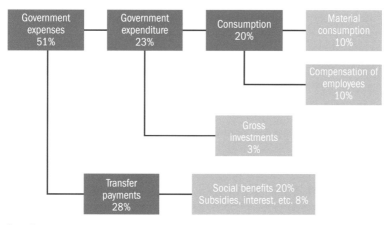

Source: Eurostat

6.3.2   Government income

During 2015, government income in the EU amounted to 45% of the GDP: around €6,500 billion. This proportion has remained relatively stable over the years. In Japan and the USA, government expenses are about 35% of the GDP. In the countries of the EU the government has a greater number of duties (for instance, in the field of distribution of income). This is why taxes in the EU are higher than in Japan or the USA. Government income is derived from various sources as Figure 6.7 shows.

FIGURE 6.7   Main categories of government revenue EU, 2015, (% of GDP)

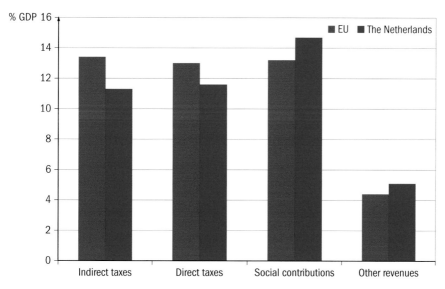

Source: Eurostat

Aim of taxation

The main aim of taxation is, of course, the financing of government spending. But the government pursues a few other objectives as well. In most countries, the government uses taxation and social security contributions to reduce the difference in income between its citizens.
As can be deduced from Figure 6.7, taxes on income, value added tax and social contributions each provide approximately 30% of the government's income.

Consequences for the economic process

The major role played by the government in the production and the distribution of income has consequences for the economic process. Taxes and social security contributions make up about 40% of the total wage costs. A high level of taxes and contributions leads to high wage costs. This makes industry less competitive compared to countries where taxes are lower. Apart from the effect high taxes have on the competitive position of industry, a high taxation level imposed on the national income also gives rise to certain mechanisms for passing taxation costs on, avoiding or evading tax.

Passing on taxation costs

Passing on taxation costs is a way of getting somebody else to pay for the taxation that the government imposes. Entrepreneurs may try to avoid any reduction in their profits by trying to pass on a rise in tax on profits to customers through a price increase. Similarly, employees may attempt to pass on an increase in social security contributions to their employers by demanding a pay rise. This is also a type of price increase. Whether an attempt to pass on taxation is successful is, of course, dependent on

Market power

Weakest market party

Tax avoidance

the market power of the market players. This could result in the taxation ultimately being carried by the weakest market party. Tax avoidance can be defined as someone adjusting his economic conduct in such a way that he pays as little tax as possible while staying within the bounds of the law. Sometimes the avoidance is desired by the government, as is the case with environmental levies. Environmental levies are an incentive for people to pollute less because they can then save on the levies. Sometimes, however, tax avoidance is not intended, as is the case when companies or citizens leave the country for fiscal reasons.
Tax avoidance is also encouraged by adjusting the labour supply. Working less means that one has to pay less tax, potentially making it difficult for companies to obtain employees. This effect is not likely to be very great, because the opposite might also occur. In order to reach a certain desired income, one might have to work longer than would have been necessary without taxation. In such a case, taxation has a positive influence on labour supply.
Passing on and avoiding tax are legally allowed. Some ways of responding

Tax evasion

to taxation levies are, however, not allowed. These are in the realm of tax evasion and fraud.

Not declaring sales

A common way in which companies evade tax is by not declaring sales to the tax authorities. Similar in kind is wage earners not divulging extra

Black money economy

income. This is referred to as the hidden economy or the black money economy. Some areas, such as drugs production and domestic help services, fall almost entirely within this category.

Governments are sometimes tempted to stimulate employment by company taxation measures such as lowering of the tax on profits or the granting of other privileges. 'Policy competition' is the term applied to governments attempting to outbid each other.

6.3.3   Government and the business cycle

There are two opinions about the role the government could and should play in the business cycle. In the vision of the Keynesian economists, the government should play an active role in the business cycle. They lay great emphasis on the role that expenditure has on the economic process. In the vision of the classical economists, the government should interfere with the economy as little as possible. These economists are of the opinion that the supply side of the economy should be disturbed as little as possible by government action.

In the Keynesian view of economics, the government is responsible for realising the objectives of economic policy and should be actively involved in the business cycle. According to this philosophy, the specific duty of government is to make sure there is full employment and economic growth. In order to reach full employment, the output gap (the difference between expenditure and production capacity) must be kept as small as possible. If the private sectors spend too little, the government ought to compensate this by increasing its expenditure and providing more services to the public, or lowering taxes to keep private expenditure at an acceptable level. This so-called counter-cyclical policy slows down the cycle and prevents an excessive downturn in the business cycle.
A large public service will have a natural dampening effect on business cycles. Government expenditure is laid down by law and expenditure cuts are often not possible in the short term. During a downturn, it keeps expenditure up. Since unemployment will increase during a recession, if there are ample social benefits the unemployed will be able to keep up their expenditure, and production will not suffer much in consequence. These are described as the automatic stabilisers of the business cycle.
Some governments carry out a structural fiscal policy which exerts a stabilising influence on the business cycle. The simplest form of this is expenditure planned on the basis of the economy's long-term growth (structural growth). Government income follows a cyclical pattern. During a revival, it will increase more strongly and during a recession the increase will be far less than the structural growth.

The taxes derived from decreasing production and expenditure drop during a recession. If expenses are kept at a steady level, the government deficit will develop naturally during a recession, which in turn has a stimulating influence on the business cycle. During a period of recovery, a budget surplus will develop. This will have a moderating effect on the business cycle.

In the classical view of economics, the government's role should be restricted as much as possible. The government's duties should be restricted to guaranteeing safety for its citizens and taking care that property is protected and contracts fulfilled. A large public service is inefficient because of the bureaucracy that creeps into every large organisation. Bureaucracy inhibits private initiative by its profusion of rules and regulations. When this happens the public sector is, in fact, impeding the economy's capacity to grow. The matching of supply and demand on the labour and other markets is best left to market mechanisms. When this happens, prices will effectively reflect the scarcity of products and production factors. Individuals will seize their opportunity and be rewarded according to their productivity.

Keynesian view

Counter-cyclical policy

Automatic stabilisers

Structural fiscal policy

Classical view

Safety

Property is protected

6

Except where it involves investments that will provide future income, the government should not run up a deficit. According to the classical economists, there are three reasons why an active cyclical policy will not work.

The first is that while politicians are prepared to stimulate the economy during a depression, they are not prepared to put on the brake during an economic boom. Taken over the whole of the cycle there will be a deficit, and debts will therefore keep mounting up. The second reason is that there is usually insufficient insight into the cyclical situation at any particular point. During a depression, it is difficult to tell when the lowest point will be reached and how low that point will be. Measures are thus often taken too early or too late. The third reason is that certain deceleration factors mean that government measures take effect too late. Policy making and reducing or increasing expenditure, with the subsequent effect of this on the business cycle, involves a lot of time, and consequently the measures will be too late and have the wrong effect on the business cycle.

The Keynesian approach to economics has been the basis from which most European governments have operated. However, in order to reduce the disadvantages of a large public sector, over the last few decades policies
Privatise
to privatise public enterprises and to dispose of as many government tasks as possible have been implemented. The European Commission is encouraging the privatisation of steel industries, airlines, electricity companies, telecommunication companies and the like. Under the terms of the EMU, governments have also agreed not to allow government deficits to amount to more than 3% of the GDP and to reduce the government debt to a maximum of 60% of the GDP (the Maastricht Treaty). These agreements
Stability Pact
have been delineated further in the Stability Pact.

6.4 Macroeconomic basis statistics

Macroeconomic planning bureaus such as those of the OECD use models to estimate changes to various kinds of macroeconomic variables.

These models provide an insight into changes to expenditure, production and the like and consist of the variables and the mutual relationships between them that have been treated in Chapters 4, 5 and 6 (see Figures 6.8 and 6.9). The models consist of innumerable mathematical formulas, but they can also be represented in the form of a diagram. Figure 6.8 shows the variables themselves and their mutual dependencies and Figure 6.9 shows prices and how they change.

FIGURE 6.8 Macroeconomic relations I: the volume of expenditure, production and employment

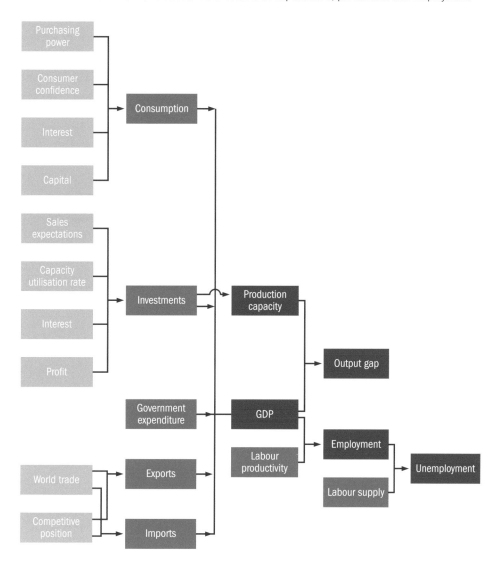

Table 6.4 combines predictions relating to the development of some variables in the economies of the Euro zone and the US.

In Table 6.4 the changes are compared to the previous year unless otherwise stated. If consumption was 8,000 billion euros in 2015 it was therefore 8,184 billion euros in 2016 (8,000 + 2.3%). All the other variables for which a change in relation to the previous year is given can be calculated in a similar way. Most of these variables have already been dealt with in previous chapters; others will be dealt with in this chapter. A short explanation follows.

FIGURE 6.9 Macroeconomic relations II: prices and price changes

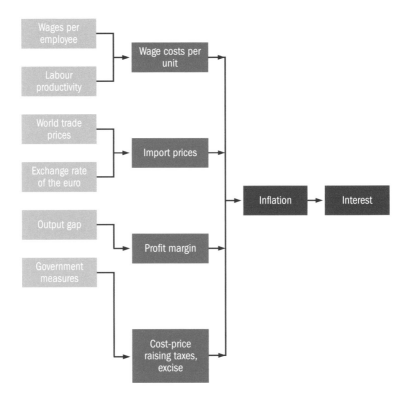

International

Table 6.4 lists firstly a number of variables that have a bearing on the international environment of the Euro zone. The volume of world trade consists of the exports of all of the countries in the world. It reflects the general state of the world's economy. If world trade increases strongly this is the result of an economic revival either in the world at large or in the main regions. A considerable increase in world trade will stimulate European exports, which in turn will stimulate an increase in production. A comparison of world trade with EU exports can tell us whether the EU is doing better or worse in relation to the increase in world trade.

World trade

TABLE 6.4 Basic statistics of the EU and the US (percentage changes from the previous year, unless otherwise indicated)

	2015	2016	2017	2018
International				
World trade volume (goods)*	3.6	3.8	4.4	4.5
World trade price (goods, €) *	6.2	-1.3	0.2	0.2
Oil price ($ per drum)	52.4	42.9	45.0	45.0
Resource price (2010 = 100)	72	71	75	75
Effective Euro exchange rate (2005 = 100)	99.9	98.9	96.9	96.9
Exchange rate (1$ = ...€)	0.901	0.901	0.921	0.921

TABLE 6.4 Basic statistics of the EU and the US (percentage changes from the previous year, unless otherwise indicated) (continued)

		2015	2016	2017	2018
Volume of expenditure and production					
Consumption	EU	2.1	2.1	1.6	1.5
	US	3.2	2.6	2.7	2.8
Gross investments	EU	3.5	2.8	2.5	3.1
	US	3.7	0.6	2.3	5.3
Export of goods and services	EU (€)	6.2	3.0	3.5	4.2
	US ($)	0.1	0.3	3.6	3.7
Import of goods and services	EU (€)	6.1	3.2	3.6	4.1
	US ($)	4.6	1.2	4.1	4.0
Current account (% GDP)	EU	1.8	2.1	2.1	2.2
	US	-2.6	-2.5	-2.6	-2.9
Government expenditure (% GDP)	EU	1.4	1.8	1.2	1.3
	US	1.6	6.9	1.3	3.2
Government surplus (% GDP)	EU	-2.4	-2.0	-1.7	-1.6
	US	-4.4	-4.6	-4.2	-4.0
Gross domestic product	EU	2.2	1.8	1.6	1.8
	US	2.5	1.6	2.1	1.9
Wages and prices					
Pay rises	EU	1.2	1.6	2.0	2.3
	US	3.0	2.1	3.5	4.0
Wage costs per unit of output 2010 = 100	Eurozone	97.8	98.0	97.9	97.5
	US	100.4	101.2	101.5	101.9
Inflation	Eurozone	0.0	0.2	1.2	1.4
	US	0.1	1.2	1.9	2.2
Current interest	Eurozone	-0.0	-0.3	-0.3	-0.3
	US	0.5	0.9	1.5	2.3
Non-current interest	Eurozone	1.1	0.8	0.6	0.6
	US	2.1	1.8	2.4	3.6
Production and labour market					
Employment opportunities	EU	1.8	1.2	0.5	0.3
	US	1.7	1.7	1.0	6.5
Unemployment (% of working population)	EU	9.8	9.1	8.8	8.5
	US	5.3	4.9	4.6	4.6
Labour productivity	EU	1.1	0.4	0.7	0.9
	US	0.5	-0.2	0.7	1.5
Labour offer	EU	0.2	0.8	0.6	0.5
	US	0.8	1.4	1.4	1.2
Output gap	EU	-1.2	-0.6	-0.4	-0.1
	US	1.2	-1.2	-0.4	1.1

Source: CPB, *MLV 2018-2021*; European Committee, *European Economic Forecast – Autumn 2016*; OECD, *Economic Outlook*, November 2016

The world trade price reflects the international trade in goods. The price of oil can fluctuate considerably. Oil is the main source of energy and is processed into many products. After a while, changes in the price of oil have an effect on private consumption, which is taken by the ECB as a guide for the interest policies that should be followed. The exchange rate of the euro in terms of the dollar has been included in Table 6.4 because of the dominance of the trade connections between the Euro area and the US. The prices of major raw materials are also quoted in dollars. A rise in the exchange rate of the dollar will mean that these materials will become more expensive in the Euro area. This will eventually result in a rise in prices in the Euro area.

World trade price

Volume of expenditure and the GDP

The volume of expenditure and the GDP are the most important variables of the basis statistics. In previous chapters it has been explained that these variables are at the core of prosperity, production and income. The GDP is the variable that is most suited to measure economic growth. Of a number of variables, the growth figures of the Euro area and the US are both given, because the performance of the Euro area can best be measured in comparison to that of the US. For most of these variables, the performance of the US is better than that of the Euro area and can be used as a benchmark for the Euro area.

Wages and prices

Wage costs per employee is an important indicator of the costs of the production factor of labour. Labour costs in the market sector is an important indicator of company costs.

The price development of private consumption indicates the level of inflation. The policy of the central bank is triggered by inflation. The European Central Bank will take measures if inflation exceeds two percent.

Interest rates

The long and short term interest rates are the prices of long-term and short-term loans. Loans are used for expenditure. They are a cost item for households and companies that finance their spending with borrowed capital. A high interest rate indicates a large demand for money and occurs during a period of economic boom. If the central bank raises the short-term interest rate, this will have the effect of restricting expenditure.

TEST 6.5

How much can the consumption rate be expected to increase in 2018? What items are consumers likely to consider most important?

Production and the labour market

By how much employment has increased is an important criterion for judging macroeconomic policy. Any increase in employment will be the result of growth in production and labour productivity. The figures for labour productivity are taken from industry (public sector labour productivity is not included).

Output gap

The output gap is the difference between actual production and production capacity. A positive output gap indicates that production and expenditure are higher than the production capacity. This means that supply and availability of production factors is being choked, which causes prices to rise. If there is a negative output gap, the opposite situation applies.

Miscellaneous

Public sector balance

The public sector balance is the difference between the income and the expenditure of the public service. The income is made up of taxation levies, social service contributions and income from government property. The expenditure consists of government spending and social services benefits.

Current account

The balance on the current account is the sum of the export balance and the income balance (see Chapter 9). This indicator is important for gauging how interest and exchange rates are developing.

6.5 **Industry and the business cycle**

The business cycle is not only important for governments but also for industry. During a recession, an increasing number of companies will be reported as being in severe difficulties. During a revival, sales and profits increase. Not all branches of industry are equally susceptible to cyclical changes. Section 6.5.1 deals with the criteria that determine susceptibility to cyclical trends and the policies of companies to reduce susceptibility. Section 6.5.2 deals with the effects susceptibility to cyclical trends has on company results.

6.5.1   Susceptibility to cyclical trends and policy

A number of criteria can be used to determine a company's susceptibility to cyclical trends. In the first place, the susceptibility is determined by the nature of the market to which the company ultimately delivers its products. The aspects of that market that warrant attention are as follows:

Nature of the market

- The type of product or service that is being provided. The difference between durable and non-durable goods is particularly significant. The purchase of durable goods can be postponed. Consumers will purchase fewer of these goods if their income cannot be maintained at its current level during a recession.

Postponed

- The level of income elasticity. Products with high income elasticity (luxury goods) are more susceptible to cyclical change than products with a low income elasticity (necessary goods).

Income elasticity

- The product's life cycle phase. This is especially relevant for durable consumer goods. The sales of durable consumer goods are particularly susceptible to cyclical change during the saturation phase. During this phase, most sales consist of replacement purchases that can be postponed if the consumer's purchasing power or willingness to buy warrants it.

Life cycle phase

TEST 6.6
What are some products with a high income elasticity that are nevertheless not durable?

One way for companies to reduce their susceptibility to cyclical change is to tailor their production to less susceptible final markets, or to spread production more equally over susceptible and non-susceptible products.

- -

EXAMPLE 6.1
A chemical manufacturer such as Akzo produces raw materials for the car industry as well as pharmaceutical end products. The car industry is a cyclical industry, the pharmaceutical industry is not. In order to reduce the company's overall cyclical susceptibility, management might decide to expand sales on the stable final market to the detriment of sales on the cyclical market.

- -

In the second place, cyclical susceptibility is determined by the stage of the production chain the company operates at. Basic producers such as the base chemical, base metal and base paper industry are cyclically more susceptible than the producers of final products, because they are faced with the effect of stock-building in the production chain. During a recession, companies that are closest to the consumer will be the first to notice a drop

Stage of the production chain

in demand. They themselves will pass on the decrease in demand to their own suppliers. But they will also reduce their stock. If all the links in the production chain reduce their purchases by the drop in demand as well as the reduction in stock, the basic producer will face a far greater reduction in sales than the original drop in consumer expenditure.

A company can reduce cyclical susceptibility by producing further along the production chain.

EXAMPLE 6.2

The steel industry (take Mittal, for instance) is very sensitive to cyclical trends. Steel and aluminium are used for various kinds of products (machinery, durable consumer goods), the purchase of which can be easily postponed if the economic situation demands it. Not only sales but prices will be quickly under pressure during an economic depression. Of all prices for raw materials, metal prices are the most affected by cyclical changes. The profits of a company like Mittal are for a large part determined by the economic climate. In order to reduce this dependency, the company is trying to sell products with a higher added value.

These include such things as steel treated to make galvanised or painted sheets, or new alloys for the car industry. The prices and profit margins of these products are not as vulnerable in the event of a decline in the economy.

Capital intensity

The third factor is the industry's capital intensity. The higher the capital intensity, the greater the share of constant costs as part of the total costs. A high proportion of constant costs in the cost structure gives rise to strong price competition during a recession. The drop in sales that is the outcome of this cannot be adequately compensated for by lowering the cost level. One way of lowering the proportion of constant costs is to farm out the company's most capital-intensive activities.

Investment policy

The last factor determining the cyclical sensitivity of an industry is the investment policy (counter or procyclical). The more procyclical the investments in an industry, the more susceptible the industry will be to cyclical trends.

The question is whether it is possible for companies to carry out countercyclical policies in order to reduce cyclical vulnerability. A countercyclical policy would involve increasing investment and promotional activities during an economic decline and restraining from investment and promotional activities during the upturn. The advantage to the company would be that it is cheaper to invest during a downward trend than during an upward trend. When the cyclical downward trend starts and the confidence of entrepreneurs in the future drops, the drop in prices on industrial markets will be relatively strong.

In practice, it is far more common to invest and budget in a procyclical way than in a countercyclical way. In other words, during an economic depression investments and promotional budgets are reduced and during an economic boom they are expanded. Turning points in the business cycle can even be explained in terms of procyclical investment behaviour. The main reason for this behaviour is, of course, the necessity to attune costs to returns.

The sensitivity of industries to cyclical trends can be classified on the basis of the four criteria mentioned (see Table 6.5).

TABLE 6.5 Industry sensitivity to cyclical trends

Agriculture and horticulture	1	Shipbuilding	3
Fishery	1	Aircraft manufacture	3
Offshore North Sea	2	Instruments and optical industry	2
Food, tobacco and beverages industry	1	Electricity companies	1
Textile industry	2	Building industry	2/3
Clothing industry	2	Building installation trade	2
Leather & shoe industry	1/2	Wholesale trade agricultural products	1
Wood & furniture industry	3	• wood & building materials	2/3
Paper industry	3	• capital goods	3
Graphic industry	2	• consumer goods	1/2
Petroleum industry	2/3	Retail trade	
Chemical industry	3	• foodstuffs	1
Rubber & synthetics manufacturing industry	2/3	• non-food	2/3
Building materials industry	3	Car trade	3
Base metal industry	2/3	Hotel & restaurant trade	3
Metal products industry	2/3	Road transport	3
Machinery industry	2/3	Sea transport	3
Electrotechnical industry	2	Inland shipping trade	3
Transport industry	3	Air transport	3
Car and truck manufacture	3	Business services	1

Key:
1 = Light sensitivity to cyclical trends
2 = Average sensitivity to cyclical trends
3 = Considerable sensitivity to cyclical trends

Source: ABN/Amro, *Enkele actuele risico's en hun invloed op Nederlandse bedrijfstakken in 1991*

On the whole, industries that produce raw materials, semi-finished products, capital goods, means of transport and luxury consumer goods are highly sensitive to cyclical trends. There are differences in the degree of sensitivity between industries, but also between sectors of the same industry. The chemical industry's results are closely connected to the business cycle. At the same time, there are considerable differences between individual chemical producers. In order to explain these differences, not only should a variety of criteria be examined, but more particularly, those criteria that are specific to the industry.

The first important criterion is product diversification. If a company's sales are spread over a larger number of product groups with a low – or at least a varied – income elasticity, sensitivity to cyclical trends will decrease. Chemical producers that aim their sales at the medical sector or the foodstuffs industry will be less sensitive to cyclical trends than base chemical producers.

Product diversification

For instance, chemical producer Akzo / Nobel profits greatly during a depression from the stable sales of pharmaceutical products.

A further way of spreading cyclical risks is geographical diversification. Cyclical trends do not occur at the same time in Asia, America and Europe. A chemical producer who has spread his sales over a number of countries in various continents will have more stable results than a competitor who is dependent on sales in various countries within the one continent.

Geographical diversification

Market position   Last but not least is the market position of a company. It has been shown that the market leader in a particular industry has less of a disadvantage during a recession than the smaller competitors. This is partly due to the fact that a large market share and a strong brand name reputation provide good protection against diminishing sales and decreasing profit margins. Another advantage of a dominant market position is the scale on which production takes place. Because of advantages of scale, a market leader has a lower cost level than the smaller suppliers on the market. Increasing price competition (a characteristic feature of a recession) will therefore have less of an impact on the market leader. Customers will not be able to shift easily to another supplier either, because that might force prices upward. A dominant position can be the result of a merger or a takeover. The merger between Akzo and Nobel made the coatings division of the firm one of the largest concerns in the paint market. The merger created advantages of scale and higher profit margins, which increased the merged company's chances of being able to weather adverse cyclical conditions.

Table 6.6 shows the factors that determine the sensitivity of companies to cyclical trends and policy measures that can be taken to counteract it.

TABLE 6.6 Company sensitivity to cyclical trends

Causes	Policy
Type of final market	Diversification
• durable/non-durable	
• income elasticity	
• product life cycle phase	
Stage in the production chain	Produce closer to the ultimate customer
Capital intensity	Outsourcing
Investment policy	Countercyclical investments
Product diversification	Concentrate on products that are less sensitive to cyclical trends
Geographical diversification	Exploiting business cycle differences
Market position	Attempt to obtain a larger share of the market

6.5.2   The consequences of business cycle sensitivity

Why should a company be worried about high sensitivity to cyclical trends? After all, a strong decline in profits during a recession will be followed by a strong increase in profits during the economic boom. Taken over the whole of the business cycle, a cyclical activity could provide a good return, and even a return that is comparable to that of a company in a less sensitive industry. Why then do companies try to reduce their sensitivity to cyclical trends? The main reasons follow.

Little control over financial results   A company's financial results depend on an interaction between factors that cannot be influenced by the company's own efforts. With a company that is sensitive to cyclical trends, the former will dominate. The company will to a certain extent be a toy of the business cycle. There will be limited possibilities of influencing the results of one's own company. The company management will, however, be judged on the company's results. When it presents the annual figures, management will not hesitate to mention the bad economic climate of the past year. This makes it look as though bad returns are by definition the result of an economic recession, and good results the natural consequence of good management.

An associated problem is the difficulty of predicting sales and profits, which then makes the financial planning of activities problematical. When there is an economic downturn, planned activities will have to be annulled or postponed. The planned acquisition of a promising company may be at stake. Reducing the sensitivity to cyclical trends increases security and the manageability of costs and returns, which makes planning less risky.

TEST 6.7

What is the likely effect of a high sensitivity rate to cyclical trends on the interest that a company has to pay on bank credit?

During a period of economic boom, the sky seems the limit for a company that is sensitive to cyclical trends. Production facilities are fully in use, the utilisation rate is high and there seems to be no end to the demand for goods and services. In the recession which is bound to follow, there will be a decrease in demand and overcapacity. Policies will have to be aimed at surviving the economic crisis.

Required organisational flexibility

Some of the symptoms of such a crisis management situation are a freeze on recruitment, spending cuts and restrictions on investments. These recurring measures require a considerable amount of organisational flexibility.

Crisis management

Companies can either finance their activities from their own resources (business savings) or they can resort to the financial markets. During a recession, the resources of a company sensitive to cyclical trends will usually not be sufficient. External financing either by attracting borrowed capital (usually bank credit) or by attracting shareholders equity (by issuing shares) will become necessary.

Financing activities

During a recession, companies that are sensitive to cyclical trends will have a weak position on the money market. Banks will require a lot of security from these companies and will put a high risk premium on the interest rate. Companies that are sensitive to cyclical trends will therefore face high costs for borrowed capital.

The stock exchange differentiates between cyclical stocks and defensive stocks. Cyclical stocks, such as airlines, base metal industries and chemical companies have less stable profits, which is reflected in the height and stability of the exchange listing. The profits of defensive stocks such as foodstuffs companies and retail trading companies are much more stable and are therefore more attractive to low-risk investors.

Cyclical stocks/ defensive stocks

The low stock exchange listing of companies whose profitability fluctuates strongly makes their shares less suitable for attracting shareholders equity. If the exchange listing is low, the company will have to issue a lot of shares in order to obtain the required capital from the market. This is undesirable from the point of view of the existing shareholders, because they will have to share future dividends with a large number of new shareholders. This is sometimes termed dividend dilution. During a recession, the company policies of many companies that are sensitive to cyclical trends are put under a considerable amount of pressure by banks and other financial institutions.

TEST 6.8

Is it possible to identify companies that are sensitive to cyclical trends and those that are not by comparing the share prices of two different periods?

Glossary

6

Budgetary deficit	The negative difference between government expenditure and income.
Burden of taxes and social security contributions	Taxes and social security contributions as a percentage of the gross domestic product.
Business cycle	The more or less regular swing of expenditure and production in relation to capacity. There are three types of business cycle: *Kitchin* (lasting 3-5 years) *Juglar* (lasting 7-11 years) *Kondratieff* (lasting 47-57 years).
Consumer price index	The weighted average of the increase in prices of consumer goods.
Economic boom	A period in which the increase in expenditure is greater than the increase in production capacity.
Economic downturn	A period in the business cycle in which the increase in expenditure lags behind the increase in production capacity.
Economic indicator	An economic entity that precedes the actual business cycle development.
Evasion	Avoiding paying taxes by illegal means.
Inflation	A condition of constantly increasing prices or monetary depreciation. There are three types of inflation: • *Hyperinflation*: a situation with very high percentages of inflation • *Demand-induced inflation*: inflation caused by overexpenditure • *Cost-induced inflation*: price increases as a result of cost increases.
Public-sector spending ratio	The expenditure of the public sector as a percentage of the GDP.

Recession	A situation in which the GDP decreases during two consecutive quarters. The term is frequently used when GDP growth decreases.
Turning point	The moment in the business cycle at which the period of economic upturn turns into a period of economic decline, and vice versa.
Upturn phase	The period in the business cycle in which the growth of production increases.

6

PART 3

The monetary environment of companies

7

Money

The main issues that we will address in this chapter are as follows:
- How is a country's inflation affected by the money supply?
- What role does the central bank play in combating inflation?

Money affects everyone. People receive their income in money, exchange goods for money and they express their wealth in terms of money. Money has several functions within the economic process. These are dealt with in Section 7.1.

Money is brought into circulation by financial institutions. They create money in various shapes: coins, banknotes and demand deposits. The degree of confidence in the monetary system depends on the financial position of the monetary institutions. These aspects of the supply of money are dealt with in Section 7.2.

People have various reasons for holding their money. They need money to buy things with or as part of an investment portfolio. Demand for money is the central theme of Section 7.3.

The quantity theory of the demand for money, a theory that plays an important part in the monetary policy of the European central bank (ECB), is discussed in this section.

Inflation affects money's functionality. It causes the costs associated with the exchange of goods in an economy to rise. One of the tasks of the central bank is to fight inflation.

Section 7.4 deals with the instruments the ECB has to do so.

7

CASE
Money and inflation are interrelated. A rapid increase in money supply and a high inflation rate is a common situation in many countries. A high inflation rate is detrimental to a company since it makes rapid inroads into consumer purchasing power, causes customers to pay late and necessitates regular adjustment of prices and the book value of assets. A company needs a lot of staff to deal with the consequences of high inflation.
For example, when there is a high rate of inflation, additional staff will be needed in the marketing department. Price lists will have to be constantly adjusted and customers will have to be notified of the changes. In the financial department, additional staff will be required to adjust their bookkeeping to regular price changes and to urge debtors to pay in time. This will cause costs to rise. Sales will also be put under pressure because high inflation affects the purchasing power of consumers and the competitiveness in relation to companies in other countries. A high rate of inflation is therefore bad for the entrepreneurial climate in a country.

7.1 The functions of money

Money

Money is a generally accepted means of exchange. People use it to pay for things. In primitive economies that are largely dependent on agriculture, fishery, or hunting, the need for money is small. Households produce few products and each household consumes its own production to a large extent. Since trading on markets is very limited, there is little need for a generally accepted means of exchange.

Division of labour

If the division of labour increases in an economy, people will start focussing more on the production of a particular product for the market. A baker for example, only requires a small portion of his production for his own use. The rest he will trade on the market for vegetables, meat and milk. The use of money is very convenient. The more the division of labour increases in an economy, the more important the role of money becomes.

Transaction costs

As we will see hereafter, the introduction of money has resulted in people losing less time to (future) exchange their products. The transaction costs of the trade are much lower in an economy with money than in one without. The time gained by the use of money can be used to produce more products.

Labour productivity

Trading with money therefore, leads to an increase of labour productivity. In this paragraph, the functions of money as a means of exchange (subparagraph 7.1.1), evaluation (subparagraph 7.1.2) and storing wealth (subparagraph 7.1.3) are discussed.

7.1.1   Money as a means of exchange
Using money as a means of exchange has two great advantages. The exchange can be separated into two parts and the two transactions do not have to take place simultaneously.

Split the exchange of goods

Using money makes it possible to split the exchange of goods into two parts. In a barter economy, a carpenter who wants meat will have to find a butcher who has a need for a carpentry product (a table, say). In a money economy, he sells the table to whoever he wants to in return for money and he subsequently buys meat with that money from any butcher he likes. In a complex economy with many businesses and products, it will obviously be impossible to find a customer who has in turn another useful product to trade for every product. The costs of looking for a suitable customer would be far too high. The unrestricted use of money as a means of exchange is therefore a precondition for the efficient functioning of a modern market economy. Separating the exchange into two parts also has the consequence that there can be a time difference between the sale of one item and the purchase of the other. The carpenter can sell the table and keep the money until such time as he needs the meat from the butcher. Unlike bartering, the sale of one item does not have to coincide in time with the purchase of the other item. Money represents undifferentiated purchasing power. The person who exchanges goods for money can make a choice between any of the goods that are available for money, can decide when he will exercise his purchasing power and who with. As such, money is also termed a liquid asset.

Time difference

Undifferentiated purchasing power

A high level of inflation affects the exchange function of money because it makes the splitting of a transaction into two parts more difficult. The purchasing power of money decreases as inflation increases. With a high inflation rate it is important that there be virtually no time lapse between the sale of one item and the purchase of another. Companies have to spend the returns on their sales as quickly as possible on goods and services. Very high inflation (hyperinflation) in a country sometimes has the effect that sellers will only accept goods or foreign currency in return for their products. Such a country is in effect either reverting to a barter economy, with all the disadvantages for productivity that this brings, or replacing the local currency by a foreign currency.

Effects of a high inflation

Hyperinflation in Zimbabwe (2008)

TEST 7.1
It is sometimes said that money can buy everything. Look at how money has been defined. Is it true that everything in our society can be bought with it?

7.1.2   Money as a means of evaluation
The second function of money is as a standard for expressing the value of goods and services. Goods also have to be given a value for purposes that have nothing to do with an exchange situation (for instance, in connection with making up a balance or a profit and loss account). Using money as a means of evaluation has the effect of dramatically limiting the number of prices in an economy. An economy with say 100 saleable items, one of which takes on the role of money, has 99 prices. The values of these 99 items can be compared to each other because they are all expressed in terms of an amount of money. This will reduce transaction costs considerably compared

Number of prices

to a barter economy, where every item has to be expressed in terms of all other goods. In this case, there would be almost 5,000 prices to compare (100x99/2). This makes data flows very complicated and consequently transaction costs will be high.

Effects of a high inflation

Using money as a means of evaluation becomes problematic with high inflation levels. In countries with high inflation, prices are an indication of the real value of goods for only a very short time. The planning of the production process in these countries is hampered by the constant uncertainty about the level of buying and selling prices, the valuation of assets and liabilities and the level of future expenditure and income. In countries with a very high inflation rate, the balance and profit and loss account often give a false impression of the actual level of assets and results. In a situation of hyperinflation, money clearly has virtually no significance as a means of evaluation. The costs associated with that monetary system will mount up because the constant adaptation of price lists and the constant revaluation of assets and liabilities will require the deployment of factors of production.

For this reason, some countries with hyperinflation resort to replacing the local currency by a foreign currency (the dollar or the euro, for example). Figure 7.1 shows that only a few countries encountered a rate of inflation of over 25% in 2017. In that year, Venezuela was the only country that had to deal with hyperinflation. The International Monetary Fund (IMF) estimated Venezuelan inflation to be at least one million percent on an annual basis.

FIGURE 7.1 Inflation in the world (2017)

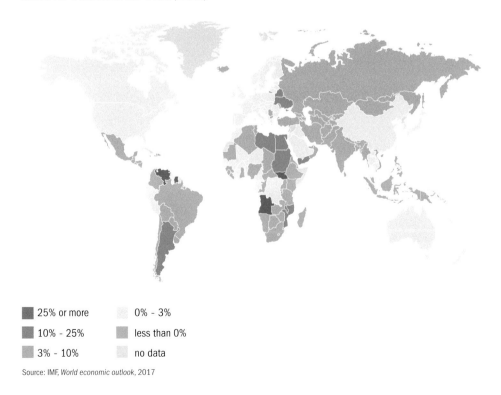

- 25% or more
- 10% - 25%
- 3% - 10%
- 0% - 3%
- less than 0%
- no data

Source: IMF, *World economic outlook*, 2017

7.1.3 Money as a means of storing wealth

The third function of money is as means of storing wealth. By saving, households build up assets during the course of time. They can hang on to these assets in the form of real estate, shares, bonds, savings accounts or in the form of liquid assets (coins, banknotes or a demand deposits at the bank). Cash that is kept as an asset is termed 'hoarded money'.

Hoarded money

In a country with a high inflation rate, using money as a means of storing wealth is ineffective. Households that keep part of their assets in the form of cash will notice that the purchasing power of their cash is decreasing rapidly. They will therefore be forced to invest their liquid assets in gold or foreign currencies. There are transaction costs associated with this plus a risk that the value of the investments might fluctuate. Table 7.1 sets out the various functions of money and the effect of a high inflation rate.

Effects of a high inflation

TABLE 7.1 The functions of money and the effect of a high inflation rate

Function	Characteristics	Effect of high inflation	Means of exchange
Splits exchange of products into two parts	Any time gap between sales and purchases is disadvantageous	Means of evaluation	Unambiguous value criterion for products
Uncertainty about the true value of products	Means of storing wealth	Money as a liquid asset	Cash loses its purchasing power quickly

TEST 7.2
Why will a high inflation rate have a less disastrous effect on a developing economy than on a highly developed economy?

7.2 Money supply

This section will deal with institutions that regulate money supply. Section 7.2.1 deals with the question of who is responsible for introducing the various types of money. Section 7.2.2. deals with how the amount of money in an economy can be measured. Monetary confidence is directly linked to trust in the institutions that create money (the banks). The role of banks and assessment of their financial state is treated in Section 7.2.3. Finally, in paragraph 7.2.4, the European banking union is discussed.

7.2.1 Types of money

In most countries, money comes in several forms: coins, banknotes and demand deposits. Money has developed from pieces of precious metal via standard coins to banknotes and demand deposits. It has synonymously acquired greater functional ability.

Coins

Throughout the course of history, many goods have been used as money. Bits of precious metal such as gold or silver have proved to be most suitable. Precious metals are generally prized and accepted, and not being perishable

Precious metal

means that they are eminently suited to the role of a means of exchange, a means of evaluation and a means of storing wealth.

Precious metals used to be either used as means of payment or for other purposes (manufacture into jewellery, for example), depending on the choice of the owner. Their value was dependent on supply and demand. Demand depended on the need for precious metals for the purposes of exchange and for jewellery. Supply was determined by the availability – location, mining and processing – of precious metals. The market determined the value. The market value of the material that money is made from is termed the intrinsic value of money.

Intrinsic value

From the moment that the government started to interfere actively in the money supply, transaction costs decreased considerably. The introduction of pieces of precious metal (coins) stamped to guarantee the value of the coin simplified trading. Money acquired a nominal value thereby: the value that was stated on the coin. This did away with the necessity to weigh and assess the quality of each quantity of precious metal at every transaction in order to determine its intrinsic value.

Nominal value

In the present system, the link between intrinsic value and nominal value has been severed. Precious metals no longer play a role. In fact, it is only the nominal value of coins that means anything.

Banknotes

The introduction of coins was as important an innovation as any technical invention. However, although the coining of precious metals was a great step forward, it had a disadvantage. Coins are relatively heavy and production and transport costs are high.

Euro coins and banknotes

During the course of time, banks developed. They issued banknotes in return for coins that their clients gave them for safe keeping. Initially, clients exchanged their banknotes for coins if they had to make payments. Later, the banknotes themselves were used as a means of payment. Banks subsequently started to lend out banknotes to private persons and companies that needed money. Lending out banknotes created new money. Ultimately, the value of the money depended on the confidence clients had that they could exchange their banknotes at any time for precious metals. The trust in the value of money no longer depended solely on the intrinsic value of the precious metals, but also on the reliability of the bank's balance sheet.

TEST 7.3
Just as in the past, banks can go bankrupt. What consequences could this have for the reliability of the monetary system?

At the moment, the issuing of banknotes is the monopoly of the central bank. In the past, customers could demand the counter value of their banknotes in gold, but this is no longer possible. As a result, bank notes (and coins) are now considered fiduciary money. Fiduciary money is a type of money whose value is not derived from its intrinsic value, but purely from the fact that people are able to rely on it to buy products. Or, to quote the founder of economic science, Adam Smith: 'All money is a matter of belief.'

Central bank

Fiduciary money

Demand deposits and the role of banks
In modern monetary economies, people keep the major part of their money in the form of demand deposits in a bank. Banks create demand deposits. A certain understanding of a bank balance sheet is necessary in order to gain an insight into the main problems associated with the creation of demand deposits. We will now go through a bank balance sheet step by step. Let us assume that a person has a capital of 15 and he is keeping this capital in the form of banknotes. His balance sheet will look like Figure 7.2.

FIGURE 7.2 Balance sheet with Cash and Equity

Assets		Balance sheet	Liabilities
Cash	15	Equity	15

Such a capital is completely liquid and yields no returns. Income from interest can be obtained by providing credit from the cash reserves. Interest is a remuneration that the borrower (debtor) has to pay to the lender (creditor) for making liquid assets available. For the lender, extension of credit brings with it a certain amount of risk. He runs the risk that the debtor will not or cannot repay his loan. This risk is reflected in the interest rate. Lending an amount of 5 will lead to the balance sheet in Figure 7.3.

Interest

FIGURE 7.3 Balance sheet with Cash, Debtors and Equity

Assets	Balance sheet	Liabilities
Cash	10	Equity	15
Debtors	5		

The interest is initially put on to a profit and loss account and can be added to the individual's own equity at the end of a book year.

In the next step, the private person lending out his money becomes a money-creating banker. As well as lending money in the form of banknotes, a banker can also lend money in the form of a demand deposit. The borrower receives his money in the form of an amount payable on demand by the banker. The banker guarantees the client that he can make payments from this amount to third parties or that it can be transferred into banknotes.

Money-creating banker

Let us assume that a client wants to borrow 50 from the banker. He receives a demand deposit from the bank that he can use to make his payments. What this gives the bank is a claim on the client. The client has to pay interest, and after a while will have to repay his loan. This is shown in the balance sheet in Figure 7.4.

FIGURE 7.4 Balance sheet with Cash, Debtors, Equity and Demand deposit

Assets	Balance sheet	Liabilities
Cash	10	Equity	15
Debtors	55	Demand deposit	50

Because the bank accepts a debt payable on demand to the borrower and the borrower accepts a debt to the bank over a period this way of creating money is sometimes called a mutual debt agreement. A mutual debt agreement entails a risk for banks. The more demand deposits they create, the less cash resources there are proportionally to cover the deposits: the liquidity of the banks worsens. If clients demand their deposits en masse in the form of banknotes ('a bank run') the banks will not be able to comply and will go bankrupt.

Mutual debt agreement

Bank crisis

A bank crisis is detrimental to economic growth because lending operations within the economy will come to a standstill. We call this a 'credit crunch'. The bankrupt banks can, of course, no longer extend any credit and the remaining banks will be very reluctant to provide new credit. Monitoring of banks by the central bank is thus clearly essential. (See also Sections 7.2.3 and 7.2.4).

TEST 7.4

A bank can provide a loan based on a mutual debt agreement or attracted savings. Which of these two will contribute the most to the bank's profit?

7.2.2   Monetary aggregates: M1 and M3

Money is not neutral in an economy. It has a major influence on inflation and various other economic variables. This is the reason why the central bank meticulously monitors the development of the money supply in a country. The narrow money supply and broad money supply will now be further discussed.

Narrow money supply: M1

In the previous section we dealt with three types of money that can be used to make payments. Coins, banknotes and demand deposits are collectively referred to as primary liquid assets.

The European central bank (ECB) determines the amount of primary liquid assets within the euro area by analysing the balance sheets of the monetary financial institutions (MFI). The MFI are those financial institutions that constitute the money-creating sector of the eurozone, namely the ECB and the money-creating private banks. The ECB refers to the parties that use the money (the millions of consumers and the businesses) simply as 'the public'. The primary liquid assets *that the public holds* are called the money supply. Banknotes and coins in the vaults of banks provide cover for the demand deposits and are not used for public transactions. If these banknotes and coins were to be counted as well, it would mean counting them twice: the deposit money is, in fact, nothing but a claim on the bank for banknotes and coins.

The symbol M1 is used internationally to represent the money supply used for payments that is in the hands of the public. It is also termed narrow money supply.

Primary liquid assets

Monetary financial institutions

Money supply

M1

Broad money supply: M3

The money supply is in the possession of households, businesses and government. They often receive money without needing it immediately for expenses. Companies, for instance, may receive liquid assets from sales but they may not have to pay out salaries until sometime later. When this happens, what they have is termed a temporary liquidity surplus. Other parties may have a temporary liquidity shortfall if they have to spend before they receive income. Parties with a liquidity surplus can lend that surplus to the bank, who in turn can lend the liquid assets to parties with a liquidity shortage.

Banks offer their clients a variety of ways of lending their surplus liquidity, depending on length of time. If the time span is less than two years the investments are regarded as secondary liquid assets. Secondary liquid assets consist of claims by the public on monetary financial institutions that can be turned into money at short notice, en masse and without loss of value. Some examples of this are short-term savings deposits and short-term time deposits with banks. A short-term savings deposit cannot be used for payments – it is not a primary liquid asset – but it can be turned into a primary liquid asset very quickly. A short-term savings deposit is therefore 'near money.

Secondary liquid assets

Near money

It is important for the central bank to monitor the secondary money supply. Households that lend liquidity surpluses to banks in the form of savings often intend to use that amount for purchasing products in the near future. If a lot of households convert their secondary liquid assets into primary liquid assets at a given moment in time and make purchases with them, the risk of inflation will increase. The ECB has a policy of examining the secondary as well as the primary liquid assets in order to ascertain whether

Broad money supply: M3

there is a danger of inflation in the eurozone. The primary and secondary liquid assets in a country are jointly termed the broad money supply and are indicated by the symbol M3. M3 is the main monetary aggregate for the monetary policy of the European central bank (see Section 7.4).
Table 7.2 lists the components of M3 in the eurozone. The supply of 'near money' in the Euro zone is not much less than M1.

TABLE 7.2 Size and composition of M3 in the eurozone (January 2017; amounts in billions of euros)

Coins and banknotes in circulation	1,082
Demand deposits[1]	6,156
M1	**7,238**
Secondary liquid assets	4,198
M3	**11,436**

[1] All deposits that can be converted into cash either immediately or at the end of the day, or that can be withdrawn relatively cheaply using a PIN card, cheque or the like, including call money and foreign currency deposits.

Source: ECB, *Monetary developments in the euro area*, January 2017

TEST 7.5
During 2016, the GDP in the eurozone was about one-and-a-half times M1. How is it possible for the supply of money within a country to be less than the value of the goods and services produced?

7.2.3   The role of banks and the bank balance sheet

Money is always a claim on a monetary financial institution. Monetary confidence depends ultimately therefore on confidence in monetary financial institutions. In turn this confidence is dependent upon the financial position of these institutions. This section deals with the composition and assessment of the bank balance sheet based on financial indicators.

Financial institutions
Financial institutions are companies that raise and lend money. They include banks, insurance companies, pension funds, social funds and investment institutions. They are part of the financial system of the economy, which can be described as the way in which the flow of money within the economy is organised. An economy's financial system fulfils several functions, each of which is important for healthy economic growth.

Creation of money

The first function – the creation of money – has already been dealt with in some detail. A growing economy needs an increasing amount of money to finance the increase in production and expenditure. Creating money by means of mutual debt agreements is very profitable for banks. Banks receive debit interest on the money they have lent. They usually do not pay credit interest on the public's demand deposits. The difference between debit and credit interest (the interest margin) is therefore considerable. The interest margin is, however, slightly offset by the costs of payment transactions associated with demand deposits.

Interest margin

Passing on of money

The second function of the financial system is the passing on of money from those with a liquidity surplus to those with a liquidity deficit. This function has also been treated already. Because banks do pay credit interest on attracted savings the interest margin on passed-on liquid assets is less than it is for mutual debt agreements. The interest margins that banks earn by passing on liquid assets and by mutual debt agreements are termed interest-rate dependent operations.

In the third place, the financial system has to ensure that payment transactions function smoothly. Households and companies expect their financial transactions to be carried out quickly and against low costs. The more efficiently payment transactions are carried out, the lower the transaction costs of the exchange of goods.

Smooth payment transactions

Finally, the financial system provides all kinds of other financial services. These include various types of insurance, such as life, pension, damage, burglary and fire insurance as well as stockbroking and advisory services. Financial institutions ask a commission for these services which is why they are called commission operations.

Other financial services

There are monetary and non-monetary financial institutions. The difference between the two is that monetary financial institutions have primary liquid assets on the credit side of their balance sheet (such as deposit money in the case of banks and banknotes in the case of the central bank). Non-money-creating institutions do not have these items on their balance sheet. Table 7.3 lists the various financial institutions.

Monetary financial institutions

Non-money-creating institutions

TABLE 7.3 Financial institutions

Monetary	Non-monetary
Central bank	Mortgage banks
Money-creating private banks	Pension funds
	Insurance companies
	Investment funds
	Social funds

The balance sheet of a monetary financial institution
The balance sheets of monetary financial institutions give an impression of their financial position. The financial situation of the banking system is essential for judging the quality and reliability of the monetary system. In table 7.4, the consolidated balance sheet of Rabobank, a Dutch bank is presented.

Balance sheet

TABLE 7.4 Consolidated balance sheet of the Rabobank (situation at the end of June 2016, amounts in billions of euros)

Assets		Liabilities and equity	
Cash	73.2		
Banks	24.4	Banks	21.9
Loans to clients	463.7	Client accounts	342.9
Financial assets	98.6	Issued debt securities	171.4
Other assets	26.7	Other liabilities	109.9
		Equity	40.8
Total assets	686.6	Total liabilities and equity	686.6

Source: Rabobank

Just as with other companies, liquidity, solvency and profitability determine how financially sound a bank is regarded. These indicators also have a macroeconomic significance, since confidence in the monetary system is based on the financial position of banks. We shall deal with the liquidity, solvency and profitability of a bank respectively.

Liquidity

The liquidity of a bank is an indication of the extent to which the bank can fulfil its short-term obligations. The central bank ensures that the available liquidity of a bank during a certain period is greater than the liquidity required.

Liquidity present

The liquidity present consists of the liquid assets and the money receipts of a bank during a certain period. To calculate the liquidity present, the central bank determines what items from the debit side of the balance a bank may include and to what extent. Banknotes in reserve and the demand deposits with the central bank are regarded wholly as liquid assets. The share portfolio only counts for 50 percent of its value because it is by no means certain that in times of crisis – a run on the bank, for example – the bank can convert the shares into cash quickly and without too much loss in value.

Required liquidity

The required liquidity is a function of the expected obligations of the bank during a certain period. Here too, the central bank applies a certain weighting depending on the likelihood of whether a short-term liability will, in fact, lead to expenditure. For example, for short-term debts to the central bank the required liquidity is 100% and for demand deposits of private clients it is 20%, because the chance that account holders will withdraw more than 20% of their deposits is extremely small.

Solvency

Solvency means that a bank is able to guarantee any loss from debtors with its own capital. The Bank for International Settlements (BIS) in Basel is the main organization for mutual consultation by countries about world-wide solvency requirement standards. These consultations have resulted in the Basel accords.

Basel I and II

The Basel I-accord of 1988 laid down that the ratio of the capital of a bank (consisting of equity capital and subordinated loans) to risk-weighted debtors should be at least 8%. In calculating this BIS-ratio, Basel I did not differentiate between a high-risk rate and a low-risk rate for loans to businesses and private clients. The Basel II Accord of 2004 does do so.

BIS-ratio

Capital buffer

The capital buffer that a bank must maintain increases according to the potential risk of a loan. If a bank grants a high-risk loan it has to retain a lot of capital and therefore incur high costs. Providers of capital are last in line for repayment in the event of a bankruptcy. They bear more risk than common creditors and therefore require higher compensation for making capital available. Basel II therefore made high-risk lending operations less attractive.

Basel III

During the global financial crisis of 2007 and 2008 it became clear that the size as well as the quality of the capital of many banks was insufficient. The

Basel III accord of 2010 obliges banks to maintain larger capital buffers that in addition have to consist for a larger part of their own equity.

Own equity is namely the highest quality capital buffer, because it is always available and is not encumbered by payment obligations. A new demand of Basel III is that a bank's own equity has to be at least 3% of all assets, whether they are high-risk or not. This so-called leverage ratio means that the total of the assets of a bank is not allowed to be more than 33.3 times its own equity capital. Before the credit crisis this was often 50 times or greater.

Own equity

Leverage ratio

In Figure 7.5, the development of the bank capital as a percentage of risk-weighted assets in the Euro zone is presented. It indicates that the solvency of banks in the Euro zone significantly improved over the past few years. This is mainly due to profit retaining.

FIGURE 7.5 Total capital as a percentage of risk weighted assets in the euro area (2010–2016)

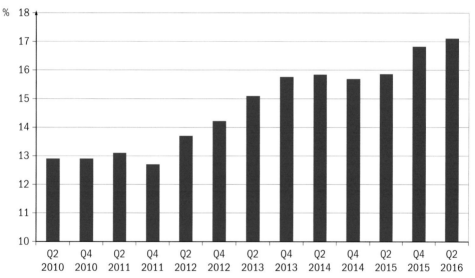

Source: ECB

Profitability

The profitability reflects the relationship between profits and the equity capital. The bank uses profits for paying dividends to shareholders and for increasing its equity capital. A sufficient level of profitability is therefore necessary for solvency and future lending operations. As has been mentioned before, most of a bank's returns are derived from interest margins and commissions. Its costs are mainly personnel costs.

Liquidity, solvency and profitability and the bank balance sheet

Figure 7.6 shows the main components of a bank balance sheet and the concepts of liquidity, solvency and profitability in diagrammatic form.

7

FIGURE 7.6 Bank balance sheet and commercial indicators

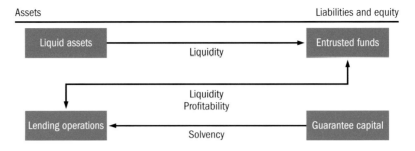

Liquid assets serve as a covering for obligations that include demand deposits. The funds entrusted to a bank are made up of demand deposits, time deposits and savings. These assets are necessary for lending operations and their profitability derives from the interest margin received from them. Banks have to adjust the funds entrusted to them to their lending operations in such a way that future liquidity problems are avoided and obligations are complied with. The guarantee capital is a solvency buffer against those debtors who cannot or will not meet their obligations.

7.2.4   European Banking Union

During the bank crisis of 2007 and 2008, it became apparent that many banks are 'too big to fail'.

'Too big to fail'

If a large bank runs into trouble, a crisis of the entire financial system is imminent. Large banks actually lend each other large amounts of money. Problems at one large bank will therefore, soon be transferred to another. Furthermore, due to threatening bankruptcy of a mega bank, the trust in the entire banking system diminishes. Even healthy banks will no longer be safe from a 'bank run'.

Systematically important banks

Banks which are 'too big to fail', are called systematically important banks. They are crucial for the survival of the financial system. The government must support failing systematically important banks. However, systematically important banks are so large that rescuing them can even bring governments into financial problems.

To limit the influence of failing banks on a government's finances, the euro countries have agreed to a banking union (other EU-countries are free to join if they wish to do so).

Banking union

A banking union organises bank supervision and the resolution for failing banks at a central level. The European banking union rests on four pillars:
1 Single Supervisory Mechanism
2 Single Resolution Mechanism
3 Single Resolution Fund
4 Harmonised deposit guarantee schemes

These four pillars of the European banking union will be further discussed.

1 Single Supervisory Mechanism (SSM)

According to Basel III, banks must conform to stricter requirements with regard to liquidity and solvency. The supervision of all banks in the euro zone, concerning adherence to these requirements, is in the hands

of the European Central Bank (ECB). The ECB directly supervises the
systematically important banks. For the smaller banks, the ECB delegates
the supervision to the national central banks. The ECB however, remains
ultimately responsible.

It is quite obvious why the ECB supervises the systematically important
banks. These banks are of a European size and are sometimes even world
players. A level playing field is created for all banks, by uniform and central
supervision.

European Central
Bank (ECB)

Level playing
field

2 Single Resolution Mechanism (SRM)

In spite of central supervision, banks sometimes still run into financial
problems. For this purpose the resolution for failing banks, was drawn up.
Simply put, this procedure determines whether failing banks survive or fail.
A specially assembled Single Resolution Board, draws up the resolution
plans for failing banks. The European Commission (the civil service of the
EU) must approve these plans.

So far the national governments have rescued their systematically important
banks by providing them with additional capital. This is called a bail-out. It
is not the capital providers, but the taxpayer who pays the bill for recovery
of a bank. In future, the costs of a rescue will be for the account of the fund
providers of the bank. This is called a bail-in. It implies that shareholders
and certain creditors have to accept their loss, for a bank to become healthy
again. Small savers will be spared.

Resolution for
failing banks

Bail-out

Bail-in

3 Single Resolution Fund

A bail-in must prevent that the taxpayer foots the bill for the recovery of a
bank. A second buffer for the taxpayer is the European bank fund. Failing
banks can call on this fund if a bail-in offers insufficient options for a
recovery. Banks have to contribute to this resolution fund until it contains
approximately €55 billion. This amount however, is very low in proportion
to the balance sheet total of the banks in the euro zone. The collapse of a
large bank would dwarf the available funds. According to some critics, the
banking union is bound to fail if national governments are not prepared to
automatically and jointly, fill the Resolution Fund with public funding if
required. Without a large public safety net, the single resolution mechanism
loses its credibility.

4 Harmonised deposit guarantee schemes

The guarantee of saving deposits is important for a stable bank sector. If
savers realise that their savings are guaranteed, they will be less inclined
to panic and cause a 'bank run' in the event of a failing bank. By centrally
setting the guaranteed deposit amount to €100,000 per person per bank, a
level playing field is created. This furthers fair competition between banks
in the euro zone.

Guaranteed
deposit amount

There is no joint European deposit guarantee scheme (yet). The participating
countries do not jointly guarantee the deposits of all savers in the EU. The
deposit guarantee scheme of a euro country therefore, is as good as the
creditworthiness of the national government which guarantees the saving
deposits.

In Figure 7.7 the workings of the European banking union are shown
schematically.

FIGURE 7.7 European Banking Union

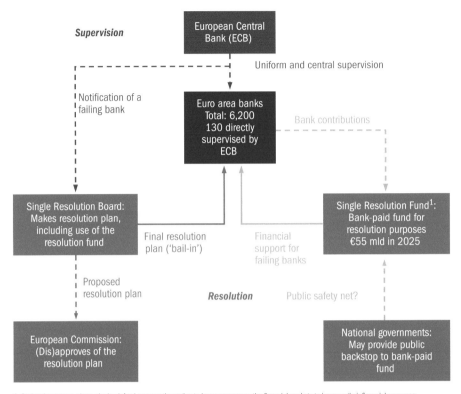

1 During the start-up phase, the bank fund reserves the option to borrow money on the financial markets to increase their financial resources
   and therefore the credibility of the fund.

Source: European Commission, Financial Times (www.ft.com; consulted on 17 December 2013)

7.3 Demand for money

Households, businesses and the government need money for several reasons. In this section the reasons for holding money (7.3.1) and the quantity theory relating to demand for money (7.3.2) are dealt with.

7.3.1   Motives for holding money

When the term 'demand for money' is used, it refers to the public need to hold liquid assets. The reasons for businesses and households holding money are closely related to the function of money as a means of exchange and storing wealth.

The most obvious reason for holding money relates to transactions. People need money to buy things. They thus retain a certain amount of liquid assets in order to be able to pay for their purchases (transactions).

The amount needed depends on the value of the transactions they intend to make during a given period. In an economy where production is growing or prices are rising, the transactions demand for money will increase. The transactions demand is also termed 'demand for active balances'.

Transactions demand for money

In addition to needing money for transactions, households and businesses may have another reason for holding money: precautionary or speculative motives.

Households frequently put money aside as a precaution against financial setbacks. When they budget, many households take account of the fact that durable consumer goods such as cars or consumer electronics can break down suddenly and have to be repaired or replaced. Companies also often keep a certain amount of liquid assets on hand as a buffer against a sudden drop in sales. The liquid assets that households keep on as a precaution against unfavourable financial developments are referred to as the 'precautionary demand for money'. **Precautionary demand for money**

Lastly, households and businesses alike hold money for investment purposes: money as a means of storing wealth. Liquid assets are part of the household investment portfolio and offer an alternative to investment in bonds, stocks or real estate, for example. If households expect a rise in the price of bonds, stocks and real estate, they will invest more money in those. This means they will hold a smaller part of their capital in the form of liquid assets. Conversely, the expectation that stock exchange prices will drop will induce investors to keep a larger proportion of their capital in the form of liquid assets. The demand for money for reasons of investment is termed the 'speculative demand for money'. **Speculative demand for money**

Precautionary and speculative demand for money is jointly known as a 'demand for idle balances', indicating that the money is not immediately used for the financing of transactions.

TEST 7.6

We will assume that there is the likelihood of a war in the Middle East. What influence is this likely to have on the speculative demand for money?

The demand for idle balances depends largely on the interest rate. Holding liquid assets that are not immediately required for transactions is associated with a loss in returns. Households and businesses could use these idle balances for investments in bonds, or put them into an interest-bearing bank account. Changes in the interest rate affect income derived from cash in hand. The higher the interest rate the higher the missed income. When interest rates are high, investing liquid assets in interest-bearing ways makes sense. Conversely, when the interest rate is low there will be a considerable demand for idle balances. Holding cash supplies only involves a small loss of income in such a situation. **Demand for idle balances** **Interest rate**

Not only the level of the interest rate but also the expected interest rate has an effect on the demand for idle balances. Changes in the interest rate have an important effect on the prices of shares and bonds. An increase in the interest rate leads to a decrease in the prices of shares and bonds on the stock exchange. The prices of existing bonds drop because investors prefer newly issued bonds at the higher interest rate. A decrease in share prices has two causes. The first is that a rise in interest rates is bad for the profit prospects of companies and the second is that a rise in interest reduces the attractiveness of shares as compared to, for instance, a savings account. Investors who expect a rise in the interest rate will therefore do away with the whole or part of their investments in shares and bonds in favour of liquid assets. After the interest has risen and the stock exchange prices have dropped they will move back to the stocks and bonds markets. **Expected interest rate**

In short: the demand for idle balances is high when the interest rate is low or there is an expected increase in the interest rate. The reverse applies when there is a high interest rate or a decrease in the interest rate is expected (see Figure 7.8).

FIGURE 7.8 Demand for money and the interest rate

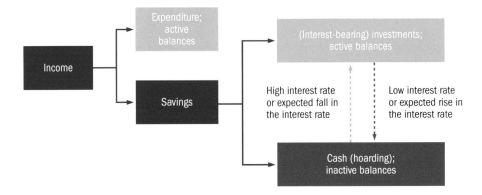

7.3.2 The quantity theory of money

We can analyse the need for liquid assets in an economy using the quantity theory of money. According to this theory, the amount of money that is needed in an economy is dependent on the nominal value of production and the velocity of circulation:

$$M \times V = P \times Q$$

in which:
M = Money supply (required)
V = Velocity of circulation (number of times per year a euro is spent on buying goods and services that make up GDP)
P = Price level of GDP
Q = Volume of GDP

The demand for active balances depends on the nominal value of the goods and services produced during a given period. This is the same as the quantity of goods and services produced (Q) multiplied by the average price of goods and services (P). If production increases, the number of transactions will increase, causing the demand for money to grow. If prices rise there will also be more money required to carry out the transactions because more money will be required for the same quantity of goods. Although the demand for money is dependent on the nominal value of production in an economy, it is not identical to that amount. During a given period, money can be used more than once to buy goods and services. This is expressed by the velocity of circulation (V). This variable indicates the number of times a year a given monetary unit is used to buy goods and services. The greater the velocity, the smaller the amount of money required.

Velocity of circulation

The velocity of circulation of money depends firstly on the level of technical advancement (for instance, developments in the field of electronic payments) and on payment habits. In an economy where wages are paid once a week, the velocity of circulation is greater than in an economy where wages are paid once a month. At a monthly pay rate, the money is dormant longer than at a weekly pay rate. This implies that in an economy where wages are paid monthly a larger amount of money is needed than in a similar economy where wages are paid weekly. The technical aspects of payment traffic and payment habits are not subject to short-term change. Some economists consequently assume that the velocity of circulation is constant in the short term.

TEST 7.7
What effect would electronic payments have on the velocity of circulation and the money supply needed?

The velocity of circulation is also dependent on the interest rate. As has already been mentioned in the previous section, the demand for idle balances is determined by the interest rate. If the interest rate is low, the income lost from holding an idle balance will also be low. Moreover, the chances that the interest rate will rise in the near future are also greater at a low level of interest. So when the interest rate is low, the demand for idle balances is high. This means that an important part of the money supply is not being used for the purchase of goods and services. Consequently the velocity of circulation will be low.
A low interest rate will therefore cause a low velocity of circulation and a high interest rate a high velocity of circulation. In Section 7.4 the quantity theory is applied to monetary policy.

7.4 **Monetary policy**

A high rate of inflation interferes with monetary functions. Businesses, households and the government will face high transaction costs when making payments. In most countries the government considers a well functioning monetary system so important that monetary policy aimed at curbing inflation is one of the cornerstones of its economic policy.
In this section, the subject is the monetary policy in the eurozone. Section 7.4.1 and 7.4.2 subsequently deal with the objectives and the instruments of monetary policy.

7.4.1   Monetary policy objectives
In the eurozone, the European Central Bank is responsible for implementing monetary policy. Together with the central banks of the 28 member states, it is part of the European System of Central Banks (ESCB) whose main task is to promote price stability in the European Union. Alongside the ESCB is the Eurosystem, which consists of the ECB and the national central banks of the euro countries. *European Central Bank*

The main tasks of the ECB are: *Tasks of the ECB*
- carrying out monetary policy
- the issue of banknotes
- management of the currency reserves of the countries of the eurozone
- intervention in the currency market

- stimulation of efficient financial traffic in Europe
- stimulation of the stability of the European financial system.

Most of the above tasks will be treated elsewhere in the book. This section deals with the main task of the ECB: monetary policy.

Monetary policy is aimed at preventing the money supply having a detrimental effect on economic growth in the medium term. Both too great and too little an increase in the money supply is undesirable. Too great an increase in the money supply is accompanied by a high rate of inflation and a too slow increase in the money supply is accompanied by a level of expenditure that is too low.

Price stability
In the euro area, monetary policy aims at price stability. Only after price stability is guaranteed do objectives such as stimulating economic growth come into the picture. In this regard, the European monetary policy differs from the American monetary policy (see Table 7.5). In the USA, the objective of monetary policy is also a low rate of inflation, but it has to contribute to a high rate of employment as well.

TABLE 7.5 Monetary policy in the United States and in the eurozone

	United States	**Eurozone**
Objectives	To promote the goal of maximum employment, stable prices and moderate long-term interest rates	Maintaining price stability
Definition price stability	Economic decisions are not disturbed by expected inflation	Inflation at, or just below 2%
Policy based on	A variety of economic indicators	Two 'pillars': • The money supply (M3) • Other inflation indicators (such as business cycle, prices of raw materials, wages and exchange rate)
Main official interest rate	Federal funds target rate	Refinancing rate
Independence of the central bank	Responsible to Congress	Completely independent

Source: *Kwartaalbericht De Nederlandsche Bank*, March 2001

The objective of the monetary policy of the ECB is an inflation rate at, or just below 2% (see Table 7.4) Strictly speaking, price stability occurs at an inflation rate of 0%. The ECB accepts a limited amount of inflation, however, because on some markets there will always be a degree of imported inflation or some cost inflation. If it were not possible to 'finance' this inflation by a limited increase in the money supply, other markets would be forced to accept price decreases, which would have a detrimental effect on the growth of production. The ECB makes its policy on the basis of inflation

Inflation expectations
expectations. It constantly studies those economic features that have an influence on price development. The bank bases its inflation expectations on two so-called pillars (see Table 7.4). The first allots an important role to

the growth of the money supply (M3). The second pillar is an analysis of inflation indicators such as the business cycle and the development of costs.

The first pillar of the ECB's monetary policy presupposes that M3 is a reliable leading indicator for medium-term price development. The quantity theory easily demonstrates this. An increase in the money supply will of necessity lead to price increases if the velocity of circulation and the production remain the same. If the public has increasing amounts of money at its disposal, there is a good chance that they will be used for purchasing goods and services. This causes expenditure to increase – assuming that the production remains constant – and this will cause a price increase. Put simply, inflation is the result of too much money chasing too few goods.

Headquarters of the ECB in Frankfurt

Source: *website* ECB (new premises media centre)

The ECB publishes an annual reference value for M3. This represents the growth ratio of money that is compatible with medium-term price stability. The ECB uses the quantity theory to determine the reference value for M3 (see figure 7.9).
The European Central Bank looks first at the increase in the amount of money that is necessary to finance trend-related growth in production. The ECB assumes that production (Q) in the eurozone grows yearly by 2% in line with the trend. At an admissible inflation of 2% yearly, the demand for money (PxQ) will increase by 4% per year (see Fig. 7.8). The amount of money (M) would also have to increase by 4% if it were not for the fact that the velocity of circulation changes too. Let us assume that the velocity of circulation in the eurozone (V) decreases by about 0.5% per year. When money does not go from hand to hand that fast anymore more money is needed to pay the same quantity products. The decrease in the velocity of circulation is compensated by the ECB, which determines the reference value for monetary growth not at 4% but at 4.5% per year.

Reference value for M3

FIGURE 7.9 Determining the reference value of M3

Actual growth of M3

If the actual growth of M3 exceeds the reference value the ECB will scrutinise the causes carefully. If the ECB is of the opinion that exceeding the reference value is the result of an incidental increase in demand for idle cash it will not take any measures. After all, idle balances are not used for expenditure but are kept for investment purposes. If, however, the ECB is of the opinion that the public is using the increased amount of money for expenditure, it will take measures to prevent demand-pull inflation.

TEST 7.8
If the productivity growth in the EMU region increases structurally, what will the effect be on the M3 reference value?

The second pillar of monetary policy is comprised of inflation-indicators such as the business cycle, the prices of raw materials, wages, exchange rates and actual inflation. An economic boom, rising prices of raw materials, increasing wages, a depreciation of the euro and a high actual inflation bring with it the increasing danger of inflation (see Chapter 6).
Figure 7.10 summarises the monetary policy of the European central bank.

FIGURE 7.10 Anti-inflationary policy of the European bank

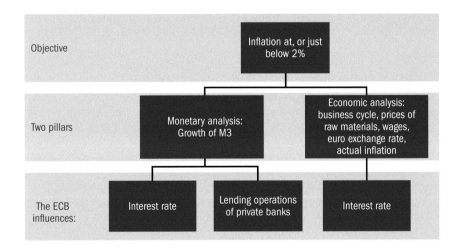

If the ECB expects an inflation rate that goes beyond its objectives the bank will want to take measures. These will normally be aimed at curbing the money growth. To a large extent, money growth is the result of lending operations by the banks. The ECB will be able to halt the increase in money by putting a brake on lending operations by banks. The instruments that the ECB can use to do that are dealt with in Section 7.4.2.

7.4.2   Instruments of monetary policy
In this section we deal firstly with the usual or conventional instruments of the monetary policy of the ECB. Next we shall deal with unusual or unconventional instruments that the central banks have deployed during the GFC (the global financial crisis) and the subsequent debt crisis in the eurozone.

Conventional monetary instruments
The ECB strives to maintain its control over the money supply and the interest rate by influencing the liquidity position of banks. This is why it makes sure that the banks have a permanent shortage of liquid assets. The banks can borrow this so-called money market deficit from the central bank at an interest rate determined by the ECB.

Money market deficit

The instruments that the ECB uses can be divided in quantity and pricing instruments (See Figure 7.11). The ECB can take quantity measures by influencing the size of the money market deficit. It can also take measures to alter the interest rate that banks have to pay. Both types of measure eventually have an effect on the costs that banks incur in their lending operations to their clients. They will pass on those costs in the form of interest. When the interest rate is high, clients borrow less and money-creating will decrease. This reduces the risk of inflation.

FIGURE 7.11 The ECB's anti-inflation policy instruments

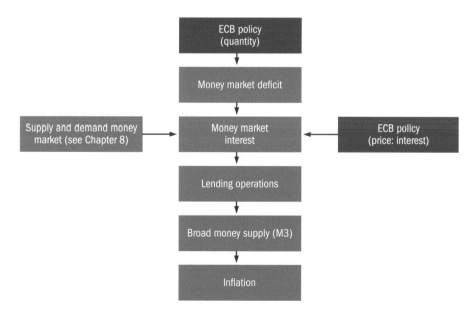

Quantity instruments: influencing the money market deficit

With its quantity policy the ECB aims at influencing the liquidity position of the banks. The main tool for this is the reserve requirement. The reserve requirement states how many liquid assets a bank has to deposit in an ECB account. The central bank determines the reserve requirement on the basis of the liquidity position of all banks in the eurozone during one month. If banks have a large amount of cash money and the money supply threatens to increase rapidly because of this, the ECB will increase the reserve requirement.

The main purpose of the reserve requirement is to make sure that banks have a constant shortage of liquid assets. In order to make up the deficit, banks have to borrow from the credit facilities of the ECB.

Sometimes it is necessary for the ECB to respond swiftly to a sudden change in the money market. This is done by trading securities or currencies on the financial markets with other banks. This is called an open market operation. An open market operation is very convenient for fine-tuning the money market deficit. If the liquidity position of banks for example, temporarily worsens, the ECB will buy securities (such as bonds) or currencies from these banks. The ECB will pay in euros, which improves the liquidity of the banks immediately. As the ECB only wishes to improve the liquidity position of the banks temporarily, there is often a reverse transaction linked to it. The securities or currencies will return to the banks in exchange for euros, which will worsen the liquidity position of the banks again.

Price instruments: setting official interest rates

Banks will make up their shortage of liquid assets by refinancing transactions. This means that banks can borrow money from the ECB with securities as collateral. The ECB determines the amount of money that banks may borrow and charges a refinancing rate for that loan. This rate is passed on by the banks to their clients. In this way the ECB keeps its grip on the interest level in the economy and can use the interest rate to combat inflation.

If banks still have a liquidity deficit after borrowing from the central bank, they will want to cover their liquidity requirements with other parties. These are usually banks with liquidity surpluses. The interest that European banks charge each other is the Euro Interbank Offered Rate (Euribor). The ECB makes sure that the liquidity requirements of the banks is so great that the Euribor is just above the refinancing rate. The refinancing rate is thus the basis for the Euribor.

The ECB determines the maximum amount that banks can borrow at the policy rate. Furthermore, banks have two permanent facilities at the ECB at their disposal: the marginal lending facility and deposit facility. These facilities can be used permanently and unlimitedly by the banks.

A bank that has not fully covered its liquidity deficit with the ECB by the refinancing facility can draw on the marginal lending facility. The ECB automatically covers bank deficits by providing additional loans. For this the banks pay the marginal lending rate. This rate is considerably higher than Euribor and banks will therefore borrow the deficit from the interbank market as soon as possible (usually the next day). Because banks may make unlimited use of the marginal lending facility, the marginal lending rate represents the ceiling for interest rates on the money market.

Margin notes:

Reserve requirement

Open market operation

Fine-tuning

Refinancing rate

Euro Interbank Offered Rate (Euribor)

Permanent facilities

Marginal lending rate

Meeting of the Governing Council of the ECB in Frankfurt

Source: ECB

A bank with a temporary surplus of liquid assets can make use of the
deposit facility of the central bank. We have seen that as a rule, the reserve
requirement causes banks to be in the red with the ECB. There is, however,
the possibility of averaging. The amount that banks have in their reserve
account is allowed to vary. At the beginning of the reserve period, banks
often deposit more in their accounts than is strictly necessary. They may
therefore have a very temporary surplus in liquid assets at the end of the
reserve period. This temporary surplus they can put into a deposit account
with the ECB. This makes the deposit rate the absolute floor for interest   **Deposit rate**
rates on the money market (Euribor).

The refinancing rate, the marginal lending rate and the deposit rate are the
official interest rates available to the ECB. The marginal lending rate and the   **Official interest**
deposit rate form the highest and lowest interest rates respectively. Within   **rates**
this interest corridor, the ECB manages the money market interest via the
refinancing rate (see Figure 7.12).

As shown in Figure 7.12, the market rate in the euro zone was below the
policy rate for quite some time, due to the crisis. During the crisis, the ECB
opened the money gates to support the banks. Banks received - against
collateral - unlimited credit and also for a much longer period than usual.
The mutual trust between banks was so low that the interbank market had
almost come to a standstill. Banks preferred to deposit their money with the
ECB rather than lend it to another bank. Under these special circumstances,
the Euribor could remain for a long period of time below the policy rate.

FIGURE 7.12 Official interest rates and Euribor (2005-2017)

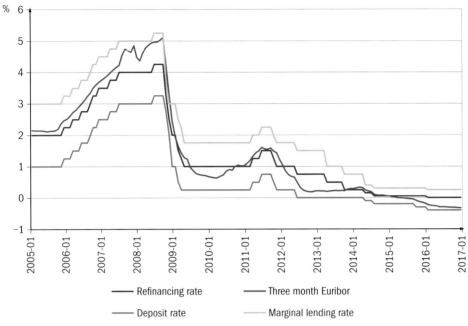

Source: ECB (www.ecb.int)

Unconventional monetary instruments

Deep recession

In a deep recession the usual monetary policy is inadequate. The official rate is then so low that a further decrease is not possible or worthwhile. Despite the low official rate, the interest rate in certain credit markets can remain high, because during a deep recession banks tend to avoid credit risks as much as possible. When they do grant new credit the client will have to pay a high interest rate.

Deflation

If monetary policy is no longer effective during an economic crisis there is a real chance of deflation occurring. Deflation is disastrous for economic growth. When prices drop, consumers postpone purchases, causing demand, production and prices to fall even further. The central banks want to avoid deflation at all costs and in achieving that sometimes resort to unconventional measures. The exceptional consequences of the GFC of 2008-2009 have led to unconventional monetary policy all over the world. The British and the American central banks (the Federal Reserve) resorted

Quantitative easing

to quantitative easing. This means that the central bank purchases securities (mostly bonds) from banks with new money that it creates electronically. The new money finds its way into the economy via the banks. As a result, expenditures and economic growth increase. On top of that, the additional money ensures a greater availability of a particular currency on the currency market. This causes the exchange rate to go down. A cheaper currency stimulates export, thus ensuring additional economic growth.

Credit easing

The European Central Bank resorted to credit easing. With this method, the central bank buys securities stocks from a selected segment of the financial markets with new money that it creates electronically. If the ECB for example, wishes to keep mortgage loans going, it buys mortgage bonds from banks. The additional money injected into the mortgage market by the ECB, will lead to a lower mortgage rate. In this way the central bank stimulates mortgage lending specifically. The central bank can then decide to absorb the money that the banks receive for the mortgage bonds – for instance, by selling other bonds to the banks – or not. Credit easing can therefore be accompanied by an increase in the amount of money though this is not inevitable. Initially, the ECB did 'mop up' the extra money. Later, it turned to quantitative expansion at a major scale. At one point, the ECB purchased no less than €80 million in securities per month, using new scriptural money. Quantitative easing is a contested practice. Its opponents argue that it is inadequate. During a crisis in particular, the money ends up in a 'real' economy hardly, if at all. You can pump as much money into an economy as you like, but if the people who are part of that economy will not use it to buy things, your efforts will have been for nothing. In fact, you run the risk of making things worse if people start to use the extra money to buy shares, real estate, or resources. That sort of thing leads to bubbles in the prices of these investment objects. And if those bubbles should burst, you would be looking at a new crisis.

Bubbles

The quantitative easing by the ECB did result in a lower exchange rate for the Euro. This stimulated economic growth within the Eurozone at the cost of the economic growth outside it. This is another contested issue. Foreign central banks might take a page from the ECB, thinking: 'Two can play that game'. A currency war, with countries individually trying to escape the crisis through export using a cheaper currency, would be right around the corner.

Currency war

Lastly, there is substantial criticism aimed at the purchasing of government bonds of countries with large government deficits. The purchasing scheme allows these countries to more readily access money, decreasing the need for them to work on their government finances. In that way, the ECB undermines the budgetary discipline of countries within the Eurozone. Moreover, the ECB's purchasing scheme attracts more and more high-risk government bonds. Possible losses incurred on these bonds are suffered by the tax payers in the Euro countries. Critics say that only elected politicians should be allowed to take such drastic financial risks on behalf of their citizens. A politician can be held accountable by the electorate; the same cannot be said for the management of the ECB.

The ECB's defence in the face of all of this criticism is simple: desperate times call for desperate measures. The president of the ECB, Mario Draghi, claims that the ECB's policy is the reason the crisis in the Eurozone did not get further out of hand.

Table 7.6 summarizes the main differences between quantitative easing and credit easing.

TABLE 7.6 Unconventional monetary policies

	Quantitative easing	Credit easing
Description	The central bank buys securities from banks to pump new money into the economy	The central bank buys specific securities in certain areas of the financial markets
Primary aim	Increasing liquidity in an economy	Influencing the interest rate and extension of credit in a particular segment of the economy
Monetary expansion	Yes	Either yes or no (depending on compensating liquidity action by the central bank)

Glossary

Active balances	The demand for money for the purpose of carrying out transactions.
Bail-in	Rescue of a bank, owing to the existing capital providers accepting their losses.
Bail-out	Rescue of a bank, owing to new capital providers, usually the government, who provide the bank with fresh capital.
Banking union	A union which centrally organises the supervision of banks and an orderly process of the rescue or bankruptcy of a bank.
BIS-ratio	Ratio of the equity of a bank and the risk-weighted assets. This ratio should be at least 8%.
Credit easing	The central bank buys securities in a specific section of the financial markets with new money it has created electronically. Its aim is to exert an influence on the interest rate and on the extension of credit in that section.
Demand deposits	Claims by the public against a monetary financial institution. These are payable on demand and can be used to make payments (in the EMU, demand deposits include deposits in foreign currencies).
Deposit rate	The interest that a bank receives if it temporarily deposits a liquidity surplus in the ECB.
ECB certificates	Negotiable financial assets issued by the ECB that are aimed at changing the money market deficit.
Entrusted funds	Debts such as demand deposits, savings deposits and time deposits that banks owe the public.
Euribor	Euro interbank offered rate. The interest that banks within the eurozone charge each other.
European central bank (ECB)	The central bank within the EMU that is responsible for formulating and implementing monetary policy.
Financial system	The way in which the money flows within an economy are organised.

Idle balances	Money held for precautionary and speculative reasons.
Interest margin	The difference between the interest that a bank receives for loans (debit interest) and the interest the bank has to pay for the deposits it has received (credit interest).
Interest	Remuneration for liquid assets that the borrower (debtor) has to pay to the lender (creditor).
Intrinsic value	The market value of the material that money is made from.
Leverage ratio	Ratio of the bank's own equity to the total assets of a bank. This ratio should be at least 3%.
Liquid assets	See Money.
Liquidity (liquidity position)	The extent to which the short term obligations of banks are covered by liquid assets.
M1	Primary liquid assets in the hands of the public.
M3	The sum of the primary and secondary liquid assets (=M1 plus claims by the public on monetary financial institutions that can be turned into money at short notice en masse and without loss of value).
Marginal lending rate	The interest that a bank pays to the ECB for a 24 hour liquidity deficit.
Means of evaluation	The possibility of measuring the value of goods and services that money offers.
Means of exchange	The possibility of dividing a transaction into two parts that money offers.
Means of storing wealth	The possibility of holding capital that money offers.
Monetary financial institutions	Financial institutions that have primary liquid assets on the credit side of their balance sheet.
Monetary policy	Policy aimed at preventing monetary variables such as the money supply having a detrimental effect on medium term economic growth.
Money	Generally accepted medium of exchange.
Money market deficit	The net debt position with the ECB of monetary financial institutions in the eurozone.

7

Mutual debt agreement	A lending operation in which a monetary financial institution agrees to an immediately payable debt (i.e. a demand deposit) and the client agrees to a debt that he has to repay after a ° period.
Nominal value	The value that is stated on money.
Official interest rates	The interest rates that the ECB uses to carry out monetary policy, the refinancing rate, the marginal lending rate and the deposit rate.
Primary liquid assets	See M1.
Profitability	The relationship between profits and equity capital.
Quantitative easing	The central bank purchases securities from banks with new money that it creates electronically in order to increase the amount of money.
Reference value for M3	The rate of growth of M3 that is compatible with medium-term price stability.
Refinance rate	The interest that banks have to pay for credit from the ECB to cover their money market deficit.
Reserve requirement	The amount of money that banks in the eurozone are obliged to keep with the ECB.
Secondary liquid assets	The claims by the public on monetary financial institutions that can be turned into money at short notice, en masse and without loss of value.
Solvency	The extent to which a bank can guarantee payment from its capital base for debtor losses.
Systematically important bank	A bank, which is crucial for the functioning of a financial system in a country, due to its size.
Transaction costs	Costs that are associated with the exchange of goods and services.
Velocity of circulation	Number of times a year that a unit of currency is used to purchase goods and services that are part of the GDP.

8

Money and capital markets

8

The main issues to be addressed in this chapter are as follows:
- What factors have an influence on the interest rate?
- How can a company protect itself against unfavourable interest rate developments?

If companies, consumers or the government need money, they approach the money and capital markets. Section 8.1 will deal with the way these markets work and will also deal with the difference between the money market and the capital market.

If a company needs money for a short period only, it will approach the money market. This market will be treated in Section 8.2, which examines the factors that determine the money market or short-term interest rate.

If companies need money for a period longer than two years, they will approach the capital market. Section 8.3 deals with the capital market and the factors that determine the capital market or long-term interest rate.

The term structure of interest rates, the relationship between the interest rate of a loan and the remaining time to maturity is the subject of Section 8.4. In normal circumstances, the long-term interest rate is higher than the short-term interest rate. This situation is termed a normal term structure of interest rates. It does occasionally happen, however, that the term structure is reversed: the long-term interest rate is lower than the short-term interest rate. Section 8.4 will deal with the circumstances in which this situation occurs.

Fluctuations in the interest rate can put companies under risk. A rise in the interest rate could cause sales to decrease, or costs to increase, causing a lowering of profits. The risk of interest rate fluctuations having an effect on the future profits of a company is called the interest rate risk. Section 8.5 deals with the factors that determine interest rate risk and how a company can minimise the risk.

8

Businesses invest in production resources such as buildings and machines. They often have to take out a loan to buy these capital goods. The amount a bank will provide depends on the interest rate. The higher the interest rate, the higher the future interest expenses and the lower the amount the business can borrow.
When the business has obtained a loan it will have to choose an interest type. Should it choose a variable interest or a fixed interest and if it chooses a fixed interest, for what period of time? The choice of either of these interest types depends on the expected interest rate movements. If management thinks that the interest rate will rise sharply in the short term it will choose a fixed interest rate and vice versa.
During the period to maturity of a loan the interest rate can rise or fall. A business with a variable interest rate will seek to protect itself against an interest rate rise. To do this they can make use of a number of interest rate instruments that the banks offer.

8.1 Functions and classification of the money and capital markets

What the functions of the money and capital markets are is dealt with in Section 8.1.1, and how they can be classified is treated in Section 8.1.2.

8.1.1   Functions of the money and capital markets
The money and capital markets are the markets on which (debt) securities are exchanged for money. Market parties that need money offer debt securities (bonds, for example) and demand liquid assets in return; market parties that have a surplus of money buy these (debt) securities in exchange for liquid assets (see Figure 8.1). The interest rate insures that demand equals supply on the financial markets.

FIGURE 8.1 Supply and demand on the financial markets

The main function of the financial markets is to bring together the deficits and surpluses of liquid assets within an economy. This is illustrated in Figure 8.2, which represents a simplified balance sheet of a financial institution.

FIGURE 8.2 The functions of money and capital markets

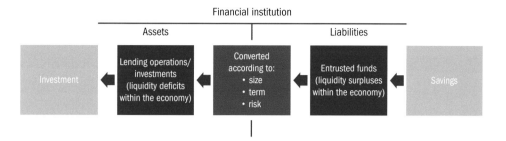

Market parties with a surplus of money (savings) entrust this surplus to financial institutions. With these entrusted funds, credit can be extended to market parties that are short of money. Monetary financial institutions (and they only) can also extend credit through a mutual debt agreement. Financial institutions bring the deficits and surpluses in liquidity in an economy together in the way that has been described. They match the needs of the lender in terms of size, time span and risk with those of the borrower. This may, for example, involve financial institutions converting a number of small savings deposits by individual customers into large loans to companies.

8.1.2 Classification of the money and capital markets

There are two criteria for classifying money and capital markets: residual maturity and whether there is a trade in new or existing financial assets. The term of a financial asset can vary from one day to a very long time indeed (in, for example, the case of shares and perpetual bonds). The residual maturity of the financial asset is used as a criterion for dividing the market into the money market and the capital market. Financial assets with a residual maturity of less than two years are traded on the money market. It is the remaining maturity that is the determining factor: ten-year bonds with a residual maturity of one year fall under the money market. The money market is dealt with in Section 8.2.

Money market

Financial assets that have a residual maturity of more than two years are traded on the capital markets. The capital market matches long-term liquidity deficits and surpluses. Companies often call on the capital markets to finance their investments. The capital markets are the subject of Section 8.3.

Capital market

The second criterion for classifying the money and capital markets is whether the financial assets are new or existing.
The primary market deals with newly created financial assets. One example of a transaction on the primary market is the emission of shares or bonds. Existing financial assets (mainly securities) are traded on the secondary market. The trade in shares on the stock exchange is a good example of trade on the secondary market. The secondary market plays an important role in the financial system. It enables market parties with a temporary surplus of liquid assets to buy securities with a long maturity, such as bonds. After all, long-term securities can be turned into money at any time on the secondary market.

Primary market

Secondary market

8.2 The money market

The money market is the market for financial assets with a remaining maturity of two years or less. The money market consists of two parts.

Wholesale money market

The wholesale money market is only accessible to big market parties such as banks, the government, institutional investors (pension funds and life insurance companies) and some very large companies. A characteristic of this mainly interbank market is the size of both the market parties and the traded amounts. The interest rate on the wholesale money market is the

Euribor

Euribor (Euro interbank offered rate). As can be deduced from the name, the Euribor is the interest rate that banks charge each other. The interest rate on loans made to large companies and on the deposits they make is based on the Euribor. The interest rate movements on the wholesale market are dealt with in Section 8.2.1.

Retail money market

Small and medium-sized businesses and consumers have no access to the wholesale money market. They use the retail money market. The interest rates on the retail money market are the credit and debit interest rates of

Credit and debit interest rates

banks. The interest rate movements on the retail money market are dealt with in Section 8.2.2.

8.2.1   The wholesale money market

Financial institutions have a wholesale function on the money market. They make an inventory of the liquidity surpluses and deficits of their clients. Balancing these two amounts will produce a net deficit or a net surplus. If there is a net surplus, the bank can deposit the surplus liquid assets with another bank. If there is a net deficit the bank will have to borrow liquid assets from another bank. If all of the banks are faced with a net liquid assets deficit at the same time, they will have to borrow from the ECB (see Chapter 7). We shall now look at the factors that determine the interest rate level on the money market.

The Euribor is the interest rate that banks charge each other for short-term loans. There are different Euribor rates depending on the period to maturity

Three-month Euribor

of the loan. The three-month Euribor is usually used as an indicator for the level of the money market or short term interest rate (see Figure 8.3).

The level of the money market interest rate is determined by the demand for and the supply of money for a short term. If the demand for money increases, the interest rate will rise; if the supply of money increases, the interest rate will drop. In order to explain or forecast the level of the money market interest rate we need to know what factors determine the demand and supply of money in the short term.

There are three groups of factors that determine the level of interest:
1 Monetary policy
2 International capital flows
3 Economic fundamentals.

Monetary policy

The main determining factor for the level of money market interest is monetary policy. In Chapter 7 it was said that banks constantly have to make use of the lending facilities of the ECB. Over these loans they pay the refinancing rate. Under normal circumstances, the Euribor will be just above that official interest rate. Figure 8.3 illustrates this very well.

FIGURE 8.3 Three month Euribor and the official interest rate (2001-2017)

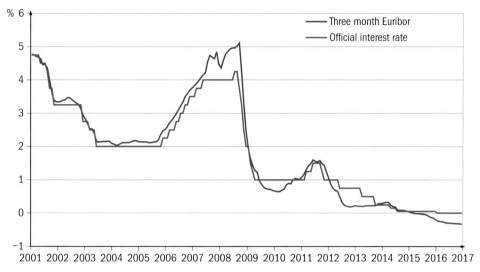

Source: ECB (www.ecb.int)

The Euribor is therefore highly dependent on the objectives of the monetary policy of the ECB. The priority that the ECB gives to achieving price stability results in the fluctuations of the official interest rates, depending largely on inflation expectations. If the ECB expects inflation to rise (for instance, because the supply of money is rapidly increasing) it will increase its interest rates. The interest rate level on the money market will also then rise.

TEST 8.1
Investors find it important that the central bank can make monetary policy independent of political institutions. What reasons can you think of for this?

Although the short term interest rate is mainly dependent on monetary policy, it is also influenced by international capital flows and economic fundamentals. International capital flows make the difference between the Euribor and the refinancing rate larger or smaller. If short-term capital flows out of the eurozone, the supply on the European money market will decrease and the Euribor will rise. On the other hand, the Euribor will drop if short-term money flows into the euro area. _{International capital flows}

Capital flows between countries develop mainly as a result of international interest rate developments and exchange rate expectations. If, for instance, the short term interest rate in the USA rises, investors will decide to invest more short-term capital in the USA. This will cause the supply of liquid assets on the European money markets to decrease, which will cause a rise in the interest rate. A similar capital flow will occur if international investors expect a rise in the exchange rate of the dollar compared to the euro. _{International interest rate developments}

The direction of the international capital flow is also determined by political and economic news that affects the interest rate expectations of market parties. Statements by monetary authorities on economic developments have an important effect on the interest rate expectations of the market (otherwise known as 'market sentiment'). If, for instance, the president of the ECB says that the rate of inflation in the eurozone is developing _{Political and economic news}

favourably, market parties will expect a lowering of the interest rate in the near future. Market parties with a liquidity surplus will try to put their money into a deposit before the lowering of the interest rate takes effect. Market parties with a liquidity deficit will, on the other hand, want to wait until the interest rate has been lowered before taking out a loan. The statement by the ECB president will cause supply on the money market to increase, demand to decrease and the interest rate to drop. The expected interest rate development thereby becomes a reality.

8

Economic fundamentals

Economic fundamentals have an indirect effect on the money market interest rate. The monetary policy of the ECB is fully dependent on one economic fundamental alone, namely inflation. Inflation is, in turn, influenced by economic variables such as the business cycle and the wage costs. The central bank uses these economic variables as the basis of its interest rate policies. Table 8.1 summarises the factors that determine the interest rate on the money markets.

TABLE 8.1 Determining factors for the money market interest rate

Category	Determining interest factors
Monetary policy	Objectives central bank
	Official interest rates ↑
Economic fundamentals	Inflation (expected)
International capital flows	Foreign money market interest rate
	Short-term exchange rate expectations
	Political and economic news

TEST 8.2
Assume that the ECB has announced that employment in the eurozone is increasing at such a rate that there is a danger of labour shortage. What effect is this news likely to have on interest rate expectations?

8.2.2   The retail money market

The wholesale money market is only accessible for large market parties. Smaller market parties such as private individuals and small and medium sized businesses deposit temporary liquidity surpluses with banks in the form of short term deposits, short savings deposits and the like. They cover temporary liquidity deficits by taking out short-term bank credit.

Bank credit and debit interest
The interest rates on the retail money market are the debit and credit rates of banks. The bank interest rates are determined by three factors:
1 The Euribor
2 The interest margin
3 A credit risk surcharge.

Interest margin

The Euribor rate is the basis for bank credit and debit interest rates (see Figure 8.4). The credit rate is lower than the Euribor rate and the debit rate is higher. The difference between the debit interest and the credit interest is the interest margin that banks receive. The interest margin depends largely on the intensity of competition on the financial markets. If competition increases, the interest margin of banks will decrease. To take an example, during recent times, large financial institutions have entered the savings market via the Internet, among other things. A number of these new competitors do not have a large network of offices and the costs associated with them. For this reason they are able to give a higher interest rate on demand savings deposits. In order to keep their share of the savings market, the general banks have to go along with the competitive battle, resulting in a decrease in their interest margin.

FIGURE 8.4 A view of the debit interest of banks

The surcharge that the individual borrower has to pay will depend on his financial position and the securities that he provides to the bank. A company with a strong financial position and business assets as security will have a high credit standing. If so, the bank's credit risk surcharge can be low. A customer who has already taken out a number of loans and who cannot provide the bank with security will be in a different position. Such a client has a lesser credit standing, which means that he will have to pay a large credit risk surcharge.

Surcharge

8.3 The capital market

If a company needs money for an extended period it approaches the capital market. This market trades in financial assets with a residual maturity of more than two years. Section 8.3.1 treats the various segments of the capital market. The long-term interest rate is the subject of Section 8.3.2.

8.3.1   Market segments

The essential division within the capital market is between the official and the private market (see Table 8.2).

TABLE 8.2 Capital market segments

Official market	Private market
Shares	Private loans
Bonds	Home mortgage loans
Bank and mortgage bonds	Real estate investments

The official market (the stock exchange) trades mainly in shares and bonds. A share is a certificate of participation in a joint stock company. A shareholder is co-owner of the company and receives – depending on the company's results – an annual share in the profits, called dividends.

Official market

Share

Bond

A bond is a debt security that is part of a loan issued by a government, company or institution. The bondholder receives a fixed interest payment and gets his money back at the end of the maturity period. There are also bank and mortgage bonds that are issued by banks and mortgage banks.

Private market

On the private market, transactions are made by direct negotiation between lender and borrower. If, for instance, a company wants bank credit, they will negotiate the lending conditions jointly. These conditions, including the interest rate, the repayment terms and the security provided, are usually not made public.

The stock exchange differs from the private market in several ways. In the first place, the trade in shares and bonds is public, which means that information about demand, supply and prices on the stock exchange is available to all parties. This makes the stock exchange a very transparent one. Lending conditions on the private market are not made public, which limits availability of information about size, price and maturing time of transactions on the private market considerably.

Public trading

Negotiability

The second difference is the negotiability of financial assets within both market segments. A bond loan of a hundred million euros is divided into certificates of debt of a smaller amount (a thousand euros, say) on the stock exchange. The number of subscribers to a bond loan may be very large. On the other hand, a private loan of a hundred million euros will be arranged between a set number of parties and the loan will not be split up into smaller units. The negotiability of a bond loan of a hundred million euros is clearly greater than that of a private loan of equal size. It is, after all, easier to find buyers for bonds for a multiple of a thousand euros than it is to find a single party to take over a private loan of a hundred million euros.

Trading Floor Deutsche Bank in Frankfurt

Price of the financial asset

The third difference is the way in which the various market segments arrive at their prices. Prices on the stock exchange are based on two things: the price of the financial asset and the nominal yield. Since shares and bonds are traded on the secondary market, the price fluctuates. This will provide a profit or a loss to the owner of these shares and bonds. The original issuers of the shares and bonds also provide a nominal yield in the form of a dividend or interest. On the private market, the only yield is the interest. The financial assets on this market are not traded under the auspices of an official exchange and there is no official quotation.

The following sections require an understanding of the various types of yield on the capital market. These types of yield will be explained first.

Nominal yield

Capital market yields

A share has a nominal value. This is the value that is given on the share certificate. The actual price of the share is different to the nominal value. The price is the result of supply and demand on the stock exchange market. The annual profits paid on a share is termed the dividend. If we divide the dividend by the stock price we will obtain the dividend yield on a share. This yield and the possible price gain on a share jointly determine the investment result on a share.

Nominal value

Dividend

State of the Netherlands

1/2% bond 2016 due 15 July 2026
re-opening

Issued under the authorization to contract bonds borne by the State of the Netherlands, given by the Comptabiliteitswet 2001
(Government Accounts Act 2001)

Issuance method	**Tap Auction**
Issuance period	**8 November 2016; starting from 10:00 CET**
Payment date	**10 November 2016**

Bond	1/2% bond 2016 due 15 July 2026 issued by the State of the Netherlands
Interest	1/2% per annum
Interest due date	15 July 2016 and annually thereafter on 15 July
Initial maturity	10 years and 113 days
Remaining maturity	9 years and 247 days starting from 10 November 2016
Initial payment date	24 March 2016
Redemption date	on 15 July 2026 the principal of the bond will be made redeemable at par; early redemption either in whole or in part is not permitted
Issue price	the issue price will be announced via MTS Netherlands by 10.00 a.m. on 8 November 2016 and may be revised at any time
Announcement	the total accepted amount and the average auction price will be announced after the close of the issue

Announcement of a new government bond of The Netherlands (www.dutchstate.nl)

Like shares, bonds have a face or nominal value and a market price. The face value of a bond is the amount that is printed on it. It is also the same amount as that which will be paid out at the end of the maturity period. The price of a bond is determined by supply and demand on the bond market. A bond with a face value of €1,000 can thus have a price of €1,040.

Coupon rate   The interest that is paid annually on a bond is termed the coupon rate. An 8% bond with a nominal value of €1,000 brings in a coupon rate of €80. Because the bond price may vary during the bond's lifetime, the coupon yield may differ from the coupon rate.

Coupon yield   The coupon yield is calculated by dividing the annual interest receipts by the bond price. If a bond with a face value of €1,000 and a coupon rate of 8% has a market price of €1,040 at a particular time, the coupon yield will be 7.69%. The coupon yield and the dividends yield are somewhat similar in this regard. In both cases, the remuneration received in a given year and the investment made to obtain it are taken into consideration.

There is, however, an important difference between shares and bonds. Bonds are redeemed at the end of their maturity against their face value and shares are not. If the bond price is lower than the nominal value at a certain moment, the investor who buys it will make a profit when it is redeemed.

Yield to maturity   The yield to maturity or market yield of such a bond is greater than its coupon yield because of the redemption profit. The reverse holds for a bond with a price that is higher than its nominal value. The yield to maturity of a bond is equal to the sum of the coupon yield and the redemption yield. Example 8.1 shows how the different yields of a bond can be calculated.

- -

EXAMPLE 8.1

Yield on bonds

The government issued a bond loan on 1 April 2015. The nominal value of the bonds is €1,000. The period to maturity of the loan is six years. It will be redeemed in full on 1 April 2021. The coupon rate on the bond is 8%. On 1 April 2017, the market price of the bond is €1,040.

Calculation of the coupon yield and the yield to maturity.
An investor who buys this bond will have to pay €1,040 on 1 April 2017 to receive an annual coupon rate of €80. The coupon yield can be calculated by dividing the annual interest (€80) by the invested amount (€1,040). The coupon yield therefore equals 7.69%.

The bond loan is redeemed four years from now (on 1 April 2021). The bondholder will receive the face value of the bond (€1,000) even though he paid €1,040 for it. During the remaining period of maturity, he suffers a redemption loss of €40. If we divide that by the time to maturity the annual loss is €10. This annual loss we divide by the invested amount of €1,040. The redemption yield will therefore equal –0.96%. The yield to maturity of the bond is the sum of the coupon yield and the redemption yield: 7.69% – 0.96% = 6.73%

- -

The calculation described in the example is an approximation of the yield to maturity. If we want to calculate the yield to maturity exactly we have to take the present value of future interest payments and redemption of the principal amount into account. The present value takes the liquidity preferences of investors into account. This implies simply that investors value an interest payment of €80 now higher than an interest payment of €80 in, say, four years' time. If we take this into account, the yield to maturity in the previous example will turn out to be 6.82%. A calculation using the present value is beyond the scope of this book. The simple way of calculating the yield to maturity suffices to understand interest developments.

The bond market eliminates differences between the yield to maturity of newly issued bonds and existing bonds with the same period to maturity. This is explained in Example 8.2.

8

EXAMPLE 8.2

Yield to maturity and the market interest rate

On 1 February 2016 an investor buys a newly issued bond of €1,000 with a coupon rate of 6% and a maturity of 10 years. One year later the interest rate has dropped and the market interest for bonds with a maturity term of 9 years is now 5%. The interest payments on these bonds is therefore €50, while existing bonds with the same maturity term will pay out an interest of €60 per year. The demand for 6% bonds will increase and the price of these bonds will rise. The price rise will result in a lower coupon yield and the yield to maturity on the 6% bonds will drop. The yield to maturity of the 6% bonds will eventually finish up somewhere near the market interest of 5%.

We can therefore draw the conclusion that a drop in the market interest rate will cause the prices of existing bonds with a higher coupon rate to increase. The yield to maturity of these bonds will therefore drop to about the rate of the current market interest.

TEST 8.3
What effect will a rise in the long-term interest have on stock prices?

8.3.2   The long-term interest rate

There is no single long-term interest rate. The interest rate depends on the period to maturity, the securities offered, the credit standing of the loan applicant and so on. There are, in fact, several interest rates, depending on the conditions of the capital transfer. Nevertheless, for the sake of convenience, the term 'long term interest rate' is used. It is, however, based on an indicator. In the European Union, the market yield on the most recent ten-year government bond is used as an indicator for the long-term interest rate. The reason for this is that the government is in most countries the main issuer of bonds. Government bonds are also easily negotiable and have a negligible credit risk, at least in the industrialised countries. The interest rate on government bonds forms the bottom interest rate because of its negligible credit risk. Companies that want to issue a ten-year loan will have to pay the long-term interest rate plus a surcharge that is related to their credit standing. The changes in the long-term interest rate are illustrated in Figure 8.5.

Market yield on the most recent ten-year government bond

FIGURE 8.5 Long term interest rate in the euro area and the United States (% per annum, 1999–2016)

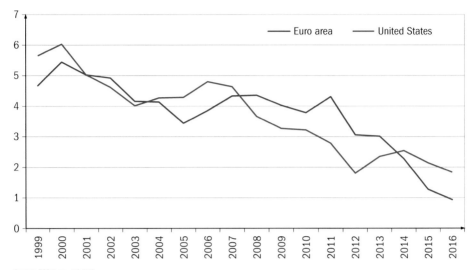

Source: ECB (www.ecb.int)

Unlike the short-term interest, the long-term interest rate depends mainly on supply and demand and not on monetary policy. This means that of the three types of interest rate determining factors that are mentioned in Section 8.2 the economic fundamentals and the international capital flows have a particularly important effect on the long-term interest rate. In small open economies such as that of Denmark, the main determining factors for the interest rate are the international capital flows. In larger, relatively closed economies such as those of the eurozone or the USA, domestic economic development is the main determining factor. In the following we will treat the influence on the long-term interest rate of economic developments, international capital flows and monetary policy.

Economic fundamentals

In large economies like the Eurozone or the USA the interest rate is mainly determined by domestic economic developments. The two main economic fundamentals behind the long-term interest rate are as follows:

1 The propensity to save and invest within an economy
2 The expected inflation

1 The propensity to save and invest

In the long term, the interest rate on long-term debt securities is a reflection of the propensity to save and invest in an economy. If – other things equal – there is little saving or a lot of investing going on in a country, the long-term interest rate will be high.

The private sector's (households and businesses) readiness to save and
Business cycle   invest is to a large extent dependent on the phase of the business cycle. During a phase of economic boom, the demand for money by households and businesses is on the increase. Demand on the capital market will

increase and consequently the interest rate will rise. Conversely, during an economic recession, households and businesses will spend less, causing the demand for money and the interest rate to decrease.

The government budget reflects the propensity to save or investing by the government. If the government runs a budget deficit it has to borrow on the capital market. This will cause the long-term interest rate to rise (assuming all other things remain the same). In the eurozone, the influence of the government on the long-term interest rate is dependent on the budget balances of nineteen national governments. There is a danger that the government of a country with an extreme deficit will cause an interest rate rise in the whole of the eurozone. To avoid this happening, the Stability Pact stipulates that EU members must aim for a budget balance somewhere in the vicinity of the equilibrium (see Chapter 10). *Government budget*

An important indicator of the propensity for saving and investing within a country is the balance on current account of the balance of payments. This balance represents the national savings balance of a country (see chapter 5). A surplus on the current account means that national savings exceed national investment. A country with a long-term surplus on the current account has therefore a relatively large supply of liquid assets, which may keep the interest rate low. *Balance on current account of the balance of payments*

2 The expected inflation

The long term interest rate is very sensitive to the expected inflation. Investors tie up their liquid assets for a long time on the capital market. Inflation reduces the purchasing power of the main capital and the future interest returns of a bond. Bondholders demand a higher interest rate to compensate the loss of purchasing power. Countries with a high inflation rate therefore, have a high long-term interest rate.

International capital flows

Capital flows have a considerable effect on the interest rate. The inflow and outflow of capital is mainly dependent upon international interest rate differences. *International interest rate differences*

In the eurozone, interest in the USA is especially important. If there is an increase in the interest rate in the USA, the market parties will invest a larger part of their money in the USA. The smaller supply of liquid assets on the European capital market will also cause the interest rate to rise in the euro area. In practice there is therefore usually little difference between the long-term interest rates of the USA and Europe (see Figure 8.5).

International capital flows are not only affected by differences in interest rates between countries, but also by differences in risk.

An important risk in international investment is the currency risk. For a foreign investor in the euro area, a depreciation of the euro will mean that principal and interest receipts are worth less in his or her own currency. Exchange rate expectations have an important influence on the long-term interest rate, therefore. If international investors expect a depreciation of the euro, they will demand a higher interest rate on the European capital market. *Currency risk*

Finally, just as on the money market, economic or political news plays an important role. Unfavourable economic or political news leads to an outflow of capital, causing the interest rate to rise. *Economic or political news*

TEST 8.4

Assume that American investors expect the euro exchange rate to drop in relation to the dollar. What influence is this likely to have on the price of bonds and the long-term interest rate in the euro area?

Monetary policy

The central bank exerts a major influence on interest rates on the money market. On the capital market this influence is much less. The influence of monetary policy on the long-term interest rate is indirect: through inflation expectations. It is the main task of the ECB to combat inflation and inflation expectations. The more effective the ECB is in doing so, the lower the long-term interest rate. Monetary policy credibility plays a major role in the inflation expectations of investors, and therefore also for the long-term interest rate.

Monetary policy credibility

Table 8.3 sets out the factors that determine the long-term interest rate.

TABLE 8.3 Factors that determine long-term interest rates

Category	Interest-determining factors
Economic fundamentals	Propensity to save and invest • Business cycle • Government deficit • Current account balance • Expected inflation
International capital flows	Foreign long-term interest rate Long-term exchange rate expectations Political and economic news
Monetary policy	Credibility inflation control

The factors shown in Table 8.3 determine the average long term interest rate in the eurozone. Unlike the short term interest rate, the long-term interest rate is not uniform throughout the whole of the eurozone. The difference in long-term interest rates between two countries within the eurozone reflects the difference in bond market liquidity and the difference in the financial position of the government. Countries in the eurozone with a large bond market (Germany, for example) have a greater market liquidity than countries with a small bond market (Portugal, for example). Because of the larger size of the German bond market, this means that the negotiability of government bonds is greater than in Portugal. Investors in Portugal will demand a higher interest rate in compensation for the lesser negotiability of Portuguese bonds.

Market liquidity

The financial position of the government determines its credit rating. If, for instance, the government has a large debt, the credit rating will drop. The chance that a government will run into financial problems increases at the rate that interest and repayment obligations relating to the debt increase. Investors will want to see a higher debtor's risk on a loan to a government with an unfavourable financial position compensated by a higher interest rate.

Financial position

All big market parties have a credit rating on the financial markets which indicates their creditworthiness. Specialised institutions as Moody's or

Credit rating

Standard and Poor's determine the credit rating on the basis of an analysis of the financial position of the market party. This rating is very important, because it determines against what interest rate the market party can borrow. Table 8.4 sets out the credit rating of the governments in the eurozone, the government debt, the government balance and the long-term interest rate.

TABLE 8.4 Credit rating and long-term interest rates in a number of countries in the eurozone (January 2017)

	Rating[1]			Government finance (2017)		Interest rate
	Standard & Poor's (VS)	Moody's (VS)	Dagong (China)	Government debt (% GDP)	Government balance (% GDP)	
Germany	AAA	Aaa	AA+	66	0.4	0.25
Netherlands	AAA	Aaa	AA+	61	-0.3	0.44
Finland	AA+	Aa1	AA+	67	-2.5	0.46
Austria	AA+	Aa1	AA+	81	-1.3	0.53
Belgium	AA	Aa3	A+	107	-2.3	0.61
France	AA	Aa2	A	97	-2.9	0.75
Ireland	A+	A3	BBB+	74	-0.5	0.84
Spain	BBB+	Baa2	BBB+	100	-3.8	1.44
Italy	BBB-	Baa2	BBB-	133	-2.4	1.89
Portugal	BB+	Ba1	BB	130	-2.2	3.74
Greece	B-	Caa3	CC	179	-1.0	6.94

[1] The highest credit rating is Triple A, followed by AA, which is divided by Moody's into three categories (the higher the number, the lower the credit rating)

Sources: www.standardandpoors.com, www.moodys.com, en.dagongcredit.com, European Union *Economic Forecasts, autumn* 2016, European Central Bank (www.ecb.int)

TEST 8.5
Germany has a higher government debt expressed as a percentage of the GDP than the Netherlands. Nevertheless, the German government's credit rating is higher. Try to explain why.

Debt crisis in the eurozone
The influence that the credit rating of a government has on the interest on capital became very clear during the debt crisis in the eurozone of 2009 and 2010. During these years the government finances of Greece in particular, but also of Portugal, Ireland and Spain, got completely out of control. This was partly due to the economic crisis of 2009, but also to a lack of budgetary discipline. Investors started to doubt the tenability of government finances in Greece, Portugal, Ireland and Spain and consequently demanded an ever-increasing interest on the government bonds of these countries. Because of the higher interest rate, government expenditure in these countries increased even more, with the danger of a vicious circle with ever-increasing government deficits.

Lack of budgetary discipline

Investors in the eurozone went searching for the most creditworthy governments. They found them in Germany and the Netherlands. The difference in interest rate between these countries and the problem countries kept on increasing as a result (see figure 8.6). Because of increasing differences in interest rate within the eurozone, confidence in the euro decreased. Investors seriously reckoned on the possibility of the eurozone falling apart. This caused the exchange rate of the euro to drop from $1.50 in December 2009 to $1.20 in May 2010.

Increasing differences in interest rate

FIGURE 8.6 Long term interest rates in Germany, The Netherlands, Portugal, Ireland, Greece and Spain (2007–2017)

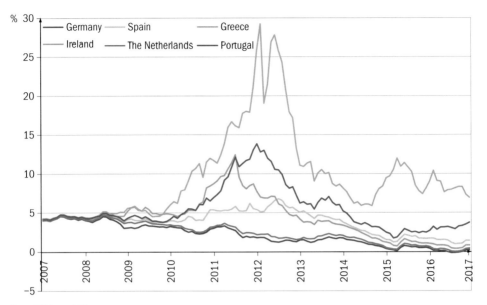

Source: ECB (www.ecb.int)

The strong euro countries refused to come to the aid of the weak ones initially. This was to avoid a situation in which tax payers in countries with a strong budgetary discipline would pay for problems in countries with a weak budgetary discipline. At the end of April 2010 the Greek government threatened to go bankrupt. This would not only hit Greece, but also many banks that had invested in Greek government bonds, potentially starting a new banking crisis (following on from that of 2007 and 2008). The Greek crisis also threatened to have a flow-on effect in other euro countries. At the beginning of May 2010, the European heads of state made, in co-operation with the International Monetary Fund, money available for euro countries in financial difficulties. This gave the problem countries time to regularise their financial affairs.

As shown in Figure 8.6, the differences in interest rates in the euro zone have become much smaller since the height of the credit crunch, and indicates that international investors are increasingly confident that problem countries will be able to regularise their affairs. Ireland is a prime example of this. Nevertheless, the restoration of confidence is fragile and very sensitive to unfavourable political and economic news.

8.4 The interest rate structure

The short-term interest rate was dealt with in Section 8.2 and the long term interest rate in Section 8.3. The difference between the two interest rates is expressed in the term structure of interest rates. The following section deals with a normal and an inverse term structure of interest rates.

8.4.1　Normal term structure of interest rates

Interest represents remuneration for making funds available. This remuneration consists of two elements. It represents both payment for making liquid assets available, and it is a fee which the lender receives for running a risk.

The remuneration for making liquid assets available (the liquidity premium) becomes higher proportional to the remaining time to maturity of the loan. The lender demands a higher liquidity premium for long-term loans because he will have no access to his money for a long time.

Liquidity premium

The risk that a lender runs consists of several elements. The debtor may not be able to repay his debts. Another uncertain factor is the level of inflation in the remaining time to maturity of the loan. Fluctuations in the rate of inflation will cause the real value of interest and repayments to become uncertain. The longer the term of the loan the higher these risks will be. The risk premium that a lender demands will therefore also be higher the longer the term of the loan. Both aspects of the interest payments – the liquidity premium and the risk premium –increase with the length of the term of the loan. This is why, under normal circumstances, the long-term interest rate will be higher than that the short term interest rate.

Risk premium

The term structure of interest rates is the relationship between the remaining time to maturity of debt securities and the interest rate. The yield curve is the graphical representation of the term structure of interest rates (see Figure 8.7). The yield curve is normal if the interest rate increases with the remaining time to maturity.

Normal yield curve

FIGURE 8.7　The euro area yield curve in January 2017

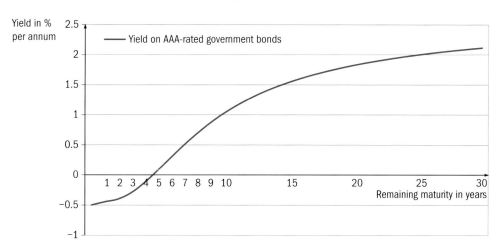

Source: ECB (www.ecb.int), January 2017

8.4.2　Inverse term structure of interest rates

The term structure of interest rates is usually normal. But sometimes the short-term interest rate is higher than the long-term rate. This is called an inverse term structure of interest rates and it is characterised by a yield curve with a downward slope. An inverse term structure of interest rates is associated with the interest expectations on the market.

Expectations and term structure of interest rates

We can explain the term structure of interest rates with the aid of the expectation theory. This theory is based on the premise that short- and long-term debt securities are substitutes. In this view, one four-year investment on the capital market is an alternative for four subsequent one-year investments on the money market. In order to make a choice between the alternatives, the investor compares the present long-term interest rate with the present and expected short term interest rates. The following example illustrates the relation between the long-term interest rate and the expected short term interest rate.

We shall assume that investors are expecting a decrease in the one-year money market interest rate (see Table 8.5).

TABLE 8.5 Expected short term interest rates and the long-term interest rate

	Year			
	0	**1**	**2**	**3**
Short term interest rate (1 year)	9%	8%	7%	6%
Long-term interest rate (4 years)	7.5%			

The expected decrease in the short-term interest rate means that investors will reinvest four one-year investments against a diminishing interest rate. For a money market investment, investors expect an average interest of 7.5% per annum. The alternative, the four-year investment, will have to bring a comparable yield. As long as this is not the case, investors will make use of the difference in interest between the two types of investment. If the long-term interest is 9%, for instance, investors will invest their surplus liquid assets for a long term and will withdraw investments from the money market. This will cause the long-term interest rate to drop and the interest rate on the money market to rise until both alternatives yield a similar return. According to the expectation theory, the level of the long-term interest rate is therefore

Expected short-term interest rate

dependent on the current and the expected short-term interest rate. It will now be easy to deduce when an inverse term structure of interest rates will develop. Table 8.5 shows that an inverse term structure of interest rates occurs when investors expect a drop in the short-term interest rate. A normal term structure occurs when investors expect the money market interest rate to rise. Any conclusions drawn from the expectation theory have to be modified in the light of the fact that short- and long term investments are not perfect substitutes. A long term investment is less liquid. An investor who makes a choice for one four-year investment ties up his money for a longer period than an investor who chooses four subsequent one-year investments. This

Liquidity premium

difference needs to be reflected in a higher liquidity premium on long-term investments. In Table 8.5, the average short-term interest rate is 7.5%. The long-term interest rate will be somewhat higher than 7.5% because of the liquidity preferences of investors.

Consequently, if investors expect a small drop in the short-term interest rate, the term structure of interest rates may remain normal because the higher liquidity premium is included in the long-term interest rate. The determining factors of term structure of interest rates are summarised in Table 8.6.

TABLE 8.6 Determining factors of the term structure of interest rates

Normal term structure of interest rates	Inverse term structure of interest rates
A longer maturity period is accompanied by higher liquidity and risk premiums	
Market parties expect a stable or increasing money market interest rate	Market parties expect a drop in short term interest rates after: • temporary exchange rate unrest • inflation that is regarded as being temporary

The term structure of interest rates in practice

An inverse term structure of interest rates is to be found when investors expect a strong decrease in the short-term interest ratee. The higher the money market interest rate, the greater the chance of this happening. The central bank exerts a considerable influence on the money market interest rate. An inverse term structure of interest rates will therefore only occur when the central bank regards a high short-term interest rate as necessary. There are at least two circumstances, both related to the external and internal value of the country's currency, that make this necessary: unrest on the foreign exchange market and inflation that is regarded as being temporary.

Within a system of fixed exchange rates, the central bank has the obligation to stabilise the exchange rate of its own currency. If investors speculate against the currency, the central bank has to increase the short-term interest rate to attract capital flows (see Chapter 10). This could create an inverse term structure of interest rates. Unrest on the currency market is usually of a temporary nature. If things become normal again, the central bank may lower its rates again. This will cause the term structure of interest rates to revert to normal.

A second reason for an inverse term structure of interest rates is a difference between the long-term and the short-term inflation expectations. If investors expect a high short-term inflation they will demand a higher interest on short-term investments. At the same time the central bank will increase its interest rates to counteract the expected inflation. The market and policy will contribute in this case to a high short-term interest rate. The expected short-term inflation will usually be high if the business cycle is nearing its peak. Fear of inflation among investors will be great because of the rapid increase in expenditure. If investors expect that a cyclical turning point is imminent they will be of the opinion that the inflation rate will diminish in the longer term. If they also have confidence in the anti-inflation policies of the central bank, investors will regard the rise in inflation as a temporary phenomenon. The long-term interest rate will, in that case, need less of an inflation compensation than the short-term rate. In these circumstances, the long-term rate may be lower than the short-term rate, which will result in an inverse yield curve. Sometimes, therefore, an inverse yield curve is regarded as a leading indicator of an economic decline.

Leading indicator of an economic decline

8.5 Interest rate risk

Interest rate developments have an effect on the profits of companies. For many companies, a higher interest rate means, for instance, that sales will drop and costs increase. The risk of the potential profitability of companies being influenced by fluctuations in the interest rate is called 'interest rate risk'.

Interest risk management

8

FIGURE 8.8 The interest risk management cycle

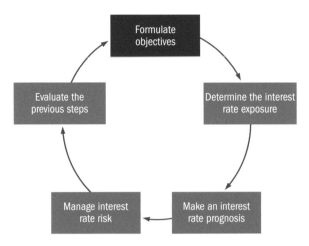

Companies often want to take action to prevent the interest rate affecting profits unfavourably. Figure 8.8 shows how a company could go about interest risk management. In the next subsections we will deal with the steps in the interest risk management process.

8.5.1 Formulating objectives

The first step in the management of interest rate risks is the formulation of objectives. Senior management should indicate if, and if so, to what extent, an interest rate risk is considered acceptable.

Active interest rate policy

If a company desires to exclude interest rate risks as much as possible, it will carry out an active interest rate policy. The company will cover itself as much as possible against unfavourable interest rate fluctuations. To do this they will make use of the interest rate instruments that the banks provide. The disadvantage of an active interest rate policy is that it may involve high costs. A company can also choose to manage its interest rate policy passively. It will try to manage the interest rate risk by internal measures only. Spreading the maturity times of loans is one such measure. The company will under no circumstances make use of the interest rate instruments provided by the banks. Companies may have two reasons for pursuing a passive interest rate policy. In the first place, accurately determining the interest rate exposure of a company is not a simple matter. The influence of interest rates on sales and profits cannot always be readily estimated. The second reason for a passive interest rate policy is the assumption of interest rate unpredictability.

Passive interest rate policy

If both interest rate exposure and interest rate developments are uncertain, the benefits of an active interest rate policy will also be uncertain. This is why some companies are of the opinion that the uncertain benefits of an active interest rate policy are no compensation for the certain costs involved. An active interest rate policy is especially important for companies with a weak financial and a weak market position. The interest rate exposure of these companies is great because of their financial position, and because of their weak market position they are not able to pass on the results of an unfavourable interest rate development to their customers (see Table 8.7).

TABLE 8.7 Objectives of interest rate risk management

Active interest rate policy aimed at *risk minimisation*	Passive interest rate policy aimed at *cost minimisation*
Necessary in case of:	Possible in the case of:
• Weak financial position	• Strong financial position
• Narrow profit margins	• Broad profit margins
• Weak market position	• Strong market position
• High risk aversion	• Low risk aversion

8.5.2   Determining the level of interest rate exposure

Interest rate exposure indicates the extent to which the profits of a company are sensitive to interest rate fluctuations. The interest rate has a number of direct and indirect effects on the profits of an organisation, and it is therefore not an easy matter to determine the interest rate exposure.

Interest rate exposure

The interest rate exposure depends firstly on the financial structure of the company. The financial structure determines to what extent interest income and interest expenses fluctuate with the interest rate. The sensitivity of interest expenses to changes in the interest rate will become evident from an analysis of the liability side of the company's balance sheet.

Financial structure

An analysis of the asset side of the balance sheet will show to what extent the interest income is sensitive to changes in the interest rate. An analysis of the financial structure will also demonstrate which interest rate will affect the company (see Figure 8.9).

FIGURE 8.9 Sensitivity of the capital stucture to the interest rate

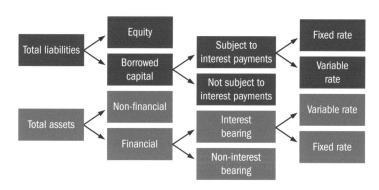

TEST 8.6
Will the profits of a company with a low solvency always be sensitive to short-term interest rate changes?

Future cash flows have a bearing on interest rate exposure as well. A company's cash flow prognosis will show when liquidity surpluses or deficits can be expected. Management can use this to determine when to borrow money and when to deposit money on the financial markets.

Future cash flows

A cash flow prognosis is based on an estimation of expenses and receipts. Expenses and receipts are themselves sensitive to interest rate changes. The

8

cash flow prognosis is therefore not only a determinant of the interest rate sensitivity of a company, but is itself also dependent on the interest rate (see Figure 8.10). Receipts in, for instance, the building trade or the capital goods sector are strongly susceptible to interest rate changes.

FIGURE 8.10 Determining the interest rate exposure of a company

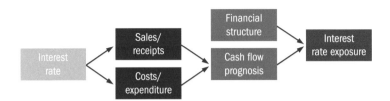

8.5.3   Developing an interest rate prognosis

We have dealt with the determining factors of interest rates in Sections 8.2 to 8.4. In order to make an interest rate prognosis, a company will have to analyse those interest rate determining factors that were treated there. While making a prognosis of the interest rate level is not easy, the direction in which the interest rate is moving can usually be estimated. The biggest problem is to predict the interest rate turning points. We saw in Sections 8.2 to 8.4 that the interest rate is among other things dependent upon inflation. Inflation is in turn dependent on the business cycle phase. While predicting a cyclical turning point is difficult, it is even more difficult to predict when interest rates will turn as a precursor to a cyclical turning point. The problem is that the interest rate is not only determined by rational but also by irrational factors. The inflation and interest rate expectations on the financial markets are not only the result of more or less objective cyclical indicators but also of market sentiment. Investors appear to think in waves of optimism and pessimism, during which they tend to exaggerate the consequences of economic developments. To gauge these irrational aspects of price formation on the financial markets is extremely difficult.

The uncertainty in an interest rate prognosis can be expressed in terms of interest rate scenarios. An interest rate scenario is a conditional prediction of the interest rate (see Table 8.8). The prognosis is the most likely scenario (the basic scenario). A pessimistic (worst-case scenario) and an optimistic (best-case) scenario could also be taken into account. Management may decide which measures if any should be taken in respect of each of these scenarios. A scenario with a substantial increase in the interest rate may have an unacceptable effect on interest expenses and profits. In the event of the scenario becoming reality, management might decide, for instance, that the proportion of fixed interest liabilities in the portfolio should be increased. The sensitivity of the interest rate to economic and political news is so great that scenarios quickly lose their validity. Interest rate scenarios should therefore be updated regularly: at, say, three-monthly intervals.

Interest rate scenarios

TABLE 8.8 Interest scenarios for the coming year at the present three-month Euribor of 6%

Assumption	Effect	Action
Basic scenario Average economic recovery	Interest rate rises slightly: 6.5%	Increase the proportion of fixed interest loans slightly
Pessimistic scenario Rapid economic recovery giving rise to fears of inflation	Interest rate rises quickly: 7.5%	Increase the number of fixed interest loans dramatically
Optimistic scenario No economic recovery	Interest rate is stable or drops slightly: 6%	No action for the moment

8.5.4 Interest rate instruments

Interest rate exposure and interest rate volatility determine jointly the extent of interest rate risk. Depending on what its objectives are, the company should implement an effective interest rate policy. There are a number of instruments available to the company, the most important of which we will treat in this section.

Interest rate risk depends on the type of loan that the company chooses. Loans may be classified according to time to maturity or interest type. With short-term loans, variable interest that bears a relationship to the money market interest rate is paid. With long-term loans there is a choice between a fixed interest rate or a variable interest rate. A loan with a variable interest rate is desirable if a decrease in the interest rate is anticipated; a loan with a fixed interest rate is to be preferred if there is the expectation of an increase in the interest rate. Table 8.9 shows the various types of loan according to time to maturity and interest type.

Type of loan

TABLE 8.9 Loans according to time to maturity and interest type

Time to maturity	Interest type	
	Variable (money market interest rate)	Fixed (long-term interest rate)
Less than two years (money market)	• Short term credit (cash loan and overdraft facility)	n.a.
More than two years (capital market)	• Roll-over loan • Floating rate notes	• Private loan • Bond loan

The main types of money market loans are the overdraft (with a credit limit) and the cash loan. Long-term loans can have either a variable or a fixed interest rate. A roll-over loan is a long-term loan with a variable interest rate. This type of loan is essentially not negotiable: the lender and the borrower remain the same. Floating rate notes are like roll-over loans issued for a period longer than two years. As the name suggests, the interest rate on these financial assets is variable. Unlike roll-over loans, floating rate notes are negotiable.

Roll-over loan

Floating rate notes

Except for the interest rate, the private loan and the bond loan can be compared to the roll-over loan and the floating rate notes respectively. The private loan and the bond loan have a fixed interest rate for the whole maturity period of the loan.

TEST 8.7
An entrepreneur needs a three-year loan for an investment. He anticipates that the economic boom will finish shortly. What type of loan would be the most favourable for him to take out?

Early repayment clause

If an entrepreneur has had an early repayment clause included in his loan conditions he can redeem the loan wholly or in part when the interest rate drops. At the same time he can take out a new loan against the lower market interest rate. The early repayment clause offers the borrower extra flexibility to react to interest rate changes. He does have to pay a price for this, however, either in the form of a higher interest rate or a penalty for early repayment. The higher interest rate and the prepayment penalty protect the lender to a certain extent against unfavourable early repayment terms. Management can also diminish interest rate sensitivity by spreading the size and term of loans. By spreading the maturity structure of the credit portfolio, management will have to refinance part of the loans during a period of economic boom and part during a period of economic recession. Refinancing is expensive during an economic boom and cheap during a period of economic recession. By spreading the credit portfolio, the average interest rate is paid during the whole of the economic cycle. Without a spreading of the credit portfolio, it could happen that the major part of the loans have to be refinanced in a year at a high interest rate.

Spreading the maturity structure

The possibilities of reducing the effect of interest rates on profits that we have looked at so far proved to be inadequate at the end of the 20th century. Liberalisation of international capital flows caused an increase in the potential of the interest and currency rates to fluctuate. Financial institutions have reacted to this by offering new instruments for controlling interest and currency risks. The main financial instruments for managing interest rates are the forward rate agreement (FRA), the interest rate option and the interest rate swap.

The forward rate agreement
The forward rate agreement (FRA) enables a company to stipulate in advance the interest rate that it will pay on a future loan or will receive on a future deposit. The FRA is a forward contract between two parties to offset at some time in the future the difference between the interest rate decided on and the market interest rate at the time the loan is taken out. The way an FRA works is best illustrated by an example (see Example 8.3).

- -
EXAMPLE 8.3

The FRA

In six months' time, an entrepreneur will need a loan with a term of three months. During the coming six months he expects a rise in the interest rate from 6% to 7.5%. On the basis of this interest rate prognosis he buys an FRA in which the following conditions are laid down:

- The forward period: the entrepreneur needs the loan after six months, so-the forward period is six months
- The interest period: the period over which interest is paid (three months in this example)
- The contractual interest rate: in this example, that may be 6.5%
- The reference rate (the future market interest rate) to which the contractual interest rate is compared.

Let us assume that the interest rate expectations of the entrepreneur turn out to be correct.

The market interest rate rises to 7.5%. He takes out a loan with his bank at 7.5%. At the same time he cashes in on his FRA. The buyer pays him the difference (1%) between the market interest rate (7.5%) and the contracted rate in the FRA (6.5%). His interest expense is therefore 7.5% − 1% = 6.5%. If the interest rate had been lower than 6.5% the entrepreneur would have had to pay the difference between the market interest rate and the contracted rate to the seller of the FRA. In that case, too, his interest rate would have amounted to 6.5%.

Example 8.3 shows how an entrepreneur can fix his future interest liability or asset by means of a FRA. The example also shows that the buyer profits from an interest rate increase and a seller from a decrease in the interest rate.

The interest rate option
An interest rate option is an agreement between two parties in which the seller grants the buyer the right to a specified interest rate. Unlike the FRA, the buyer does not have to make use of his right if it would be detrimental to him.

Right

There are two main types of interest rate option. The interest rate cap gives the buyer the right to a reimbursement if the interest rate rises above an agreed on ceiling (cap rate). An interest rate floor gives the buyer the right to reimbursement if the interest rate drops below a certain agreed interest rate (floor rate). We will explain the way an interest rate option works at the hand of a cap rate example (Example 8.4).

Interest rate cap

Interest rate floor

EXAMPLE 8.4

The interest rate cap

An entrepreneur has a loan with a remaining time to maturity of two years. The interest rate is the same as the Euribor: 6%. He expects an increase in the interest rate, but is by no means certain of it. He therefore decides to buy an interest rate cap.

The interest rate cap guarantees the entrepreneur a ceiling for his interest rate payments.

There are conditions in the agreement for the following:
- The height of the ceiling (cap rate): say 7%
- The term of the option; in this example, two years
- The reference interest rate: in this example, the Euribor

For the right to an interest rate ceiling the entrepreneur pays a price to the seller of the option.

The price (the option premium) depends among other things on the volatility of interest rates, the current interest rate and the term structure of interest rates.

If the Euribor rate exceeds the cap rate of 7%, the entrepreneur will exercise his option. The seller of the option will pay him the difference between the Euribor rate and 7%. The entrepreneur can thus put a ceiling on his interest payments. If the interest rate stays below 7% he will not make use of his option. He will profit from the lower interest rate and will only have lost the option premium.

Example 8.4 shows how an interest rate cap protects the buyer against a rise in the interest rate while allowing him to keep on profiting from a lower interest rate. Analogously, the interest rate floor protects the buyer against a decrease in the interest rate.

The interest rate swap

An interest rate swap allows a company to change the interest rate type of a loan without repaying it. An interest rate swap is an agreement between two parties to exchange a variable interest obligation against a fixed one. The way an interest rate swap works is illustrated in Example 8.5.

EXAMPLE 8.5

The interest rate swap

An entrepreneur has a loan with a remaining time to maturity of four years against a fixed interest of 8%. He expects a drop in the interest rate and would therefore much prefer to have a variable interest rate. Early repayment of the loan is no alternative because of the unfavourable penalty conditions in the loan agreement.

The entrepreneur enters into an interest rate swap with a another party who prefers a fixed interest rate.

The interest rate swap contains the following conditions:
- The term of the interest rate swap: in this example, four years
- The variable interest rate that the entrepreneur will pay: for instance the Euribor + 0.5%
- The fixed interest rate the other party will pay. This rate is related to the current market rate for securities with a maturity of four years (say, 7.5%). The interest rate swap will look like this:

Interest rate swap

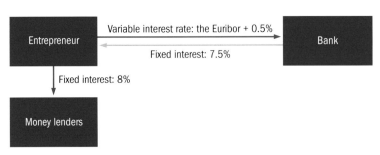

With the interest rate swap, the entrepreneur has changed his fixed interest payments to variable payments without repaying his original loan. The new interest rate is the Euribor + 1% and can be calculated as follows:

Outgoing interest flow:
- Payments to the money lenders   8%
- Variable interest rate because of the swap: Euribor + 0.5% +
                                            Euribor + 8.5%

Incoming interest flow:
- fixed interest because of the swap   7.5% −

Remaining interest liability   Euribor + 1%

TEST 8.8
Why would the other party be prepared to swap interest liabilities?

Table 8.10 summarises the main interest rate instruments. This summary is by no means complete. There are a variety of compound interest rate instruments that are a combination of the basic instruments of forward contract, option and swap. Treatment of these combinations falls outside the scope of this book.

TABLE 8.10 Interest rate instruments

Traditional measures	Financial instruments
Choice of loan type	Forward rate agreement
Early repayment	Interest rate option
Term structure loans portfolio	Interest rate swap

8.5.5   The evaluation

The last step in the cycle of interest rate management is the evaluation. The most important question at this stage is whether the objectives of the interest rate policy have been achieved. If the objectives were not met, the cause has to be ascertained. Every step in the process has to be evaluated. The first thing that may appear from the analysis is that the interest rate exposure was estimated incorrectly. The evaluation may, for instance, show that the company is consistently misjudging the future capital flows. The interest rate exposure may also turn out to be too great to realise the objectives of the interest rate management. This might force the company to decrease the interest rate exposure by, for example, debt reduction. In that case, the company might have to sell parts of the company or postpone investment plans.

Objectives

Exposure

The evaluation of interest rate expectations is all about the quality of the interest rate prognoses. Anticipation of interest rate *changes* is especially important because this is the basis for the use of interest rate instruments. An evaluation of the quality of the interest rate prognoses might, for instance, show that the importance of certain interest rate determining

Prognoses

factors has been underestimated while the impact of other factors has been overestimated. The evaluation could also make clear to the company how frequently it should adjust its interest rate prognoses. Adjusting them too often brings with it unnecessarily high costs and reviewing them not often enough might lead to the wrong decisions.

Instruments

A company should also evaluate the instruments used. Were the instruments used the most efficient and effective ones for reaching the desired objectives?
If management has to answer in the negative, it will have to decide precisely what instruments the financial department should use in the future and under what circumstances.

If the objectives were not reached in spite of management evaluating all the steps of the management cycle positively, it will be forced to conclude that the objectives were too ambitious. The company will then have to down scale its objectives. The opposite, an upgrading of the objectives, is, of course, also a possibility.

Glossary

Bond	A debt security which is part of a loan issued by a government, company or institution.
Long-term interest rate	The interest rate that is paid on financial assets with a remaining time to maturity of more than two years. The yield to maturity of the most recent1 0-year government loan is usually used as an indicator of the long-term interest rate.
Capital market	The market on which financial assets with a remaining time to maturity of more than two years are traded.
Coupon rate	The actual interest received on a bond.
Credit interest	The interest a bank customer receives on his deposits.
Credit rating	A coded indication of the creditworthiness of an institution or country.
Credit risk surcharge	A surcharge on the interest rate to cover the possibility of the borrower not being able to comply with his interest and repayment obligations.
Debit interest	The interest a borrower has to pay to the bank for a loan.
Dividend yield	The dividend on a share expressed as a percentage of the market price.
Dividend	That part of a company's profits that is paid out to shareholders.
Yield to maturity	The sum of the coupon yield and the redemption yield of a bond.
Coupon yield	The actual interest received on a bond expressed as a percentage of the market price.
Floating rate notes	A bond loan with a variable interest rate.
Forward rate agreement	A futures contract between two parties to offset the difference between the interest rate agreed on and the market interest rate at the time the loan is taken out.
Interest exposure rate	The extent to which the profits of a company are exposed to interest rate fluctuations.

Interest rate option	An agreement between a bank and a company in which the company obtains the right to a contractually laid down interest rate at some time in the future. There are two types of interest rate options: • interest rate cap: an interest rate option in which the bank guarantees the company the maximum interest rate • interest rate floor: an agreement in which the bank guarantees the company the minimum interest rate.
Interest rate risk	The risk of the profitability of a company being affected by fluctuations in the interest rate.
Interest rate scenario	A conditional prediction of the interest rate.
Interest rate swap	An agreement between a company and a bank in which a company obtains the right to exchange a fixed interest rate for a variable interest rate (or vice versa) for a certain period of maturity.
Interest rate volatility	The degree to which interest rates fluctuate.
Liquidity preference	A preference for an amount of liquid assets now instead of at some time in the future.
Liquidity premium	That part of the interest rate that is a remuneration for relinquishing liquid assets temporarily.
Market liquidity	The ease with which negotiable securities can be traded. Market liquidity increases when the market turnover on the financial market increases.
Market price	The current stock market price of negotiable securities.
Money market interest rate	The interest rate that is paid on financial assets with a maturity interest rate term of less than two years. The three-month Euribor is usually used as an indicator of the money market interest rate.
Money market	The market on which financial assets with a maturity term of less than two years are traded.
Nominal interest	The actual interest received or the actual monetary yield.
Nominal value	The value of a security as it appears on the security itself.
Overdraft	A form of credit in which a bank allows a company a certain credit limit (overdraft) in return for securities and interest payments.
Primary capital market	That part of the capital market on which newly issued financial assets are traded.

Private capital market	That part of the capital market on which the conditions of a loan are the result of direct negotiation between the borrower and one or more lenders.
Private loan	A loan with a fixed interest rate and a fixed period of maturity of at least one year.
Public capital market	That part of the capital market in which there is public trading in securities. This market is also known as the stock market.
Real interest	Nominal interest adjusted for inflation.
Redemption yield	The difference between the market price and the nominal price of a bond (taking into account the remaining maturity time) expressed as a percentage of the market price.
Risk premium	That part of the interest rate that is a remuneration for the risk that the lender is incurring.
Roll-over loan	A long-term private loan with a variable interest rate.
Secondary capital market	That part of the capital market that trades in existing financial assets.
Securities	Negotiable certificates of indebtedness or titles of ownership in a company.
Share	Certificate of entitlement in a joint stock company.
Term structure of interest rates	Relation between the time to maturity of a debt security and the interest rate
Yield curve	The graph of the term structure of the interest rate.

8

PART 4

The international environment of companies

9

International economic relations

9.1	**International economic trends**
9.2	**The theory of comparative costs**
9.3	**Free trade and protectionism**
9.4	**The balance of payments**
9.5	**International cooperation**

The central issue in this chapter is the causes and consequences of international economic trade and investment.

Section 9.1 deals with the two most important international economic developments. They are related to each other: globalisation and the expansion of emerging markets.
Proponents of globalisation usually base their arguments on the theory of comparative costs. This theory will be treated in Section 9.2.
Comparative cost differences change in the course of time. This causes trade flows to alter and at a national level companies to change from one production sector to another. This is associated with a loss of employment in sectors at a comparative cost disadvantage. These sectors will ask the government to introduce protectionist measures. Section 9.3 will deal with the arguments for protectionism, the types of protectionism that exist and the effects protectionism has.
The economic relations that a country has with other countries are reflected in its balance of payments. The way the balance of payments is set out and how it can be analysed is the subject of Section 9.4. From an analysis of the balance of payments an entrepreneur can draw important conclusions about the economy of the country concerned.
Because of the growth in international trade and international capital flows there will be an increasing necessity for international cooperation at the regional and global level. Section 9.5 treats the various forms of regional economic integration and the main organisations in the global economic arena.

9

CASE
The end of the twentieth century and the beginning of the twenty-first
century were characterised by a rapid growth in international trade
and investments (globalisation of the economy) and a rapid growth of
the economy in a number of developing countries, especially in that
potential economic giant, China. Both developments have given rise to
uneasy feelings in the advanced economies. The wage costs per hour in
the developing countries are much less than those in Western Europe.
According to the International Labour Organisation the hourly wage in the
Netherlands, for example, is more than six times as high as that in Mexico.
The differences between the wage costs in the Netherlands and in some
Asian countries such as India, China, Indonesia and Sri Lanka were even
greater still. Entrepreneurs in Western Europe are wondering whether
they are ultimately able to compete against the low-wage countries. The
government, trade unions and employees fear loss of employment because
of increasing international competition. The fear of job losses has on
occasion led to pleas for protectionism.

9.1 International economic trends

Emerging
markets

At the global level, two main economic trends are becoming evident. The
first is the increasing importance of the so-called emerging markets to the
world economy. These markets are in Latin America, Central and Eastern
Europe and in Southeast Asia, which is the largest of them. Section 9.1.1
illustrates the developments in the world economy. The other main trend is
globalisation, which will be dealt with in Section 9.1.2.

9.1.1   An overview of the world economy

The International Monetary Fund (IMF) classifies the world economy into
three categories of countries: advanced economies, emerging markets and
developing countries. The share of these categories in world output, world
trade and world population is represented in table 9.1.

Advanced
economies

Emerging
markets

Economic growth

In Table 9.1 we see that the world economy in 2015 was dominated by the
advanced economies. These 39 countries accounted for no less than 42%
of the world's production and 63% of the world's trade. Their share of the
world's production and trade is very large if we consider that only 15% of the
world's population lives in the advanced economies. The major part of the
world's population (85%) lives in the emerging markets and the developing
countries and their contribution to the world's production and trade is
relatively small.

The development of the global distribution of production is dependent on
economic growth. Table 9.2 demonstrates that the total production in the
world during the period 1998 to 2017 increased annually by about 3.5%. This
average growth rate masks quite different developments in the different
categories of countries. The economic growth in the advanced economies
lagged behind the world's average in the period from 1998 to 2017. Their share
of the world's production is therefore decreasing. The developing countries,
on the other hand, had a growth rate that was higher than the average. Their
share of the world's production is increasing. Within the group of developing
countries the high growth rates in Asia are exceptionally striking.

TABLE 9.1 Share of selected regions in world GDP, world trade and world population in 2015

	Number of countries	Share (in %)		
		GDP	Export of goods and services	Population
Advanced Economies	**39**	**42.4**	**63.4**	**14.6**
United States		15.8	10.8	4.5
Euro area	19	12.0	26.5	4.7
Japan		4.2	3.7	1.8
Other advanced economies	18	10.4	22.4	3.6
Emerging markets and developing economies	**152**	**57.6**	**36.6**	**85.4**
Sub-Saharan Afrika	45	3.1	1.7	12.8
Emerging and developing Asia	29	30.8	18.4	48.8
Middle East and North Africa[1]	22	7.6	5.3	9.1
Latin America	32	8.2	5.1	8.4
Emerging and developing Europe	12	3.3	3.4	2.4
Commonwealth of Independent States (CIS)[2]	12	4.6	2.8	3.9

[1] Including Pakistan and Afghanistan
[2] Former Soviet Union, including Russia
Source: IMF, *World Economic Outlook*, October 2016

TABLE 9.2 Average growth of real GDP in selected regions, 1998-2017 (annual percent change)

	1998-2007	2008-2017
World	**4.2**	**3.2**
Advanced Economies	**2.8**	**1.1**
United States	3.0	1.4
Euro area	2.4	0.5
Japan	1.0	0.2
Other advanced economies	3.6	1.9
Emerging markets and developing economies	**5.8**	**5.0**
Sub-Saharan Afrika	5.3	4.4
Emerging and developing Asia	7.6	7.2
Middle East and North Africa[1]	5.3	3.5
Latin America	3.1	2.1
Emerging and developing Europe	4.2	2.7
Commonwealth of Independent States (CIS)[2]	6.2	1.3

[1] Including Pakistan and Afghanistan
[2] Commonwealth of Independent States (former Soviet Union, including Russia)
Source: IMF, *World Economic Outlook*, October 2016

The importance of the Asiatic region in the world economy is rising rapidly.   Asiatic region
Figure 9.1 shows the vigorous economic development taking place in Asia.
This figure shows the ten biggest economies in the world in 1980 and in 2016
(expressed in dollars, with corresponding purchasing power). In 1980, the
US was far and away the world's biggest economy. China did not even make

BRIC-countries

the top ten back then. Thirty five years later, China has picked up the mantle from the United States. According to the investment bank Goldman Sachs, the BRIC-countries (Brazil, Russia, India and China) will dominate the world economy in the twenty-first century.

9

FIGURE 9.1 The GDP[1] of the ten largest economies in 1980 and 2016

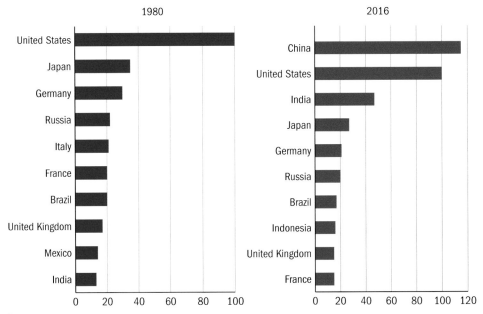

[1]Expressed in terms of purchasing power parity

Source: IMF, World economic database, October 2016

TEST 9.1

What region offers the best sales potential at the beginning of the 21st century?

9.1.2   Globalisation

One of the main global economic trends is globalisation, which can be described as the process of world-wide integration of economies caused by the rapid increase in trade and cross-border investments.

Causes of globalisation

There are two main reasons for the world-wide integration of economies: technological innovations and deregulation.

Technological innovations

In a sense, technological innovations in the areas of transport and communication have made the world smaller. The improvements in transport technology have made sea and air transport in particular much cheaper. This has made the geographical distance between two places in the world increasingly less important.

The progression in information and communication technologies (ICT) has been even more important for the process of globalisation. ICT is making the exchange of information between two places in the world faster and cheaper all the time. The Internet, for example, is making it possible to communicate in a cheap and fast way with subsidiaries, clients and suppliers over the whole world. Together with improved transport technology, ICT offers companies the possibility of, for instance, producing parts in India, assembling them in Hungary, establishing an research centre in Great Britain, and choosing Germany as a location for its headquarters. This is termed global sourcing, a strategy in which a company establishes non-location-specific business operations in those parts of the world where the costs and the added value are most favourable.

Global sourcing

The other reason for the increase in international economic transactions is the world-wide process of deregulation and liberalisation. In advanced economies this process has gone the furthest. Capital transactions between these countries is free and trade between advanced economies face a decreasing number of restrictions. World Trade Organisation (WTO) figures show that the average import tariffs on industrial products in the advanced economies has dropped from 40% in 1940 to less than 5% at present. The liberalisation of the economic transactions between the industrial countries is not only evident from the lowering of import tariffs. Business sectors such as the airlines and telecommunications, until recently protected by all kinds of government measures, have been subject to increasing international competition because of deregulation.

Deregulation and liberalisation

Deregulation of the international economic transactions has the same effect as a lowering of transport and telecommunication costs: companies have greater freedom to decide where in the world they will buy, produce or sell.

Shanghai: financial and commercial centre of modern China

Facts about globalisation

In order to assess the progress of the globalisation process, we will look at the changes that have taken place in world trade and subsequently at the changes in international investments.

World trade in goods and services

Developments in world trade

World trade   World trade is the sum of the export of goods and services in the world. Figure 9.2 shows the development of world trade as a percentage of world output.

FIGURE 9.2 World trade in goods and services as a percentage of world GDP, 1960-2015

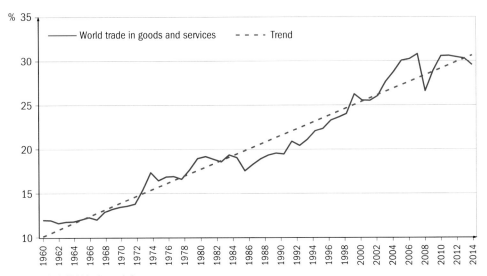

Source: Worldbank, World development indicators

World export quote

Figure 9.2 shows that global trade grew much more rapidly than global production in the period from 1960 to 2015. The world export quote, the world's trade as a percentage of the world's production, saw an increase from 12% in 1960 to around 30% now. Countries' connections to the world economy, therefore, have strengthened dramatically since 1960.
The period from the mid-eighties to the global economic crisis of 2008/2009 saw the sharpest increase in the world export quote. This was the heyday of economic globalisation. This period coincided with the spectacular (re) emergence of China onto the world's economic stage.

Intraregional trade

Interregional trade

International trade consists of trade within and outside of one's own region. If, say, a Dutch company were to export goods to Germany, this constitutes trade within its own region, or intraregional trade. If the same Dutch company were to export goods to China, this constitutes trade outside of its own region, or interregional trade.
More and more companies are taking part in trade with other countries. But are these other countries also outside of these companies' own regions? Figure 9.3 shows that this is not the case. All major regions see a growing percentage of intraregional trade in the period from 1990 to 2015. As we will discuss further on, this is mainly the result of the growing trade in intermediate products within regional production chains.

FIGURE 9.3 Intraregional trade in 1990 and in 2015

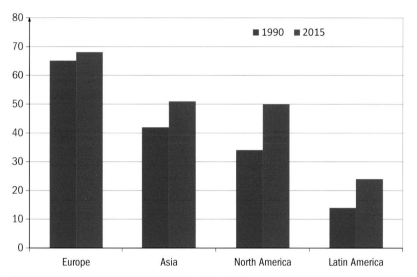

Source: World Trade Organisation, International Trade Statistics, 1990 and 2015

Developments in investment flows

Globalisation can be triggered either by export or by foreign production, of which there are two types. A company can outsource its production to a foreign company. This is known as international outsourcing. Alternatively, a company can manufacture its own products abroad. This is known as offshoring. Offshoring requires a direct investment abroad. A direct investment is defined as the acquisitioning of an interest in a company abroad, with the aim of influencing policy. There are several motives for companies to invest abroad.

International outsourcing

Offshoring

Direct investment

Firstly, a direct investment allows access to a foreign sales market should export be impossible, for example through significant import restrictions or transport costs. Even if export is a possibility, it may be helpful to produce goods near their intended buyers; it allows a company to better recognise and address local needs.

Access to a foreign sales market

Secondly, a direct investment allows access to production factors, such as resources or a competent workforce. An oil producer would invest in a country that has natural oil reserves; a software development would invest in a country that houses many well-trained IT specialists.

Access to production factors

Lastly, a direct investment may be aimed at cost reduction. Philips Lighting, for example, has moved the production of its lamps from the Netherlands to Poland, to benefit from the lower wages found there.

Cost reduction

TEST 9.2

What arguments could a company have for a direct investment in China?

Figure 9.4 shows that direct investments have increased sharply since the mid-nineties. It also shows they are highly sensitive to the business cycle. The global economic recession of 2001 and the credit crisis of 2007/2008 both led to a clear reduction in investment flows.

FIGURE 9.4 Developments in incoming foreign investments, 1990–2015

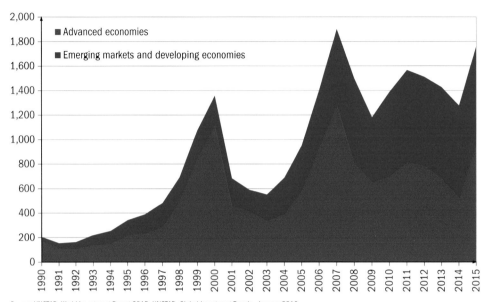

Source: UNCTAD, World Investment Report 2015; UNCTAD, Global Investment Trends, January 2016

Lastly, Figure 9.4 clearly demonstrates that more and more countries are investing in countries with emerging markets and developing economies. For developing countries, direct investments are an important drive for economic growth. There is often a readily available workforce, but capital, management expertise, and technical knowledge are lacking. Direct investments allow these countries access to both capital and the technology it embodies.

Drive for economic growth

International value chains

International production fragmentation

'Made in the world'

Globalisation has led to international production fragmentation. Blurring boundaries have allowed companies to split up the production process into smaller, distinct branches, which are spread globally. Nowadays, Boeing's aircraft are 'made in the world' rather than 'made in the USA' (see Figure 9.5). In 1967, the company manufactured 90% of the systems and components for the Boeing-737 in the United States. In 2016, no less than 80% of the systems and components of the latest model – the 787-Dreamliner – are supplied from all over the world.

Trade in tasks

International value or production chains

International production fragmentation, such as that employed by Boeing, has led to a situation where over half of the world's trade in goods consists of intermediate products. Nowadays, international trade is more a matter of trade in tasks than trade in final products.

The fragmentation of production processes has created international value or production chains ('global value chains'). A value chain is comprised of all tasks or activities that directly or indirectly contribute to a final product. The chain starts at research and development, and ends at after-sales-service (see Figure 9.6).

FIGURE 9.5 International production fragmentation at Boeing

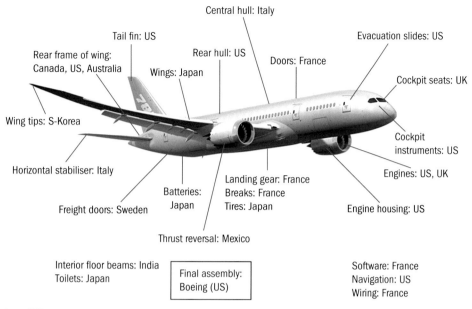

Source: OECD, *Towards measuring trade in value-added and other indicators of global value chains*, Global Forum on Trade Statistics, Geneva, 2-4 February 2011; Reuters, *A wing and a prayer: outsourcing at Boeing*, January 2011

FIGURE 9.6 The 'smile curve': added value by tasks on the value chain

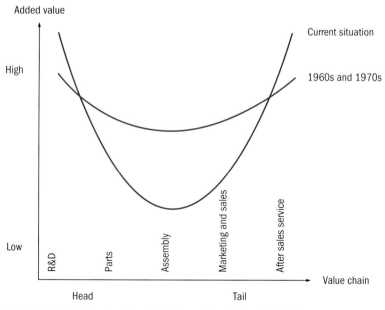

Source: *Kamerbrief versterking van de positie van Nederland in mondiale waardeketens*, 16 May 2014

Smile curve

Figure 9.6 lists the consecutive tasks on the value chain on the horizontal axis, and the added value per task on the vertical axis. Due to its shape, this curve is known as the 'smile curve'. The smile curve shows that the creative thinking at the head (R&D, design) and the tail (branding, marketing, after-sales-service) of the chain results in more added value than the basic assemly in the middle. This is nothing new: this 'smile' has always featured on the face of the value chain. Globalisation, however, has made it more pronounced. Open borders have led to fierce competition in the assembly industry. The margins in the middle of the chain have decreased sharply as a result. The added value at the beginning and the end of the chain have – partly as a result of this – actually increased (see Case 9.1).

CASE 9.1

Made in the World

The iPhone is a very fine example of the final product of an international value chain. Apple designs the iPhone in California. The device contains components from many different countries, including Germany, France, the Netherlands, the United States, Taiwan, Japan, and South Korea. Apple has the iPhones assembled in China. Even though the final product is completed in China, Apple does not print 'made in China' on it. Rather, iPhones feature the text 'Designed by Apple in California. Assembled in China'. 'Made in the World' would be even more apt. All of this raises the question of where the majority of an iPhone's added value ends up: in California, or in China. There is no mistaking what the answer is: in California. Apple manages the profitable 'head' (R&D, design) and 'tail' (marketing, branding, after-sales-service) of the value chain. The production activities in the middle are outsourced. Research conducted by OECD in 2011 showed that no less than half of the total added value of an iPhone4 saw its way into Apple's pockets. The Taiwanese company that assembles and actually exports the iPhones in China earns only a couple of dollars per assembled smartphone (which equates to around 1% of the added value).

Source: www.WTO.org

The globalisation debate

Globalisation has both supporters and opponents, locked in a fierce debate that has a major influence on elections in Europe and the US.
Supporters of globalisation argue that trade improves global prosperity. Economies that are open to the outside world, they say, fare much better than those that seal themselves off. They contrast the success of 'globalising countries' (such as South Korea or China following its economic liberalisation) against the disappointing development of 'non-globalising countries' (such as North Korea or China before its economic liberalisation). According to the supporters, we owe much to international collaboration and globalisation. In fact, they claim, these are things we are unable and unwilling to go without. International collaboration in Europe contributed to an era of peace on a continent that was the stage of two destructive conflicts during the previous century. In addition, globalisation has also presented us with a varied range of products heretofore unheard of; a range of products that is also inexpensive thanks to global production chains. Without globalisation, there would be much less to choose from; we would also be dealing with much higher prices when purchasing, for example, a TV, a car, or clothing.

Supporters of globalisation

There has always been solid resistance to globalisation. Since the financial crisis of 2008/2009, this resistance has grown even further. Criticism is mainly twofold:

Resistance

1 Globalisation leads to a loss of national decision-making powers and a loss of cultural identity.
2 Globalisation puts one-sided emphasis on the economy, and leads to a more skewed distribution of income.

Loss of national decision-making power and cultural identity

Criticism in Europe and the US is mainly concerned with the loss in decision-making power. Globalisation has resulted in national politicians having less influence on what goes on in their own country. Their grip on profit taxes is lessened. In a world without boundaries, companies can put pressure on national governments. They can head abroad, or threaten to do so, if they want to pay lower profit taxes. If, as a result, one government lowers taxation, other governments will need to follow suit. This causes an unintended race to the bottom, with tax revenues dropping further and further. And the lower the amount of tax revenue that comes in, the less politicians can accomplish.

Decision-making power

The discussion in the European Union (EU) is mostly focussed on free movement of people. Should member states be allowed to decide who does and who does not enter their country? This question played in important role in the 'Brexit' referendum held in the UK in 2016. The eventual winners of the referendum, being those who wanted Britain to withdraw from the EU, summed up their feelings in the motto: 'Let's take back control.' 'Taking back control' of decision-making is a returning theme in the globalisation debate. It demonstrates an ever-present rift between governments and their peoples. Support of globalisation and international collaboration is often stronger among members of parliament than among members of the public. A very large majority of British representatives supported the EU membership, whereas a small majority of the public voted against it. Something similar also happened during earlier referendums regarding European collaboration held in France and the Netherlands.

Most politicians accept the decrease in executive power as the inevitable result of globalisation and international collaboration. They see it as the price a society has to pay to enjoy the benefits of globalisation. The one, being a more open society with a varied and cheap range of products, cannot exist without the other, being a decrease in decision-making power: you cannot have your cake and eat it too.

But many members of the public refuse to accept this loss in national executive power. Their affinity is with their nation and their national culture. They still feel that charity begins at home. And in spite of the prevalence of globalisation, cultures are defined by national boundaries. According to cultural researcher Geert Hofstede, an expert in the field, this is not something we can expect to change in the near future. This does not make matters easier for politicians. They have to navigate between international collaboration and their voters' nationalist feelings. And politicians appealing to voters' nationalism have proven to be successful in both the US and Europe in recent years.

Anti-globalists

According to anti-globalists, globalisation affects the cultural identity of countries. In a world in which goods, capital, persons, money, and data can move freely, maintaining national norms and values has become increasingly difficult. According to critics, globalisation leads to cultural homogenisation: cultures start to look more and more alike. The dominance of US culture is a thorn in their sides. They point out the influx of American made films, TV shows, music, fashion, and fast food the world over.

Own culture should be preserved

Anti-globalists feel that culture should not be a 'product' subject to a free trade agreement. On the contrary, one's own culture should be preserved if it is threatened by the prevalence of a dominant foreign culture. The chances of national cultures to fade away as a result of opening up the borders are slim. As we have observed before, cultural differences are simply too persistent.

One culture worldwide?

One-sided emphasis on economy and increasing equality

Critics say the supporters of globalisation overemphasise its positive macroeconomic effects. Even though global production may increase as a result of globalisation, its consequences for the environment and society as a whole are not given enough attention. The limited interest in the social consequences of globalisation, anti-globalists say, comes at the cost of the weakest of us. Purchasing power (here: money) instead of needs or requirements dictate the direction in which research and development in a market economy are driven. As such, companies will spend more attention on developing a new line of cosmetics, or tomatoes that are slower to go off, instead of looking towards developing drought-resistant crops or a vaccine to prevent malaria. And it is the latter two of these innovations that would be of benefit to the poorest among us.

Social consequences of globalisation

9

Macroeconomically speaking, globalisation leads to increased prosperity. But that does not detract from the fact that there are those who do not benefit from globalisation. Think of older, lower schooled employees losing their jobs as the result of offshoring production. Younger, more highly educated employees well-versed in more than one language can benefit greatly from the opportunities presented by globalisation, on the other hand. The same applies for investors; globalisation opens doors and allows access to better interest rates. Even though globalisation reduces the differences in income *between* countries, the differences in income *within* countries have increased. The income distribution has become more skewed in nearly all developed industrial countries since 1985. According to the World Bank, the difference between the wealthy and the poor in communist China has become greater than in the United States. Anti-globalists feel that the free movement of goods, services, people, money, and data should be reined in to combat the harmful consequences of globalisation. Indian Nobel Prize winner Amartya Sen feels this would not be the way forward. In a 2002 report for developmental organisation Oxfam, he stated that: 'It is not isolationism, but global interaction that offers the basis for economic progress. The challenge lies in uniting the major trade benefits pointed out by many supporters of globalisation on the one hand, with overall need for fairness and equality.' Amartya Sen can be counted among the 'alterglobalists': they do not reject globalisation outright, but aim to have its advantages distributed more evenly. According to alterglobalists, market liberalisation cannot occur without a strong government in charge of redistributing income. Moreover, governments may sometimes need to reduce the rate of liberalisation in order to protect the weakest members of society.

Differences in income

Need for fairness and equality

Alterglobalists

9.2 The theory of comparative costs

The advocates of globalisation maintain that trade goes hand in hand with a world-wide increase in prosperity. They base that view on the theory of comparative costs that we will look at in this section. In Section 9.2.1 the influence of differences in comparative costs on trade between countries is treated. In Section 9.2.2 we will discuss how differences in comparative costs come about.

9.2.1 Absolute and comparative costs

The differences in costs between countries gives rise to international trade. To illustrate this we will look at the situation in two countries (the Netherlands and Thailand) and at two groups of products (dairy products and textiles). The production costs are given in Table 9.3.

TABLE 9.3 Absolute costs of dairy products and textiles (expressed in the same currency)

	Dairy products	Textiles
Netherlands	100	140
Thailand	140	100

Absolute cost advantage

As Table 9.3 shows, the Netherlands has an absolute cost advantage in the production of dairy products and Thailand in the production of textiles. If the Netherlands specialises in producing dairy products and Thailand on producing textiles there will be fewer total production costs in both countries. Without trade, one unit of dairy products and a unit of textiles will together amount to 240 in Thailand as well as in the Netherlands. Two units each will therefore cost 480 to produce. If, however, the Netherlands concentrates on producing dairy products and Thailand on producing textiles, the total production costs for two units of dairy products and two units of textiles will only be 400. Specialisation and trade therefore mean an increase in prosperity.

If one country has an absolute cost advantage in respect of the one product and the other country in respect of the other product, the advantage in terms of international trade is obvious. It is more difficult to understand in those cases where one country has an absolute cost advantage in respect of both products. This situation is represented in Table 9.4.

TABLE 9.4 Absolute and relative costs of cheese and grain

	Absolute costs		Relative costs	
	Cheese	Grain	Cheese	Grain
Poland	40	50	1C=0.8G	**1G=1.25C**
France	50	100	**1C=0.5G**	1G=2C

Table 9.4 shows that Poland has an absolute cost advantage in respect of both the production of cheese and grain. While it would appear that Poland would be unlikely to profit from trade with France, this is not true. Poland can profit from trade with France by specialising in the product for which the cost advantage is the greatest, namely grain. In order to see how this works we need to transform the absolute costs into relative costs. The right-hand side of the table shows the cost relationship between both products. In Poland one unit of cheese or 0.8 unit of grain can be produced for 40. The relative cost of a unit of cheese is therefore equal to those of 0.8 unit of grain.

In France the relative cost of a unit of cheese is 0.5 unit of grain. Cheese is relatively cheap in France and grain is relatively cheap in Poland. On the basis of these differences in comparative costs, France specialises in cheese and Poland specialises in grain.

France exchanges cheese for grain from Poland. In return for one unit of cheese France wants to receive at least 0.5 unit of grain (the price in France). Poland is prepared to pay a maximum of 0.8 unit of grain for one unit of cheese (the price in Poland). If the international exchange rate for a unit of cheese is between 0.5 and 0.8 unit of grain, both countries will profit from trade.

Let us assume that the international price will ultimately be 1 unit of cheese = 0.6 units of grain. The trade advantage can be demonstrated by calculating what both countries can consume for a fixed budget (say 3000) before and after trade (see Table 9.5).

Comparative costs

TABLE 9.5 Consumption possibilities at an international price of 1 unit of cheese = 0.6 units of grain (budget = 3000)

	Before trade	After trade
France	60 Cheese or 30 Grain	60 Cheese or 36 Grain
Poland	75 Cheese or 60 Grain	100 Cheese or 60 Grain

In terms of the absolute costs of cheese and grain it follows that France can produce and consume a maximum of 60 units of cheese or 30 units of grain with a budget of 3000. After commencing trade with Poland France starts to specialise in the production of cheese The 60 units of cheese that France produces it can exchange for 36 units of grain. By trading with Poland France can consume more grain with the same budget. But Poland will also benefit from the trade with France, despite the fact that in absolute terms both products are cheaper there. Without trade, Poland can produce and consume 75 units of cheese or 60 units of grain with a budget of 3000. The 60 units of grain that Poland can produce for 3000 it can then exchange for 100 units of cheese according to the international price. By trading with France, Poland can also achieve a higher level of consumption.

TEST 9.3
In Ghana it costs €10 to produce a pair of jeans and €20 to produce a pair of shoes. In the Netherlands the production costs are €20 and €40 respectively. Is there any possibility of trade between the two countries which will be to the benefit of both?

9.2.2 How differences in comparative costs come about

The production costs in a country depend on the prices and the productivity of the factors of production. This means that there could be two reasons for comparative differences in costs: differences in prices or differences in the productivity of the production factors. The price of a production factor is related to its availability. In most developing countries, labour for example is relatively abundant whereas capital and know-how are relatively scarce.

Price of a production factor

The result is that labour in developing countries is relatively cheap and capital is relatively expensive. If we assume that there are no differences in productivity, the wage costs per unit will be low in developing countries and for this reason these countries will specialise in the production of labour-intensive goods and services.

Cheap labour

Figure 9.7 shows the wage costs per hour in a number of countries. We see that the wage costs in the Netherlands are about six times as high as those in Mexico. Disregarding productivity differences for the moment it would be advisable for Mexico to specialise in the production of labour-intensive goods and services (such as textiles), while the Netherlands should specialise in capital-intensive goods and services (such as the specialty chemical industry).

Figure 9.7 shows that there are considerable differences in wages between countries. In the developing countries labour is relatively cheap.
Despite this the wage costs per unit can be higher for some goods and services in the developing countries than in the advanced economies. This brings us to the second reason for differences in costs: differences in the **Productivity of production factors** productivity of production factors. Labour productivity is on the whole higher in the industrial countries than in the developing countries, because of the higher input of capital and knowhow in the production process and the higher level of education of the population. This partly compensates the differences in wage level.

Experience has shown that constant changes in prices and in the productivity of factors of production mean that the relative cost advantages of countries will also change constantly. This causes constantly changing **Product's life cycle** trade patterns. This process can be explained in terms of the product's life cycle (see Table 9.6).

FIGURE 9.7 Hourly wages costs and labour productivity[1] (2015, The Netherlands = 100)

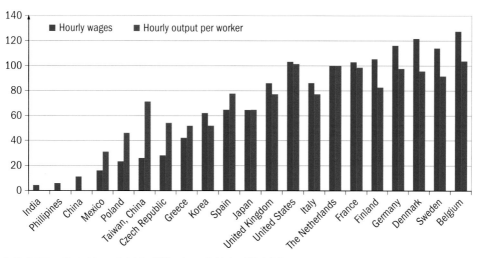

1 Hourly compensation costs in manufacturing and GDP per hour worked (not available for India, Phillipines and China)

Sources: ILO, Key Indicators of the labour market 2015; US Bureau of Labor Statistics, The Conference board, Total Economy database

TABLE 9.6 Product life cycle theory and trade flows[1]

	Trade flows			
	Technology	**Production location**	**Main markets**	**Example**
Introduction Phase	• Knowledge and labour intensive high-skilled labour • Series production	Advanced economies	Advanced economies	Advanced medical equipment
Growth and maturity phase	Transition: • Labour-intensive to capital-intensive • High-skilled labour to low-skilled labour • Series to mass production	Transition: Advanced economies to emerging markets	Advanced economies and emerging markets	Shaving appliances
Decline phase	• Capital intensive • Low skilled labour • Mass production	Emerging markets and developing countries	World-wide	Light bulbs

1 Trade flows from production location to the main markets.

Product innovation usually takes place in the industrial countries. During the introduction phase, the level of technology of the product and the production process is high. The productivity advantage of the industrial countries during this phase is consequently high, which is why production is very often located in those countries. Location in industrial countries has the added advantage that it is easy to react to rapidly changing market

Introduction phase

9

demands, which during the introductory phase is almost exclusively located in the industrial countries.

Growth and maturity phases

During the growth and maturity phases, gradual standardisation of the product and the production process will occur, accompanied by a decrease in technology level and an increase in the capital intensity of the production process. The initial productivity advantage of the industrial countries compared to the developing countries will become smaller because of this.

As well as this, because the product becomes cheaper through mass production, markets outside of the industrial countries will become more attractive. In the maturity phase, we very often see companies relocating parts of their production process to developing countries.

Decline phase

During the decline phase, the fully mechanised and standardised production process often only requires unskilled labour. In this phase the productivity advantage of the industrial countries will have almost completely disappeared and production will be concentrated in the developing countries.

9.2.3   Shortcomings of comparative costs theory

Comparative costs theory demonstrates that international trade is a win-win situation. This makes it an important and favourable argument for free trade. This does not mean that the theory does not have any shortcomings.

Argument for free trade

Homogenous products

The first of those, is that comparative costs theory is based on homogenous products, such as grain or wool. To buyers, it appears as though grain or wool suppliers provide virtually the same product the world over. If that is the case, cost difference determines product location. Comparative costs theory, therefore, is perfectly capable of explaining why one country would export grain and why another would export wool. In other words, it is eminently suitable for explaining international trade *between* lines of business ('inter-industry trade').

Trade between lines of business ('inter-industry trade')

Trade within lines of business ('intra-industry trade')

Comparative costs theory, however, is less equipped to explain trade *within* lines of business. Europe, for example, exports aircraft (Airbus) and cars (BMW), while simultaneously importing aircraft (Boeing) and cars (Toyota) as well. The trade within lines of business ('intra-industry trade') is growing rapidly, and is found particularly between countries with comparable income per capita. Both the Netherlands and Belgium, for example, produce beer. Comparative costs theory is not able to properly explain why the Netherlands would export Heineken to Belgium while Belgium is exporting Jupiler to the Netherlands. Either country ought to have a relative cost advantage in beer. But buyers feel that not all beers are created equal.

Heterogenous product

Since beer is a heterogenous product, cost differences are not necessarily a deciding factor in production location. In order to explain international trade within lines of business, we should pay more attention to product differentiation than comparative costs theory is able to do. Porter's diamond (see Chapter 3) is an example of a theory that does not use costs along to determine the comparative advantages of a line of business.

Advantages of scale or experience

Another shortcoming of comparative costs theory is that it does not take into account advantages of scale or experience. The theory states that the costs per unit of output do not change if production increases. If that is the case, the point at which a new company enters a line of business does not matter. Latecomers producing on a small scale encounter the same costs per unit of output as first movers producing on a major scale. In practice, this does not tend to be the case. Lines of business like the automobile industry and aircraft construction, for example, enjoy major advantages of scale. Higher production allows companies to spread out the fixed costs of, for example, developing a new model across several units. Early arrivals in a line of business also profit from advantages of experience. These are advantages from 'learning by doing': the more cars you make, the better and the more efficient you will be at making them.

Aircraft construction: major advantages of scale and experience when manufacturing a heterogenous product

According to 'new trade theory' early arrivals or 'first mover'-advantages play a huge role in international trade. This applies in particular to the trade in products that companies with high fixed costs are part of. First movers in these lines of business will develop more and more advantages of scale and experience as time goes on. They begin to dominate lines of business for which the world has only limited room, for example aircraft construction or the automobile industry. Latecomers from developing countries, as a result, are virtually unable to successfully enter into those lines of business. They are unable to compete with the 'first movers'. This is an important reason for developing countries to take protectionist measures.

'New trade theory'

Lastly, the theory does not sufficiently take into account various costs. One clear example is transport costs. The comparative costs of a product in Europe may be lower than those in Australia, but this does not automatically ensure trade between these areas due to the high costs of transport. A bigger problem is that the theory does not take into account adjustment costs. According to comparative costs theory, countries continually have to switch from sectors with comparative costs disadvantages to sectors with

Transport costs

Adjustment costs

comparative costs advantages. In theory, this switch is easy – an employee goes on to work in a different company – but in practice it is not. The switch creates unemployment since, for example, textile workers cannot simply get up and start doing accountancy. The temporary influence of free trade on unemployment can become so great as to force a government to take protectionist measures.

9.3 Free trade and protectionism

Differences in comparative costs can change during the course of time. While this causes business sectors to come into being or grow within a country, other business sectors will disappear, accompanied by loss of employment. This is an important incentive for a government to protect a threatened business sector against competition from abroad. In this section we will look at the arguments in favour of protectionism (Section 9.3.1), we will discuss the protectionist measures a government can take (Section 9.3.2) and we will look at the consequences this will have for the economy (Section 9.3.3).

9.3.1   Arguments in favour of protectionism

We use the term 'protectionism' to refer to the protection by the government of domestic producers against the consequences of international competition. The arguments that countries use to justify protectionism can be divided into two groups: unfair competition and independence.

Unfair competition

Governments often defend protectionist measures by pointing to the loss of employment that would result from 'unfair' competition from other countries. We will look at a few variations on this argument in detail.

International price discrimination or dumping

One of the main arguments in favour of protectionism is international price discrimination or dumping. Dumping is when a country sells products in other countries for a price that is lower than the price at home. Dumping is a clear example of unfair competition. If, for instance, a Korean car manufacturer dumps cars on the European market in order to improve his share of the market compared to his European competitors, he will only do so if the Korean market is protected against the import of cars. Should this not be the case, a Korean car salesman would be able to buy Korean cars cheaply in Europe and sell them for a higher price in Korea. Because Europe allows free entry to the market and Korea does not, the World Trade Organisation will allow Europe to protect its own industry against the consequences of dumping by Korean traders.

Low wages

Another important argument in favour of protectionism in advanced economies is the low wages in other countries. Unfair competition is not the issue here. Comparative cost differences depend on the price and productivity of production factors. The one country derives a cost advantage from low wages, the other from a high level of productivity. If an advanced country closes its borders because of low wages in other countries and a developing country closes its borders because of high labour productivity in other countries both will be worse off than in a free trade situation.

Social dumping argument

The low wages argument very often goes hand in hand with the social dumping argument. We use the term social dumping if one country

Protest against dumping on the European shoe market

artificially produces more cheaply than another country because of a difference in norms and values in respect of labour. Government regulations pertaining to child labour, working times, social security and working conditions differ from country to country and this has a considerable effect on production costs. Anti-globalists are of the opinion that protectionism against social and environmental dumping is justified in order to maintain a country's own views on labour and the environment and to protect foreign employees (children for example) against exploitation. It is debatable, however, whether child labourers in developing countries are helped by protectionism in the industrial countries. To take one example: an Indian girl who loses her job in the textile industry because of protectionism in the industrial countries could be forced to work in a local business sector such as the brick-making industry or prostitution, which would mean that she would be even worse off than before.

The social dumping argument makes it very clear that a plea for protectionism usually derives from the observation that there are international differences of opinion about the role of government, and consequently different government policies (the foreign government might, for instance, provide subsidies or have less stringent environment regulations). These differences in policy have what some would term an unfair effect on cost levels and because of this on international competitiveness. Protectionist measures are very often taken in retaliation for trade restrictions in other countries. If, for instance, the United States subsidises the steel industry or imposes import duties on European steel, the European Union will see this as an unfair influence on the competitiveness of American steel producers.

In retaliation the EU will subsidise its own steel industry or impose **Retaliation** restrictions on imports from America. In this way a retaliation spiral could be created that would be detrimental to the prosperity of both countries.

9

Independence

The second main argument in favour of protectionism is independence from other countries. In this view protectionism is allowed if national security, cultural identity, food safety or the independence of the food supply is endangered. The independence argument is the main reason for protecting film industry (cultural identity), the European import prohibitions on genetically manipulated food (food safety) or the European agriculture policies (independent food supply). The independence argument is a political argument, one that can be based on historical and cultural traditions, but sometimes also on opportunism. Economists cannot invalidate the argument; they can at most point to the effects the implementation will have.

Political argument

TEST 9.4

The agricultural policy of the United States and the EU protects some of the national producers against foreign competition. What is the effect of this on developing countries?

Strategic trade policy

A modern variation on the independence argument is the strategic trade policy. The strategic trade policy of a country aims at obtaining a prominent position in those sectors of industry that are regarded as being of great importance for future growth and employment. Countries are therefore inclined to stimulate innovative sectors of industry and to protect them against foreign competition. The national companies can then be the first to appear on foreign markets, which enables them to set the standard for the product and to profit from scale and experience advantages.

Infant industry-argument

The infant industry-argument is an important argument for protectionism in developing countries. The argument is based on 'new trade theory.' This theory states that first movers in a particular line of business build up virtually unsurpassable advantages of scale and experience. For developing countries, this is often a reason to protect a line of business in its 'infancy' from foreign competitors. There is, however, a danger involved in protecting emerging sectors of industry. The chance exists that the industry will become accustomed to government protection, making it more or less permanent.

9.3.2   Types of protectionism

There are many ways in which a government can give preferential treatment to national producers as against foreign producers. Trade restrictions can be subdivided into tariff barriers and non-tariff barriers.

Tariff barriers

Import tariff

The most common form of a trade barrier is the import tariff. An import tariff is a tax that a foreign supplier has to pay to the government if he wants to bring his product onto the market. Because the foreign supplier will pass on the tariffs in his price, imported goods will become more expensive and the quantity imported will be reduced. The reduced import and the higher price on the market will enable the domestic producer to produce and sell more. Production and employment on the domestic market is protected in this way. Sometimes a government will impose tariffs that are so high that a profit-yielding import becomes impossible. In such a case we speak of a prohibitive tariff. It virtually has the same effect as an import ban. Figure 9.8 shows the average import tariffs in the world. In the major part of the world, average import rates are below 10% now. Although this average rate also covers much higher rates for 'sensitive industries', such as agriculture, textile, clothing and shoes.

FIGURE 9.8 Average import tariffs (%) in 2015

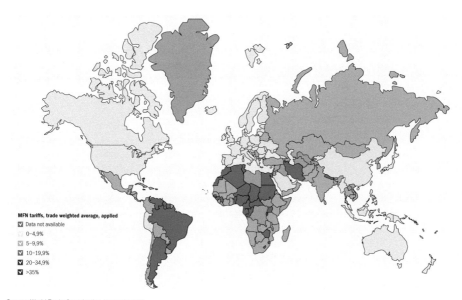

MFN tariffs, trade weighted average, applied
- ☑ Data not available
- ☐ 0–4,9%
- ☑ 5–9,9%
- ☑ 10–19,9%
- ☑ 20–34,9%
- ☑ >35%

Source: World Trade Organisation (www.wto.org)

TEST 9.5
Can we conclude on the basis of Figure 9.8 that industrial nations are more open to trade than the developing nations?

The income a government receives from import duties it can use to finance part of government expenditure. Import duties can be an attractive source of income for a government because they are paid by foreign suppliers. Ultimately the consumers pay the duties in the form of a higher price for the product, but most consumers do not know this or are insufficiently aware of this. There is a danger of imposing tariffs lightly or rashly and making them more or less permanent. A lowering of import taxes will have to be compensated by higher domestic taxes or a cut in government spending. Neither of these options is electorally attractive.

Non-tariff barriers
As well as import duties the government has a large number of non-tariff barriers at its disposal. The most important of these are: import quotas, voluntary export restraints, product regulations, subsidies and government purchasing policy.
A government determines the maximum quantity of a particular product that may be imported by means of import quotas. If the quotas have been put at zero there is in fact an import ban. Import quotas have the same effect as import tariffs: import drops and prices rise, causing domestic production to rise and consumption to drop. The only difference is that the government does not receive any income.

Import quotas

A voluntary export restraint is a variation on import quotas. In this case the one country does not impose restrictions on another country but there is an agreement to restrict their mutual trade. In this way they can circumvent the international trade rules of the WTO. The trade restriction is, after all, not imposed unilaterally, but is the result of a 'voluntary' agreement.

Voluntary export restraint

Product restrictions

'Local content requirements'

Product restrictions can severely limit trade, for example if a government sets demands for 'local content requirements'. If the Indian government were to stipulate that a smartphone produced in India would need to consist of components from India for at least 30%, it limits trade. Apple saw this demand as an important reason not to assemble the iPhone in India, choosing China instead. Another, more folkloristic example of a product restriction is the protected designation of origin found in the EU. It stipulates that champagne should be produced in the Champagne region of France, that feta cheese should be produced in Greece, and that Parma ham should be produced around the Parma region of Italy. Companies can be allowed to produce similar products elsewhere, but that means they would not be permitted to use the protected designation of origin.

Designation of origin

The government can stimulate exports and impede imports by deliberately keeping the exchange rate of its own valuta low. The American government is of the opinion that the low exchange rate of the Chinese yuan is an important reason for the large balance of payments deficit the US has with China. It believes that the low rate of the yuan puts American businesses at an unfair disadvantage. Americans are threatening counter measures in the form of import restrictions on Chinese goods if the Chinese government takes no or too little action against the undervaluation of the yuan.

Undervaluation

Undervaluation of the yuan as a non-tariff barrier?

Export subsidies

Discriminatory purchasing policy

The government can also take various kinds of measures that increase the sales and profits of domestic companies artificially. These include measures such as export subsidies that are only provided to national companies or a discriminatory purchasing policy by the government in which a government gives national companies preferential treatment when buying goods and services. US president Trump made 'buy American, hire American' the basis of his trade policy in 2017. This, he felt, should not be limited to the government; US citizens also ought to purchase more US products.

9.3.3   Consequences of protectionism

The main objection to protectionism is that a country may be using scarce production factors to produce goods and services that can be produced more efficiently elsewhere. In the 19th century the French economist Bastiat compared protectionism with a law that prohibits importing sunlight into buildings. Because of the import ban on sunlight the demand for artificial light will increase, causing the sales and the employment of lighting manufacturers to improve. While everyone will see that it is foolish to replace a product that is freely available (sunlight) by a product (artificial light) that requires production factors to manufacture and therefore involves costs, many politicians, entrepreneurs and trade unions do plead for protectionist measures as prices of foreign products near the zero line. What are the practical consequences of protectionism for the economy? Let us assume that the EU puts a restriction on the import of cars. Because of the drop in supply of cars on the European market the price will rise. European car manufacturers can profit from this, causing production and employment in the European car industry to increase. The European consumer, however is the victim. He pays a higher price for a car and has less choice. But the redistribution of income between car producers and consumers is not the only effect for protectionism also has a number of indirect effects.

Price will rise

Redistribution of income

The first is that the increase in the price of cars not only affects consumers, but also other industries in the EU. The higher price that the European consumer has to pay for his car has a negative effect on his purchasing power. This means that he can spend less money on products of unprotected industries. And those unprotected industries that need cars for their production process will see a rise in their costs, which has a negative effect on their competitiveness.

Employees will also attempt to pass on part of the price rise to their employers. If they are successful, wage costs will also rise. Protection of the car industry will therefore not only affect consumers, but also industries with comparative cost advantages.

In the second place, protectionism is detrimental to innovation in the car industry. Warding off international competition is no stimulus for product and process innovation. The chances are that the European car industry will lag even further behind the rest of the world, which would mean that the tariff walls have to be even higher. This will increase the negative effects of protection.

In the third place, other countries will not stand by and watch the interests of their car industry being damaged. It is very probable that retaliation measures will follow and they might affect other industries as well. It could happen thus that an efficient European brewery is confronted by US trade sanctions imposed in a reaction to import barriers aimed at defending inefficient car manufacturers.

The rise of international production chains means that protectionism has become much more complicated. We are long past the point where a country imported iron ore at one end, and spat out a complete car from the other. Nowadays, the international intertwining of car manufacturers is vast. Components come from all over the world. Intermediate products may cross borders more than once. Screws from Mexico, for example, are shipped to the US, where they are used to make components for a car (such as a seat). These components are then sent to Mexico to assemble the actual car. This car is then exported by Mexico to the US. Restricting import in a world of international production chains is comparable to walling up parts of a company – components cannot be transported from one department to the next (or: from one country to another), causing production to halt.

Production chains

Table 9.7 gives a summary of the direct and indirect effects of protectionism.

TABLE 9.7 The effects of protectionism

Direct	Indirect
Higher prices	Higher costs for unprotected industries
Less freedom of choice	Less innovation in the protected industry
Lowered consumption	Retaliation that affects unprotected industries
Preservation of production and employment in the protected industry	Lower production and employment in nonprotected industries

9.4 The balance of payments

International transactions between companies, consumers and governments lead to cross-border cash flows. These cash flows are registered in the balance of payments. Section 9.4.1 deals with the layout and the balances of the balance of payment. Section 9.4.2 gives an analysis of the balance of payments from the point of view of an entrepreneur.

9.4.1   Layout and balances
The balance of payments of the euro area in 2016 is given in Table 9.8. The balance of payments is subdivided in a current account, a capital transfer account and a financial account.

TABLE 9.8 The balance of payments in the euro area in 2016 (in billions of euros)[1]

Account	Balance	Sub balance
1. Current account	362	
1.1 Goods		374
1.2 Services		69
1.3 Income		50
1.4 Income transfers		-131
2. Capital transfers	6	
3. Financial account excluding international reserves	-373	
3.1 Direct investment		-279
3.2 Portfolio investment		-467
3.3 Other financial transactions		373
4. Increase (-) in international reserves	-15	
5. Errors and omissions	20	
Total	0	

1 A '+' signifies an income flow of money; '-' signifies an outgoing flow of money. On a financial statement, '-' signifies an increase in receivable due from foreign entities.
Source: ECB, *Monthly Bulletin*, March 2017

Current account
The balance on the current account registers the net amount a country earns by trading with other countries. The current account consists of a goods and services account, an income account and an income transfer account.
All income and expenditure associated with the export and import of
Goods and services account goods and services is entered on the goods and services account. The trade in services consists for the major part of transport, travel and business services. If the earnings from the export of goods and services are greater than the expenditure on goods and services we refer to it as a surplus on the

goods and services account. As we see in Table 9.8 the goods and services account in the euro area showed a surplus in 2016.

The income account shows the cross-border payments for the use of production factors. A deficit on the income account means that the amount in wages, rental, interest and profits received from abroad is lower than the amount paid out to other countries for wages, rental, interest and profits.

Income account

The income transfer account records the cross-border payments that have no service in return. These are things like donations in money and in kind such as development aid or transfer of money by migrant workers to their family back home. The income transfer account of the advanced economies is usually negative and that of developing countries positive.

Income transfer

Capital transfer account

The capital transfer account can be compared to the income transfer account. This account contains the cross-border transactions in the capital domain without a service in return. These consist mainly of transfers between governments for investment projects, often within the framework of cooperation for infrastructure development purposes.

Financial account

A country with a deficit on the current account (including the capital transfers) pays more to other countries than it receives from abroad. On the financial account we can see how the deficit has been financed. In other words, the financial account registers the changes in the net external claims. A country with a surplus on the financial account will see an increase in its net external claims and a country with a deficit will see a decrease in its net external claims. The financial account (excluding international reserves) consists of three parts.

The balance of direct investments registers the difference between the incoming and the outgoing direct investments. Financial transactions between subsidiaries of multinational companies are also shown in this account.

Balance of direct investments

The balance of portfolio investments registers the cross-border transactions in shares, bonds and the like. A surplus in securities transactions in the euro area means that foreigners have invested more in the euro area than the inhabitants of the euro area have invested in other countries.

Balance of portfolio investments

The item: 'other financial transactions' consists mainly of changes in the assets and liabilities that banks have in other countries. This account plays an important role in the settlement of transactions on the accounts 1.1 to 3.2. Let us assume that a European exporter supplies goods to a company in the United States. The transaction is entered in the goods account as export earnings. Payment is made via the banking system. The American importer instructs his bank to transfer euros to the exporter's bank. The importer's bank buys euros from a bank in the euro area in exchange for dollars. This causes the dollar deposits with banks in the euro area to increase (see Figure 9.9). As well as the cross-border transactions by banks, the financial settlements of transactions in other sectors are also entered in the 'other financial transactions' account. Entries on the accounts 1.1 to 3.2 have a contra entry in the other financial transactions account.

Other financial transactions

The contra entry could also be booked in the account international reserves. The international reserves are kept with the central bank and mainly consist of claims on foreign banks in foreign currencies. If a deficit on the current account is not compensated completely by a surplus on the financial

International reserves

account (excluding international reserves) the international claims of the central bank are reduced.

FIGURE 9.9 Settlement of an export transaction (the exporter is paid in euros)

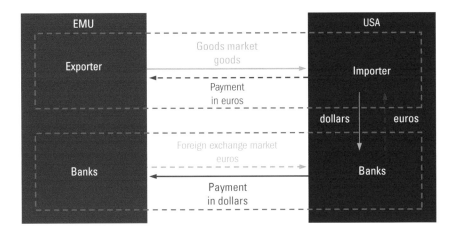

Because of the fact that every transaction on the current account has a contra entry on the financial account, the balance on the current account and the transfer account (items 1 and 2) will have to be equal to the balance of the financial account (items 3 and 4). Table 9.8 shows that this was not the case in the euro area in 2016. The explanation for this lies in statistical discrepancies when drawing up the balance of payments (errors and omissions, item 5). Apart from the errors and omissions, the balance of payments is formally always balanced. In other words the sum of the current account, the capital transfer account and the financial account is always equal to zero. The sub-balances do not have to be balanced. Per sub-balance there could be a surplus or a deficit. Analysis of these surpluses and deficits is important for judging the economic situation of a country.

TEST 9.6
The advanced economies fear that because of the lower production costs in the emerging markets, these countries will show a surplus on the current account because of high export levels and a surplus on the financial account because of the high influx of direct investments. Is this fear justified?

9.4.2   Analysis of the balance of payments
We take the balance of the current account as the basis of an analysis of the balance of payments. A surplus on the current account is regarded as being positive and a deficit as being negative. The reason for this is that the balance of the current account is regarded as an indication of a country's competitiveness. In this view, a surplus represents a strong competitiveness

Competitiveness and a deficit a weak competitiveness.
A surplus on the current account, however, does not always have to be the result of a strong competitiveness. A surplus can also be the result of a slow increase in expenditure in a country. In this case the low level of imports will

not be caused by a strong competitiveness, but by a low level of consumption and investments. A surplus on the current account is in that case a sign of weakness rather than of strength. Conversely, a deficit on the current account can be caused by a high level of expenditure, including investments. Emerging markets very often show a large deficit on their current accounts during the first phase of their economic development. Such a deficit is not the result of a weak competitiveness, but of a rapid growth of expenditure (especially investments) which high import (of capital goods) necessitates.

Emerging markets

Evaluation of a deficit on the current account is also dependent upon the way the deficit is financed. A deficit that is financed by an influx of direct investments is much less serious than a deficit that is financed by short-term loans. In the former case, the incoming investment flow indicates that foreign companies have confidence in the competitive capacities of the country. They are therefore prepared to invest their capital for a long time in that country. Because of the influx of direct investments, the production capacity of the country will also increase. In the latter case the deficit is accompanied by a mounting foreign debt. As the debt increases, the country will have to pay increasingly high interest rates in order to attract new loans. Ultimately, the foreign debts will mount up so high that the country will not be able to fulfil its interest and repayment obligations any more. This risk (the country risk) is the subject of Chapter 11.

Foreign debt

The current account also provides an insight into the exchange rate risk. The exchange rate risk is greatest in a country with a low level of expenditure and a deficit on the current account. Under normal circumstances, low expenditure is accompanied by low imports and a surplus on the current account. If a country has a deficit on the current account despite low expenditure, it is referred to as a fundamental disequilibrium. This means that fiscal policy is unable to reach an internal equilibrium (a stable price level and low unemployment) and an external equilibrium (a balance on the current account) at the same time. If, for instance, a government puts a curb on expenditure, the balance on the current account will improve but the domestic economic situation will worsen.

Exchange rate risk

Fundamental disequilibrium

The concurrence of low domestic expenditure and a deficit on the current account points toward an overvaluation of the country's currency. Because of the high value of the currency exports are low and imports are high. The exchange rate risk in a country with a fundamental disequilibrium is consequently very high.

Overvaluation

Chapter 10 will deal in more detail with the relationship between the balance of payments and the currency exchange rate.

As we have already seen a deficit on the current account that is financed by short-term loans leads to upward pressure on the interest rate. As the amount of a country's debt increases, capital providers will increasingly demand high interest rates for new loans. A persistent deficit on the current account will have a detrimental effect on the confidence that international capital providers have in a country. If the confidence wanes, they will no longer be prepared to finance the deficit. The result will be that the interest rate will rise steeply. The value of the currency will drop as well because the decrease in capital influx will lead to a decrease in demand for the currency in question. In developing countries it occurs frequently that a deficit on the current account via an increase in foreign debt leads to a confidence crisis. The negative effects of such a crisis on the country's economic development

Confidence crisis

are great and long-lasting, because once confidence has been lost it is not easily regained.

Figure 9.10 gives a summary of the main conclusions of this section.

FIGURE 9.10 Causes and effects of a deficit on the current account[1]

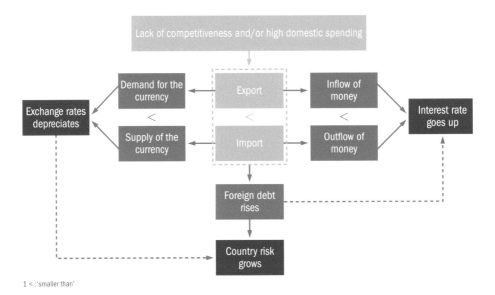

1 < :'smaller than'

TEST 9.7

A country has a surplus on the current account and is experiencing a rapid increase in domestic expenditure. What conclusion can be drawn in relation to the economy of the country in question?

9.5 International cooperation

Because of the increase in international economic transactions, international cooperation has become increasingly important. Section 9.5.1 deals with various types of economic cooperation between countries at the regional level. The most far-reaching form of cooperation between independent countries is the European Union (EU). The EU is treated in Section 9.5.2. Section 9.5.3 deals with the role played by some of the main economic organisations in the world.

9.5.1   Regional economic cooperation

Intensive economic transactions between neighbouring countries make the creation of a regional trade bloc attractive. All regions of the world exhibit some form of regional economic cooperation. We can differentiate between the following types of regional economic cooperation: a free trade zone, a customs union, a common market and an economic and political union.

Free trade zone

In a free trade zone, the participating countries have abolished their mutual tariffs. Each participating country maintains its own import tariffs in relation to countries outside of the free trade zone. This creates the problem that goods will be imported in the country with the lowest external tariff. The United States, Canada and Mexico jointly form the North American Free Trade Agreement (NAFTA). Let us assume that the USA and Canada impose import tariffs of 20% and 5% respectively on machinery from other countries. European machinery for the American market will then be exported via Canada. This undermines the trade policy of the United States, because a European exporter pays only 5% import duties by using the Canadian detour. Border controls are therefore still necessary in a free trade zone if only to determine the origin of products coming into the country. Entrepreneurs wishing to export goods from Canada to the United States against a zero tariff will have to prove that those products have, in fact, been produced wholly or largely in Canada. Determination and control of the origin of products involves a lot of paper work and delay at borders. Countries can overcome this problem by forming a customs union.

North American Free Trade Agreement

Customs union

In a customs union, the participating countries not only abolish their mutual import tariffs but they also impose the same tariffs on countries outside of the customs union. The effect that a customs union has on the prosperity of a country is not clear. On the one hand, a customs union does lead to an increase in mutual trade. Domestic production is replaced by imports from the country with the lowest cost level within the customs union. This is called trade creation and has a positive effect on prosperity within the union. On the other hand, a customs union is likely to lead to import from countries outside of the union being replaced by imports from countries within the customs union. This is termed trade diversion, and causes loss of prosperity. Imports from a country with low costs outside the customs union will be replaced by import from a country with higher costs within the union. We can illustrate the concepts of trade creation and trade diversion by an example based on figures (see Figure 9.11). Let us assume that the production costs of a unit of grain is €4, €6 and €8 in the United States, France and the Netherlands respectively. To start with, we shall assume that the Netherlands levies a prohibitive import tax on grain of €5. Before a customs union is formed there will be no trade in grain between the Netherlands (price €8) and France (price €11) or the United States (price €0). If the Netherlands and France form a customs union, the Netherlands will import grain from France. The price of a unit of grain in the Netherlands will drop from €8 to €6. Trade creation will therefore have caused an increase in prosperity.

Trade creation

Trade diversion

If the import tariff before the customs union is not €5 but €3, the picture changes (see Figure 9.12). Before the formation of the customs union, the Netherlands trades with the United States (costs for the consumer per unit of grain €7). If the Netherlands and France form a customs union, the import of American grain (€7 per unit) will be replaced by the import of French grain (€6 per unit). Trade will shift from the United States, which has the lowest production costs (€4), to France, which produces grain against a higher cost (€6). The trade diversion from the lowest-cost producer outside of the union to the lowest-cost producer inside of the union will cause a

FIGURE 9.11 Trade creation

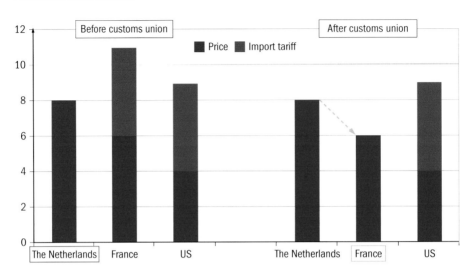

prosperity loss of €2. The import tariff of €3 is irrelevant here because it is not a net costs entry for Dutch society. The consumer admittedly pays €3 more for American grain, but the government receives the same amount.

FIGURE 9.12 Trade diversion

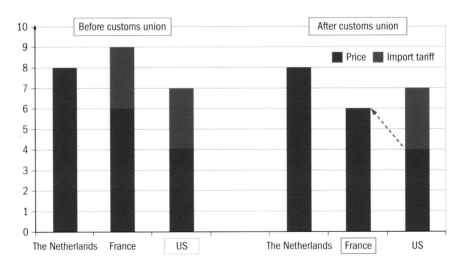

Common market

In a common market there is not only free transfer of goods and services but also free movement of production factors; that is, all restrictions on the movement of people and capital have been lifted. The markets for goods, services, labour and capital are now common. The creation of a common market is a complex process. Liberalising capital transactions does not usually cause many problems, but the free traffic of people certainly does.

Free movement of production factors

In order to prevent undesirable migration within the common market, some coordination in the fields of crime prevention, safety, employment policy and social security is necessary. These are, however, the very fields in which countries value their national sovereignty. The British felt that free movement of people in the European Union was the most important reason to vote for Britain's withdrawal from the European Union in 2016 (Brexit). Although the European Union has been a common market in name since 1993, there are still a number of restrictions in the fields of traffic of people and services. Some countries within the Union still have border controls and permission to settle within the Union is not completely free either. The consequence of this is that regardless of language problems there is unlikely to be a unified European labour market for some time.

Brexit

Economic union

National policy disrupts the functioning of a communal market. A clear example of this is taxation policy. If Ireland lowers its profit tax, Irish companies will be at an advantage compared to their competitors in the rest of Europe. This increases production and employment in Ireland at the cost of production and employment in other European countries. Governments can prevent the disruptive influence of national policy on the functioning of a communal market by coordinating policy or by entering into a communal economic policy. Taking this step creates an economic union.
An economic union could ultimately become a political union. This is the case when political decisions no longer take place on a national, but on a supranational level. Supporters of a politically unified Europe would like to see the European Union become a United States of Europe. They feel it would increase Europe's power and effectiveness on the international stage. Opponents of a political union counter this argument by saying that a political union would increase the distance between citizens and governments. They wish to return decision-making powers to member states. Table 9.9 shows the main regional trade blocs in the world's economy.

National policy

Communal economic policy

Political union

United States of Europe

TABLE 9.9 Important trade blocs in the world economy

Trade bloc	Participating countries	Aim
Asia Pacific Economic Cooperation (APEC)	21 countries in Asia and America that border on the Pacific Ocean	Economic cooperation and ultimately a free trade zone
North American Free Trade Agreement (NAFTA)	United States, Canada, Mexico	Free trade zone
Association of South East Asian Nations (ASEAN)	Brunei, Cambodia, Indonesia, Laos, Malaysia, Myanmar, Philippines, Singapore, Thailand, Vietnam	Free trade zone
Mercosur	Argentina, Bolivia, Brazil, Paraguay, Uruguay and Venezuela (suspended in 2016)	Customs Union
European Union	Austria, Belgium, Croatia, Denmark, Finland, France, Germany, Great Britain[1], Greece, Ireland, Italy, Luxemburg, Netherlands, Portugal, Spain, Sweden, Cyprus, the Czech Republic, Estonia, Hungary, Latvia, Lithuania, Malta, Poland, Slovenia, Slovakia, Bulgaria and Rumania	Economic and political union

[1] Great Britain triggered the negotiations for its withdrawal from the EU in 2017

9.5.2   The European Union
The European Union (EU) is the most far-reaching form of regional economic cooperation in the world. In this section we treat in turn the objectives, the organisation, the results achieved and the future of the EU.

Objectives
In the twentieth century, Europe was beset by two devastating world wars. After the Second World War, it was clear to most Europeans that the best way to achieve peace and prosperity in Europe is through cooperation rather than nationalism. In 1957, six countries – Germany, France, Italy, Belgium, the Netherlands and Luxemburg – signed the Treaty of Rome and founded the European Economic Community (EEC). From the original six member states in 1958, the EU has grown to a total of twenty-eight member states today. The substantial growth in the number of member states has been coupled with an increase in the number of policy areas in which the EU is engaged. Today, issues such as basic human rights, the environment or foreign policy are as high on the European agenda as economic issues. In 2016, a small majority of Britons choose for the UK's withdrawal from the

Brexit

European Union ('Brexit'). In 2017, negotiations regarding the conditions of Britain's withdrawal commenced. These should be concluded within two years. Figure 9.13 shows the population and GDP of the European Union and the UK's share in the two.

FIGURE 9.13 Population and GDP[1] of the European Union in perspective, 2016

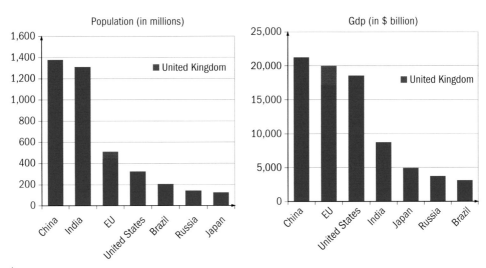

[1] The GDP is expressed in purchasing power parity, meaning it
has been corrected for differences in costs of living between countries.

Source: IMF, World economic outlook database, 2016, Eurostat

The original objective of European economic integration was the creation of a common market. In the Maastricht treaty (1992), government leaders took this one step further: in time the EU should become an economic, monetary and political union.

FIGURE 9.14 Growth of the European Union*

- 1958:
  Benelux, Italy, Germany,
  France

- 1973:
  Denmark, Ireland,
  Great Britain

- 1981: Greece

- 1986: Spain, Portugal

- 1995:
  Austria, Sweden, Finland

- 2004:
  Estonia, Latvia, Lithuania,
  Poland, Hungary, Czech Republic,
  Slovakia, Slovenia,
  Malta, Cyprus

* In 2016, Great Britain announced its withdrawal from the European Union.

- 2007:
  Bulgaria, Romania

- 2013:
  Croatia

Government and organisation

The government of the EU is based on the subsidiarity principle. This means that the EU undertakes to restrict itself to policy areas that have a cross-border effect, such as environmental, trade and competition policies. National matters such as education, culture and health are left as much as possible to the national governments. This keeps government close to the people and allows the national governments to cater to local preferences. The European Council and the Council of the European Union are the decision-making bodies of the EU. The European Council consists of the government leaders of the member states. There are a number of European summit meetings a year. During a European summit meeting important topics about the future of the EU are discussed, such as the introduction of the euro and the expansion of the EU.

Subsidiarity principle

Depending on the topic under discussion, the Council of the European Union consists of the relevant departmental ministers of the member states. They work out the agreements that the government leaders have reached on a certain subject. The introduction of the euro, for example, has been a major point on the agenda of the Council of Ministers of Finance in recent years. The Council of the European Union represents the interests of the member states.

Council of the European Union: voice of the member states

The preparation and execution of policies is the task of the European commission (EC). The EC represents and upholds the interests of the EU as a whole. The members of the EC are appointed by the governments of the member states. The EC has a considerable influence on the running of the Union. It prepares European legislation and monitors the implementation

European commission: promoting the common interest

9

by the national governments. As well as this the EC is responsible for implementation of the budget and for external trade relations.

European parliament: the voice of the people

The European parliament represents the voice of the people in the EU. The European parliament (EP) has as its main task endorsement of the European regulations, supervision of the European commission and allocation of the budget. The parliament is elected directly by the citizens of the member states. Although the European parliament has obtained some more tasks over the years, it does not have the same power as the national parliaments.

European Court of Justice: the rule of law

Citizens, companies, member states or EU organisations can bring conflicts relating to compliance with EU agreements before the European Court of Justice. The task of the Court is to guarantee consistent interpretation and application of the European regulations.

Unity in diversity

Results obtained and the future

Table 9.10 shows the main milestones of European economic integration. At the moment the EU is a common market and in some policy areas it is an economic union. Agricultural policy, trade policy and monetary policy, for example, are for the main part determined jointly. In other fields, including taxes, there is no economic union at all as yet. Both the rate of direct taxation (income tax and profit tax) and indirect taxation (VAT and excise) differ greatly.

TABLE 9.10 Milestones in European economic integration

Year	Progress in European integration
1958	European Economic Community (EEC) founded, consisting of Belgium, France, Germany, Italy, Luxemburg and the Netherlands
1962	The common agricultural policy is introduced
1968	The European community (EC) becomes a customs union
1973	Denmark, Great Britain and Ireland join

TABLE 9.10 Milestones in European economic integration (continued)

Year	Progress in European integration
1979	The Exchange Rate Mechanism, aimed at stable exchange rates within the EC, is put into effect
1981	Greece joins
1986	Portugal and Spain join
1992	In the Maastricht treaty, the name is changed to European Union (EU). The aim of the EU is the forming of an economic, monetary and political union
1993	The common European market takes effect
1995	Austria, Finland and Sweden join
1999	The Economic Monetary Union takes effect. The common currency, the euro, is introduced
2004	Cyprus, Czech Republic, Estonia, Hungary, Latvia, Lithuania, Malta, Poland, Slovakia, Slovenia
2007	Bulgaria and Rumania join
2009	Treaty of Lisbon, aimed at a more efficient, more democratic and more decisive Europe, comes into force
2013	Croatia joins
2016	Great Britain announces its withdrawal from the EU

Member states need to answer the question of whether the EU's future is to be found in greater unity or in greater diversity.

A choice for unity means that member states should take further steps towards political unification. On the international scene, the EU is a giant economically, but a dwarf politically. During recent international crises, the EU proved to be limited in its political and military decisiveness. But getting that many countries to all face in the same direction is no small task.

It is, however, unlikely that the EU will turn into a political union (a 'United States of Europe') in the short term because the opposition to this is great within the member states. A number of EU member states feels it is important to maintain the diversity within Europe. According to these states, integration in certain areas has overshot its mark. As a result, they wish to reclaim decision-making powers from Brussels.

An intermediate solution would be a 'Europe of two speeds'. This would mean that members states looking for increased unity strive to achieve that goal together, while EU member states looking for increased diversity refrain from taking part in the unification effort.

A different question is whether future European collaboration can be expected to become broader or more narrow.

Broadening of European co-operation implies that more countries join the European Union. In 2017 Albania, Macedonia, Montenegro, Serbia and Turkey are candidate countries. The EU is currently negotiating with these countries on accession. The candidate countries have to apply to the accession criteria. These criteria concern:

- The political situation (a stable democracy with respect for human rights and a well-functioning constitutional state)
- The economic situation (a well-functioning market economy and macroeconomic stability)
- The extent to which EU regulations have been adopted and applied.

Narrowing European collaboration by member state withdrawal is also a possibility. The possibilities for departure of an EU member state were not formalised until 2009. Article 50 from the Lisbon convention dictates

Margin notes: Unity · Diversity · 'Europe of two speeds' · Broadening · Candidate countries · Narrowing · Article 50

the withdrawal procedure. Following the Brexit referendum, Great Britain was the first to trigger article 50 in 2017. Once the article is triggered, the departing member state and the remainder of the EU have two more years to come to a withdrawal agreement.

9.5.3   International organisations

In this section we look at the main international organisations involved in trade and capital flows.

World Trade Organisation

Promotion of free trade

The main aim of the World Trade Organisation (WTO) is the promotion of free trade. In 2017 there were 164 countries that were members of the WTO.

Non-discrimination

The basic principle of the WTO is non-discrimination. A country cannot differentiate between WTO members when lowering trade barriers. If, for example, the EU lowers the import tariff on American meat from 20% to 15%, then the new tariff must also apply to Argentinean or Moroccan meat. Another consequence of the non-discrimination rule is that governments have to treat foreign companies in the same way as domestic companies.

Reciprocity

The second principle of the trade regulations is reciprocity. Under the terms of this principle a lowering of import tariffs by one country requires a corresponding tariff concession by the other country.

Transparency

The third principle is transparency. According to the WTO protectionism should be visible and quantifiable. According to the terms of the transparency principle tariffs are to be preferred to hidden and not quantifiable trade limitations such as product regulations.

The WTO promotes free trade by regularly organising multilateral discussions on reducing trade limitations. These discussions, in which all the members take part, are called trade rounds. Since 1947 there have been

Trade rounds

nine trade rounds. The first few were mainly about lowering import tariffs in goods transactions. During the course of time, sensitive subjects such as non-tariff restrictions, agriculture, services transactions and protection of intellectual property have been on the agenda. As well as organising trade

Mediating in trade conflicts

rounds, the WTO also has a role in mediating in trade conflicts between countries. These conflicts are usually about whether a country is allowed to implement protectionist measures or not. Under the rules of the WTO, the following reasons for protectionism are sanctioned:

- Safeguarding: countries are allowed to introduce trade restrictions temporarily if a sudden increase in imports causes severe damage to domestic industries.
- Combating unfair trade practices such as dumping
- Compensating export subsidies in other countries ('countervailing duties')

International Monetary Fund

When the International Monetary Fund (IMF) was established it was allotted four tasks: promoting stable exchange rates, supervising international monetary transactions, creating new international means of payment and providing credit to member states with a temporary balance of payments deficit. Of the original four tasks only the last has, in fact, remained.

When they joined, all member states had to provide an amount in their own and in a foreign currency. From these deposits the IMF provides credit to countries with a deficit on the current account. This gives the country concerned some time to combat the causes of the deficit.

Provides credit to countries with a deficit on the current account

There are conditions attached to the credits the IMF provides to countries with a deficit on the balance of payments. The severity of the conditions increases with the amount the country wants to borrow. The measures the IMF usually insists on are a devaluation of the nation's currency and other measures that curb expenditure such as a reduction in the government deficit or a reduction in monetary supply. The consequences for the countries concerned can be far-reaching. A devaluation, for instance, leads to a rise in import prices in the country's own currency. This causes inflation to increase and the purchasing power of the population (which is usually poor) to decrease even further. A reduction in government spending or an increase in taxes is usually very painful for the poorer population groups. The conditions that the IMF attaches to its support are controversial. For this reason, IMF policy has been the subject of massive and sometimes violent protests in the last few years.

Conditions

TEST 9.8
One of the conditions that the IMF usually imposes on credits is a reduction in government subsidies. Why would the IMF impose that condition and why does this condition often meet with a great deal of resistance?

World Bank
The International Bank for Reconstruction and Development was founded in 1945. As the name would suggest the task of the bank was originally to finance post-war reconstruction and economic development in Europe. Today, the World Bank provides credits to developing countries that desire to strengthen the supply side of their economy by, for example, improving their physical infrastructure. The World Bank derives its creditworthiness from guarantees by the industrial countries. This enables it to provide the less creditworthy developing countries with loans against relatively low interest rates.

Provides credits to developing countries

Favourable economic development in East Asia, Eastern Europe, and Latin America has begun to shrink the working area of the World Bank. Due to the low income per capita, sub-Saharan Africa and Southern Asia are currently the major operating range of the World Bank (see Figure 9.14).

G7, G8 and G20
The 'Group of 7' consists of seven big industrial countries, namely the United States, Japan, Germany, the United Kingdom, France, Italy and Canada. Russia joined in 1998, thus forming the G8. Russia was expelled in 2014 when it annexed the Crimea peninsula. This caused the Group of 8 to – temporarily? – revert to the Group of 7.

G8

The main task of the G7 is international policy coordination. The government leaders of the G7 come together every six months to discuss developments in the world economy. One of the main points on the agenda of these meetings is coordination of economic policy in order to avoid large balance of payment imbalances and exchange rate fluctuations.

International policy coordination

The growing importance of the emerging industrial countries in the world economy led to the formation of the G-20 in 1999. The aim of the G-20 is to bring about a dialogue between the advanced and the emerging economies

FIGURE 9.15 Gross domestic product per capita in the world (in international dollars, 2017)

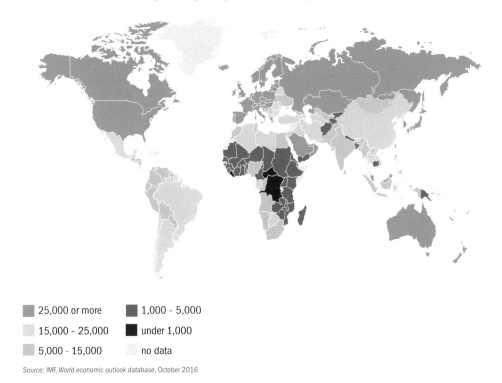

25,000 or more	1,000 - 5,000
15,000 - 25,000	under 1,000
5,000 - 15,000	no data

Source: IMF, *World economic outlook database*, October 2016

in respect of financial and economic matters. The participants in the meetings of the G-20 are the finance ministers and representatives of the central banks of nineteen countries: Argentina, Australia, Brazil, Canada, China, France, Germany, Great Britain, India, Indonesia, Italy, Japan, Korea, Mexico, Russia, Saudi Arabia, Turkey and the United States. The twentieth participant is the European Union, represented by the president of the Council of Economic and Financial Affairs and the president of the European Central Bank. Representatives of international organizations like the IMF and the World Bank also take part in the deliberations. Because of the economic weight of the G-20 – the countries account for about 90% of world production – and the broad membership, the G-20 has considerable legitimacy and influence (see figure 9.15).

OECD
The Organisation for Economic Cooperation and Development (OECD) has 35 industrial countries as its members. The main purpose of the OECD is exchange of information. Government representatives of the participating countries meet regularly to discuss the economic situation and policy proposals. This makes the governments of the participating countries better prepared for economic developments abroad that have an effect on the national economy. As well as a platform for the exchange of information, the OECD is also an advisory body. The OECD regularly issues publications that analyse the economies of the participating countries. The recommendations

Exchange of information

Advisory body

FIGURE 9.16 G-20 countries

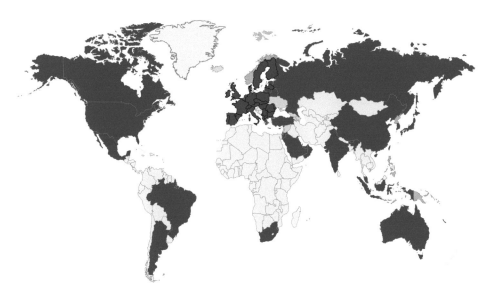

that follow from them receive a lot of attention in the press because of their relatively objective character.

Table 9.11 gives a summary of the main international organisations and their tasks.

TABLE 9.11 International organisations

Organisation	Task
WTO	Promoting free trade
	Settling trade disputes
IMF	Providing credit to countries with a deficit on the balance of payments
World Bank	Providing credit to developing countries that desire to strengthen the supply side of their economy
G7, G8, G20	Coordinating international policy
OECD	Information exchange
	Advising the participating countries.

Glossary

Advanced economies	Industrialised countries with a high per capita income.
Balance of payments	A survey of the cash flows between the inhabitants of a country and other countries. The balance of payments is divided into: • The current account • The capital transfer account • The financial account.
Common market	An agreement between countries to achieve free movement of goods, services, persons and capital.
Comparative costs	The cost ratio between two products.
Council of ministers	Decision-making body of the European Union made up of departmental ministers of the participating countries.
Current account	The balance of the export of goods and services together with the balance of the primary incomes and the balance of income transfers.
Customs union	An agreement between countries in which mutual tariffs are abolished and a common tariff in relation to other countries is established.
Developing countries	Countries with a relatively low pro capita income.
Direct investments	Obtaining property rights in a foreign company with the objective of exercising control.
Dumping	Selling products abroad at a lower price than that paid on the domestic market.
Economic union	A common market in which economic policy is coordinated or in which there is a common economic policy.
Emerging markets	Developing countries that are experiencing a very fast economic growth. Also known as newly industrialising countries.
European Commission	The policy-making and executive body of the European Union.
European Council	The government leaders of the European Union.

European Court of Justice	The body that ensures the consistent application and execution of European regulations.
European parliament	Directly elected representatives of the European population with a limited authority over the European Commission.
European Union	Economic union between the countries of France, Belgium, Luxemburg, Germany, Austria, Italy, United Kingdom, Ireland, Denmark, Finland, Sweden, Greece, Portugal, Spain, the Netherlands, Cyprus, Czech Republic, Estonia, Hungary, Latvia, Lithuania, Malta, Poland, Slovakia, Slovenia, Bulgaria, Romania, Croatia.
Export ratio	Export expressed as a percentage of the Gross Domestic Product.
Formal equilibrium	Accounting equilibrium of the balance of payments, obtained by having the banks compensate the balance of the current account, the capital account and private financial transactions.
Free trade zone	An agreement between countries to abolish their mutual import tariffs.
Fundamental disequilibrium	A situation in which the simultaneous reaching of internal equilibrium (full employment and a stable price level) and external equilibrium (balance on the balance of payments) is not possible without adjusting the exchange rate.
G7, G8, G-20	A group consisting of the seven main industrial countries: the United States, Canada, Japan, Great Britain, France, Germany and Italy. When Russia takes part it is termed the G8. The G-20 consists of Argentina, Australia, Brazil, Canada, China, France, Germany, Great Britain, India, Indonesia, Italy, Japan, Korea, Mexico, Russia, Saudi Arabia, Turkey, the United States and the European Union.
Global sourcing	A strategy whereby a company locates non-location-bound activities in those parts of the world where costs and added value are most favourable.
Globalisation	A speeding up of the process of world-wide integration by means of a strong increase in international trade and direct foreign investments.
Import quota	Maximum quantity of imports permitted.
Import tariffs	Tax on imported products.
Infant-industry argument	Protectionist argument which states that industries in the introductory phase need protection against foreign competitors with lower costs.

International Monetary Fund (IMF)	International organisation which has as its main task the promotion of free financial transactions and credit provision to countries with a temporary deficit on the balance of payments.
International price discrimination	See: dumping.
Multinational companies	Companies with subsidiaries in other countries.
OECD	An organisation consisting of 34 industrialised countries which has as its main task advising the participating countries on socio-economic matters.
Political union	Economic union in which political policy making takes place supra-nationally (i.e., at the union level).
Prohibitive tariffs	Tariffs that are so high that they prevent all import.
Protectionism	Protecting the national producers against competition from abroad.
Social dumping	Artificially producing more cheaply than other countries because of differences in norms and values in the labour field.
Strategic trade policy	A national policy of stimulating important innovative industries and protecting them against foreign competition.
Subsidiarity principle	The principle that states that the main policies of a regional cooperative body should be restricted to policy areas that have a cross border effect.
Trade creation	Increasing the mutual trade between countries by abolishing trade restrictions in a customs union (or a free trade zone).
Trade diversion	Shifting trade movements from countries outside the union to countries within the union by abolishing trade restrictions in a customs union (or a free trade zone).
Trade round	Consultation between the members of the WTO aimed at a reduction of trade restrictions.
Voluntary export restraints	Agreement between countries aimed at curbing mutual trade.
World Bank	International organisation with the task of providing credit to developing countries that want to strengthen the supply side of their economy.
World trade	The sum of all the exports of the world put together.
World Trade Organisation (WTO)	International organisation with as its main tasks the promotion of free trade and resolving trade conflicts between countries.

10

The foreign exchange market

The main issues that we will address in this chapter are the following:
- What factors induce changes to the exchange rate?
- How can companies reduce the detrimental effects of exchange rates on profits?

Exchange rates are determined on the foreign exchange market. Section 10.1 deals with some aspects of that market.

The foreign exchange market is divided into a spot market and a forward market. On the spot foreign exchange market transactions are concluded within two working days. Exchange rate developments in this part of the market are treated in Section 10.2.

Exchange rates may be determined by free market forces. If so, they are termed flexible exchange rates. Alternatively, the exchange rate of one currency may be pegged to another currency. In that case, they are termed fixed exchange rates. Section 10.3 treats the advantages and disadvantages of these two exchange rate systems.

In 1999, the year that the Economic and Monetary Union (EMU) came into force and a common currency – the euro – was introduced, the European foreign exchange market changed drastically. Section 10.4 deals with the exchange rate policy of the European Union.

On the forward exchange market, transactions are concluded after a period of time. The determining factors of the forward exchange rate are the subject of Section 10.5.

Since fluctuating exchange rates can have a major effect on the profits of a company, many companies have policies aimed at reducing the exchange rate risk. The instruments for doing this are dealt with in Section 10.6.

CASE

The euro: success or failure?

The euro was introduced in 1999. The initial exchange rate between the new currency and the dollar was €1 = $1.17. In the first two years of its inception, the euro fell sharply against the dollar. The exchange rate reached its lowest level of €1 = $ 0.82 at the end of 2000. Many saw the introduction of the euro as just another example of a failed European project. An important disadvantage of the low exchange rate of the euro versus the dollar was higher import prices, which fuelled inflation. In 2002 the euro entered upon a period of major growth, breaking one record after another. Its highest rate so far was achieved in July 2008, when 1 euro fetched almost $1.60, causing criticism of the euro to subside somewhat. A high euro rate also carries disadvantages as it worsens the competitive situation of entrepreneurs in the eurozone. This can lead to a loss of production and employment. Since 2008, the Euro has suffered a severe relapse. This was eventually due to the credit crisis in the Eurozone. Later, the Euro was impacted by the ECB monetary policy. Due to quantitative easing, the amount of Euros on the financial markets experienced a strong increase.

10.1 Characteristics of the foreign exchange market

Exchange rate

The currency of one country is traded against the currency of another country on the foreign exchange market. The equilibrium price on this market is the foreign exchange rate, which we can define as the price of the currency of one country expressed in the currency of another country. This section deals with the various segments of the foreign exchange market and the quotation of the exchange rate (Section 10.1.1), as well as some important aspects of foreign exchange trading (Section 10.1.2).

10.1.1   Market segments and the quotation of the exchange rate

The foreign exchange market consists of two segments: the spot exchange market and the forward exchange market.

Spot exchange market

The spot exchange market delivers currencies within two working days. The equilibrium price on this market is the spot exchange rate. The exchange rate between two currencies can be listed in two different ways:
- EUR 1 = USD 0.8 (direct quote of the euro, indirect quote of the dollar).
- USD 1 = EUR 1.25 (direct quote of the dollar, indirect quote of the euro).

Direct and indirect currency quotes

Within the euro area the euro is usually directly listed against the dollar. Newspapers frequently publish exchange rates in the form of a cross rates table (see Table 10.1).
The advantage of a cross rates table is that it shows both the direct and indirect currency quotes. The direct quotes of the euro, for example, are shown from left to right (e.g. EUR 1 = USD 1.0632) and the indirect quotes from top to bottom (e.g. USD 1 = EUR 0.940557).

TABLE 10.1 Spot exchange rates[1] on 20 January 2017

	EUR	USD	GBP	CHF	JPY
1 EUR	1	1,0632	0,8659	1,0727	122,47
1 USD	0,940557	1	0,814428	1,008935	115,189992
1 GBP	1,154868	1,227855	1	1,238827	141,436656
1 CHF	0,932227	0,991144	0,807215	1	114,169852
1 JPY	0,008165	0,008681	0,00707	0,008759	1

[1] EUR = euro; USD = US dollar; GBP = British pound; CHF = Swiss franc; JPY = Japanese yen.

Source: *Het Financieele Dagblad*, January 21th 2017

It is important to know the reference exchange rate when converting foreign currency into euros. For example, if an entrepreneur wants to buy or sell foreign currencies, he will need to know the buying and selling prices in bank transfers (indirect quotation of the dollar):

Currency	Official code	Buying rate	Selling rate
US dollar	USD	1.0625	1.0639

A company that sells $200, 000 to its bank will receive €187,987.59 (= $200, 000/ $1.0639) in return. A company that simultaneously time buys $200, 000 from its bank will pay €188,235.29 (= $200,000/$1.0625). The difference between the buying and selling rates is termed the spread.

Banks publish buying and selling rates for banknotes as well as buying and selling rates for non-cash exchanges. The spread in the rates for banknotes is greater than that for bank transfers. This can be explained by cost differences. Keeping a stock of banknotes involves high costs in transport, storing and insurance. Moreover, unlike foreign exchange deposits, banknotes do not generate interest. The higher cost involved in keeping a stock of banknotes is reflected in the buying and selling rates.

The foreign exchange market has its own terminology for exchange rate increases and decreases. It varies according to the type of exchange rate system. A rise in the rate of a system with flexible exchange rates is termed appreciation; a drop in the exchange rate is termed depreciation. In a system with fixed exchange rates, the exchange rate is not determined by market forces. This means that a change in the value of a currency will occur only following a decision made by the monetary authorities. A decision to increase the value of the local currency is termed revaluation; a decision to decrease the value is termed devaluation.

Spread

Cost differences

Appreciation
Depreciation

Revaluation
Devaluation

Forward exchange market

Currencies on the forward market are exchanged after a period of time. The settlement of a forward contract (in other words, the actual exchange of currencies) takes place sometime in the future. The exchange rate against which the currencies are exchanged is set when the forward contract is entered into. This rate is called the forward rate. In general, these forward contracts can be taken out for one, two, three, six, nine or twelve months. There is a forward rate for each of these terms.

Premium/ discount

The forward rate is often expressed in relation to the spot rate. The difference between the spot rate and the forward rate is described as either a premium or a discount. If the forward rate is higher than the spot rate it is described as a premium, and conversely a discount. The factors that determine whether the forward rate is at a premium or a discount are discussed in Section 10.5. At this time we are only looking at the quotation of the forward rate. Table 10.2 shows that the spot rate of the euro against the dollar was $1.0632 on 20 January 2017. The amount that has to be added to the spot rate to determine the forward rate has been listed underneath the spot rate. In Table 10.2, the forward rate of the euro against the dollar shows a premium. To take an example, the twelve month forward rate is at a premium of $0.0198. A currency trader who sells euros for dollars on the twelve month forward market on 20 January 2017 will receive $1.0830 (= $1.0632 + $0.0198) per euro one year months later.

TABLE 10.2 Spot and forward rates of the euro on 20 January 2017

	USD	GBP	CHF	JPY
Spot rate	1.0632	0.8659	1.0727	122.47
1 month	0.0010	0.0005	-0.0004	0.04
3 months	0.0037	0.0016	-0.0011	0.10
6 months	0.0085	0.0033	-0.0023	0.16
12 months	0.0198	0.0095	-0.0043	0.28

Source: *Het Financieele Dagblad*, 20 January 2017; global-rates.com

Trade 24 hours a day

10.1.2   Market size and characteristics of the exchange trade

Average daily turnover

Turnover on the international exchange markets is very large indeed. According to the Bank for International Settlements, the average daily turnover in 2016 was $5,100 billion. In that year a four-day turnover on the international exchange markets would have been enough to finance the whole of the world's trade in goods.

The exchange market is a highly transparent market. This means that the currency traders can be aware of the prices in the various financial centres at any time of the day. The rapid availability of exchange rate information makes it virtually impossible for there to be any difference between London and Frankfurt in the exchange rate of the euro against the dollar. Any exchange rate difference will disappear through arbitrage. Arbitrage is taking advantage of the difference between the exchange rate at different financial centres at one moment in time. If the exchange rate of the euro in Frankfurt is $1.25 and $1.24 in London at a certain time, currency traders will buy euros in London and sell them in Frankfurt. This will lead to an appreciation of the euro in London and a depreciation of the euro in Frankfurt. The exchange rate difference (not counting transaction costs) between the two financial centres will eventually disappear through arbitrage. Arbitrage does not involve any risk because it is based on the exchange rate difference between financial centres at a given moment in time.

Speculation is a different matter. Speculation involves making use of anticipated exchange rate differences over a period of time. Because the future exchange rate is never certain, unlike the arbitrage dealer, the speculator does run a risk.

Transparent market

Arbitrage

Speculation

10

TEST 10.1
What will happen to the exchange rate of a currency if speculators expect an exchange rate rise?

The American dollar is the most traded currency in the world. The dollar serves as the main medium of exchange and the means of evaluation of the exchange market. There is hardly any direct trade between the currencies of relatively small economies. Most of these transactions are made via the dollar. Trade via the dollar is termed cross trading. If, for instance, a bank has to exchange Norwegian crowns into Indonesian rupiahs for a multinational company it will split the transaction into two parts. Firstly the bank will purchase dollars in return for Norwegian crowns. Then it will purchase Indonesian rupiahs in return for dollars. The bank can deduce the exchange rate of the Norwegian crown expressed in rupiahs on the basis of the exchange rates of the crown and the rupiah against the dollar. The result is termed the cross rate. If the rate of the dollar is 9 Norwegian crowns in Oslo and in Jakarta a dollar is equal to 11,250 Indonesian rupiahs, the cross rate of the Norwegian crown expressed in rupiahs will be 1,250 (= 11,250/9).

Most traded currency

Cross rate

10.2 Spot exchange rate

The spot exchange rate is determined by supply and demand on the foreign exchange market. Demand and supply are dependent on a large number of factors. These will be set out in this section. The balance of payments will be used as the basis for analysing exchange rate changes.

Transactions with other countries are registered within a country's balance of payments. These transactions lead to a demand for and a supply of domestic and foreign currencies on the exchange market. If, for example, we want to account for changes in the exchange rate of the dollar we have to take the balance of payments of the United States as our starting point (see Table 10.3).

Balance of payments

10

Dollars

TABLE 10.3 The balance of payments of the USA and the exchange market

Demand for dollars or supply of foreign currencies	Supply of dollars or demand for foreign currencies
1 Current account	
Export of goods and services + income received	Import of goods and services + income paid out
2 Financial account (excluding official reserves)	
Capital imports • Long-term investments in the USA • Direct investments in the USA • Short-term investments in the USA (including speculation in favour of the dollar)	Capital exports • Long-term US investments in other countries • Direct US investments in other countries • Short-term US investments in other countries (including speculation against the dollar)
3 Official reserves	
Sale of foreign currencies in return for dollars	Purchase of foreign currencies in return for dollars

Demand for dollars

Supply of dollars

The left-hand side of the table lists all the international transactions of the United States that lead to a demand for dollars. An increase in US exports, for instance, will lead to a demand for dollars. The right-hand side of the table lists all the international transactions of the USA that lead to a supply of dollars. For example, a direct investment by an American company in the euro area will lead to a supply of dollars and a demand for euros. Every change in one of these balance of payment items will cause a change in the demand for or the supply of dollars on the foreign exchange market. This will also affect the exchange rate of the dollar.

The reasons for a change in the exchange rate of a currency will therefore have to be sought in details relating to the balance of payments. Since

changes in the official reserves are the result of monetary policy decisions, the exchange rate indicators will have to be deduced from the following:
- The current account (Section 10.2.1)
- The financial account (Section 10.2.2)
- Monetary policy (Section 10.2.3)

A survey of the exchange rate indicators (Section 10.2.4) follows.

TEST 10.2
Large European airline companies invoice part of their turnover in American dollars. Will the export of airline services by these companies lead to a demand for euros on the exchange market?

10.2.1   Exchange rate indicators and the current account

The current account of a country registers export and import of goods and services. Exports lead to a demand for the domestic currency and a supply of foreign currencies; imports lead to a supply of the domestic currency and demand for foreign currencies. So, other things equal, a deficit on the current account of the USA will lead to a drop in the rate of the dollar. A deficit on the current account develops when national expenditure rises more quickly than national production. Too rapid growth of expenditure can have a number of causes. Taxation measures or a rapid increase in money supply can cause the increase in expenditure to exceed the increase in production. The result will be a negative effect on the current account balance and depreciation of the currency of the country involved, or at least if all other conditions remain the same.

Current account

TEST 10.3
What effect will a lowering of taxes have on the current account and on the exchange rate (assuming that all other conditions remain equal)?

Purchasing power parity
The purchasing power parity theory is one of the most important exchange rate theories. This theory explains the exchange rate on the basis of the price differences between countries. The purchasing power parity theory maintains that exchange rates ensure that prices of internationally tradable goods are the same everywhere in the world (this is termed the law of one price). The following illustrates this.
Let us assume that a certain product costs €100 in the eurozone and $125 in the United States. This represents a purchasing power parity of €1 = $1.25. At this particular rate there is no price difference between the USA and the eurozone because one euro represents the same purchasing power as $1.25. As long as there is a difference between the actual exchange rate and the purchasing power parity profitable trade between the two regions is possible. Let us assume that the actual exchange rate at a certain moment is €1 = $1.50. A European trader buys the product in the USA for $125 / $1.50 = €83.33 and then sells it in the eurozone for €100. This causes an increase of exports from the USA to the euro area, which causes a demand for dollars and a supply of euros on the exchange market. The exchange rate of the dollar will rise until purchasing power parity is reached at the rate of €1 = $1.25.
In actual fact, purchasing power parity is not calculated on the basis of just one product, but on a representative range of goods. Nevertheless, the

Purchasing power parity theory

Purchasing power parity

principle remains the same: exchange rate adjustments cause international price differences to disappear.

So far we have only looked at the importance of absolute price levels for the exchange rate. This is termed the absolute version of the purchasing power parity theory. The relative version of the purchasing power parity theory explains the difference in terms of international differences in inflation. The following example will demonstrate how this version of the purchasing power parity theory works.

Let us assume that at the beginning of a certain year, an identical range of consumer goods costs €1,000 in the euro area and $1,250 in the USA. The purchasing power parity of the euro is therefore $1.25. We will also assume that the rate of inflation in the euro area is 2% and in the USA 4%. At the end of the year the prices of the range of goods have risen to €1,020 in the euro area and $1,300 in the USA. The purchasing power parity of the euro has therefore risen to $1.2745 (see Table 10.4).

Absolute version

Relative version

TABLE 10.4 Calculating purchasing power parity

	Purchasing power parity	
	This year	Next year
United States	$\dfrac{\$1{,}250}{€1{,}000} = \$1.25$	$\dfrac{\$1{,}250 \times 1.04 = \$1{,}300}{€1{,}000 \times 1.02 = €1{,}020} = \$1.2745$
Eurozone		

Table 10.4 shows that the difference in inflation between the USA and the euro area leads to about the same amount of appreciation of the euro in relation to the dollar. The appreciation of the euro is caused by the improved competitiveness of European companies in comparison to their American competitors. This causes the demand for euros on the exchange markets to increase and the demand for dollars to decrease. The ultimate result is that the difference in inflation between the USA and the eurozone is compensated for by approximately the same change in the exchange rate.

The limitations of the purchasing power parity theory

If we applied the purchasing power parity theory we would see that it has quite a few limitations. In the first place, the theory only applies to tradable goods and services. However, the country's inflation figures that we use to calculate changes to the exchange rate also contain the prices of goods and services that are not tradable. Consequently, international trade will not lead to purchasing power parity in relation to these goods and services (see Example 10.1)

- -

EXAMPLE 10.1

The Big Mac Index

The periodical *The Economist* has been publishing an annual Big Mac index since 1986. This index takes its name from the hamburger that is sold worldwide in McDonalds, the American franchise. Comparing the Big Mac prices will enable us to calculate the purchasing price parity of various currencies.

Big Mac-index (January 2017)

	Big Mac Price in local currency	Implied purchasing power of the dollar	Actual dollar exchange rate (January 2017)	Over- or undervaluation of the dollar
US	USD 5.06	-	-	-
Eurozone	EUR 3.88	EUR 0.77	EUR 0.96	Overvaluation
Japan	JPY 380	JPY 75.1	JPY 116.7	Overvaluation
China	CNY 19.60	CNY 3.87	CNY 6.93	Overvaluation

Source: *The Economist*, January 2010

The table shows us that a Big Mac in the eurozone costs €3.88 and in the United States $5.06. There would be purchasing power parity if the dollar were worth €0.77 (= €3.88 / $5.06). In January 2017, the market rate of the dollar was higher than this. The overvaluation of the dollar compared to the euro is partly caused by the fact that the Big Mac is a typical example of a product that is not traded. A consumer from the United States cannot use the international price difference to make a profit by going to a restaurant in the euro area with the express purpose of consuming Big Macs. In this instance, there can be no question of international trade leading to purchasing price parity.

- -

Example 10.1 shows us that international price differences for non-tradable products will not lead to trade between countries, and hence there will be no change in the exchange rate. Nor will there be any change in the exchange rate if the price differences derive from different VAT rates and excise duties in the various countries. We are therefore forced to conclude that if we use general inflation figures (which will include price rises in non-tradable goods and the effect of price raising tax levies) we will only be able to get an approximate idea of exchange rate changes.

Non-tradable products

VAT rates and excise duties

The second objection to using purchasing power parity theory to explain and to predict exchange rates is based on the existence of trade restrictions and transport costs. Purchasing power parity presupposes free trade between countries since this causes international price differences to disappear. In practice, however, international trade is frequently restricted by protectionist measures, and these keep the price differences intact. High transport costs between countries can also be a cause for continuing price differences between countries.

Trade restrictions and transport costs

One final limitation that needs to be mentioned is that the purchasing power parity theory bases its explanations of exchange rate changes solely on goods and services being traded between countries. In view of the increased importance of international capital movements, a convincing explanation of changes in the exchange rate will have to include capital transactions in the analysis.

International capital movements

The limitations to the purchasing power parity theory that have been mentioned can sometimes cause the actual exchange rate of a currency to diverge considerably from purchasing power parity. This is termed an overvaluation if the actual exchange rate of a currency is higher than purchasing power parity and undervaluation if the actual exchange rate is lower than purchasing power parity (see Case 10.1).

Overvaluation

Undervaluation

CASE 10.1

The purchasing power of the euro compared to the dollar

Since the introduction of the euro there has been a lot of attention paid to the question of what constitutes acceptable parity between the euro and the dollar. A version of the purchasing power parity theory can provide an explanation. Purchasing power parity has to be established on the basis of tradable goods and services. Alternatively, purchasing power parity can be determined on the basis of the prices of goods and services that are part of the GDP. The OECD uses this calculation method to compare the GDP of countries.

According to the OECD, in 2016 the purchasing power of the euro on the basis of GDP was $1.34. The actual exchange rate of the euro at the end of 2016 was $1.05. At the end of 2016 the euro was therefore undervalued against the dollar (see the figure below).

Market rate and purchasing power[1] of the euro against the dollar (1999-2016)

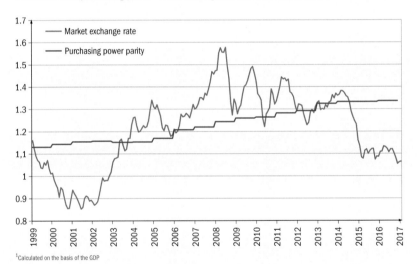

[1]Calculated on the basis of the GDP

Source: ECB (ecb.int), OECD (oecd.org)

TEST 10.4

What are the advantages to a country of having a currency that is overvalued?

Long-term equilibrium value

We can conclude that the purchasing power parity theory is able to provide an insight into the long-term equilibrium value of a currency. The short-term exchange rate is far less easily predicted: considerable short-term over or undervaluation of currencies may take place. As suggested above, the causes of short-term fluctuations in the exchange rate should primarily be sought in international capital flows.

10.2.2   Exchange rate indicators and the financial account

International capital flows are made up of direct investments and portfolio investments in securities. We shall now look at these components in turn.

Direct investments

How one country's investment climate compares with the investment climate in other countries will influence the amount of direct investment in that country. Multinational businesses look all over the world to find countries that offer the best opportunities for establishing their business. They will base their choice of country on a number of different factors, including the proximity of markets, economic growth, whether the country is politically and socially stable, whether the existing production conditions are qualitatively and quantitatively suitable, and the state of the infrastructure. These factors will jointly determine the investment climate. If a country has a poor investment climate, this will restrict foreign investment, leading to a net supply of the country's currency on the foreign exchange market and a decline in the exchange rate.

Investment climate

Portfolio investments

Return and risk are the key words for explaining the size and direction of portfolio investments. Just as multinational businesses are constantly on the look-out for the best location climate, international investors are always searching for the best climate for investing their excess liquid assets. A country with a favourable climate for portfolio investments is one in which high returns on investments can be made combined with low risks.

Return and risk

How much return can be made on an international investment is primarily determined by interest rates. If an investor has to choose between an investment in the eurozone and one in the United States, the first thing he or she will do is find out what interest rates are like in both regions. If interest rates are higher in the United States than in the eurozone, investors will express a preference for investing in dollars (as long as the exchange rates remain unchanged). The changes in the international interest rates are an important indicator of the short-term exchange rates.

Interest rates

The investor's choice will not only depend on the difference in the interest rate between the two countries. If, for example, the interest rate in the United States is 6% and in the eurozone 4%, it is by no means certain that the investors will invest in dollars. Compared to an investment in euros, an investment in dollars carries an additional risk. The risk is that the dollar will drop in value during the period of maturity, causing the return in euros to decrease. The investor will have to weigh up the interest rate difference between the USA and the euro area against the exchange rate risk that he is running with the dollar. International capital flows also depend therefore on the exchange rate expectations in the market. These expectations are known as market sentiment.

Exchange rate expectations

TEST 10.5

At a certain moment, the one-year interest rate in the USA is 1.5% and in the eurozone it is 3%. The exchange rate of the euro is $1.025. In a year's time, at what euro/dollar exchange rate will it make no difference to investors whether they invest in the USA or in the eurozone?

10

Market sentiment

Market sentiment is largely influenced by economic or political news. Economic news will only have an influence on the exchange rate if it deviates from what the market had forecast. If the economic news is exactly as the market had forecast there will be no change in the exchange rate because the news will already have been priced in. The following will illustrate this. Imagine that at a certain moment in time it is made known that the economic growth in the United States has improved slightly. We could expect the dollar to appreciate because greater economic growth will attract investors. The reverse would occur if the currency traders had counted on a greater improvement in economic growth. They would have invested in dollars already, causing the expectation of greater growth to be already reflected in the exchange rate. If the real growth then turns out to be disappointing, the currency dealers will sell part of their dollar investments again. This will cause the exchange rate of the dollar to drop and market sentiment in relation to the dollar to deteriorate. This could mark the start of another drop in the dollar rate. The publication of a rise in economic growth in the United States will, in fact, ultimately result in a sizeable drop in the dollar exchange rate! Such an overreaction to economic or political news items is commonly known as overshooting.

Overshooting

10.2.3   Exchange rate indicators and monetary policy

The central bank also carries out currency transactions. If a country's currency falls under a fixed exchange rate system, the central bank will be obliged to stabilise its own currency's exchange rate. This means that the bank will intervene by buying or selling its own currency in order to steer the exchange rate in the desired direction. The central bank may even intervene in a flexible exchange rate system. In such an event, intervention will not take place because of any formal obligation, but because the central bank wishes to send signals indicating the direction it wants the exchange rate to move in. The central bank sometimes tries to influence the exchange rate by issuing public statements ('verbal interventions'). Statements such as 'the euro is undervalued compared to the dollar' and 'the ECB attaches great importance to a strong euro' are aimed at positively stimulating market sentiment in relation to the euro.

Intervention

Verbal interventions

Exchange rate system

What exchange rate indicators can we derive from the central bank's monetary policy? In the first place, the exchange rate system itself is a factor of importance. A fixed rate system in which monetary authorities maintain the rate at a particular level will provide greater certainty about exchange rate movements than a system in which the exchange rate is left up to demand and supply on the exchange market. A fixed exchange rate system is, however, no protection against unexpected revaluation or devaluation. These are usually caused by the fact that the central bank is not always willing or able to support its own currency's exchange rate. The credibility of monetary policy with regard to exchange rate policy is thus at stake. A credible exchange rate policy implies that the central bank has to be prepared to intervene or raise the interest rate if a country's own currency rate comes under pressure. Any negative consequences to the country's own economy will have to be taken for granted. In countries where the central bank is under political control, this condition for a credible exchange rate policy is usually not complied with. If raising the interest rate is not adequate, the central bank has to be both willing and able to intervene. The central bank will then buy up its own currency in exchange for foreign currencies.

Credibility of monetary policy

The size of its foreign reserves will set limitations on how far it can go in doing this, however. The size of the foreign reserves are therefore important in assessing the reliability of a country's exchange rate policy.

10.2.4 Overview of exchange rate indicators

In sections 10.2.1 up to and including 10.2.3 we have looked at the balance of payments of a country in order to find the most important exchange rate indicators. We have summarised these in Table 10.5.

10

TABLE 10.5 Exchange rate indicators

	Exchange rate indicators	**Background cause**
Current account	National expenditure	Business cycle
	Inflation differences	Monetary growth
		Wage costs per unit of output
Capital account	Investment climate	The economy's competitiveness
		Economic growth
	Interest rate differences	Monetary growth Business cycle
	Exchange rate expectations (market sentiment)	Political and economic news
		Historical exchange rate movements
Monetary policy	Exchange rate system	Monetary policy priorities
	Credibility of exchange rate policy	Size of official reserves

Short-term exchange rate forecasts should primarily be based on changes in interest rate differences, market sentiment and monetary policy. Long-term exchange rate predictions should be based on purchasing power parity and the long-term economic growth potential. In the long run, the level of the exchange rate reflects the competitiveness of an economy. Countries with a limited ability to compete on the world market will not export a great deal and will not attract much direct investment or portfolio investment. This will be reflected in a tendency for the exchange rate to drop. The opposite applies for countries with a strong competitiveness.

10.3 Exchange rate systems

In the previous section we referred in passing to the role of the exchange rate system in analysis and prediction of the spot rate. In this section we will make a distinction between two exchange rate systems: one with flexible rates and one with fixed rates (Section 10.3.1). Section 10.3.2 will subsequently address the question of to what extent both systems are compatible with the internal economic aims of price stability and full employment.

10.3.1 Fixed and flexible exchange rates

In a system of fixed exchange rates, the participating currencies are pegged to each other. Every currency has an official value expressed in terms of a certain means of evaluation (for example, the dollar or the euro). The official value is termed the central rate. A small margin of fluctuation around the central rate is usually allowed. Within this margin, the exchange rate is determined by market forces. If there is any danger of a certain currency

10

Flexible exchange rates

moving outside the tolerated margin, the exchange rate system participants are obliged to intervene. What this means is that a currency that is decreasing too much will be bought and a currency that is rising too much will be sold. In a system of flexible exchange rates, the price of a currency is determined by supply and demand. The exchange rates of the main world currencies (dollar, euro) are determined by supply and demand on the international exchange markets.

10.3.2   The advantages and disadvantages of flexible exchange rates

In this subparagraph, the advantages and disadvantages of a flexible exchange rate system will be discussed.

Automatic adjustment of balance of payments disequilibrium

One of the major advantages of a flexible exchange rate system is that a deficit or surplus on the balance of payments will disappear automatically when there is a change in the exchange rate. Let us assume that a certain country has a deficit on the current account. The demand for the currency is smaller than the supply, which causes the exchange rate to drop. This improves the competitiveness of that country's producers. Exports increase and imports decrease until an equilibrium on the current account is reached (the external equilibrium). In a system of flexible exchange rates, the government or the central bank do not have to take measures to restore the external equilibrium. They can concentrate fully on maintaining the internal equilibrium, which involves full employment and a stable price level.

External equilibrium

In a system of fixed exchange rates, expenditure cutting measures are necessary to reduce imports and to restore the external equilibrium. The expenditure cuts can, however, disturb the internal equilibrium even more. This will occur if a country is simultaneously faced with unemployment and a deficit on the current account of the balance of payments. To diminish the deficit on the current account, the government has to curb expenditure, which it will do by, for instance, raising taxes. However, raised taxes will also lead to an increase in unemployment. Such a situation can be characterised as one of a fundamental disequilibrium, because simultaneously achieving internal and external equilibrium by means of policies geared towards increasing or decreasing expenditure is not possible. Solving a fundamental disequilibrium requires a revaluation or a devaluation.

Fundamental disequilibrium

No import of inflation

The second advantage of a system of flexible exchange rates is that it prevents importing inflation. Let us assume that there is a high rate of inflation in Great Britain and the prices of British export goods rise sharply. Because of the intensive trade between Great Britain and the Continent, the rise in British export prices will carry through into the eurozone unless the exchange rate compensates the difference in inflation rate. In a system of flexible exchange rates this is what will happen. The high inflation rate in Great Britain will cause the British exports to drop, causing the demand for British pounds to decrease and thereby causing the pound to depreciate. The depreciation of the pound will compensate for the raised import prices in pounds in the eurozone, and consequently there will be no effect on inflation in the eurozone. In a system of fixed exchange rates this adjustment of rates is not possible and imported inflation is unavoidable.

Imported inflation

Independent monetary and fiscal policy

The third advantage of a flexible exchange rate system is that the government is not dependent on other countries for policy making. Because the government is not aiming at a fixed exchange rate in relation to other countries it does not have to take into account the policies of other countries. In a system of fixed exchange rates the government and the central bank cannot implement budgetary and monetary policies independently. Convergence of the policies of the participants is a necessary prerequisite for a successful fixed exchange rate system. Let us imagine that two countries within a fixed exchange rate system establish monetary policy independently of each other. Economic growth and inflation are low in one country, and so the central bank decides to lower the interest rate. The other country, however, has high economic growth and high inflation, which is a reason for the central bank to increase the interest rate. The changed interest rate differences between the two countries will cause a capital flow in the direction of the country with the increased interest rate. This is irreconcilable with exchange rate stability between the two countries. As we have seen, a system of fixed exchange rates cannot function without convergence of policy. In turn, convergence of policy is not really feasible without convergence of economic development in the participating countries. This is especially important if the system of fixed exchange rates evolves into a common currency. We can therefore deduce that ideally, a currency area will consist of countries that do not differ greatly in terms of their economic development (growth and inflation) and economic policy (especially budgetary policy). This is why convergence criteria have been formulated for admission to the eurozone.

Convergence of the policies

Convergence criteria

Exchange rate risk

The main disadvantage of the system of flexible exchange rates is that the exchange rate will be a constant source of uncertainty in international trade and investment transactions. Exchange rate fluctuations are accompanied by risks for entrepreneurs. In order to protect themselves against these risks they have to incur costs. As a rule, these are not necessary in a system of fixed exchange rates.

Exchange rate risk

Table 10.6 summarises this section.

TABLE 10.6 Distinguishing features of exchange rate systems

	Exchange rate system	
	Flexible	Fixed
Rapid and automatic adjustment of a balance of payment imbalance	yes	no
Imported inflation	no	yes
Independent monetary and budgetary policy possible	yes	no
Uncertainty in international trade, payment and investment transactions	yes	no

⑩④ Exchange rate policy in the European Union

The Economic and Monetary Union (EMU) came into force in 1999. A common currency – the euro – was introduced. Section 10.4.1 will discuss the main advantages and disadvantages of the EMU. Those countries that are not a part of the euro area are expected to peg their currency to the euro. The exchange rate mechanism operating between the euro and the other EU currencies (ERM-II) is dealt with in Section 10.4.2. Section 10.4.3 treats the relationship between the world's three main currencies: the euro, the dollar and the yen.

Euro symbol in the official colours

10.4.1   The Economic and Monetary Union

In the Maastricht Treaty (1992) the decision was made to replace the national currencies of the EU member states by one common currency. In this section we will firstly discuss the safeguards for a stable euro and subsequently the advantages and disadvantages of the EMU.

Safeguarding the stability of the euro

An effective anti-inflationary policy is of prime importance in maintaining the internal and external value of the euro. To ensure that anti-inflation policies are not thwarted by the individual member states a number of safeguards have been built into the EMU. The main ones are the convergence criteria, the Growth and Stability pact and the independence of the ECB.

Convergence criteria

The treaties that form the basis of the EMU all contain convergence criteria. These criteria relate to a low level of inflation and interest rates, sound government finances and (for potential participants) exchange rate stability. The purpose of the criteria is to prevent any country endangering the effectiveness of the euro area by a too high inflation rate or an excessive government deficit. A high inflation rate in one country increases the average inflation rate in the whole of the eurozone. This could force the ECB to raise the interest rate in all the countries, even in those countries that have a low inflation rate. Table 10.7 shows the extent to which the convergence of EU government finances has advanced. As demonstrated in the table, the levels of government debt are especially varied. Southern European governments in particular are heavily in debt.

TABLE 10.7 Government finances in the EU in 2017

	Government balance (% GDP)	Government debt (% GDP)		Government balance (% GDP)	Government debt (% GDP)
Norm	−3	60	*Norm*	−3	60
Euro area			*Other EU countries*		
Belgium	−2.2	107	Bulgaria	−0.5	27
Cyprus	−0.2	103	Hungary	−2.4	72
Germany	0.4	66	Croatia	−2.1	83
Estonia	−0.5	10	Poland	−2.9	55
Finland	−2.3	66	Romania	−3.6	41
France	−2.9	97	Czech Republic	0.1	37
Greece	−1.1	177			
Ireland	−0.6	74	Denmark	−1.6	38
Italy	−2.4	133	Sweden	−0.2	39
Latvia	−1.0	37			
Lithuania	−0.7	44	United Kingdom	−2.8	88
Luxembourg	0.2	23			
Malta	−0.6	58			
The Netherlands	0.2	60			
Austria	−1.2	81			
Portugal	−2.0	129			
Slovenia	−1.7	79			
Slovakia	−1.4	52			
Spain	−3.5	100			

Source: European Union, Economic forecasts, Winter 2017

Growth and Stability Pact

The Growth and Stability Pact was introduced in order to ensure that all the countries that are part of the EMU continue to comply with the criteria for government finance. The terms of the Stability Pact stipulate that in the medium term, countries should aim at a government balance that is in equilibrium. This will create a budgetary safety margin which will ensure that during difficult economic times the deficit does not exceed the 3% norm. The Pact also has an excessive deficit procedure whereby the government finances of the EU member states are closely scrutinised. If there is any threat of an excessive deficit the government of that country will be urged to take measures. If measures are not taken, in extreme cases, a fine can be imposed.

The Stability and Growth Pact was not able to prevent the sovereign debt crisis of 2009 and 2010 in the eurozone. The Pact became a paper tiger after France and Germany failed to accept sanctions because of an excessive deficit. In particular, Germany's refusal to stick to the rules put paid to compliance to the Stability Pact.

Political independence

The third important guarantee for a stable euro is complete ECB political independence. This means that neither the president of the ECB nor the presidents of the national central banks are allowed to accept directives from politicians. Many politicians are of the opinion – an opinion voiced particularly during an election year – that growth of production and employment should take precedence over combating inflation. They consequently often put pressure on the central bank to stimulate the economy by lowering the interest rate. The ECB is not permitted to relax its vigilance in the fight against inflation.

Advantages of the EMU

One common currency means that the economic decisions made by entrepreneurs and consumers are no longer hampered by uncertainty about the exchange rates in Europe. Cross-border transactions no longer require currencies to be converted, and costs relating to exchange rate risk insurance within the eurozone have disappeared. As well as lowering transaction costs, the euro also had some indirect benefits.

Lowering transaction costs

In the first place, it has made the European market more transparent. It is easier for producers and consumers to compare prices if the same means of evaluation is used everywhere in the eurozone. The transparency of the European market has stimulated competition, forcing European companies to produce more efficiently.

Transparency of the European market

In the second place, the introduction of the euro provided the European Union with the same sort economies of scale as their American and Japanese competitors. With the formation of the eurozone a European market was created in which more than 300 million people pay with the same currency. European companies always used to have a disadvantage in relation to their American and Japanese competitors because they had to operate on a fragmented home market in which there were a lot of different currencies. Thirdly, since the euro has the capacity to become as major an invoicing currency as the dollar, European companies can save on the costs of currency management.

Invoicing currency

Disadvantages of the EMU

The main objection to a common currency is that the individual member states can no longer use the interest rate and the exchange rate as economic policy tools. Such tools are particularly useful for crises in the eurozone that are country-specific: a crisis – economic or non-economic – that affects mainly one country, such as a disastrous flood in the Netherlands. Before the introduction of the EMU the affected country could decide to lower the value of the domestic currency (devaluation) in order to maintain its competitiveness. The introduction of the euro put a stop to this and countries now have to find other ways to improve their competitiveness. Cost management and innovation are two options available.

Economic policy tools

Another major objection to the EMU lies in the loss of national sovereignty in budgetary matters. The Growth and Stability Pact compels countries to work toward a budgetary equilibrium or even a budgetary surplus. It must be remembered that the Pact does not set a norm for the *amount* of government expenditure and income but for the *balance*. The national governments remain responsible for the expenditure on public goods as long as it is financed in such a way that it does not result in an excessive deficit.

Loss of national sovereignty

The third major objection to the EMU concerns the limited democratic control over monetary policy. The European Central Bank operates quite independently of democratically elected politicians. In the monetary area, democracy has been put on a side line, though admittedly with the assent of democratically elected politicians (in the political independence provisions of the Maastricht Treaty). The independence of the ECB can be interpreted

Limited democratic control

in various ways. Some see it as evidence of the democratic shortcomings of the EU in its policies. On the other hand, others see in political self-restraint a sign that the need for price stability is being taken seriously.

Convergence in the Eurozone?

A monetary union between independent countries can only work if their economies grow closer, also known as convergence. So what, if anything, is happening in terms of convergence in the Eurozone after two decades? Table 10.8 shows the economic achievements of four North European countries (Germany, Finland, the Netherlands, and Austria) and those of four South European countries (Greece, Italy, Portugal, and Spain).

Convergence

TABLE 10.8 Convergence in the Eurozone[1]

	1981-1989		1990-1998		1999-2007		2008-2016	
	North	South	North	South	North	South	North	South
Economic growth (%)	2.3	2.4	2.3	2.4	2.6	2.8	0.5	-1.2
Inflation (%)	3.9	14.2	2.3	6.8	1.8	2.9	1.6	1.3
Unemployment (% of working population)	5.6	10.5	7.3	11.3	6.7	8.9	6.2	15.6
Balance on current account (% GDP)	0.6	-2.2	0.6	-1.5	3.5	-5.9	4.3	-3.2

[1] North: Germany, Finland, the Netherlands, Austria; South: Greece, Italy, Portugal, Spain; figures are annual averages.

Source: IMF, World Economic outlook database (October 2016)

Prior to the introduction of the Euro in 1999, economic growth in the countries in both groups was similar. South Europe scored much worse in terms of inflation and unemployment.

Following the introduction of the Euro, North and South seemed to be growing closer. The southern Euro countries initially saw an increase in economic growth. But there was another side to that coin. Due to high inflation in South Europe, its competitive position compared to North Europe worsened. And the introduction of the Euro prevented the South European countries from devaluing their currencies.

Competitive position

The difference in inflation caused the Euro to become undervalued (too cheap) in North Europe, while at the same time it became overvalued (too expensive) in South Europe. The result: a growing deficit on the current account in the south, and a growing surplus in the north (see Table 10.8). During and immediately after the economic crisis of 2008-2009, things went pear-shaped. The southern Euro countries got into trouble financially, and had to make extensive cuts. This resulted in a shrinking economy and increased unemployment (see Table 10.8). The crisis did hit the northern countries as well, but the impact was much less severe. In all, economies within the Eurozone are diverging rather than converging. The income inequality between North and South has therefore increased instead of decreased compared to the situation in 1999.

Economic crisis

Apart from just continuing in the same vein and hoping that convergence will happen along the way, there are two other solutions to the lack of convergence:
1 fully or partially undo the monetary collaboration
2 forming a political union.

Ad 1 Fully or partially undoing the monetary collaboration

National currencies

One option is to reintroduce national currencies. If, in retrospect, the Eurozone does not prove to be a viable stage for a common currency, that would be a logical step. Countries would be returned their interest and exchange rate instruments, but would lose the advantages of a common currency.

Unrest

Reintroducing national currencies would be costly, would cause unrest on financial markets, and would lead to a steep decrease in the value of South European currencies. It is less than certain that southern Euro countries would still be able to meet their obligations to their creditors. It would likely result in a new debt crisis.

Another, less far-reaching solution could be found in the introduction of a North European Euro (the 'Neuro') and a South European Euro (the 'Seuro'). The difference in competitive power between the northern and southern countries would be expressed in the value of both currencies. This means the 'Neuro' would become more expensive than the 'Seuro'. Something similar to the 'Neuro' already existed in the 1980s and 1990s. Known as the D-Mark bloc, it saw the Benelux countries along with Switzerland, Austria, and Scandinavia link their respective currencies to the Deutsche Mark. For all intents and purposes, this meant the northern countries all had the same currency. The currencies in the D-Mark bloc continually appreciated relative to the currencies in the southern countries.

Ad 2 Forming a political union

The Eurozone does not have political unity. Setting budgets falls under national authority. That means it would not be appropriate for tax payers in one country (e.g. Germany) to have to bail out those of another country (e.g. Greece) in times of financial distress; it would mean that the Greek government would indirectly be setting the height of the taxes in Germany which, in turn, would contradict German sovereignty or decision-making power.

Budgeting union

Should the decision be made to have budgeting decided at the European level, things would be different. In a budgeting union the budget no longer falls under the authority of any single individual country, but under European authority. In the United States of Europe, it would be much easier to achieve convergence through budgeting. In many countries, this is part and parcel of economic policy. West and East Germany, for example, formed a political and monetary union in 1990. As a result, the west supported the east in terms of finance for many years. The monetary union in the United States also involves having tax payments move from stronger, richer states to the government and then on to weaker, poorer states. Yet it is highly unlikely that a similar fiscal union will be formed within the Eurozone.

10.4.2 The Exchange Rate Mechanism II

Nineteen EU countries have already introduced the euro (see table 10.7). The remaining countries have committed themselves to join the eurozone in the near future. Only Denmark and Sweden have stipulated an exemption. They determine whether, and if so, when they join the euro. There is thus a potential danger that exchange rate fluctuations between the euro and the other EU currencies will hamper economic transactions within the common market. To avoid this, an exchange rate mechanism linking the euro to the other EU currencies was created. This mechanism was called ERM-II since it replaced the European Monetary System (EMS) that ensured (though with varying success) the exchange rate stability in Europe between 1979 to 1999.

ERM-II: principles

The main principle of ERM-II is that all EU countries must take mutual responsibility for the successful functioning of the European market, undisturbed by any uncertainty about exchange rates. For this to happen, the ECB and the central banks in the other EU member states have to coordinate their monetary policy.

Mutual responsibility

Another principle of ERM-II is voluntary participation. Compulsory membership of countries is likely to lead to tension within the EU and to speculation on the exchange markets, with an ensuing detrimental effect on the objective of exchange rate stability. At the beginning of 2017 only Denmark participated in ERM-II.

Voluntary participation

10

The way ERM-II operates

A central rate in relation to the euro is established for every currency in the ERM-II. Under the terms of ERM-II there is a standard deviation margin of +/– 15% from the central rate. It is possible for a country to agree to work with a narrower deviation margin. The Danish central bank has made an arrangement with the ECB that the fluctuation margin of the Danish crown in relation to the euro may not be more than +/– 2.25%.

Central rate in relation to the euro

Deviation margin

If the market rate is in danger of moving outside the fluctuation margins, both the ECB and the central bank of the country concerned are obliged to intervene. If, for instance, the Danish crown depreciates too much, both the ECB and the Danish central bank will buy Danish crowns in return for euros. An intervention of this type will result in an increased demand for crowns on the exchange market, causing the exchange rate of the crown to rise. Because of the fact that at any given moment, the maximum deviation of a currency compared to the euro is equal to +/– 15%, the maximum deviation possible over a period of time is double that, namely +/– 30%. During a given period, it is theoretically possible for a currency to move from the highest value permitted to the lowest value permitted.

Intervention

In some cases, the central rate becomes impossible to sustain. Relatively high inflation, for example, can result in a coin becoming overvalued. An expensive currency is detrimental to a countries competitive position, resulting in a multitude of negative consequences to the economy. In that case, a reduction of the central rate, or devaluation, is required.

Devaluation

10.4.3 The euro and the other currencies

The ECB does not have any exchange rate policies in relation to currencies such as the dollar or the yen. As the ECB sees it, changes in, for example, the euro / dollar rate are determined in the long run by the inflation in the eurozone compared to that in the USA. If the inflation in Europe is consistently higher than that in the USA, the value of the euro compared to the dollar will drop. Consequently, in the long run, the external purchasing power of the euro (the exchange rate) is dependent on the internal purchasing power of the euro, which is determined by the level of inflation. If the ECB succeeds in keeping inflation low, the result will automatically be a strong euro compared to the dollar and the yen. The exchange rates of the world's three major currencies – the euro, the dollar and the yen – are therefore flexible in relation to each other. This does not take away from the fact that monetary authorities in the three regions have an interest in balanced exchange rate developments in respect of the three currencies.

Flexible

Table 10.9 summarises this section's main conclusions.

TABLE 10.9 Exchange rate systems in the EU

Countries	System	Policy consequences
Eurozone	Single currency	Common monetary policy
ERM-II	Fixed, but adjustable	Limited independence for the monetary policies of those countries of the EU that do not have the euro (eurozone – rest of the EU)
Eurozone – USA, Japan	Flexible	• ECB can implement independent monetary policies • Coordination of policy is desirable

10.5 Forward exchange rate

On the forward exchange market, currencies are exchanged against the forward exchange rate at some time in the future. The most common terms for a forward contract are one, two, three, six, nine and twelve months. The forward exchange market allows entrepreneurs to tie the value of future foreign currency cash flows to the domestic currency.

An exporter who expects to receive a payment of $1 million in three months' time can sell that amount on a three-month term against the three-month forward rate. This ties the future value of the export order to the euro. He is thus protected against a sudden drop in the exchange rate of the dollar. Section 10.5.1 deals with the factors that determine the forward rate and Section 10.5.2 deals with the question of whether the forward rate is a good indicator of the future spot rate.

10.5.1   Determining the forward rate: interest rate parity

The forward rate of a currency originates in an action by market parties that we term covered interest arbitrage. Interest arbitrage means making use of the interest rate differences between countries. There are two types of interest arbitrage: covered and uncovered interest arbitrage. Uncovered interest arbitrage is what takes place when an investor invests in a particular currency because of the high interest rate, though does not act to avoid exchange rate risk. In such a case, the investor is, in fact, acting speculatively. Covered interest arbitrage is what occurs when an investor makes use of international interest rate differences, but excludes any exchange rate risk in the forward market. This type of interest arbitrage is illustrated in Example 10.2.

Covered interest
arbitrage

- -
EXAMPLE 10.2

Covered interest arbitrage and the forward rate

During the course of a year, a European investor has built up a liquid assets surplus of €1 million. He has a choice between investing it in dollars or in euros. If he elects to invest in dollars he wants to avoid any exchange rate risk.

We will assume that at the time the liquid assets are to be invested the dollar interest rate has risen from 6% to 8%. The other interest rate and exchange rate data relevant for the investor are as follows:
- Dollar interest rate: 8% per annum (was 6%)
- Euro interest rate: 6% per annum
- Spot rate: €1 = $1.00
- One year forward rate: €1 = $1.00

The investment return on both alternatives
An investment in euros yields the following return:

$$€1,000,000 \times 1.06 = €1,060,000 \qquad [1]$$

Covered interest arbitrage, which involves the following three simultaneous transactions, guarantees the return on the investment in dollars.
- Converting €1 million into $1 million on the spot market
- Putting $1 million in a dollar deposit against 8% interest. After a year the dollar investment grows to $1,080,000
- In order to avoid running any exchange rate risk, the $1,080,000 is sold on the forward market at a year's term against the current one year forward exchange rate which is €1 = $1.00.

The guaranteed return on the dollar investment is therefore:

$$\frac{(\$1,000,000 \times 1.08)}{\$1.00} = €1,080,000 \qquad [2]$$

Investors' preferences and the consequences for the forward exchange rate
A risk-free euro investment yields less than a risk-free dollar investment. International investors will therefore invest in dollars.[1] The supply of dollars and the demand for euros on the forward market will increase in response to the need to avoid any exchange rate risk on dollar investments. The forward exchange rate of the euro compared to the dollar will also increase. The one year forward rate of the euro will therefore rise above the level of $1.00. Equation [2] demonstrates that an investment in dollars will become progressively less attractive. The question is how great the rise of the one-year forward rate of the euro compared to the dollar will ultimately be.

The equilibrium price of the forward market: interest rate parity
The forward exchange rate of the euro against the dollar is in equilibrium when risk-averse investors have no preference for either of the two investments. This rate is referred to as the break-even rate or interest rate parity. In our example, the one-year forward rate is therefore equal to:

$$\frac{\text{Investment in dollars: } \$1,080,000}{\text{Investment in euros: } €1,060,000} = \$1.0189 \qquad [3]$$

At a one-year forward rate of the euro of $1.0189, both investments will yield the same amount. In such a situation, covered interest arbitrage no longer offers the international investor risk-free profit opportunities. The premium on the euro will be about two dollar cents, which is about 2% of the spot rate. The premium on the euro is, however, compensated by the euro's interest rate handicap (8% − 6% = 2%).

[1] The assumption here is that interest rates and the spot exchange rate will remain the same. In actual fact, the spot rate of the dollar will rise because of the dollar interest rate rise. However, this will not affect the inevitability of a discount on the dollar and a premium on the euro developing.

- -

TEST 10.6
Calculate whether there was any interest parity before the increase in the dollar interest rate.

As Example 10.2 shows, the forward rate is the result of the spot rate and the interest rate difference between two countries. By covered interest arbitrage the forward rate automatically reaches the level at which it makes no difference to the investors where they make their investments. This stage will be reached when the premium/discount in the forward rate is the same as the interest rate difference. The currency of a country with a high interest rate therefore always has a discount in the forward rate and the currency of a country with a low interest rate always has a premium in the forward rate.

Discount

Premium

10.5.2 The forward exchange rate and the future spot exchange rate

The forward exchange rate is the rate for exchanging currencies in the future. This raises the question of whether the forward rate is a reliable indicator of the future spot exchange rate. To answer that question requires an understanding of the notion of market efficiency. An efficient exchange market is one in which the exchange rates respond rapidly and rationally to information. Experience tells us that currency traders usually react quickly but not always rationally to new information. Emotions and unwarranted reactions to political and economic news facts sometimes play an important role in price-making (see Section 10.2.2). Nevertheless, the foreign exchange market is one of the most efficient financial markets. The more efficient a financial market, the better the forward exchange rate of, say, the dollar reflects all the available information about the way in which the dollar can be expected to develop in the future. This makes the forward market into the most logical predictor of the spot rate. Research has shown that the forward exchange rate is an unbiased estimate of the future spot rate. This means that over a long period of time, the forward rate gives a reliable picture of the future spot rate. While the forward rate can overestimate or underestimate the spot rate temporarily, the chances of overestimation or underestimation are the same. In fact, banks often use the forward rate as a basis for their exchange rate prognoses.

Market efficiency

Figure 10.1 shows the main causal relationships described in this section. The first relationship – that of the inflation and interest rate differences between two countries – is known as the Fisher effect. This effect is named after the American economist Irving Fisher, who came to the conclusion (in 1930) that a rise in inflation was followed after a while by a rise in the nominal interest rate. Investors want any rise in inflation compensated for in the interest rate.

Fisher effect

FIGURE 10.1 The relationship between the Fisher effect, interest rate parity and the future spot exchange rate

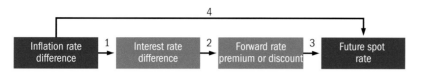

1 = Fisher effect
2 = Interest rate parity
3 = Premium or discount as an indicator of the future spot rate
4 = Purchasing power parity

The second relationship represents covered interest parity. Whether a currency is at a premium or a discount in the forward rate depends on the difference between the interest rates of the countries in question. The forward rate of a country with a high interest rate will show a discount whereas the reverse holds for a country with a low interest rate.

The third relationship related to the extent to which the forward rate can be regarded as an indicator of the future spot rate: exchange market efficiency. If viewed over a long enough period of time, a premium in the forward rate will indicate a rise in the spot rate, a discount will indicate a drop. However, in the short term, the forward rate can over- or underestimate the spot rate considerably. Some caution must therefore be exercised if the forward rate is used as an indicator of future exchange rate movements.

If we compare the three relationships we can conclude that the future spot rate is ultimately determined by the difference in the inflation rate in one particular country compared to that in another. A country with a high inflation rate will also have a high interest rate, which causes the forward rate of the currency concerned to show a discount. If we assume that the forward rate can be used to accurately predict the future spot rate, we can expect a depreciation in the currency concerned. A conclusion that the difference in inflation between two countries determines exchange rate developments is consistent with the purchasing power parity theory (see arrow 4). This theory, however, deduces the relationship between inflation and the exchange rate via trade in goods and services.

TEST 10.7
Let us assume that the inflation rate in the euro area is lower than that of the USA. What prognosis can be made in relation to the future spot exchange rate of the dollar?

10.6 Exchange rate risk

Exchange rate risk can be defined as the risk of a company's profitability being affected by fluctuations in the exchange rate. Many companies have a policy aimed at managing the exchange rate risk.

Exchange rate risk management is done in a similar way to interest rate management (see Figure 10.2). In the following sections we will deal with the first four steps of exchange rate risk management. The last step, evaluation

Exchange rate risk management

10

of the cycle as a whole, has been treated in the section on interest rate management (see Chapter 8).

FIGURE 10.2 The exchange rate risk management cycle

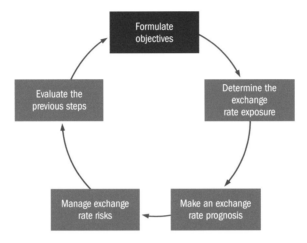

10.6.1   Exchange rate risk management: objectives

The objectives of exchange rate risk management reflect to what extent a company is prepared to accept exchange rate risk. The company has a choice between a full cover, no cover and a selective cover policy. With a **Full cover policy** full cover policy, a company has covered itself against all possible foreign exchange developments, thus avoiding unexpected currency setbacks. However, a full cover policy involves high costs. Proponents of a full cover policy advocate the avoidance of financial risks as much as possible. They believe that companies should concentrate on their core tasks and not behave like speculators on the foreign exchange market.

No cover means complete vulnerability to all foreign exchange developments. Such a policy saves on the costs associated with exchange rate risk **No cover policy** management. Proponents of a no cover policy usually refer to the (in their eyes) unpredictable nature of exchange rates. In their view the certain costs of exchange rate risk management do not weigh up against the uncertain advantages of risk management. Another likely reason for not taking out a cover against exchange rate risk is a strong market position. If a company has a strong market position it can pass on any unfavourable exchange rate developments in its selling prices. Companies usually choose a selective cover **Selective cover policy** policy which means that they will hedge part of the total currency exposure. Which part of the exposure is hedged, will depend upon a cost/benefit analysis. For example, an exporter within the euro area will probably cover his transactions in dollars but not in Danish crowns, because the volatility of the dollar in relation to the euro is much greater than that to the Danish crown.

10.6.2   Determining the extent of foreign exchange exposure

Foreign exchange exposure is the extent to which present and future profits are subject to exchange rate fluctuations. There are three main types of exposure: transaction exposure, translation exposure and economic or structural exposure.

Transaction exposure is the type of exposure a company is vulnerable to when it concludes a contract in a foreign currency with payment to follow later. If, for example, a European exporter signs a contract to the value of $1 million with a payment in three months' time, the profit margin on the order is exposed to fluctuations in the euro-dollar exchange rate until the payment date. If the contract is preceded by a tender the exporter will have exchange rate risk exposure during the term of the tender. This is termed pretransaction exposure. Companies pay particular attention to avoiding transaction exposure because it is easy to gauge and it affects short-term cash flows.

Transaction exposure

Pretransaction exposure

10

Translation exposure is the type of exposure a company is vulnerable to when it has items in foreign currencies on its balance. If, for example, a European company takes over an American firm and finances the takeover with euros, it will be vulnerable to translation exposure. If the dollar depreciates during a particular book year, the value in euros of the American firm will drop. Companies rarely pay much attention to translation exposure. While the conversion of balance items at the end of the year will produce an exchange result for accounting purposes, it has no bearing on the company's cash flow. It will only affect it if the exchange results are realised (for instance, if the foreign firm is sold).

Translation exposure

TEST 10.8
A European company with a subsidiary in a country with a weak currency decides to finance the foreign branch locally. What advantages and disadvantages will this entail?

The third type of exchange rate exposure is economic or structural exchange rate risk exposure. This type of exposure is the vulnerability of future profits to fluctuations in the exchange rate. A European brewer with an American competitor is vulnerable to dollar economic exposure. This is because the competitiveness and the future profits of the brewer depend on the dollar exchange rate. Economic exposure is important, but difficult to gauge. The reason for this is that the competitiveness of a company depends not only on fluctuations in the currencies it deals in itself, but also on fluctuations in the currencies its competitors do business in.

Economic exposure

10.6.3 Making an exchange rate prognosis
There are two ways of forecasting the exchange rate: fundamental analysis and technical analysis.
Fundamental analysis is the type of analysis done in order to make a prognosis based on a country's economic developments. In Section 10.2, exchange rate indicators were derived from a country's balance of payments. A fundamental analyst makes an exchange rate prognosis on the basis of the way these indicators develop. The main determiner of short-term rate changes are changes in interest rate differences between two countries. The main long-term exchange rate indicators are purchasing power parity and a comparison of the growth potential of two countries. Fundamental analysts often base their forecasts on the forward rate. A forward premium is a possible indication of currency appreciation, a forward discount of a possible depreciation. A fundamental analyst has only proved his worth if his prognosis is more accurate than a prognosis based on the forward rate, which, after all, can be had for free.

Fundamental analysis

With a technical analysis, the forecast is based on past changes to the exchange rate. Technical analysis is based on the following assumptions:

- The exchange rates have taken account of all available information (opinions, events, expectations).
- Exchange rates follow certain trends, and these trends will continue until the contrary is shown.
- History repeats itself: that is, past exchange rate patterns will repeat themselves in the future.

It is the task of the technical analyst to detect exchange rate patterns – trends – in historical data and from them extrapolate to the future. Technical analysts do not make use of economic forecasts in making their prognoses since they assume that all available economic information will already have been included in the exchange rates.

Chart reading Technical analyses may take one of two forms: chart reading and time series analysis. With the chart reading technique, a currency's past changes are shown in graph form. The technical analyst seeks to detect typical exchange rate patterns in the diagram, and on the assumption that the same patterns will reoccur in the future, makes an exchange rate forecast (see Example 10.3).

EXAMPLE 10.3

Chart reading

Technical analysis: chart reading[1]

(Exchange rate of the euro in dollars May 2016-January 2017)

[1] Green rectangle: appreciation; Red rectangle: depreciation; Green line: support; red line: resistance; blue line: 40 weeks moving average

Source: FXstreet.com, 24 January 2017

Financial market technical analysts often look for so-called support and resistance lines in exchange rate graphs. These lines are based on the idea that there are psychological upper and lower limits to the various exchange rate levels. Both lines are obtained by connecting the various exchange rate dips and peaks respectively (see the figure; support at $1.035, resistance at $1.175). The support line indicates the lower limits of the exchange rate, the resistance line the upper limits. The space between each respective line is termed the trend canal. Depending on the time frame in question, both long and short-term trend canals can be identified.

When the actual rate approaches the support line, this is an indication that the lower rate limit is about to be reached. A currency trader would be advised to buy up the currency in question.
The reverse applies when the actual rate approaches the resistance line.

Technical analysts also use statistical time series analysis to process past rate data in order to make them suitable for making prognoses. For example, they can calculate quarterly or half-yearly moving averages and so detect exchange rate trends. Another possibility is using statistical techniques to find a relationship between a past currency rate and the prospective rate. The various statistical techniques that are used in time series analysis are, however, beyond the scope of this book.

Statistical time series analysis

TEST 10.9
What is likely to happen to the exchange rate if all currency traders use the same support and resistance levels?

Table 10.10 summarises the backgrounds and ways in which the methods of prognosis can be used.

TABLE 10.10 Methods of exchange rate forecast

Method	Basis/background	Suitability
Technical analysis • chart reading • time series analysis	Past exchange rate movements	Forecasts up to half a year
Fundamental analysis	Economic developments	Forecasts longer than half a year
Forward rate	Market efficiency	Forecasts from one month to one year

10.6.4 The use of exchange rate instruments
The instruments of exchange rate risk management can be divided into internal and external instruments. Internal instruments are instruments that a company can use more or less independently. External or financial instruments require a transaction with another party on the foreign exchange market (for example, a bank).

Internal instruments
Internal measures to manage foreign exchange risk may be either strategic or operational measures.
The extent of a company's exposure to foreign currency is determined by the foreign currency component of its costs, returns, assets and debts. In the final analysis, therefore, the extent to which it is exposed to exchange rate

Strategic decisions

risk will depend on the strategic decisions that the company makes with regard to purchases, production (where it is sited) and sales. Table 10.11 lists the main decisions.

10

TABLE 10.11 Strategic decisions and exchange rate risk

Purchase	Production	Sale
Choice of procurement market	Production location	Choice of export markets invoicing
Invoicing	Financing	Strengthening of market position

If possible, the strategic policy should be aimed at matching the future revenues and costs in foreign currencies. For instance, if a European company has a large turnover in dollars, it would be logical to increase the dollar share of the costs. This may be done by making more of its purchases in dollars. The company might decide ultimately to relocate its production to the USA or to a country that has pegged its currency to the dollar. These measures reduce the amount of dollar exposure and result in changes to the exchange rate of the dollar having less effect on the profitability of the company. The problem is that strategic decisions involve many more factors than currency considerations alone. When choosing the location, the considerations of availability, price and quality of the production factors are just as important.

Dominant market position

A company can also reduce its exchange rate risk by adopting a strategy geared to a dominant market position, since a company with a large share of a foreign market is more able to pass unfavourable exchange rate changes on in the sale price. A European exporter with a dominant position on the American market can absorb a depreciation of the US dollar by raising the sale prices in dollars. In fact, a dominant position on the market provides the only real protection against exchange rate risk. A company can use currency instruments such as the forward rate contract to protect it against short-term depreciation of a foreign currency, but it does not provide protection against long-term depreciation. Only by gaining a dominant market position can entrepreneurs protect themselves against long-term unfavourable exchange rate changes.

By making strategic decisions, companies are fixing the foreign exchange structure of costs and revenues for the long term. To neutralise the effects of sudden exchange rate fluctuations on profits, management can take operational measures that are aimed at keeping the external cover the company needs as low as possible.

Netting

Netting involves the company offsetting all exposure of foreign currencies against each other within the company, which means that it only has to protect itself against net external exposure. If one subsidiary of a multinational firm has a claim of $400,000 and another subsidiary has a debt of $100,000, then the net exposure will be $300,000, for which external cover needs to be taken out. Netting does not reduce the total exchange risk exposure that a company runs, but it does cut down on the costs of exchange risk management.

The objective of matching is coordinating the time frames within which there is incoming and outgoing cash flow in foreign currencies. Let us assume that a company has to pay $100,000 to a supplier. The same amount is due to be received from a customer in a week's time. By postponing payment to the supplier by a week, the company will save on the costs associated with covering itself against transaction risks (and moreover, the company will avoid transaction costs when the euros are converted into dollars and vice versa). An instrument that bears a strong resemblance to matching is leading and lagging. Leading and lagging involves the business entrepreneur accelerating or slowing down incoming or outgoing payments in foreign currencies based on exchange rate forecasts. An exporter who expects a depreciation of the dollar will want accelerated payment of amounts owed (leading). On the other hand, faced with the same exchange rate expectations, an importer would prefer to postpone payment in dollars (lagging). In both cases, there is a real threat of the relationship with the business partner suffering serious damage.

Matching

Leading and lagging

10

If a European exporter demands to be paid in euros, the importer will run an exchange rate risk. If the payment is in the currency of the importer, the exchange rate risk lies with the exporter. If an exchange rate clause is included in the contract, both parties will share the risks. An exchange rate clause makes the cost expressed in a foreign currency dependent on the rate of the foreign currency in question. Depreciation of the foreign currency will have the effect of raising the price in that currency; appreciation will have the effect of lowering the price in that currency. The possibility of including an exchange rate clause is dependent on the other party's willingness to accept such a clause in the contract.

Exchange rate clause

External or financial instruments

Strategic and operational measures are aimed at minimising exchange risk exposure. The remaining exposure can be combated by external or financial instruments. The main ones are the forward contract, the option and the exchange rate swap.

Forward contracts

A forward contract is, as we have seen in Section 10.4, a binding agreement between two parties to exchange currencies at some time in the future. The exchange rate at which the currencies will be exchanged in the future, the forward rate, is determined in advance. An exporter who will receive payment in dollars in three months' time will cover his exchange risk by selling dollars via a forward contract, and an importer who has to pay an amount in dollars in three months' time will cover himself by buying dollars via a forward contract. Using a forward contract means that both the exporter and the importer will know beforehand how much they can expect to receive or will have to pay in euros. The forward contract is the most used external instrument for managing exchange rate risk. The reasons for this instrument's popularity are its relatively low costs and the forward contract's simplicity.

Currency options

A currency option is the right to buy a particular currency (a call option) or to sell (a put option) for a rate fixed in the options contract (the strike or exercise price). The purchaser of a currency option has this right for a certain period of time or at a future date. A price is charged for a currency option; this is called the option premium.

Option premium

Let us assume that a certain exporter can expect to receive $1 million in three months' time. He can cover himself against the exchange rate risk by buying a put option on the dollar. In doing so he is buying the right to sell $1 million for the exercise price in the option contract (for instance, $1 = €0.95). The risk of the dollar dropping in price is now covered. If the exchange rate of the dollar drops, the exporter will exercise his option. He will receive the guaranteed return of $1,000,000 × 0.95 = €950,000. This amount less the option premium is the net revenue in euros.

The real advantage of a currency option compared to a forward contract is that the exporter can still profit from a rise in the exchange rate of the dollar. If the dollar increases in price the exporter will not exercise his option. He will, of course, have lost his premium. A currency option consequently offers greater flexibility than a forward contract. The disadvantage is that the costs of a currency option are usually greater than those of a forward contract.

Currency swaps
The currency swap is an agreement between two parties involving the exchange of interest and foreign currency obligations. There are three stages to a currency swap:

1   At the commencement of the term, amounts of principal are exchanged at the spot exchange rate.
2   During the term of the foreign currency swap, the entrepreneur pays interest in the currency obtained. He receives interest in the currency that he has relinquished to the other party under the terms of the exchange.
3   When the contract expires, the principal amounts are again exchanged at the original rate.

The currency swap is a currency instrument that can be used to obtain cover against long-term foreign currency exposure. It is usually used when the exposure lasts for between two and ten years. Forward contracts are not usually available for such time frames. How a currency swap works is demonstrated in the following example.

EXAMPLE 10.4

How currency swaps work

A European company has a large amount of his turnover in dollars. Financing the enterprise with US dollars could lessen his exposure to the dollar. The income in dollars will then be offset by greater expenditure in dollars.

However, the company has limited access to the American capital market since it is relatively unknown in the United States, and consequently would have to pay too much interest on a loan in dollars. An American company with a large turnover in euros will face a similar problem.

For both companies, the currency swap will be most advantageous (see the figure). The European company borrows euros relatively cheaply on the European capital market and the American company borrows dollars relatively cheaply on the American capital market. At the start of the term they exchange the principal amounts against an agreed rate (say, €100 million against $102 million). During the term of the contract the European company pays the interest in dollars (over $102 million). In return, it receives

Flexibility (margin note)

interest in euros (over €100 million) from the American company. This enables both companies to fulfil their interest obligations to their capital providers. On expiry of the contract's term, the principal amounts are again exchanged at the original rate. The European company pays $102 million to the American company and receives €100 million in return. The companies then use these amounts to redeem their original loans.

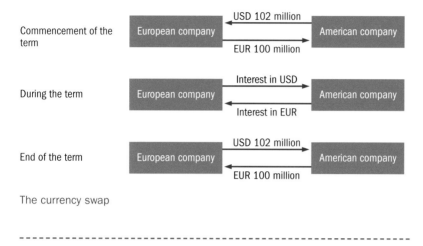

The currency swap

- -

In short: a currency swap enables companies to profit from differences in credit standing on national capital markets, reducing at the same time the exchange rate risk.

Glossary

Appreciation	An increase in the exchange rate within a flexible exchange rate system.
Arbitrage	Making use of exchange rate differences between exchange markets at a particular point in time.
Central rate	The official value of a currency within a fixed exchange rate system.
Cross rate	The exchange rate relationship between two currencies that is derived from the exchange rate of both currencies expressed in terms of a third currency.
Depreciation	A decrease in the exchange rate within a flexible exchange rate system.
Devaluation	A decision to lower the central rate of a currency in a system of fixed exchange rates.
Economic exchange risk	The risk that a company's future profitability will be affected by fluctuations in the exchange rate.
ERM-II	Exchange Rate Mechanism-II: a system of fixed but adjustable exchange rates between the euro and the other EU currencies.
Exchange rate	The price of a currency of one country expressed in terms of the currency of another country.
Exchange rate clause	A clause in a trade contract in which the height of the agreed price is subject to the exchange rate at the time of payment.
Exchange rate indicator	A variable that precedes an actual change in the exchange rate.
Exchange rate quotation	The way in which the price of a currency (e.g. the euro) is published • direct: the price of the euro expressed in the foreign currency • indirect: the price of the foreign currency expressed in euros.
Exchange rate risk	The risk that a company's future profitability will be affected by fluctuations in the exchange rate.

Exchange rate system	• Fixed exchange rates: an exchange rate system in which every participating currency is allotted a fixed value, allowing a limited amount of fluctuation around that value • Flexible exchange rates: an exchange rate system in which the price formation is the result of supply and demand on the exchange market.
Foreign currency exposure	The degree to which a company is exposed to fluctuations in the exchange rate.
Foreign currency option	The right to buy a foreign currency (call option) or to sell it (put option) at the strike price fixed in the option.
Foreign currency swap	An agreement between two parties to exchange foreign currency obligations.
Forward exchange market	The foreign exchange market in which currencies to be delivered at some time in the future are traded.
Forward rate discount	The negative difference between the forward rate and the spot rate of a currency.
Forward rate premium	The positive difference between the forward rate and the spot rate of a currency.
Fundamental analysis	A method of forecasting changes in the exchange rate in which the prognosis is based on a country's economic developments.
Interest arbitrage	Making use of the difference in interest rates between two countries at a particular moment. If the exchange rate risk is not hedged this is termed uncovered interest arbitrage. If the difference in interest rate is made use of while simultaneously excluding the exchange rate risk, it is termed covered interest arbitrage.
Interest rate parity	A situation in which the difference in the interest rates of two countries is exactly offset by a premium or discount in the forward rate.
Intervention rate	The minimum and maximum exchange rate within the set margins at which the central bank is obliged to intervene.
Intervention	Buying or selling of foreign currency by the central bank in exchange for the domestic currency.
Leading and lagging	Adjusting the due dates of payment of outstanding accounts or obligations according to exchange rate forecasts.
Market efficiency	A financial market situation in which all of the information is rapidly and lucidly incorporated within the exchange rates.
Market sentiment	Those expectations relating to a particular financial and economic variable that are current in the market.

10

Matching	Coordination of incoming and outgoing foreign currency cash flows.
Netting	Offsetting of amounts owed and debts in foreign currencies.
Overshooting	A situation in which the exchange rate of a currency reacts to economic or political news in an unwarranted way.
Overvaluation	A situation in which the actual rate of the currency is higher than the value calculated on the basis of purchasing power parity.
Pretransaction risk	The type of exchange rate risk deriving from offers expressed in foreign currencies.
Purchasing power parity	The exchange rate relationship between two currencies in which the purchasing power of both currencies is the same.
Reference exchange rate	The equilibrium price of a foreign currency as published daily by the ECB.
Resistance line	A line in an exchange rate graph showing the exchange rate's short-term upper limits.
Revaluation	A decision to raise the central rate of a currency within a system of fixed exchange rates.
Speculation	Making use of an expected change in the exchange rate of a currency over a period of time.
Spot market	The exchange rate market on which currencies that are immediately delivered (i.e., within two working days) are traded.
Spread	The margin between the buying and the selling price of a currency.
Support line	A line in an exchange rate graph showing the exchange rate's short-term lower limits.
Technical analysis	A method of forecasting the exchange rate in which the prognosis is based on past changes in the exchange rate.
Transaction risk	That type of exchange rate risk a company is vulnerable to if it concludes transactions in foreign currencies.
Translation risk	That type of exchange rate risk a company is vulnerable to if it converts balance sheet items to its own currency.
Trend canal	The gap between the support and the resistance line.
Undervaluation	A situation in which the actual rate of the currency is lower than the value calculated on the basis of purchasing power parity.

11

Country selection and country risk

11.1   **Country selection**
11.2   **Country risk**

The main questions to be addressed in this chapter are as follows:
- How can a company select an export market?
- How can a company analyse the risk it is running on that market adequately?

For European entrepreneurs it has become increasingly easy to sell and produce goods and services outside their own region. An entrepreneur selects a country to do business in on the basis of demographic, political, cultural and economic criteria. If a country scores low on one or several of these criteria it will not qualify. Country selection can be compared to a filtering process: the entrepreneur filters the most attractive sales market out of a large number of countries using a set of predetermined criteria. Section 11.1 deals with country selection using the filter method.
Doing business outside the advanced economies is not without risk. Country risk is the risk that companies and private individuals in that country are not able to meet their international financial obligations because of measures their government has taken. These measures usually involve the restriction on or a prohibition of payments in foreign currencies to other countries by the inhabitants of the country because of a currency shortage. A European company with a claim on a customer in the country concerned may not be paid therefore, even if the customer is prepared to pay. Section 11.2 deals with analysing country risk.

CASE

Unilever is a British-Dutch firm that is active world-wide on the markets for food and beverages, and home and personal care. The firm calls itself a multilocal multinational.

This means that Unilever adapts its world-wide marketing and distribution models to local patterns and habits in the country, or at least if the market is large enough.

According to Unilever they take this approach in Vietnam. Although the Vietnamese population is poor, the market shows potential: there are 90 million people, most of whom are younger than 25. As well as this, illiteracy is low and the government of this socialist republic is increasingly open to foreign investment.

The success of Unilever in Vietnam is based on what the firm calls localisation, the adaptation of world-wide Unilever products to the local market. Because of the low purchasing power of the Vietnamese, products are packaged in small quantities.

Unilever also incorporates local ingredients in its products, thus increasing their acceptability.

11.1 Country selection

In this section we will treat the basis and the procedure for a country selection by an exporter. Country selection for the purpose of direct investment will not differ essentially from a selection for the purpose of export. The contents of both analyses will differ, however. A country selection for the purposes of direct investment will have to be more detailed and more in-depth. In the case of a direct investment a company is tied to the country in question for a long period. An exporter has the opportunity to withdraw from a foreign market immediately should the economic and political situation give cause to do so.

11.1.1   Selection based on risk and return

The purpose of a country selection is to find out what geographical sales markets are attractive to an entrepreneur. The attractiveness of an export market is determined by two factors: the expected return and the expected risk (see Figure 11.1).

Country matrix In the country matrix (Figure 11.1) the economic growth in a country is the indicator for the expected return. The higher the economic growth in a country, the higher the expected sales and profits will be. The level of social consensus in a country is an indicator of the risk involved. A low level of social consensus means that the various social groups are relatively polarised. Opposition between employers and employees, for instance, might lead to labour conflict and a wage/price spiral. The situation is even more serious if the dichotomy between population groups is so great that there is a threat of social, ethnic or religious conflict. A low level of social consensus is therefore associated with a considerable chance of unfavourable national economic or political developments.

The criteria of economic growth and social consensus allows us to identify four categories of countries (see Figure 11.1). Countries in the A category (for example Singapore) are characterised by high economic growth and a high level of social consensus. This is the optimum situation: the country

FIGURE 11.1 Country matrix based on economic growth and social consensus

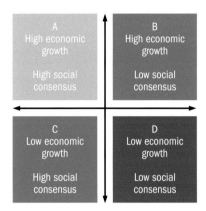

Source: J.G. Wissema, *De kunst van strategisch ondernemerschap*, 1993

offers good sales perspectives at a low risk. To do business in or with these countries is an attractive proposition. The reverse hold for countries in category D (for example, Afghanistan or many African countries). Both the social consensus and the economic growth in these countries are low. The return / risk profile of these countries is very unfavourable. To do business with or in these countries is not recommended.

An evaluation of countries in the categories B and C is more difficult. A country in the B category will be experiencing high economic growth but a low level of social consensus. This situation often occurs in emerging markets. Modernisation and internationalisation of the economy will rock the foundations of these societies which are often still traditional. Some population groups will oppose the consequences of modernisation and internationalisation, which may lead to social and political conflict. Countries in the B category are mainly to be found in Southeast Asia. Most Western European countries can be put in category C. The economic growth in Western Europe is relatively low, though social consensus is high. A large growth in sales is therefore difficult to achieve on most Western European markets, though on the other hand the risk is limited.

Emerging markets

The matrix is mainly useful for developing scenarios. B-category countries such as India have a relatively high economic growth. At the same time the social and political situation in these countries is relatively unstable. Two scenarios are possible. With a pessimistic scenario, the country will move towards becoming a D-category country. This possibility may become reality if smouldering ethnic conflict comes to a head, causing economic growth to decrease sharply. With an optimistic scenario, the country will move towards becoming a country in the A category. In this scenario, economic growth provides a higher standard of living for all groups of the population. Because of this the social contrasts become less pronounced and the country will develop into an attractive sales market.

Scenarios

The matrix in Figure 11.1 is a simplified form of the filter model for country selection. Countries where the company can expect a high return and low risk are selected ('filtered') on the basis of two selection criteria: economic growth and social consensus. In the following sections, we will deal with the filter model in more detail.

Filter model

11

Heineken in Asia

11.1.2   How to set up a filter model

Country selection aims at filtering out on the basis of return and risk profiles those countries in a geographic region that are attractive markets. The filtering process is done in three steps (see Figure 11.2).

FIGURE 11.2 Country selection using the filter method

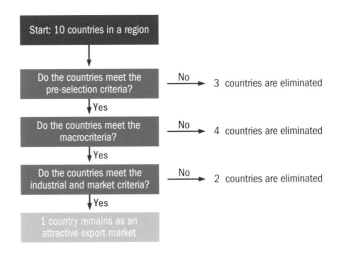

Pre-selection

A thorough analysis of a great number of countries is a time-consuming process. This is why most companies will make a pre-selection on the basis of criteria that would severely limit or even completely exclude export to a certain country. Even without analysis, countries with an Islamic culture obviously will be eliminated in the pre-selection for producers of pork products and alcoholic beverages. Apart from such industry-specific pre-selection criteria, there are also criteria that all companies should take into account, such as social consensus, GDP per head and the level of import restrictions. Countries at war or suffering from a civil war, countries with a great deal of poverty and countries with exorbitantly high import restrictions will be eliminated in the pre-selection.

The countries that are left after the pre-selection are subsequently put through a macro filter. In this part of the selection, the company analyses the countries that are left on the basis of political, socio-cultural, demographic, legal and macroeconomic criteria. This could bring up problems that could make export to that country difficult. A political analysis might show that in a particular country there are all kinds of smouldering religious and ethnic conflicts that might flare up at any time. The macroeconomic analysis may show that the country has a high foreign debt and an overvalued currency. In such a situation there is a real chance of a currency crisis and currency shortage in the near future. The macro filter is treated in Section 11.1.3.

Macro filter

After the macro selection, the countries are put through an industry and market filter. The company analyses the industry and the market the company forms part of. The analysis might, for instance, show that the level of competition in the industry is very high in a certain country. This could mean that the profit margin on the export product would be unacceptably low for the company. Even though the macro criteria yielded an acceptable score such a country would still be eliminated. The industry and market filter is treated in Section 11.1.4.

Industry and market filter

11.1.3   The macro filter

Table 11.1 sums up all the criteria that play a role in a macro filtering of the country selection. These criteria are not uniformly important for all companies. The political policy making is not or only minimally relevant for an exporter of lamps, for instance, but of the utmost importance for an exporter of military equipment. Dependent on the type of product that a company produces, the list of points to consider may therefore vary.

We will deal briefly with some political, demographic, cultural and legal criteria and subsequently deal more extensively with the economic criteria.

TABLE 11.1 The macro filter in a country selection

Macro factors	Points to consider
Politics	Form of government
	Political structure and stability
	Quality of government (corruption, nepotism)
	Membership of international organisations
	International relations
	Trade policy
Demography	Size and growth of the population
	Population breakdown (age, sex, ethnic background)
	Degree of urbanisation
	Level of education

11

TABLE 11.1 The macro filter in a country selection (continued)

Macro factors	Points to consider
Culture	Language
	Religion
	Social customs
	Hierarchical structures
	Trading and payment ethics
Legislation	Recognition of international treaties
	Quality of the legal system
	Legislation in the field of:
	• Contracts
	• Product requirements
	• Protection of intellectual property etc.
Economy	Economic system
	Size and distribution of GDP
	Domestic economic situation:
	• Main industries
	• Inflation
	• Economic growth
	• Economic policy
	International economic situation:
	• Exchange rate
	• Balance of payments
	• Foreign debt
	• International reserves

Political criteria

An analysis of the political criteria should show whether there is any short-term threat of internal or external conflict. The form of government should be considered (parliamentary democracy or not), the international connections (diplomatic relations within the region and world-wide), the political structure (what political parties there are, who is in government and who is in the opposition) and the political stability (how secure the position of those in power is compared to the opposition). The political stability of a country cannot be seen in isolation from the economic situation. For example, in 2001 Argentina was no longer able to comply with its interest and repayment obligations on its foreign debt. In order to strengthen its competitiveness, the government decided to devalue the local currency – the peso – compared to the dollar. The inflation that resulted caused the population to take to the streets. Buenos Aires became the scene of plundering and demonstrations which eventually forced the government to resign.

But even in a stable political environment, the government can restrict economic activities. For instance, a government could be corrupt, function in a bureaucratic way or favour domestic companies (see Figure 11.3).

Internal or external conflict

Political stability

Corruption

TEST 11.1

What kind of problems could European companies expect in countries in Africa or South Asia?

Trade policy

Where the point 'trade policy' is concerned, it is important to discover to what extent the country is open to imports. Not only should the type and extent of import restrictions be considered, but also the regional economic collaboration. A company that exports to Mexico will have to take account

FIGURE 11.3 Corruption in the world 2016

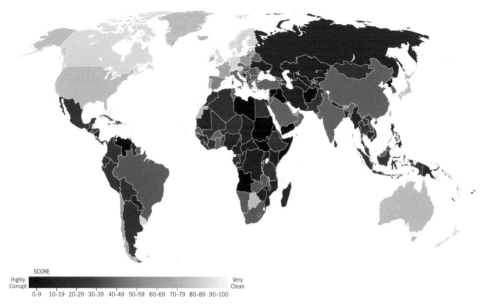

Source: Transparancy International (www.transparancy.org)

of the fact that the country is part of NAFTA. This means that American and Canadian exporters have free access to the Mexican market whereas European companies will have to pay import levies.

Demographic criteria

Demographic developments are particularly significant for exporters of consumer goods. For exporters of foodstuffs and beverages a young and fast growing population is an important criterion for a country.
The population pyramid of a country, gives an idea of the size and composition of the population by age and gender, at a glance. In Figure 11.4, the population pyramid of Senegal and the Netherlands of 2016 are shown. Left in the graph, the number of males are shown by age category and right, the number of females. The composition of the population by age has an obvious pyramid shape in Senegal: there are many young people and few elderlies. As many women are of a fertile age, the population growth in Senegal is relatively high. The population pyramid of the Netherlands shows an aging population. The pyramid is top heavy, showing that there are many elderly, relative to young people.

Population pyramid

The degree of urbanisation – the proportion of the population that lives in cities or in urban areas – is especially important for determining how easily customers can be reached. In developing countries, the degree of urbanisation is very often low, with a large part of the population living in small towns spread over the entire country. This makes it difficult for a company to get its products to the customers. It will not only be faced with logistic problems, but marketing communication will also be problematic. Because of the limited communication possibilities, it might, for instance, be difficult to introduce new products or to build brand awareness. In countries

Urbanisation

FIGURE 11.4 Population pyramid in Senegal and The Netherlands (2016)

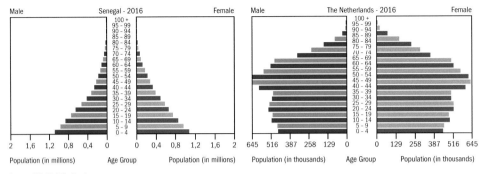

Source: CIA, World factbook

with a high level of urbanisation, customers are concentrated in cities or urban areas. In these countries, it is easier for an entrepreneur, as far as both logistics and communication are concerned, to reach his clients.

Level of education

Level of education also has a bearing on the attractiveness of a country as a sales market and a business location. If, for instance, a large part of the population is illiterate, written communication between the company and its customers is virtually impossible. This could make the export of products for which instructions for use are of vital importance, such as medicines, very problematical. The level of education of the population also has, of course, an effect on the demand for specific products such as books or computers.

TEST 11.2
Why are the levels of urbanisation and literacy significant for producers of packaged brand articles?

Cultural criteria

Culture

Culture can be described as the collective moral values that determine people's actions. People of a certain group or nationality differ from people of another group or nationality in their traditional code of behaviour. We shall illustrate this with the following example. In Western society, honesty is an important principle, not only in the private realm but also in business. In the USA and Western Europe, 'dishonest practices' such as cartelisation, corruption and insider trading are regarded as being socially unacceptable. Americans and Europeans appreciate it if business partners are direct and open during negotiations. In many Eastern societies, however, good manners are more important than honesty. An Asian business partner will not say no to a business proposal directly, even if he is not interested. Honesty is less important to him than approaching his business partner in a respectful and polite manner.

Language and religion

A firm that wants to export its products to a particular country will have to study the culture of that country. This boils down to finding out 'what's done' and 'what's not done' in communication between people. Apart from the more obvious cultural differences such as differences in language and religion, the firm will also have to develop an eye for cultural differences that are not immediately obvious. These differences – like the difference in ideas relating to the importance attached to concepts like honesty and politeness – appear during business dealings between people from different countries. They could lead to mutual annoyance or misunderstandings during negotiations about a contract or to conflict about payment behaviour. As may be obvious, cultural differences will become greater and more significant if an exporter decides to move outside Europe.

Information about cultural differences is much more difficult to obtain than demographic or economic information. As well as referring to reputable publications on cultural differences, the exporter could obtain information from national export promotion and information services, embassies and the experience of others (see Case 11.1).

CASE 11.1

Eye contact in the West and East

'Humility is the mother of all virtues.' (Confucius)

Maintaining eye contact in Western culture implies that people pay attention to one another, and are open and honest. In Western culture, parents doubting the sincerity of their children say: 'look at me'. In Western tradition, the eyes are 'the windows to the soul'.
In Asia, people interpret the maintaining of eye contact as a sign of disrespect and aggression. This applies particularly to continuous eye contact between people of a different status in society (elderly – youngsters, leader – subordinate).
Asian people feel very uncomfortable if Europeans or Americans insist on maintaining eye contact. Europeans and Americans interpret attempts to avoid eye contact as a sign that the other party cannot be trusted. Based on their principles, trading partners should literally 'look each other straight in the eye' to establish a trust base.

Legal criteria
Those who do business abroad, will encounter local rules and legislation. Legislation and law enforcement are part of the legal system of a country. The quality of the legal system depends on the quality of the laws and legislation, independent of the legal power and the available capacity to enforce it.

Legal system

The World Bank issues a publication "The ease of doing business" every year. It compares countries with regard to legal ease, for example in starting a business activity, hiring employees, acquiring building permits, acquiring financing, trading internationally, enforcing adherence to contractual obligations or wrapping up a bankruptcy. The World Bank focusses mainly on the amount of time and money spent by an entrepreneur on various legal procedures.

The ease of doing business

Figure 11.5 shows the legal problems an entrepreneur can encounter worldwide. Particularly in Africa - and to a lesser extent in Latin America and South Asia - the legal settings do not make business transactions very easy. In many African countries the legal system fails. The law and legislation is incomplete, faces bureaucracy, legal power is not independent and law enforcement is weak. This makes it very difficult to trade, even if sales prospects are good.

FIGURE 11.5 Ease of Doing Business Scores in the World[1] in 2017

Legend

- ■ 20 - 49
- ■ 49 - 57,3
- ▢ 57,3 - 63,9
- ▢ 63,9 - 73,2
- ▢ 73,2 - 88

[1] Scores from 1-100. The higher the score, the easier it is to do business

Source: Worldbank (www.doingbusiness.org)

Economic criteria
Hereafter the most important economic criteria from table 11.1 will be discussed.

Economic system

Economic system

The economic system or the economic order will partly determine the number of government regulations a company can expect in a country. A centrally planned economy is characterised by a great deal of government interference in markets. This will include price controls and restrictions on trade and capital transactions.

Convertible

Often the currency of a central planned economy is not. This means that the currency cannot be exchanged for other currencies. The government does this to control the money flows in and out of the country. For example, the Chinese Yuan is only since 1996 freely exchangeable for export and import transactions.

With a few exceptions such as Cuba and North Korea there are no planned economies left. The former planned economies, amongst which those of Russia and China, have moved on to a mixed economy in which there is a combination of market mechanisms and government control.

Size and growth of GNP (per head)
A second indicator of the attractiveness of a country as a sales market is the size and growth of the gross per capita national or domestic product (GNP or GDP). The size and growth of income per head of population is an important variable, especially for income-sensitive products. In order to enable comparison, the GNP per capita is usually expressed in dollars. The purchasing power of the dollar can, however, differ from country to country

because of differences in the cost of living. If we adjust the GNP per capita to the cost of living we obtain the GNP expressed in terms of purchasing power parity (see Table 11.2).

TABLE 11.2 Gross National Product per capita, 2015 (dollars and purchasing power parity)

High income	Dollars	Purchasing power parity (Netherlands = 100)	Low income	Dollars	Purchasing power parity (Netherlands = 100)
Norway	93,740	134	Togo	540	2,8
Switzerland	84,630	130	Guinea	470	2,3
Luxembourg	77,000	147	Gambia	460	3,3
Australia	60,070	93	Madagascar	420	2,9
Denmark	58,550	99	Congo, Dem. Rep.	410	1,5
Sweden	57,920	99	Niger	390	2,0
United States	55,980	120	Liberia	380	1,5
Ireland	52,580	108	Malawi	340	2,4
Netherlands	48,860	100	Central African Rep.	330	1,3
Canada	47,540	91	Burundi	260	1,5

Source: World Bank, *World development indicators database*, December 2016

Table 11.2 shows very clearly that the GNP per capita in dollars gives a distorted view of purchasing power. In 2015 a Dane had an income that was about 20% higher than the income of a Dutch person. Despite that a Dutch person could buy approximately the same amount of goods and services with that lower income than a Dane. This is because the cost of living is higher in Denmark than in the Netherlands.

TEST 11.3
On the basis of Table 11.2, what conclusion can be drawn about the general price level in Denmark in comparison with that of the United States?

Distribution of income
Besides the income per head of population, the distribution of income is also important. In India for example, 1.3 billion people live on a low average income. Due to the low income per head of the population, the Indian market does not appeal to Western companies. It is forgotten that India has a very unequal distribution of income. According to the World Bank, the ten percent wealthiest Indians earn thirty percent of the total income. This enormous group of people can easily afford Western imports.

Sectoral composition of production
Not only the size but also the sectoral composition of the gross national or domestic product is an important economic factor. The sectoral structure gives an insight into the stability and the strengths and weaknesses of an economy. For example, in an advanced economy, the services sector forms a large proportion of the domestic product. Most developing countries, on the other hand, are strongly dependent on income from the production and sale of one or only a few raw materials. Such a one-sided production structure means that income of these countries is very sensitive to price fluctuations on the international raw materials market. Experience shows that these prices do fluctuate strongly. In a country with a narrow export

11

structure, sales are therefore likely to fluctuate in accordance with the prices on the international raw materials market.

Exchange rate

The national currency exchange rate is also a determiner of the attractiveness of a country as a sales market. If the currency of a country is overvalued, there will be favourable short term sales conditions in that country. Because the exchange rate of the currency is too high the competitiveness of the local companies will be low and European countries will be able to sell their products easily. In the long term, sales perspectives in a country with an overvalued currency are less favourable. Depreciation of an overvalued currency is sure to occur at some stage and when that happens, the European exporter will lose his sales market.

Inflation

The level of inflation has a very big effect on the attractiveness of a country as a sales market or business location.

In the first place, a high inflation rate can be the result or the cause of social unrest. Inflation often occurs as a result of a lack of social consensus. In such a situation, groups in society such as employers and employees will pass on cost rises to each other, thereby losing sight of the common interest. Inflation can also be the cause of social polarisation. Inflation causes a relatively random redistribution of income. Some population groups will profit from this redistribution (debtors, black marketers), whereas other groups will be disadvantaged by it (lenders and population groups with a fixed income).

In the second place, inflation has an effect on the exchange rate. The higher the inflation the greater the chance of a drop in the exchange rate. Exchange rate risk in trade with that country will increase because of inflation.

Thirdly, a high inflation rate can lead to government measures that restrict the room for companies to manoeuvre. Restrictions on capital transactions in order to prevent capital flight, import restrictions in order to put a stop to a further deterioration of the balance of payments or credit restrictions to combat the inflation itself are possible countermeasures. All of them are detrimental to the sales perspectives in that particular country.

Balance of payments

Payment problems

Finally, an analysis of the balance of payments, the extent of foreign debt and the amount of international reserve assets will show whether payment problems are to be expected in the future (see figure 11.6). A company can expect problems in a country with a persistent balance of payments deficit combined with an overvalued currency, low economic growth and a rapidly increasing foreign debt. There are only two possibilities in such a situation: either the government does nothing, which will result in a shortage of foreign exchange and a payment crisis, or the government takes measures to combat the deficit, such as devaluation, introduction of import restrictions or restrictions on expenditure. In both cases the attractiveness of the country for a European exporter will diminish.

TEST 11.4
What will be the effects on the inflation rate of a country if the currency is devaluated after a long period of overvaluation?

FIGURE 11.6 Current account balance (percent of GDP, 2016)

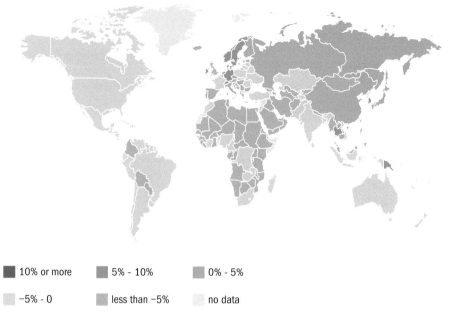

■ 10% or more	■ 5% - 10%	■ 0% - 5%
▦ −5% - 0	▦ less than −5%	▦ no data

Source: World Economic Outlook, October 2016

11.1.4   The industry and market filter

After the countries have been put through the macro filter, some countries
will remain as potential sales markets. Macro-selection takes no account of
the industry a company can be classified as falling under (for instance, the
soft-drinks industry) or the market in which the company sells its products
(for instance, the cola market). The final step in the selection process is
therefore the industry and market filter (see Table 11.3).

TABLE 11.3 The industry and market filter in country selection

Level	Criteria
Industry	Average return
	Growth of demand
	Capacity utilisation rate
	Number of competitors
	Entry barriers
	Degree of product differentiation
	Market power of suppliers and customers
Market	Market size
	Market growth
	Local requirements for marketing instruments

The purpose of the industry filter is to determine whether the industry
will be attractive in a particular country. This is mainly dependent on the
intensity of competition. The ultimate indication is the average return that   *Average return*

companies in the industry realise. If the return is high over a number of years, this is an indication that the intensity of competition between the companies is probably low (see also Chapter 3). Finally, a company should consider the individual markets within the industry he wants to operate on. In order to estimate whether a market is attractive or not, the company will, of course, look at the size and the growth potential of the market. Local marketing instruments should also be considered. This involves asking such questions as to what extent the product should be adapted to local needs and desires, what the payment customs are, what factoring currency is the common one, what distribution and promotion channels are available and which ones are used?

The Appendix following this chapter summarises this section in the form of a checklist that an entrepreneur could use should he want to analyse a foreign market.

TEST 11.5
An industry analysis shows that the growth of demand, the utilisation rate, entry restrictions and the number of competitors are all low in a particular country. Is this industry attractive?

11.2 Country risk

An exporter encounters a number of risks in other countries that do not apply to domestic transactions. If he invoices in another currency he runs an exchange risk. Another risk that applies particularly to export to developing countries is the country risk. This is the risk of government measures getting in the way of compliance with international financial obligations by trading partners in a particular country. These measures may be the result of unwillingness or incapacity on the part of the government of the country concerned.

Incapacity

Incapacity will be involved if there is a currency shortage in a country. A currency shortage is usually the result of low competitiveness on the world market, which results in a country earning too little foreign currency to pay for imports and to meet the repayment and interest obligations on its foreign debt. This aspect of country risk is largely economic risk. The entrepreneur can determine its extent by analysing the competitiveness of a country.

Economic risk

Unwillingness

Unwillingness will be involved if the government of a country has sufficient international currency at its disposal but nevertheless blocks payments to other countries. The government may choose to do this during or after a political changeover, a civil war or an external conflict. This aspect of country risk is mainly political risk. The government of a country can also cease international payments for other reasons, such as a natural disaster. In such a case the government will need all available foreign currency for emergency aid or repairing the damage. This could, however, be described as incapacity rather than unwillingness. Country risk may affect anybody who is doing business abroad. Exporters run the risk of their bills not being paid and multinational companies run the risk that they cannot transfer the profits they make to the head office. We will deal with country risk as it applies to an exporter (Section 11.2.1) and a multinational (Section 11.2.2). We shall conclude the section by discussing a number of instruments for reducing country risk (Section 11.2.3).

Political risk

11.2.1   Country risk as it applies to an exporter

An exporter runs the risk of a client in another country not being able to pay because the government of that country has declared a currency freeze. An analysis of country risk should provide the exporter with a view of the future long-term and short-term paying capacity of a country. The extent to which a country can make international payments in the future depends on the present currency reserves and the capacity to generate currency reserves. The currency generating capacity of a country is determined using the following criteria:
- The degree of political and social stability
- The domestic economic situation
- The external economic situation.

The degree of social and political stability is a major determiner of currency generating ability. Social unrest and political conflict damage international trading and capital transactions. Trading partners and potential investors are frightened off by social and political unrest. The result will be a drying up of the international cash flow. The political situation in a country can be assessed using the criteria in Table 11.1. The currency generating power of a country also depends on the state of the domestic economy. A country can only earn international currency if its home base is sound. A healthy home base implies balanced economic growth, a low inflation rate, a good economic structure and healthy government finances. These are the basic requirements for success on the international markets.

Social and political stability

State of the domestic economy

The extent of social and political stability and the state of the domestic economy have a general influence on the degree of country risk. Country risk is more particularly determined by three factors that are associated with the external economic position of a country:
- The extent of the international reserves
- The foreign debt
- The balance of payments.

The extent of the international reserves
The risk that a currency shortage might develop in a particular country increases in proportion to how low its international reserves become. The extent of the gold and currency reserves of a country is only relevant if the need for cash is considered in the analysis as well. For exporters how big the import cover is can be significant. The import cover measures the relationship between the international reserves of a country and its annual imports. An import cover of 0.5 means that the international reserves of a country are sufficient to pay for half a year of imports. An import cover of 3 months is commonly regarded as the absolute minimum (see figure 11.7)

Import cover

Foreign debt
It is not only import that causes a need for hard currency. Interest and capital repayment obligations (debt service obligations) in relation to foreign debts lead to an outgoing capital flow. To estimate the chance of a currency deficit, it is therefore also important to assess the size of the debt and the resulting debt service obligations.
In itself, the size of the foreign debt says little about country risk. It is only by comparing the foreign debt and associated obligations with other macroeconomic entities such as the GDP or exports that we can get a true indication of the extent of country risk.

FIGURE 11.7 Import cover in a number of developing and emerging economies (in months)

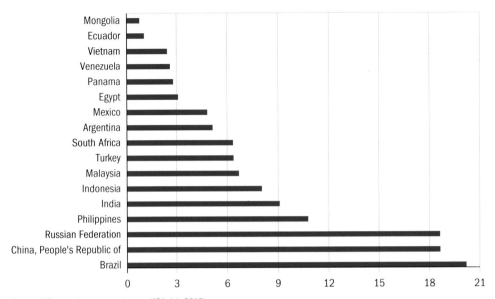

Source: IMF, *Assessing reserve adequacy* (ARA, July 2016)

Debt/export ratio

Debt service ratio

In a country risk analysis, the foreign debt and the debt service obligations are usually linked to exports. The relationship between debt and export is usually referred to as the 'debt/export ratio' and the relationship between the debt service and export as the 'debt service ratio. The debt service ratio lays a connection between an outgoing cash flow (debt service) and an incoming cash flow (exports). This ratio tells what proportion of the export earnings is flowing out of the country in the form of debt servicing. The higher the debt service ratio, the less money left to pay foreign suppliers. Not only the size but also the structure of the foreign debt is relevant for country risk. The shorter the average term of the foreign loans the sooner the repayment obligations. The need for currency in the short term will be considerable in such a situation, which will increase the country risk for European exporters.

The balance of payments

A country's balance of payments registers the origin and the destination of international currency. Currency comes into the country via export and capital import, currency leaves the country through import and currency export (including repayment of foreign debt). An analysis of the balance of payments is therefore essential for insight into the currency generating capacities of a country.

A country receives currency through the export of goods and services.

Competitiveness

The extent of the export is partly dependent on its competitiveness. It has already been shown that competitiveness is closely associated with the strength of the domestic economy and social and political stability. Only when a country has a strong domestic economy and a stable political and social climate can it generate sufficient export income.

How stable exports are is just as relevant as their extent. To determine this requires an analysis of the countries and products involved in exports. A too unilateral dependence on one or two countries increases the chance that export revenue will fluctuate strongly. The same condition applies when a country is dependent for its exports on one or two products. Many developing countries in Africa and Latin America are dependent for their exports on the sales and the price of one raw material. The income of these countries therefore depends heavily on market and price changes on the international raw materials market.

Stability of exports

A second source of currency is capital import. If a country succeeds in attracting foreign investors, currency flows into the country. The state of the domestic economy, the socio-political stability, exchange rate developments and the level of foreign debt are the factors that determine the likelihood of attracting foreign capital. Companies and investors will not be prepared to invest money in a country if it falls down in respect of one or more of these factors.

Capital import

After the origin of the currency has been ascertained, the need for foreign currency should be looked at. As we have already seen, a large part of the foreign currency may be needed to repay or pay interest on foreign debt. An exporter needs to know whether there is any foreign currency left to pay for imports.

In the Netherlands, the Atradius credit insurance company studies country risk. Figure 11.8 shows the country risk map regularly published by the company.

FIGURE 11.8 Country Risk Map (Quarter 4 2016)

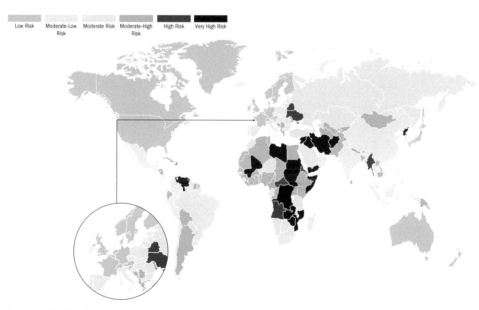

Source: Atradius (Atradius.nl)

Figure 11.8 shows that country risk is highest in Africa and the Middle East. Very high risks are found in so-called 'failed states'. These are countries

'Failed states'

11

whose central government is too weak or ineffective to exercise any substantial influence on its territory, or is unable to provide quality public services, such as safety, to its citizens. This frequently results in violence, corruption, criminality, and survival of the fittest. Not a particularly appealing area in which to conduct business.

11.2.2   Country risk to a multinational

In the previous section we looked at the country risk faced by an exporter. An exporter will want to know whether the country with which he does business has enough foreign currency to be able to continue to pay him. A subsidiary of a multinational will also want to know whether there is a threat of currency shortage in the country of its location. If this is the case, it will not be able to transfer its local currency profits into hard currency, making payment of foreign suppliers and profit transfers to headquarters impossible. The risk that a subsidiary is not able or permitted to transfer the profits (converted into hard currency) to the mother company is termed

Transfer risk

transfer risk.

For a multinational company, country risk involves more than transfer risk. The physical presence of a multinational in the host country makes the company much more vulnerable to unfavourable developments than an exporter. The most obvious example of this is the risk of nationalisation.

Risk of nationalisation

This could affect a multinational company but not an exporter. An analysis of the country risk to a multinational company will therefore have to include more aspects. BERI, a Swiss company, does research into the country risks that exporters, banks and multinationals run. For this purpose the company periodically calculates the so-called Business Environment Risk Index (Beri index), which is comprised of a number of sub-indexes. One of these

Operations Risk Index

sub-indexes, the Operations Risk Index (ORI), summarises the criteria for determining the country risk of a multinational company (see Table 11.4).

TABLE 11.4 Criteria for determining the Operations Risk Index (ORI)

Criterion	Weight
1 Political stability	3.0
2 Attitude toward foreign investments and profits	1.5
3 Likelihood of nationalisation	1.5
4 Monetary inflation	1.5
5 Balance of payments	1.5
6 Bureaucratic delays	1.0
7 Economic growth	2.5
8 Currency and convertibility	2.5
9 Wage costs and productivity	2.0
10 Short-term credits	2.0
11 Long-term credits and capital	2.0
12 Legal regulation of contracts	1.5
13 Communication and transport	1.0
14 Local management	1.0
15 Professional services	0.5

Source: Beri SA

TEST 11.6

According to the Operations Risk Index what measures should a country take in order to attract direct investments?

The Operations Risk Index is determined on the basis of a multi-criteria analysis in which all of the fifteen criteria are weighted. The sum of the separate weights equals 25. For each criterion a score is given that can vary from 4 (very good) to 0 (very bad). The determining of the score is done by using primary data (such as talking to experts) or secondary data (analysis of existing data). The country risk is determined by multiplying per criterion the score by the weight and adding all the weighted scores. A country without any country risk will obtain the maximum score of 100. A country with an extremely high country risk will be given the minimum score of 0.

Multi-criteria analysis

The question is, of course, what conclusions a company should draw from the index. A rule of thumb is that at a score of between 0 and 40 points, a country is not an interesting proposition as a business location, but at a score of between 60 and 100 it is. If the score lies somewhere in between, the country risk is high and further research will have to determine whether to expand in that country or not. This can be done by, for example, varying the weighing or adding criteria that are important to the company.

11.2.3 Managing country risk
In the previous sections we analysed the country risk of an exporter and a multinational. In the current section we will deal with how an exporter and a multinational can manage country risk.

Exporter
Doing business involves taking risks. An exporter may regard country risk as a normal business risk that is to be accepted. If so, he will take into account that a certain percentage of payments from abroad might have to be written off. This is only possible if the financial situation of the company allows it. If the financial margin is limited the exporter will have to find ways of excluding country risk or managing it.

An exporter can manage country risk by:
- The choice of mode of payment
- Taking out an export credit insurance
- Spreading sales over a larger area.

Mode of payment
The country risk is a payment risk. The choice of the way payment is made is an important way of excluding or reducing country risk. An exporter will exclude country risk by adhering to the rule of 'no delivery unless payment is absolutely certain'. Three international payment conditions conform to these terms.

The first is requiring payment in advance. A client in a country with a high country risk will only receive his order when hard currency has been put on the exporter's account. If there is a currency shortage the importer will probably not be able to pay in advance and consequently will not receive the goods. Payment in advance provides the ultimate security in international financial transactions. The problem with demanding payment in advance is that it may be detrimental to the competitiveness of the exporter. If his competitors allow payment in arrear he could lose his share of the market.

Payment in advance

The second form of payment that precludes country risk is so-called confirmed documentary credit. This type of payment is also referred to as confirmed international letter of credit (ILC).

Confirmed international letter of credit

Documentary credit means that the claim an exporter has on a foreign importer becomes a claim on a bank. In a sense, documentary credit is like a bank guarantee. Because the credit standing of a bank is usually easier to determine than that of a foreign importer, the exporter is more assured of in fact receiving payment.

A documentary letter of credit is a common way of paying for financial transactions with countries outside the advanced economies. The way a documentary credit works is illustrated in Figure 11.9.

FIGURE 11.9 The way a letter of credit (L/C) works

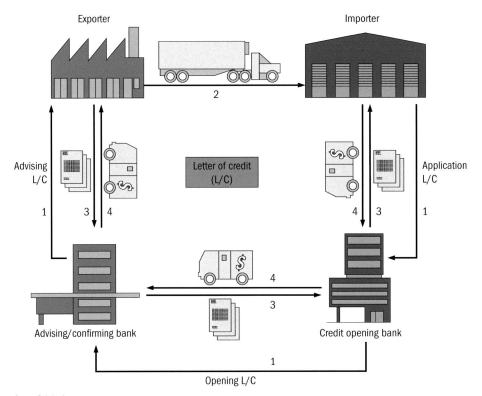

Source: Rabobank

The documentary credit procedure consists of four steps:
- Opening a documentary credit (1)
- Transfer of goods (2)
- Transfer of documents (3)
- The financial settlement (4).

In the contract between the exporter and the importer, both parties must agree that payment will take place by letter of credit. The importer will then request his bank to open a documentary credit on his account in favour of the exporter (1). The credit-opening bank now has a payment obligation to the exporter. The credit-transferring bank informs the exporter about the opening of the credit. The exporter then sends the goods to the importer (2). At the same time he sends the documents belonging to the export consignment via his own bank to the importer's bank (3). The documents represent a right of disposal in respect of the goods. If the credit-opening bank considers the documents to be in order it will pay the exporter by debiting the importer's account (4). The importer then receives the documents and consequently the goods.

A documentary credit transforms a claim on an importer into a claim on the importer's bank, which offers more security. Such a course of action does not, of course, eliminate country risk. If the importing country decides to stop all currency payments to other countries, the importer's bank will not be able or allowed to pay either. The exporter can avoid this risk by getting a bank in his own country to confirm the documentary credit. This means that a bank in the domestic market will accept a payment obligation to the exporter in return for the documents belonging to the consignment. The payment obligation to the exporter will therefore have passed on from the credit-opening bank in the other country to the credit-transferring bank in the exporter's own country. In this way the exporter will have transferred the country risk to his own bank.

A European bank will only confirm a documentary credit if it estimates the country risk to be lower than the exporter does, or if the bank has sufficient security. This security can consist of deposits that the importer's bank has with the exporter's bank. Confirmation of a documentary credit to countries with a high country risk will always be expensive.

Confirmation

A third payment condition that will reduce country risk is a bank guarantee. With a bank guarantee, the guarantee-issuing bank promises to pay a certain amount of money to a beneficiary (the exporter) if the latter declares that the other party (the commissioner of the bank guarantee, in this case the importer) has not fulfilled certain obligations. By demanding a bank guarantee an exporter can reduce debtor risk. If the bank that issues the guarantee is located abroad, country risk remains. The exporter can solve this problem by having a bank in his own country take over the bank guarantee. A taken over bank guarantee is therefore similar to a confirmed documentary credit. The costs of having a guarantee taken over is dependent on the country, the bank that issued the guarantee and the term of the bank guarantee.

Bank guarantee

An export credit insurance
An exporter who extends export credit runs debtor and country risk. It is possible to take out insurance against both risks. Insurance companies will not insure all export transactions. In their country policy they usually categorise countries on the basis of their credit worthiness.
In Figure 11.10, the country risk assessment of Argentina by the Belgian export-credit insurer Credendo, is shown schematically. For each risk type, they apply seven categories, from 1 (low) to 7 (high).

Country policy

FIGURE 11.10 Country risk assessment[1] by the Belgian credit insurer Credendo (2017)

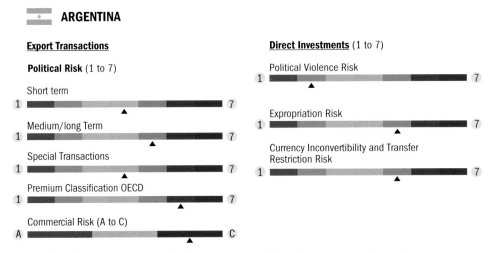

1 Commercial risk refers to the risk of accounts receivables. The rating provides a general picture of the payment behaviour in the country. This can obviously be different for specific customers.

Source: Credendo (www.credendo.com)

Figure 11.10 shows that country risk in Argentina is relatively high. An exporter to Argentina should also take into account increased commercial risk. On average, Argentinian buyers are not the most prompt to pay. Direct investors can take into account the fact that there is little risk of war in Argentina, but expropriation risk and transfer risk are high.

Export-credit insurers assess countries by risk level (see table 11.5). They apply the classification of the OECD, from 0 (very low risk) to 7 (very high risk). The classification of a country in a risk category determines whether the insurer accepts the payment risks, and if so, under which conditions. In high risk countries, insurers will for example, require a bank or government guarantee as a condition of the insurance.

Risk category

TABLE 11.5 Classification of a number of countries according to the risk classification of the OECD (start of 2017)

Country	Country classification
Taiwan, Hongkong	1
China, Saudi-Arabia	2
India, Indonesia, Romania	3
Russia, Turkey, Bulgaria	4
Brazil, Vietnam, Bangladesh	5
Nigeria, Argentina, Sri Lanka	6
Zimbabwe, Venezuela, Afghanistan	7

Source: OECD, *Prevailing country risk classification*, January 2017

The country policy of insurance companies sends clear signals. If insurance companies refuse to cover export transactions to certain countries or demand strict conditions for a cover an exporter will know he is running a high payment risk.

Geographical spreading of sales
An exporter can exclude country risk by choosing the manner of payment or taking out an export credit insurance. But what if neither of these alternatives offer a solution?
The degree of country risk will depend on the extent of the business interests in a particular country and the chance of unfavourable economic or political developments in that country. The political and economic developments in a country cannot be influenced by an entrepreneur, though the extent of the business interests can. The country risk that a company runs can be reduced by spreading of sales. Geographical diversification increases the chance of negative developments in one country being compensated for by positive developments in another country. By spreading sales, a company will achieve a 'natural cover' against country risk.

Geographical diversification

The multinational company
A multinational company has fewer ways of managing country risk than an exporter. For instance, insurance against political risk is not a possibility. Moreover, the presence of a subsidiary in a country cannot be changed in the short term. The company is tied to the country in more ways than one.

Country scenarios
A decision to invest directly in order to establish a subsidiary in a particular country is a long-term investment decision. As such, the country survey on which the decision is based or the interim evaluation of an existing business location is crucial.
Because there are many uncertainties, especially in the long term, it is wise to include all possible scenarios in the country survey (see Section 11.1). In these scenarios, the company should also include the way it intends to react to possible unfavourable developments.
A company might decide to leave a country because of continuing social and political unrest. This involves exit costs. In a sense, this is no different from a company that enters a certain industry with a high risk factor on the domestic market. That company will make its decision on the basis of the entry as well as the exit costs (in case the desired success does not eventuate). If both costs are relatively low he will enter the industry despite the high-risk factor. The same holds for a multinational company. If the national-level entry and exit costs are relatively low, the company could decide to locate to that country despite the potentially high future country.

Exit costs

TEST 11.7
Which sector in a particular country will have the higher entry and exit costs: the industry or the services sector?

Spreading and sharing risks
Multinationals and exporters alike have a variety of geographical locations open to them. By spreading production and sales over the whole world a multinational becomes less vulnerable to economic and political developments in one particular country or region.

Another way of managing country risk is to share the risk with others. By collaborating with other multinationals or with local companies is a way of ensuring that both parties share the country risk. If the collaborating parties are competitors in other places there is the additional advantage that they both will be equally open to country risk. The competitiveness of companies will not change because of unfavourable political and economic developments in the country concerned. This is one of the reasons why multinational companies often follow the market leader in their choice of location. Doing so means that every competitor faces the same country risk.

11

Glossary

Bank guarantee	A bank agrees to pay a certain amount to a beneficiary (for instance, an exporter) if another party (for instance, an importer) does not comply with his payment obligations.
BERI index	Business environment risk index: an index that provides a quantitative assessment of the level of risk in a particular country.
Convertible currency	A currency that is freely convertible into hard foreign currencies.
Country risk	The risk that international payment obligations cannot be fulfilled as a consequence of the imposition of government measures.
Country selection	A process by means of which a company selects the most favourable country for export or business location from a large number of countries.
Debt export ratio	The relationship between foreign debt and export.
Debt service	The interest and repayment obligations deriving from a foreign debt.
Debt service ratio	The relationship between debt service payments and exports of goods and services.
Documentary credit	An agreement between a company and a bank in which the bank accepts the obligation to pay upon receipt of the documents described in the documentary credit.
Filter model	A method for selecting the country that has the greatest sales potential on the basis of predetermined criteria.
Import cover	The international reserves of a country in relation to its monthly imports.
Nationalisation risk	The risk of a foreign government taking over a company's property rights (i.e. nationalising them).
Transfer risk	The risk of a subsidiary company not being able or allowed to transfer profits to the country in which the head office is located.

11

Appendix
Questionnaire for the analysis of a foreign market

Political environment
- What is the form of government?
- What is the political structure like (the main political parties and the power they have)?
- How stable is the country politically and socially (ethnic and religious conflicts, strikes)?
- Is the government effective and ethical (corruption, preferential treatment of local producers)?
- What international relations does the country have? Of what international organisations is the country a member and what is the relationship with these organisations like (WTO, IMF)?
- What is the government's trade policy (what is the government's attitude to imports and foreign investment)? Is the country a member of a regional trade bloc?
- Are the products or investments politically sensitive? Are there restrictions on foreign companies? What are they?

Demographic environment
- How will population growth and composition (age, sex, ethnic background) affect demand for the product?
- What is the population and how fast is the population growing?
- What is the population like in terms of age, sex and ethnic background?
- How urbanised is the country?
- What is the level of education of the population (degree of literacy, educational dichotomy)?

Cultural environment
- What influence will societal norms and values have on the demand for the product?
- What are the main societal and economic norms and values (trade ethics, payment ethics, attitude to foreign products and foreign companies)?
- What is the religion of the population?
- What language or languages are spoken?
- What is the perceived social standing of the target group?
- How do people deal with each other in societal and economic transactions (communication customs, importance of traditions, hierarchies)? 'What's done' and 'what's not done' (verbal and non-verbal behaviour and customs)?

Legal environment
- Does the government adhere to international treaties (on trade and investments)?
- Is the legal system effective (quality of legislation and regulation, independent judiciary, enforcement of laws and regulations)?
- How can intellectual property (patents, brand names) be protected?
- What regulations pertaining to products (product requirements, product liability, etc) are there?

Economic environment
- What is the economic system like? How great is the influence of the government on the economy?
- What is the gross national product, the income per head of population and what is the distribution of income like? What effect will these variables have on the demand for the product?
- What is macroeconomic development like (economic growth, inflation, unemployment, interest rate)?
- What are the main sectors in the economy?
- What is the economic position of the target group compared to that of the rest of society?
- What is the country's balance of payments like (current account and financial account)?
- How great is the chance that there will be payment problems in the near future?
- Is the national currency convertible? How stable is the exchange rate?

Industry environment or competitive environment
- What is the average return in the industry?
- At what rate is demand increasing? What phase of the product life cycle is the product in on the foreign market?
- How is the utilisation rate developing? Is there overcapacity in the industry?
- Who are the main competitors on the foreign market? What are their strengths and weaknesses?
- What are the main entry restrictions for the industry?
- On what basis does competition take place? Is it mainly based on price or on quality (product differentiation)?
- How great is the market power of the industry's suppliers and clients?

Market environment
- What is the size of the market for the product? Can the market be segmented?
- What is the growth rate of the market?
- What product characteristics are important on the target market (quality, packaging, brand, etc.)?
- How are comparable products being distributed at the moment? Is this manner of distribution suitable for this particular product?
- What are the possibilities for promoting the product (use of the media, trade fairs)?
- What is the usual currency for invoicing in international transactions? Is this a stable currency?
- Is there a common pricing policy? Is there a sufficient margin?
- Are there geographical or climatological circumstances that make transport and storage difficult?

Answers to Test questions

- -

1.1   There are a number of possibilities. The company could:
- Aim for a rise in labour productivity in order to cause the wage costs price per product unit to rise less than the wages per employee (see Chapter 6)
- Outsource the production that cannot be done competitively
- Transfer the production to an area with costs advantages.

1.2   The direct environment includes customers, suppliers and distribution channels. The indirect environment includes consultative wage negotiation bodies and product and packaging regulations. The macroenvironment includes such factors as income changes, the exchange rate of the dollar and the state of the economy.

1.3   Where matters relating to the rate of turnover are concerned, it should be remembered that companies that have a high turnover rate very often also make rapid organisational changes as well. They often introduce new techniques and production processes that require frequent changes to the organisation.

2.1   To the extent that all clothing satisfies a similar need, there is such a thing as a clothing market. However, the various segments of that market are rarely in competition with each other. There is a clear division into sports clothing, menswear, ladies wear and children's clothing. For the main raw materials, such as cotton, there is a global market price.

2.2   A fundamental human right is the right to self-development. This covers the right to education as laid down in the Universal Declaration on Human Rights. To make it possible, international treaties and an implementation and control agency are required. A quality standard for products is under discussion.

2.3   In our economic order, the government is a major public health stakeholder and therefore products that are a threat to public health are also its concern. An economic order in which the government has less to do with public health is also an option. In such an order, individual citizens would have to reclaim their damages from the manufacturers via civil law suits.

This would force manufacturers to bring products onto the market that comply with all safety regulations. This could be more efficient and effective than government involvement with public health. There is, of course, no certainty about this.

In both scenarios, however, the same norms apply, namely that public health must not be compromised as a result of using products. In the first scenario, it is the task of the government to prevent this, and in the second it is the task of the judiciary. The judiciary is another institution external to the economic system able to regulate the market conduct of the various parties. In this respect, there are no differences between either economic order.

2.4 The segmentation of markets results in greater product differentiation. As Chapter 1 has already shown, product differentiation lessens the intensity of internal competition. On the other hand, segmentation divides the market up into a number of smaller markets. These markets are easier to enter, which in turn increases the possibility of competition.

2.5 The decrease in the size of families and increase in the number of incomes per household means that consumer patterns are shifting from preparing and eating meals at home to eating out. This trend will no doubt cause an increase in competition in the restaurant sector. The trend-related increase in demand will, on the other hand, have a moderating influence on competition.

2.6 Such consumer purchasing behaviour – buying more of the goods when prices increase – would at first sight seem illogical. If they had increased their demand before the price rises they would have saved money. Some people (we could call them 'snobs') see an interest in art and science as sophisticated behaviour and thus feign an interest in these areas. With snob products, it is the high price that makes the product especially attractive. Products such as expensive cars and clothes are status symbols and possession of them attracts attention.

2.7 If there is a positive relationship between price and quantity demanded, then the price elasticity of demand will be positive as well. This is the case with 'snob articles'. The price of these articles is a feature that makes buying them attractive. Usually these goods are conspicuous status symbols, such as cars and expensive clothes.

2.8 At a price of 250, the demanded quantity is 100. The turnover is therefore 25,000. At a price of 247.5 the demanded quantity is 105. The turnover amounts to 25,987.50 and has risen therefore by 4%.

2.9 Among other things, Unilever produces toilet articles. In industrial countries the firm produces for saturated markets with a high level of competition, low economic growth and an income elasticity of less than 1. Because toiletry products are still regarded as luxury products in Asia, this market is a growing one for Unilever, with high income growth and an income elasticity greater than 1.

2.10 The question is how the financial department carried out its calculations. If they have included all costs in their calculations (including fixed costs, therefore) accepting the losses is a reasonable course of action as long as the returns are higher than the variable costs. If this is so, the project also covers part of the fixed costs. If, however, the financial department has only calculated the variable costs, accepting the losses is not a reasonable course of action.

2.11 The individual supply curve can shift as a result of price changes in the production factors and improving technology (see Chapter 3 for the explanation). These factors will also have an influence on the collective supply curve.
A change in the number of companies also has an effect on the curve. When the number of suppliers increases, the supply curve will shift to the right because at every price there will be a greater supply.

3.1 The firm with the highest return is performing below the average for the business sector, while the firm with the low returns is performing better than the average for its sector. The confidence in the ability to pay back will be greater for the second firm than for the first firm, therefore.

3.2 Every now and then there must be battles to win customer loyalty. With so few firms this can probably be achieved without price wars. The reason for the fierce competition is probably the lack of customer loyalty – little product differentiation – and a saturated market.

3.3 High-tech and low-tech refer to the added value. The labour costs of high-tech products are often high because a lot of knowledge is required to make them.
As well as this, a company that produces high-tech goods can often command high prices because competition is not strong yet. Profits will be high. Wages and profits are aspects of the added value.

3.4 For starting businesses, growing markets have the advantage that the returns are not to the detriment of other companies. Other companies will therefore compete less vigorously to retain their customers than in saturated markets.
They probably have insufficient capacity of their own.

3.5 Cost leadership is very risky for companies that are experiencing competition from low-wage countries. While a lower wages cost per product unit can be effected by increasing labour productivity through mechanisation, mechanisation in the Eastern European countries will quite likely soon put an end to this possibility.

3.6 The companies often defended the takeovers by claiming synergy advantages. The scale advantages of the enlarged company would warrant the high takeover prices. Overestimation of the sales on which the high takeover prices were based and hard to realise scale advantages were risk factors.

3.7 R&D costs for completely new products are so high and the potential for a financial fiasco so great that a single company is virtually unable to afford them. Collaboration with Asian competitors improves the chance that Philips' product will become the world standard, which often carries advantages.

3.8 Increasing chain building in the clothing retail business is leading to concentration. Demand seems to be saturated. Product life cycle progression is one way of viewing the changes in the clothing retail trade.

3.9   Your education will decide ultimately whether you can be regarded as being an advanced production factor. Someone's attitude to risk is related to his preparedness to change his occupation.

4.1   The division of income is a criterion for judging the stability of a country. The assumption is that the more even the division of income is, the more the cultural homogeneity of the population. This population will have access to more or less the same government provisions, cultural provisions and democratic institutions. This will lead to harmonisation of moral and social value patterns. Countries with an uneven division of income will often contain several more or less independent cultures.

4.2   Happiness is a more important aim than prosperity. In a sense, prosperity is an aspect of happiness, since in countries with a low per capita GDP the low prosperity represents a barrier to happiness. In countries with a high per capita GDP, the extra prosperity does not usually lead to a permanently higher feeling of happiness. Apart from a certain level of prosperity, happiness is also dependent on personal characteristics, good primary human companionship, health and having work and societal responsibility.

4.3   The main demographic development is the ageing of the population. This has the following effects on wages:
- The increasing scarcity of labour will tend to increase wages.
- The increasing average age and level of education will increase wages.
- The increasing pension contributions will put net wages under pressure. Employees will try to pass these contributions on to the employers, in turn causing an upward pressure on wages.

4.4
- Quantitative environmental growth is possible when hitherto unknown stocks of raw materials are discovered.
- Qualitative growth is possible when new ways of using natural resources (such as the use of alternative sources of energy) are opened up by technological developments.

4.5   Supplier industries (for instance, motors, electronic systems, materials) reserve a great deal of research capacity for developing elements for aircraft. Other products and the quality of the entire production chain profit from it. If Europe were to lose its aircraft industry there would be less technical knowhow.

4.6   Economic growth causes social damage if it is accompanied by, for example, an imbalance in the distribution of income that causes conflicts between population groups (strikes, or even worse). Social conflicts undermine the sustainability of growth.

5.1   Dividends are what companies pay to their shareholders. Shareholders are usually quite rich and therefore have a low marginal consumption ratio. They will spend only a very small proportion of the tax cuts. Production will not or only minimally be stimulated. The measure will therefore have little effect on economic growth.

5.2   Forced stock investments are an indication that demand is lower than expected. If the customers are not prepared to buy, the companies themselves will have to supply the necessary funds. Forced stock investments ensure that production and expenditure are always matched. During the ensuing period, the company will reduce production. Forced stock investments therefore set economic adaptation processes in the economy in motion.

5.3   The main factor governing investments is sales expectations. If sales expectations are high, entrepreneurs will invest, and the high interest rate that usually accompanies an economic boom period will hardly have any braking effect.

During an economic recession, investments usually are already low as a result of low sales expectations, low profits and low levels of utilisation. If under these circumstances interest rates are high as well, companies will reduce their loans even further in order to keep costs under control.

5.4   If demand is greater than supply, prices will rise. This causes supply to rise and demand to drop.

5.5   In such a situation, the demand for capital will be greater than the supply. This will cause the interest rate to rise. This will encourage foreign investors to invest in the country. This will be accompanied with a deficit on the current account of the balance of payments. The country will have an import surplus because expenditure will be greater than production. Adaptation processes will ensure that the balance of payments will regain its equilibrium, and that the public will spend less and save more.

6.1   It is theoretically possible for the supply cycle to disappear, since orders and deliveries have to coincide with production. In practice, however, the many uncertainties about sales and the reliability of transport will make a certain amount of stockpiling necessary. Fluctuations will therefore continue.

6.2   Entrepreneurs who thought that economic growth would remain at a high level invested a great deal. When growth fell short of expectations and did not meet the level of investment, they had to depreciate much more than was appropriate for the turnover. This lasted longer than during a normal economic recession. The upturn consequently came later than expected.

6.3   Such companies are common in the open sector that is subject to fierce competition on its foreign markets. Their profits will drop. They usually take measures in the form of reorganisation, resulting in an increase in labour productivity.

6.4   A government is quite capable of causing inflation and there is a real threat of this happening. A government can increase inflation by issuing more money to finance its deficit. A government that has control over the central bank can order it to print extra money, which it then spends itself. This is informally known as 'letting the money presses roll'. In order to avoid this happening, the ECB keeps itself relatively autonomous, and does not allow European governments to finance their deficits in such a way that it causes inflation.

6.5   The increase in the consumption rate is the sum of the change in volume (1.5%) and the change in price (1.4%). Consumers appreciate a change in volume more because it represents extra consumption of goods and services.

6.6   Travel expenditure has a high income elasticity, but does not involve durable goods. Expenditure on tourism can easily be postponed and is consequently very sensitive to business cycle fluctuations. Many durable goods, including furniture and audio-visual products, are traded on a saturated market. A feature of these markets is that sales increase at a lower rate than income. Purchases, however, are postponable, and sales can drop sharply during a recession and rise just as sharply during an economic boom period.

6.7   Company results fluctuate strongly during the business cycle, creating considerable uncertainty. Whether a company will survive the downturn cannot be known. This is why banks often attach a risk premium to their interest rate. Consequently, companies with a high sensitivity rate to cyclical trends have higher capital costs than defensive companies.

6.8   The share prices of companies that are sensitive to cyclical trends will fluctuate more strongly than those of defensive companies.

7.1   Money represents undifferentiated purchasing power. Money would thus seem to be able to buy anything. However, this is not the case. Trade in some goods and services via the market is viewed as morally unacceptable, and hence they are excluded from buying and selling. Every society has goods and services that fall into this category. Slavery, for instance, is not allowed in modern societies.

7.2   The division of labour in a developing economy is usually not as advanced as in an industrial economy. In many – mainly agricultural – households, consumption as well as production takes place. Less use is therefore made of money, which means that the effects of inflation will be less serious.

7.3   If a bank goes bankrupt it can no longer meet its debt obligations. Demand deposits are part of a bank's debt. If banks can no longer effect payments or exchange demand deposits for cash, the banks debt can no longer serve as a substitute for money. If banks get into trouble on a large scale, the monetary system will collapse.

7.4   Banks do not usually pay interest on demand deposits, but they do on savings deposits. The interest rate margin on a mutual debt agreement is therefore greater. The creation of demand deposits by a bank does, however, lead to financial transaction costs.

7.5   This is possible because the velocity of circulation of M1 is greater than 1, meaning that a euro is used more than once a year to buy goods and services with (see also Section 7.3).

7.6   The threat of war will lead to unrest and uncertainty on the financial markets. This is usually accompanied by falling prices of, for example, shares. Investors will play it safe and hold a large part of their capital in liquid assets.

7.7   Electronic payments mean that money can circulate much more quickly, and consequently be used more frequently for the purchase of goods and services (that is, the velocity of circulation will increase). At a higher velocity of circulation, a lesser amount of money is needed (all other things remaining equal).

7.8   If the productivity growth in the EMU region increases structurally, the potential production growth (Q) in the EMU will also increase. This will make it necessary to increase the M3 reference value. (An increase in productivity could also cause a decrease in inflation, but this will depend on wage developments.)

8.1   Inflation is the investor's greatest enemy. A rise in inflation decreases the purchasing power of their investments. If a central bank can make monetary policy independent of political institutions, the chances are great that inflation in a country will be combated effectively.

8.2   Market parties will expect the central bank to increase its official tariffs. Labour shortage brings the danger of a strong rise in wages. After a while this will lead to higher inflation. It is likely that the ECB will increase its official tariffs in order to counteract inflation in an early stage.

8.3   A rise in the long-term interest rate will make interest-bearing investments (bonds and forward deposits) more attractive than an investment in shares. As well as this, an increase in the interest rate will reduce the profits of companies, making an investment in shares even less attractive. Share prices will therefore drop.

8.4   If American investors expect the euro exchange rate to drop they will invest less in the EMU. A reduced demand for European government bonds will cause prices on the bonds market to drop. The redemption yield on existing bonds will consequently rise. The long-term interest rate on new government loans will therefore also increase.

8.5   A government's debt does not always give an accurate impression of the present and future financial position of the government. The main reason for this is that the debt does not take in account the assets that the government might have to balance out the debt. The credit rating is also dependent on whether the country is expected to be able to reduce the government debt in the future.

8.6   The profits of a company with a low solvency will only be sensitive to short-term interest rate changes if it has to pay a variable interest rate over most of its debts.

8.7   Because of the expected turn in the business cycle the interest rate is likely to drop in the next two years. This would indicate a preference for a loan with a variable interest rate. With a view to the maturity of the loan, a roll-over loan could be taken out or floating rate bonds issued.

8.8   Some possible reasons for a bank do an interest rate swap are:
- A different interest rate prognosis: if the bank is expecting the interest rate to rise it will gladly accept a variable interest rate instead of a fixed rate
- The bank may have a great deal of income from fixed interest rate obligations while for outgoing cash flows the opposite holds. In order to reduce the interest rate risk, the incoming and outgoing interest flows have to be matched. The interest rate swap in the example would contribute to this.

9.1 On the basis of the recent past, Asia, and more particularly Southeast Asia, would appear to offer the best sales potential. This region's share in global production is increasing rapidly.

9.2 The main arguments for direct investments in China are:
- Production close to the sales market (makes it easier to anticipate and react to local trends)
- Lowering the costs (for example, by producing in low wage countries)
- Spreading risks (not being dependent on production in just one country).

9.3 No, in this situation there are no comparative cost differences and there is therefore no basis for trade. The comparative cost of a pair of shoes in both countries is equal to two pairs of jeans. There is therefore no opportunity for mutually profitable trading exchange.

9.4 Many developing countries are very dependent on exports of their agricultural products. If the EU and the USA protect their agriculture, the developing countries will be restricted in their development.

9.5 No, import tariffs alone are not enough to determine the extent to which a country is open to imports. The advanced economies could impose far more non-tariff barriers than the developing countries.

9.6 Not taking account errors and omissions into account, the balance of payments should always be in equilibrium. A country with a surplus on the current account will consequently have a deficit on the financial account and vice versa. A surplus on both the current and the financial accounts is therefore not possible.

9.7 A rapid increase in domestic expenditure will lead to a rapid growth in imports. If the country nevertheless has a surplus on the current account, this will be an indication of strong competitiveness. The currency exchange rate is likely to be too low.

9.8 Government subsidies interfere with the market mechanism in a country. This is why the IMF usually demands a reduction in government subsidies. If the subsidies mainly benefit the poorest layers of the population (for instance, subsidies for basic human needs), demanding a reduction in them often leads to a lot of criticism.

10.1 Speculators make use of exchange rate differences over a period of time. If speculators expect that the exchange rate of a currency will rise, they will buy that currency, which will cause the exchange rate to rise.

10.2 Although European airline companies invoice in American dollars, a large part of their costs (such as wage costs) is in euros. They will therefore offer the dollars they receive on the currency markets in exchange for euros. There will therefore indeed be an increased demand for euros on the exchange market.

10.3 If taxes are lowered, national expenditure will rise. This will cause a deterioration of the balance on the current account of the balance of payments, which will lead to a depreciation of the currency concerned.

10.4   The advantage of an overvalued currency is that a country can import relatively cheaply. Because of this inflation can stay low.

10.5   The interest rate difference is 1.5% in favour of the euro. If investors expect that the rate of the euro at the end of the year will be 1.5% lower than at the beginning of the year, it will make no difference to them where they invest. (It will be at a euro exchange rate of $1.01.)

10.6   Prior to the increase in the interest rate, the interest rate difference between the euro and the dollar and the forward premium was zero. In other words, prior to the increase in the interest rate, investors were not able to obtain a no-risk profit from covered interest arbitrage. Therefore, there was interest rate parity.

10.7   If the inflation rate in the euro area is lower than that in the United States, the interest rate in the euro area will also be lower than that in the United States. This difference in the interest rate will lead to a forward discount on the dollar, which will be an indication of a drop in the future exchange rate of the dollar.

10.8   The advantage of borrowing in the local currency, is that returns and costs are in the same currency, which reduces the exchange rate risk. A disadvantage of borrowing in a weak local currency is that countries with a weak currency usually have high interest rates. The interest costs will thus be relatively high if money is borrowed locally.

10.9   This situation will lead to a self-fulfilling prophecy. If the computer programmes give a 'sell' signal (for instance, because a resistance level is reached), all currency traders will sell the currencies involved. This will cause the exchange rate to drop automatically.

11.1   Corruption makes a company dependent on arbitrary government acts. Employees in a corrupt environment could also start to deal corruptly themselves. This would harm the reputation of a company. This is why big multinationals have drawn up a behaviour code for their employees which includes a prohibition on accepting or offering bribes.

11.2   A high degree of urbanisation will make it easier for the client to be reached in terms of both logistics and communication. Supermarkets in developing countries are also a more important distribution channel in cities than in rural areas, where goods are often sold unpackaged on markets. The urban population in developing countries also buys a greater number of international brand products than the rural population. A higher level of literacy will also mean that packaging and press advertising will have a greater impact on the consumer.

11.3   The Danish per capita GNP is 5% above that of the USA. Measured in terms of purchasing power parity the Danish GNP per capita is 21% below that of the USA. The average price level in Denmark will therefore be higher than that in the United States.

11.4   A devaluation leads to a rise in import prices expressed in the local currency. This causes the prices of consumer goods to rise.

11.5   The low utilisation rate and the low growth of demand make the industry unattractive. The overcapacity and the low growth of demand will put pressure on prices and the returns within the industry. The low entry restrictions are not relevant in this case, because companies will not want to enter the industry.

11.6   The order of priority can be deduced from the weight of each of the criteria. Firstly, a stable political climate has to be created. Then economic growth has to be stimulated, and so on.

11.7   In industry, because the necessary investments are usually larger. Should it be necessary to exit, it is by no means sure that the investment will be recovered.

Credits

Robert Rizzo/Hollandse Hoogte: p. 37
Koolen/Nationale Beeldbank: p. 68
Sake Rijpkema/Hollandse Hoogte: p. 81
Love-Li/Nationale Beeldbank: p. 105
Shutterstock: p. 197
Avij/Euro Bill Tracker: p. 200
Markus Pillhofer/ECB: p. 215
European Central Bank: p. 219
Peter Boer/Beeldunie: p. 234
www.dsta.nl: p. 235
Marcio Machado/Getty Images: p. 265
Amet/Getty: p. 272
PictureAlliance/Lineair: p. 276
Airbus, Toulouse: p. 279
Joel Schalit, Berlin: p. 281
Alamy/Imageselect: p. 284
iStock: p. 296
Reuters/Novum: p. 310
iStock: p. 312
SergioGeorgini/Wikipedia: p. 322
Ruud Taal/ANP: p. 348

Index